MATERIAL WITNESS

Leonardo

Roger F. Malina, Executive Editor

Sean Cubitt, Editor-in-Chief

Synthetics: Aspects of Art and Technology in Australia, 1956–1975, Stephen Jones, 2011

Hybrid Cultures: Japanese Media Arts in Dialogue with the West, Yvonne Spielmann, 2012

Walking and Mapping: Artists as Cartographers, Karen O'Rourke, 2013

The Fourth Dimension and Non-Euclidean Geometry in Modern Art, revised edition, Linda Dalrymple Henderson, 2013

Illusions in Motion: Media Archaeology of the Moving Panorama and Related Spectacles, Erkki Huhtamo, 2013

Relive: Media Art Histories, edited by Sean Cubitt and Paul Thomas, 2013

Re-collection: Art, New Media, and Social Memory, Richard Rinehart and Jon Ippolito, 2014

Biopolitical Screens: Image, Power, and the Neoliberal Brain, Pasi Väliaho, 2014

The Practice of Light: A Genealogy of Visual Technologies from Prints to Pixels, Sean Cubitt, 2014

The Tone of Our Times: Sound, Sense, Economy, and Ecology, Frances Dyson, 2014

The Experience Machine: Stan VanDerBeek's Movie-Drome and Expanded Cinema, Gloria Sutton, 2014

Hanan al-Cinema: Affections for the Moving Image, Laura U. Marks, 2015

Writing and Unwriting (Media) Art History: Erkki Kurenniemi in 2048, edited by Joasia Krysa and Jussi Parikka, 2015

Control: Digitality as Cultural Logic, Seb Franklin, 2015

New Tendencies: Art at the Threshold of the Information Revolution (1961–1978), Armin Medosch, 2016

Screen Ecologies: Art, Media, and the Environment in the Asia-Pacific Region, Larissa Hjorth, Sarah Pink, Kristen Sharp, and Linda Williams, 2016

Pirate Philosophy: For a Digital Posthumanities, Gary Hall, 2016

Social Media Archeology and Poetics, edited by Judy Malloy, 2016

Practicable: From Participation to Interaction in Contemporary Art, edited by Samuel Bianchini and Erik Verhagen, 2016

Machine Art in the Twentieth Century, Andreas Broeckmann, 2016

Here/There: Telepresence, Touch, and Art at the Interface, Kris Paulsen, 2017

Voicetracks: Attuning to Voice in Media and the Arts, Norie Neumark, 2017

Ecstatic Worlds: Media, Utopias, Ecologies, Janine Marchessault, 2017

Interface as Utopia: The Media Art and Activism of Fred Forest, Michael F. Leruth, 2017

Making Sense: Art, Computing, Cognition, and Embodiment, Simon Penny, 2017

Weather as Medium: Toward a Meteorological Art, Janine Randerson, 2018

Laboratory Lifestyles: The Construction of Scientific Fictions, edited by Sandra Kaji-O'Grady, Chris L. Smith, and Russell Hughes, 2018

The Invisible Colors: The Arts of the Atomic Age, Gabrielle Decamous, 2018

Virtual Menageries: A Mediology of Animal Representations, Jody Berland, 2019

From Fingers to Digits: An Artificial Aesthetic, Ernest Edmonds and Margaret A. Boden, 2019

Material Witness: Media, Forensics, Evidence, Susan Schuppli, 2020

See <http://mitpress.mit.edu> for a complete list of titles in this series.

MATERIAL WITNESS

MEDIA, FORENSICS, EVIDENCE

Susan Schuppli

The MIT Press
Cambridge, Massachusetts
London, England

This book was set in ITC Stone Serif Std and ITC Stone Sans Std by Toppan Best-set Premedia Limited. Printed and bound in the United States of America.

Library of Congress Cataloging-in-Publication Data

Names: Schuppli, Susan, author.
Title: Material witness : media, forensics, evidence / Susan Schuppli.
Description: Cambridge, MA : The MIT Press, 2020. | Series: Leonardo | Includes bibliographical references and index.
Identifiers: LCCN 2019020112 | ISBN 9780262043571 (hardcover : alk. paper)
Subjects: LCSH: Evidence, Circumstantial. | Forensic sciences. | Evidence (Law).
Classification: LCC K5490 .S38 2020 | DDC 341.6/9--dc23 LC record available at https://lccn.loc.gov/2019020112

10 9 8 7 6 5 4 3 2 1

With gratitude to my parents, Paul and Lydia Schuppli

Due to their artifactual status within the text as "material witnesses," all transcripts and reports have been reproduced in their original form without correcting typographical or spelling errors. All are available in the public domain.

Warning: Some images depict highly disturbing events documenting scenes of violence, suffering, and atrocity and may cause consternation to certain readers.

Contents

Acknowledgments

As with any extended project, this book is the consequence of innumerable discussions and engagements across domains and contexts. Inspired by the practical and theoretical work of many colleagues, curators, students, and friends, it recognizes that such work is always inextricably collaborative. As a concept, *Material Witness* emerged out of my dissertation project, supervised by Eyal Weizman and Luciana Parisi at Goldsmiths. I am indebted to their fierce intelligence, which both challenged and guided my research. Since that time the concept has gained considerable clarity and been shaped, in particular, by my creative practice as an artist-researcher and my investigative work with Forensic Architecture, especially during the period when I was Senior Research Fellow and Project Coordinator. I actually encountered Eyal's work in the 2003 exhibition *Territories* at the KW Institute for Contemporary Art Berlin two years prior to our meeting at Goldsmiths. Never could I have imagined that our research trajectories would come together in such a consequential manner. Eyal has been a crucial figure throughout my intellectual journey, and I am forever grateful for his ongoing support, critical insights, and the considerable opportunities that have come my way as a consequence of our enduring friendship and the groundbreaking work of the Forensic Architecture agency.

Many of my peers have since become my professional colleagues, both at Goldsmiths and further afield. I have drawn great momentum from our spirited debates. In particular, Shela Sheikh has been an encouraging and generous advocate of this project. James Burton, Joel McKim, Daisy Tam, Andy Christodoulou, Sean McKeown, and Theresa Mikuriya all figure strongly in this network of peers from our formative days together in the Centre for Cultural Studies. Likewise Angela Melitopoulos, Celine Conderelli, Beatrice Gibson, and Ines Schaber were my doctoral allies in the Centre for Research Architecture when *Material Witness* was but a loose collection of conjectural ideas.

The slow burn of the project has benefited immeasurably from ongoing discussions with close friends and far-flung colleagues. Kindred spirits and fellow artists Carey

Young, Lawrence Abu Hamdan, Kodwo Eshun, Daniel R. Small, Zach Blas, Metahaven, Susanne Kriemann, Anjalika Sagar, Patrick Mahon, Kathleen Ritter, Judy Radul, Michel Daigneault, Stephen Scoffield, Tom Tlalim, Helene Kazan, James Bridle, Broomberg & Chanarin, Milica Tomić, Ayesha Hameed, Jol Thomson, Cooking Sections, Helen Knowles, Daniel Mann, Terence Gower, Mohammad Salemy, Shaunak Sen, Emanuel Licha, Nabil Ahmed, Maayan Amir, Raviv Ganchrow, Kelly Jazvac, David Merritt, Rosa Menkman, Henry Bradley, Solveig Suess, Greg McLaren, Sean Synder, Nicholas Mangan, and the wonderful, sadly missed Colette Urban have all been part of its unfolding.

Moreover, without the energizing support of colleagues Lynn Turner, Lorenzo Pezzani, Matthew Fuller, Thomas Keenan, Vikki Bell, Suhail Malik, Laura Kurgan, Keller Easterling, Michel Feher, John O'Brian, Peter C. van Wyck, Julian Henriques, Andrea Phillips, Peg Rawes, Brenna Bhandar, Irit Rogoff, Lindsay Bremner, Bridget Crone, Emily Rosamond, Wood Roberdeau, Rosalind Gray, Nicole Wolf, Jennifer Gabrys, Ryan Bishop, Jussi Parikka, Olga Goriunova, Marina Otero, Emily Pethick, Ariella Azoulay, Roma Sendyka, Antonia Majaca, Lonneke van der Velden, Danielle Celermajer, Paulo Tavares, Godofredo Pereira, Andrea Bagnato, Charles Heller, Fusun Turetken, Francesco Sebregondi, Lewis Bush, Adrian Lahoud, Jamon Van Den Hoek, Chris Woods, Christina Varvia, Sophie Dyer, Niels Schrader, Roosje Klap, Kirsty Robertson, Susan Edelstein, Lawrence Bekich, Gregory Sholette, and my MFA supervisor Geoffrey Batchen, this adventure would never have gotten off the ground.

Curators have also played a key role in helping to bring the ideas of *Material Witness* into public presence, and many of the images that populate this book are drawn from these exhibitions and commissioned projects. My immense appreciation for these creative opportunities is owed to Anselm Franke, Ele Carpenter, Ruba Katrib, Rosario Güiraldes, Adam Kleinman, Natsha Hoare, Lucas van der Velden, Brigette van der Sande, Mihnea Mircan, James Parker, Joel Stern, Doreen Mende, Maite Borjabad López-Pastor, Kevin Muhlen, Berit Fischer, María Andueza Olmedo, Antonia Alampi, Theodor Ringborg, Remco De Blaaij, Mario D'Souza, Mila Samdub, Jayne Wilkinson, and Candice Hopkins.

In my other role as a teacher and Director of the Centre for Research Architecture, I have had the great privilege of working with an extraordinary group of students over many years. Their political commitments, intellectual agility, and abiding sense of curiosity have been my constant reward, and I am deeply grateful to all who have joined me at our Roundtables.

Research for this book, too, was assisted by the archival labors of former students Nick Axel, Hannah Martin, Blake Fisher, and Jacob Burns, who helped me scour the 9.3 million evidential artifacts in the Court Records of the International Criminal Tribunal for the Former Yugoslavia. Lou Miller also contributed her skills, while Srdjan Hercigonja joined cinematographer Steffen Kraemer and me in Kosovo as a guide and translator when shooting footage for the *Material Witness* documentary. I continue to rely upon his insights into the contentious politics surrounding the Omarska mine and former concentration camp in Bosnia and Herzegovina.

A significant debt of gratitude is owed to my colleague at Goldsmiths, Sean Cubitt, who is also Editor-in-Chief of Leonardo, and Doug Sery, Senior Acquisitions Editor, both of the MIT Press, for their incredible patience and belief in the project as it evolved over the many years of its gestation. Sean may not remember the first time we crossed paths. It was at the University of Tokyo, and a series of seismic tremors cut short my lecture when I was still a student testing out ideas around material evidence and nuclear disasters—a portentous encounter. I'm also appreciative to Gillian Beaumont for her careful reading of the final draft and editorial comments. The production staff at MIT Press are to be acknowledged for their efforts on my behalf, as are the reviewers of the manuscript, whose feedback proved vital. Many image-makers have generously allowed me to include their materials. Special thanks go to Aisling O'Beirn and Martin Krenn, who provided the image of a CCTV monitor from HM Prison Maze/Long Kesh with which I open.

My parents, Paul and Lydia, and my sisters, Joan, Rosy, and Cathy, have been incredibly supportive throughout, even if the book seems perhaps a curious enterprise to them. I hope they will find some meaning within its pages. Lastly, I surely need to mention my lovely canine companions—Ori, Uschi, and Ulli—whose practical engagements with the material world have been a daily reminder of the power of matter to engender wonder. I have relied upon our long walks to keep me grounded.

1 OPENING STATEMENTS

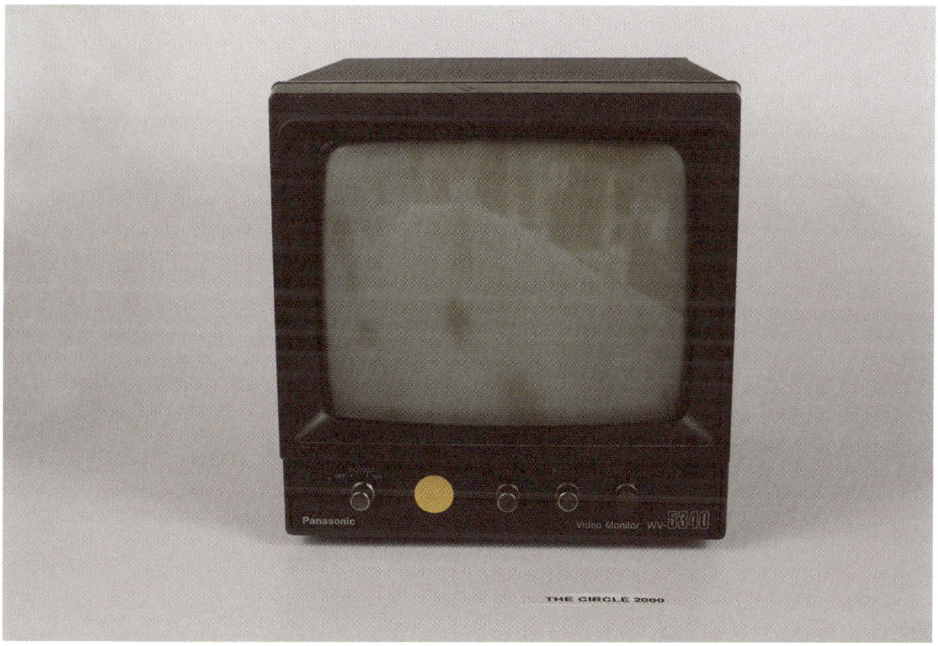

Figure 1.1
CCTV monitor as displayed in the Irish Republican History Museum, Belfast, Northern Ireland. *The Circle 2000*, Martin Krenn and Aisling O'Beirn, from the project *Transforming Maze/Long Kesh*, 2016–2018. Courtesy: Eileen Hickey.[1]

Screen Burn

A ghostly image of a corridor haunts a CCTV monitor that is no longer powered on, its phosphor compounds permanently damaged by a relentless and searing view into the notorious Long Kesh prison of Northern Ireland. The screen of this now derelict Panasonic WV-5340 surveillance system carries a materialized trace of electronic signals once relayed from a security camera mounted at a fixed vantage point within H-Block two of the prison complex. Devoid of the movement of inmates and guards, the slow burn of the prison's architectural features into the crystalline structure of the screen reveals a carceral space that no longer exists since various areas of the prison compound were demolished in 2006. It is an aggregate image composed of real-time events captured over many years; one that is saturated with the transmission of brutal histories which took place at HM Prison Maze/Long Kesh, the same prison where Bobby Sands died while on a hunger strike in 1981 along with nine other Irish Republican Army inmates. Yet it is all the more chilling because none of this violence is self-evident within the prosaic blur that remains: a cathode ray archive akin to the long exposures of early photography whose silver salts could only register the static elements of the scene, not the dynamism of bodies in movement. Burn-ins are media events that compress time when on-screen information remains motionless for extended periods: a condition of image persistence that arrests the movement of light-emitting phosphors that would normally animate its surface. This fixed electronic mediation between security camera and video monitor recalls the inexorable monotony and regulatory control of life under detention. It is as if the operations of the prison and surveillance system elide and are made manifest through the unwavering technicity of the image itself.

What evidential role could a fogged piece of glass coated in red, green, and blue phosphor dots play in a peace process as a visible proof of the powerful events that took place at HM Prison Maze throughout the many years it was in use? The representational demand to corroborate the contested versions of its history is significant, especially when experiences of prison staff and prisoners differ so dramatically. Yet evidence of what transpired in the passageways of H-Block is only partially captured by the residual traces of this particular screen. While the technical behavior of the cathode ray tube has in effect "recorded" a fixed and durational image of the prison infrastructure, the absence of any kinetic information obfuscates the presence of guards and inmates. Despite this evidential deficit, there is a stubborn resoluteness in the burnt-in image of this now dead video monitor that testifies to the simple fact that eyes and machines once conjoined to look into this very space and scrutinize its activities for years on end. Even with the closure of the prison in 2000 and the dismantling of its surveillance system, the material afterlife of the screen still retains an electronic memory of the coercive space of state power to which its infrastructural gaze was once directed. While this technical witness cannot be called forth to testify to the specific acts that might have taken place in this H-block corridor, its evidential reach—a material composite derived out of years of prison activity—reaffirms that such a place once existed, that dreadful things may have happened right here in this hallway and behind its closed doors, which are not fully available in the defunct screen's phosphorescent afterglow. Evidence for events is never simply "self-evident" and must always be painstakingly created through processes—investigative, discursive, and rhetorical—that enable the mediation of things and allow even mute entities to make convincing truth claims. The materialized inscription of this transmissional regime thus functions both as a reminder that there are those who still have knowledge of this very space and as a mnemonic device for enabling their recollection.[2] Analyzed together, they might yield information that could corroborate and further explicate the spectral testimony registered by this media object. Moreover, the very fact that such a screen image endures despite no animating electrical charge is a forceful expression of the power of materials to record and recall events. In this regard, the screen burn is both a material trace *of* and a "material witness" *to* the history of political violence known as the "Troubles."

Material as Witness

This book introduces a new operative concept—*material witness*—an exploration of the evidential role of matter as registering external events as well as exposing the practices and procedures that enable such matter to bear witness. *Material witnesses* are nonhuman entities and machinic ecologies that archive their complex interactions with the world, producing ontological transformations and informatic dispositions that can be forensically decoded and reassembled back into a history. *Material witnesses* operate as double agents: harboring direct evidence of events as well as providing circumstantial evidence of the interlocutory methods and epistemic frameworks whereby such matter comes to be consequential. *Material witness* is, in effect, a Möbius-like concept that continually twists between divulging "evidence of the event" and exposing the "event of evidence."

In pursuing this research, I examine a wide range of materials that have recorded trace evidence of the violence that generated their contexts, and explore the institutional and disciplinary protocols that enable their latent histories to be rendered intelligible and made to speak, even if their "speech acts" often fall upon deaf ears or challenge accepted truths. My case studies draw on many events in which different forms of technical media have combined to record a violation or transgression. Moreover, in initiating an account of the *Material Witness* with a media artifact produced by an automated form of "machinic vision" from a highly conflictual site and context, I wish to signal the conjunction between matter and evidence that shapes this enterprise as a particular kind of political project: one that discloses different orders of knowledge and the regimes of perceptibility that enable materials to become evidential and bear witness.[3] Indeed, what the following cases highlight is the degree to which a rearrangement of matter exposes the contingency of witnessing, soliciting questions about what can be known in relationship to that which is seen or sensed, about who or what is able to bestow meaning onto things, and about whose stories will be heeded or dismissed. Consequently, the project also reflects upon the specific requirements that must be met to secure "legitimate" acts of witnessing, from legal tribunals to climate change summits, as they adjudicate over whether certain kinds of observational practices and testimonial methods should be enlisted or rejected. It is within these institutional forums that "witnessing" can itself be witnessed, for it is here that it achieves its most prominent articulation as a distinct realm of procedural expression subject to agreed-upon conventions that turn on questions of expertise and direct experience. Inasmuch as *Material Witness* seeks to trouble settled understandings of the concepts that organize its case studies, it also engages directly with the institutional logics that structure their difference in order to expand acts of witnessing to more-than-human realms. Throughout, I have tried to account for the myriad ways in which the responsiveness of matter to external forces demands an acute and renewed sense of material specificity in order to grasp the full political implications that such ongoing changes or interactions might yield. As a conceptual imperative and practical project, my aim is ultimately to relink the material world and its affordances with the space of the aesthetic, the juridical, and the political. Consequently, my analysis often crosscuts between highly imagistic accounts and detailed technical descriptions. This is my mode of aesthetic assembly and narrative construction, which I borrow from my ongoing practice and sensibility as an artist-researcher.

While the key terms and concepts that structure this book—matter, witnessing, media, forensics, evidence, and event—are informed by philosophical thought, aesthetic considerations, legal arguments, and scientific understandings, they emerge more directly out of my practice as a contemporary artist and documentary filmmaker as well as my work with Forensic Architecture, a human rights agency directed by Eyal Weizman at Goldsmiths, University of London. Through practical engagements, investigative assignments, archival forays, remote fieldwork, and collaborative activities, my practice has always been generative of my research insights and crucial to establishing

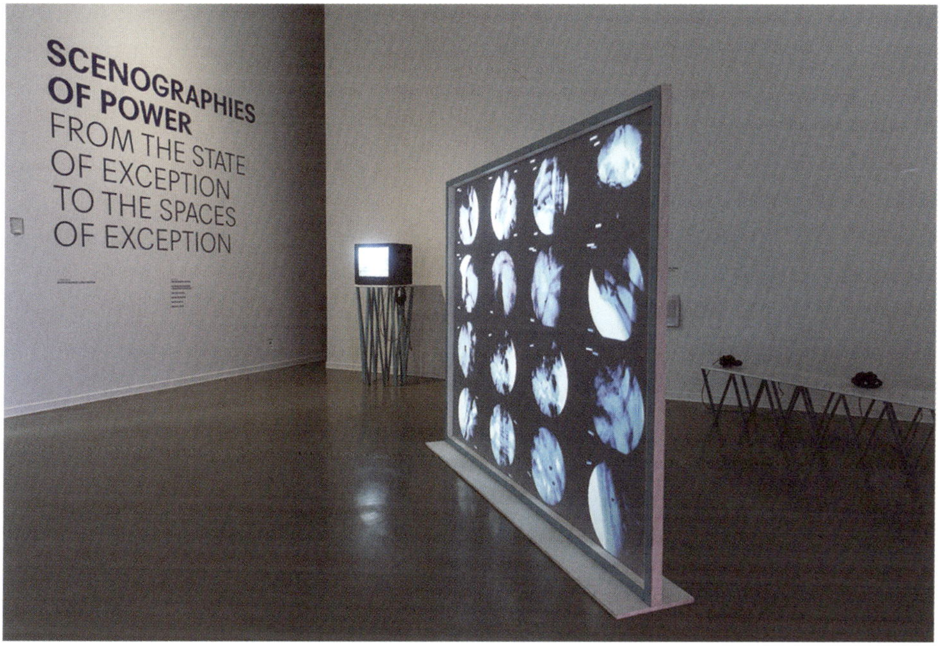

Figure 1.2
Installation view, *Scenographies of Power: From the State of Exception to the Spaces of Exception*, La Casa Encendida, 2017. Detail from *Evidence on Trial*, Sequence: X-Rays Metropolitan Police Photographic Section Zre Zre Co-op, Temp Mort, Kosovo, 01/06/99, Susan Schuppli. Curated by Maite Borjabad López-Pastor. Photo credit: Maria Eugenia Serrano, 2017.

its theoretical framework as well as foregrounding its political relevance. This remains the case in this book as I develop the concept of the *material witness* through an analysis of a series of events, some of which are also the subject of various artworks. In order to conceptualize the broader scope of the project and articulate its practical stakes, I have nonetheless had to draw upon many critical resources and disciplinary knowledges in which I have little or no formal training. I have tried to work modestly and patiently to develop some familiarity and fluency with the ways in which they both organize their debates and define certain concepts that are also mobilized within this project.

Over the course of the book's unfolding, it will become clear that even general terms such as "evidence" are being strategically recast to designate an *informed* condition, thus expanding upon conceptions that might be advanced by law or any of the disciplines from which it conventionally gains its critical purchase and traction. Under the conditions of a "post-truth" world, our notions of what constitutes material evidence for events appears to be on shaky epistemological ground, yet as has already been suggested, evidence for events is never fully self-sufficient and must always be correlated and translated across domains if it going to forward a public truth upon which a ruling, policy, or regulatory requirement can emerge, or upon which a political claim can be made. Whereas the notion of the "event" which I conjoin with that of "evidence" is specifically indebted to the theoretical work of Gilles Deleuze. Unlike other philosophers for whom the event represents a radical break in historical continuities or the commencement of something altogether different, the event for Deleuze is not a new occurrence that cuts its ties with the past, or a beginning that initiates a new story, but is, rather, a change in the intensities of relations between elements that creates a relay connecting the whole to its parts. Events are inherent to all dynamic processes, whether naturally occurring or artificially induced. Drawing upon examples from two of my nuclear case studies, one could say that within a biological system the abnormal growth in cellular tissue that mutates into a malignant tumor becomes an event. Likewise, variations in the organization of nonliving matter are also events: the atmospheric radioactivity that altered the chemistry of Vladimir Shevchenko's film stock shot at Chernobyl, or the movement of tectonic plates which generated seismic activity in the Pacific resulting in a tsunami and meltdown at the Fukushima plant. It is neither possible to determine the absolute origins of an event nor to pinpoint its moment of inception, but we can discern its effects.

> With every event, there is indeed the present moment of its actualization, the moment in which the event is embodied in a state of affairs, an individual, or a person, the moment we designate by saying "*here*, the moment has come." The future and the past of the event are evaluated only with respect to this definitive present, and from the point of view of that which embodies it.[4]

While events reveal themselves through their actualization in the present, they are always suffused by the past from which they derive their momentum and resources. Consequently, events can also reemerge in the future if their enabling circumstances prevail. For example, there was no sudden eruption of violence in the Balkans after the death of President Tito in 1980, but rather a change in the intensity of nationalist sentiments that was already a circumstance of the federated politics that had merged six republics into one Socialist state after World War II. The evidence of war crimes captured on video analyzed in chapter 8, "Cross-Examination," is a decisive capture of these ongoing ethnic tensions, which clearly have not entirely abated since the signing of the Dayton Peace Accords on November 21, 1995. Instead they are being realized in many other ways that continue the logic of ethnic discrimination.[5] During the 24 years of the International Criminal Tribunal for the former Yugoslavia (ICTY), evidence for horrific events became momentarily graspable in the form of a legal trial, which itself became an event and a further staging ground for the production of new forms of evidence brought about by the serial flows of the court and its juridical elaborations.

The term "matter" is used throughout to refer to nonhuman entities, whether they are material or dematerialized in nature. But this is not the "inhuman matter" of chattel slavery, the legacy of which endures and deeply troubles certain investments in New Materialist thought organized by simple ontological lures without any attendant politics. In my analysis, matter is a question of properties—the capacity of materials to register change resulting in an accrual of information—and not an issue of property out of which surplus value might be extracted. I borrow the notion of "informational enrichment" from geographer Andrew Barry, who usefully carries it forward from the collaborative work of Isabelle Stengers and Bernadette Bensaude-Vincent around the molecular reformulation of materials.[6] "Whether functional or structural, new materials are no longer intended to replace traditional materials. They are made to solve specific problems, and for this reason they embody a different notion of matter. Instead of imposing a shape on the mass of material, one develops an 'informed material' in the sense that the material structure becomes richer and richer in information."[7] It is this condition of informational enrichment that allows us to read history, and ultimately politics, back out of the complex material strata of our world. Information is, as Alexander Galloway argues, a process of in-forming, distinguishing it from data, which designates all that is given: "So, in contrast to data, information stresses less a sense of presence and giving-forth, and more a plastic adoption of shape. Information exists whenever worldly things are 'in-formed,' or 'put into form.'"[8] New conceptions of computational matter, too, have evolved in parallel with new understandings of algorithmic reasoning that do not assume any necessary continuity with our tangible object-world and anthropocentric logics, but locate their emergence within code.[9] I am inspired by this scholarship, but I focus more concretely on the ways in which digital entities index external events as corrupt files, glitches, transmission noise, and codec errors, which are also an expression of their internal transformation and coding modifications. Consequently matter has an analog valence in my work even when it comes to digital forms of evidence. For example, within the ICTY, all digital information from computer hard drives to data was treated as analog to prevent evidence tampering and ensure chain of custody. A series of images taken or produced with a digital camera by an OTP (Office of the Prosecutor) investigator in the aftermath of a war crime would be burned to disk, the CD carrying these images photographed and labeled, the image of this CD carrying the images taken at the crime scene filed with the Tribunals' Registry and given a unique number. A method of analogization takes places: from digital data,

Date: 20 April 2010 **Case No.: IT-04-74-T**

This is to certify that a CD-Rom has been filed with Registry page number : D59277

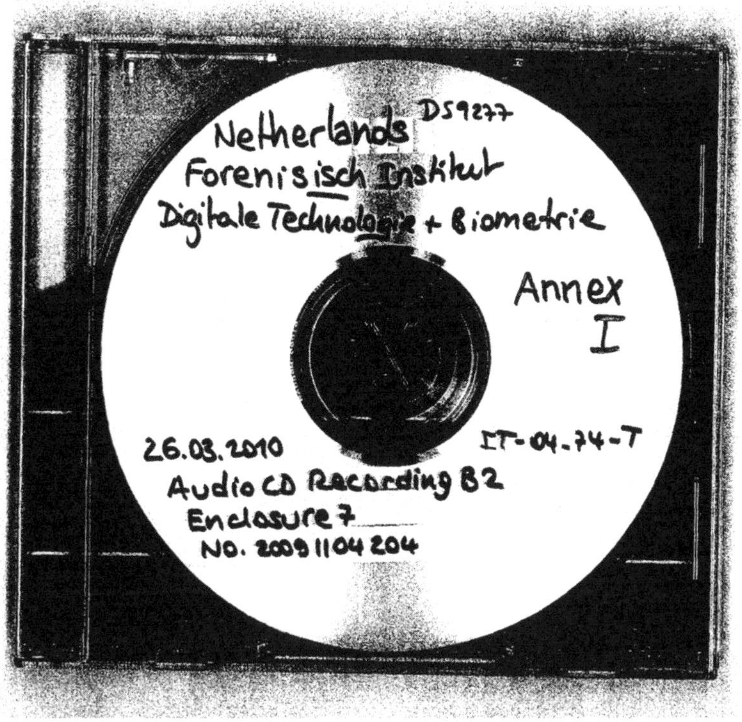

Figure 1.3

IT-04-74: Prlic and Others [TIF] Annex I (CD) to Slobodan Praljak's motion for the admission of Franjo Lozić's statement, the Bosnian Muslim press conference transcript, and associated Ministry of Justice Netherlands Forensic Institute documents. Document Type: Motions • Date: 20/04/2010 • Defense counsel. Source: ICTY Court Records.

to polycarbonate substrate, and eventual photographic proof that safeguards the integrity of information such that any tampering with the original image files (deletion or alteration) would require the physical destruction of the disk itself.

The term "media" likewise migrates and expands over the course of this book: from customary understandings that refer to the technological forms of image, sound, and data capture associated with the inscriptive capacities of film, photography, magnetic tape, and hard drives to damaged ecological systems such as an oil spill which, it is argued, are responding to environmental change in uniquely mediatic ways; a discussion with which I conclude. "Forensics," too, is employed in a manner that decouples it from its familiar uptake within criminal justice as a science in service to the law and returns it to its etymological origins in the Greek: forensis. Forensic Architecture, in particular, has repurposed this understanding to designate the persuasive skills that attend to the manufacture and presentation of evidence put before the forum.[10] Throughout I refer to the productive labor of the forensic turn as an act of imagination rather than that which merely enables deductive reasoning, the sole purpose of which is to shore up the legal use value of things: a proposition that resonates with Bruno Latour's distinction between matters of fact and matters of concern.[11] Forensics reconceptualized as such is less a means of interrogation than a mode of assembly: not a claim for the irreducibility of the object, but an ecological proposition that brings media, science, and law into new political configurations. Forensics does not get us closer to the simple truth of things, but brings us into contact with the complex realities that constitute our contemporary experiences. Rather than a search for unequivocal certainties, the work of forensics herein is oriented toward an opening-up of the expressive potential of things, including the creative retrieval and mobilization of affects. As Donna Haraway has observed, "Redistributing the narrative field by telling another version of a crucial myth is a major process in crafting new meanings. One version never replaces another, but the whole field is rearranged in interrelation among all the versions in tension with each other."[12] A culturally inflected notion of forensics also considers how nonscientific materials such as artworks, literature, and oral traditions too might enact their relevance to events by furnishing alternate forms of information—proxy data—or even countertestimonials to established understandings of events. In forensic science, every contact is perceived as leaving a trace, in forensic imagination every encounter is capable of being retraced.[13] With what I hope are some working definitions in place, I now wish to turn to the singular concept borrowed from law that guides this project.

Within a legal context, the *material witness* is a person who is deemed to have information germane to the subject matter of a lawsuit or criminal prosecution that is significant enough to affect the outcome of the trial. In other words, the witness, by means of the information they may possess, is considered sufficiently *pertinent* to the legal proceedings such that every effort must be made to procure their testimony. Humans become witnesses when their knowledge or experience positions them as semantically "material" to a case. My particular usage, in contrast, takes the concept quite literally: material *as* witness. In order to ensure its conceptual rigor, the *material witness* must remain vigilant against tendencies that might consign its operations to metaphor, which is what often happens when concepts travel from one domain to another. However, at certain points I do refer to the "testimony of things," which runs counter to the established discourse of witnessing that emerged in the mid-twentieth century organized by an ethics of becoming: a transformation from a person who can *bear* witness as a consequence of their lived experience, to a *practice* of witnessing whereby one consciously decides to become a witness in order to testify to events.[14] Primo Levi made this latter point very explicitly, stating that in surviving the camps he decided to become a writer so that he might bear witness.[15] Despite this ethical shift in the figure of the witness, the act of testimony remains a condition of human experience. Jacques Derrida too maintained that "the trace cannot bear witness" without a mediating force who can ask it the right or relevant questions, "that we need the work of the historian himself, of his living testimony as it were, in order to constitute a testimony from these traces."[16] Derrida located the act of testimony—philosophically conceived—within the speech acts of the human subject whose recall and public narration enable them to speak back to the events of history or within the interpretative apparatus of disciplinary knowledge whereby the expert "holds court" over the mediation and interpretation of things as evidence. Testimony, he argued, is of a different order than evidence because it is contracted to speech via a sworn oath to tell the truth, the whole truth, and nothing but the truth. "Consequently, where there is evidence, there is not testimony. The technical archive, in principle, should never replace testimony. It may furnish exhibits or evidence, within the theoretical order that is the order of evidence, and must be foreign to the element of credit, faith, or belief implied by the testimonial pledge."[17] This legal and philosophic distinction, which is in fact an administrative one, between the *material witness* as someone who can bear witness to an event and the technical witness as that which can offer material evidence of events but cannot testify of its own accord, is a site of continuous struggle throughout this book. While natural scientists tend to privilege "brute matters of fact as the only true origin of reality," social scientists have made language the sole condition of intelligibility.[18] Karen Barad raises this fundamental paradox when she asks: "How did language come to be more trustworthy than matter? Why are language and culture granted their own agency and historicity, while matter is figured as passive and immutable or at best inherits a potential for change derivatively from language and culture? How does one even go about inquiring after the material conditions that have led us to such a brute reversal of naturalist beliefs when materiality itself is always already figured within a linguistic domain as its condition of possibility?"[19] Invoking the speech acts of things is not to propose a recoding of materiality as a quasi-linguistic form that would bring it closer to the social sciences, nor is it a rhetorical displacement of materiality into a set of signifying relations that would compose matter into intelligible patterns.[20] It is, rather, a demand made on behalf of materials that we apprehend the potential of matter to reorganize accepted points of view and customary truths. Where there is material evidence, there is the possibility of testimony without it necessarily being contracted to the conventions of legal speech, nor indeed that of human language. This involves a conceptual realignment away from a functional understanding of "speech" toward an engagement with the expressive technicity of matter.

To borrow the legal concept of the *material witness* and then rework it through a cultural model of nonhuman agency is to consider evidence not solely with regard to what claims it might help to establish or support, but also in terms of what it can do to bear critical witness to acts and techniques of witnessing. The trial always revolves around the "questioning" of different forms of testimony; thus what emerges out of such interrogative proceedings is, as Stengers posits, a testimonial "artifact" that can tell us a great deal more about the "the device of interrogation" than the matters subject to its inquiry.[21] One of my ongoing tasks as an artist-researcher has been to highlight the ways in which legal materials can also be worked on theoretically and practically within the spheres of culture. An interest in aesthetics or legal processes should not remain exclusive to the study of art, nor the jurisdiction of law; we need, rather, to be attuned to the ways in which different knowledges and their practices are already mutually affective. Clearly the *material witness* of law cannot neatly be mapped onto a materialist conception of witnessing configured around the expressive agency of matter. However, as philosopher Brian Massumi suggests, a certain "residue" always carries over from one domain into another: "When you uproot a concept from its network of systematic connections with other concepts, you still have its *connectibility*."[22] Migrating and repurposing concepts to inhabit other domains of experimentation is one of the goals of this book, and another means by which law might enter into a productive relay with the humanities to develop alternate conceptual frameworks and open up new critical perspectives.

At the time of the International Military Tribunal at Nuremberg (1945–1946), Robert H. Jackson, Chief US Prosecutor, made the controversial decision to base the trials on the administrative archive of the Nazi regime rather than upon the testimony of survivors, thus eschewing living witnesses in favor of documentary evidence. This decision stands in my mind as perhaps the most noteworthy example of the presumed legal agency of the technical witness. Jackson's retrospective comments, made in 1954, emphasize both the sober impartiality he attributes to such material artifacts—the paper trails that would corroborate the systematic planning and implementation that went into exterminating six million European Jews—but also the implicit belief that the sheer scale and transparent ambitions of the Third Reich evidenced in these records would convert mute witnesses into fully realized agents of legal speech. In other words, the material record would speak for itself.

> The prosecution early was confronted with two vital decisions. … One was whether chiefly to rely upon living witnesses or upon documents for proof of the case. The decision … was to use and rest on documentary evidence to prove every point possible. The argument against this was that documents are dull, the press would not report them, the trial would become wearisome and would not get across to the people. There was much truth in this position, I must admit. But it seemed to me that witnesses, many of them persecuted and hostile to the Nazis, would always be chargeable with bias, faulty recollection, and even perjury. The documents could not be accused of partiality, forgetfulness, or invention, and would make the sounder foundation, not only for the immediate guidance of the tribunal, but for the ultimate verdict of history. The result was that the tribunal declared, in its judgment, "The case, therefore, against the defendants rests in a large measure on documents of their own making."[23]

While Nuremberg would make enormous contributions to jurisprudence, argues literary theorist Shoshana Felman, in "setting up a binding legal precedent of crimes against humanity," it would be the Eichmann Trial in Jerusalem (1961) that returned the living witness to the stands,[24] inaugurating what Thomas Keenan and Eyal Weizman have called the "era of the witness," in deference to Felman and Dori Laub's claim that the twentieth century was the "era of testimony."[25] Felman maintains that the two trials—Nuremberg and Jerusalem—staged the fundamental differences between nonhuman and human forms of evidence. But, as Hannah Arendt has forcefully argued in her critique of the Eichmann Trial, its focus on the testimony of survivors also shifted legal attention toward the victim and away from the perpetrator.[26] I will return to this crucial distinction in chapter 8, which explores an extraordinary videotape shot by Liri Loshi in the aftermath of the massacre at Izbica, Kosovo, in March 1999 that was presented as evidence of crimes against humanity during one of the trials of Slobodan Milošević in The Hague. In chapter 9, "Expert Witness," I detail another indictment of crimes against humanity brought before the Trial Chambers of the ICTY, in which a videotaped alibi was entered into evidence during proceedings against Slavko

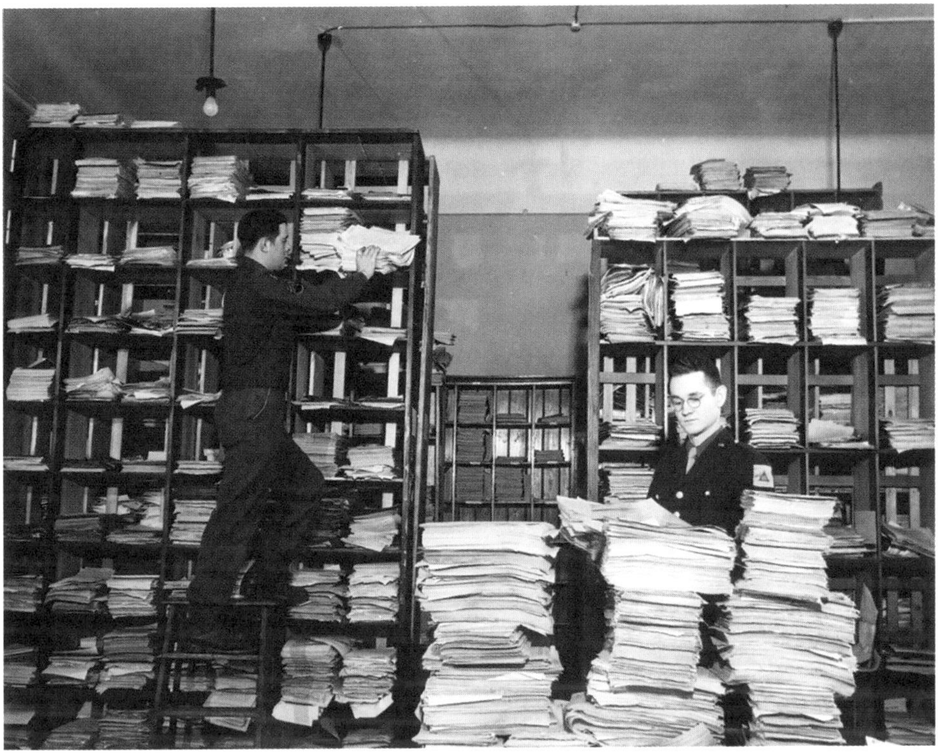

Figure 1.4
US Army staffers organize German documents collected by war crimes investigators as evidence for the International Military Tribunal. Nuremberg, Germany, November 20, 1945–October 1, 1946. Source: US National Archives and Records Administration.

Dokmanović in 1997. Dokmanović was charged with participating in the mass execution of more than 200 people at the Ovčara farm southeast of Vukovar, Croatia, on November 20, 1991. Although legal trials, especially the war crimes tribunal of the ICTY (with its 161 indictments), constitute a significant context for working through the notion of the *material witness*, the concept is not pursued as a legal one, nor does this book dwell upon questions of judgment in relation to the injustices that they mediate. But it does explore the intertwined relations between human and nonhuman forms of testimony, and the abilities of each to bear witness to powerful events as they enter into public forums as agents endowed with the capacity of [technical] speech.

The significance accorded to the affective dimensions of testimony as fundamentally human is a central provocation that the concept of the *material witness* challenges.

I assert that technical objects can account for and express their historical conditions; that artifacts can induce the affective register of testimony; and that materials can, in short, bear witness. Even Levi, when recounting his experiences as a survivor of Auschwitz, has likened his memory traces to the machinic operations of a tape recorder, which can rewind and playback history; experiences that Levi cannot fully reconcile as the properties of the human: "I still have a visual and acoustic memory of the experience that I cannot explain … sentences in languages I do not know have remained etched in my memory, like on a magnetic tape."[27] The legal primacy of human testimony is, as Keenan and Weizman argued in *Mengele's Skull*, being supplemented by a forensic, which is to say increasingly technoscientific, account of events that has shifted the emphasis toward an object-oriented juridical culture immersed in matter and in code.[28] Forensic blood work, such as comparative DNA analysis, offers an exemplary marker of this shift in juridical culture; one in which materially encoded "truths" are revealed through scientific procedures and narrated by technical experts. Yet even within highly regulated domains such as criminal tribunals, with their strict adherence to rules of procedure, the status of material evidence is still never completely fixed but must at all times remain open to cross-examination and legal reassessment.

Since its establishment by the UN Security Council on May 25, 1993, and the adoption of its rules and procedures a year later, the ICTY has regularly passed amendments (49 in total) governing its evidential protocols.[29] Amending admissibility standards allows different kinds of materials to be presented in court, and thus also different kinds of legal arguments to be made. The provisions that determine admissibility are, however, always jurisdictionally specific such that the legal frameworks of certain courts do not regard anything other than spoken testimony and written documents or technical reports as actual forms of evidence. In these contexts visual materials might be treated as aids to memory or as forms of corroborating evidence, if they are accepted at all. Despite Pakistan's legal inheritance from English common law, photographs and other forms of visual media are not easily permitted into legal proceedings due to the nature of Pakistani evidence law, said Islamabad lawyer Shahzad Akbar in a conversation we had in 2013. At other times visual evidence may be excluded because agreed-upon standards as to the handling and processing of certain kinds of media materials are not in place, or because the scientific and financial resources required for the validation of evidence such as DNA might be inadequate or unavailable. The legal admissibility of new forms of technical evidence may also turn on other considerations, such as the appropriate protections that should be in place to shield people from the undue reach of the state, especially when technologies are new or not commonplace. In 2001, a landmark judgment was reversed and the case remanded because the thermal imaging technology used to disclose evidence of a residential marijuana grow-op was "not in general public use," and therefore the plaintiff, Danny Lee Kyllo, would have had a reasonable expectation of privacy in his own home. Had the technology been more widespread, the Supreme Court of the United States might well have upheld the search warrant and indictment.[30] With this example, the question of admissibility is less an issue of the specific technical evidence produced than the social context in which such a thermal imaging device had been deployed. Given that more than two decades have passed since the inception of the ICTY, and with them extraordinary changes in technology, especially with respect to the kinds of forensic techniques that can be called upon, it is not surprising that the status of material evidence in the vault of the Office of the Prosecutor must remain open to reassessment, particularly as cases move into the latter phases of appeals, which can take place many years, even decades, after a verdict was rendered.

The specific context for many of the juridical insights developed throughout this book are drawn directly from multiyear research I conducted into the evidential

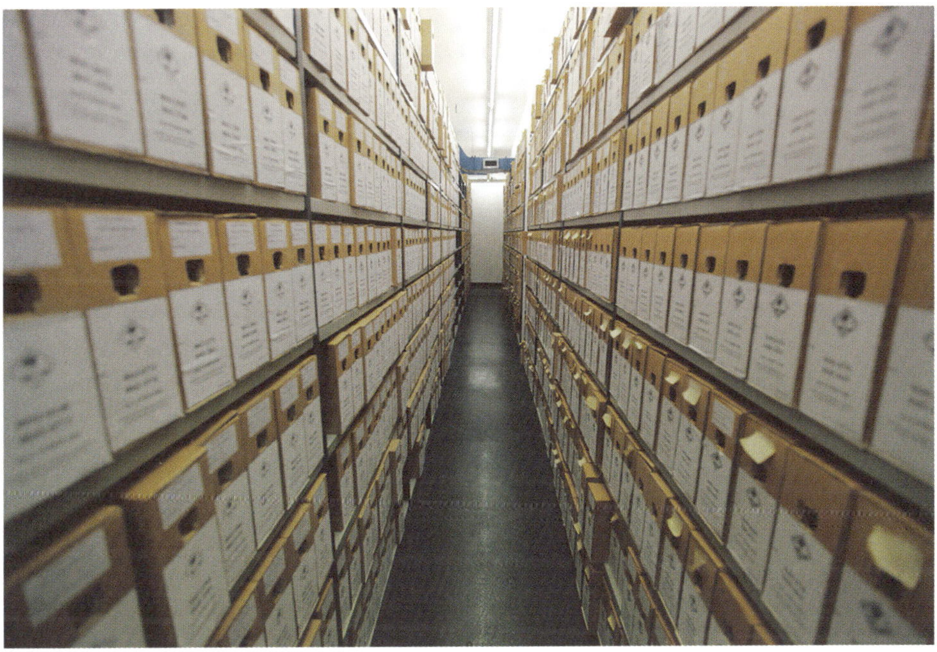

Figure 1.5
Evidence vault of the Office of the Prosecutor (OTP). Photo credit: Damir Sagolj. Source: Reuters.

holdings of the ICTY, which comprise 9.3 million documents and objects, including photographs, diaries, maps, diagrams, exhumation records, X-rays, radio intercepts, audio recordings, and videotapes, as well as physical objects such as scale models, computer hard drives, personal effects, munitions, and even remnants of charred timber and stone. All is held here, save biohazardous materials such as blood-soaked clothing, which would have been documented and then disposed of. By 2010, the ICTY Court Records required 3,704 meters of storage shelving alone. In addition to the evidential exhibits used and held by the OTP, transcripts of the cases and procedural documents are also scanned and entered into the e-court database of the Records of the Trial and Appeals Chambers. Eventually these trial transcripts, documents, and evidentiary materials become part of the public Court Records and are gradually being made fully accessible online, or can be secured upon written request.[31] As a quasi-historic body, with its cases largely completed and sentencing rendered, these evidential holdings constitute a legal record of the first international criminal law court—a process of war crimes prosecution that began with the Nuremberg and Tokyo Trials in the 1940s, and continued with the creation of the International Criminal Tribunal for Rwanda in 1994. They also provide unparalleled insight into the complex inner workings of an international court. In particular, they disclose the procedures and practices that convert testimony and artifacts into matters of legal evidence capable of presiding over questions of public truth.

However, what really astonished me throughout my investigations was the degree to which evidentiary materials carried the seemingly incongruous imprint of the Tribunal itself, often being modified to accommodate their presentation in court. While originals are safeguarded within the relatively stable environmental conditions of the OTP evidence vault, when they interface with the court as digital displays they undergo all manner of adaptation. Color photographs are marked by witnesses, duplicated, cropped, and photocopied, often reappearing as degraded black-and-white images in another prosecution. Lengthy videos might be edited and spliced with intertitles to assist with prosecutorial narration, or to clarify a complex sequence of events for a witness. While such modifications do not necessarily impinge upon the probative value of evidentiary materials, they do function as a kind of palimpsest that allows me to read the history of their transit through various legal proceedings. Through my creative practice as an artist I have explored the many ways in which the injustices of war are being managed by judicial instruments such as the ICTY through the presentation and production of evidence. Within the framework of this artistic research, I have tracked media materials sourced from the ICTY's public archive of 190,000 entries (primarily photos and videos) as they made their way through the networked legal infrastructures

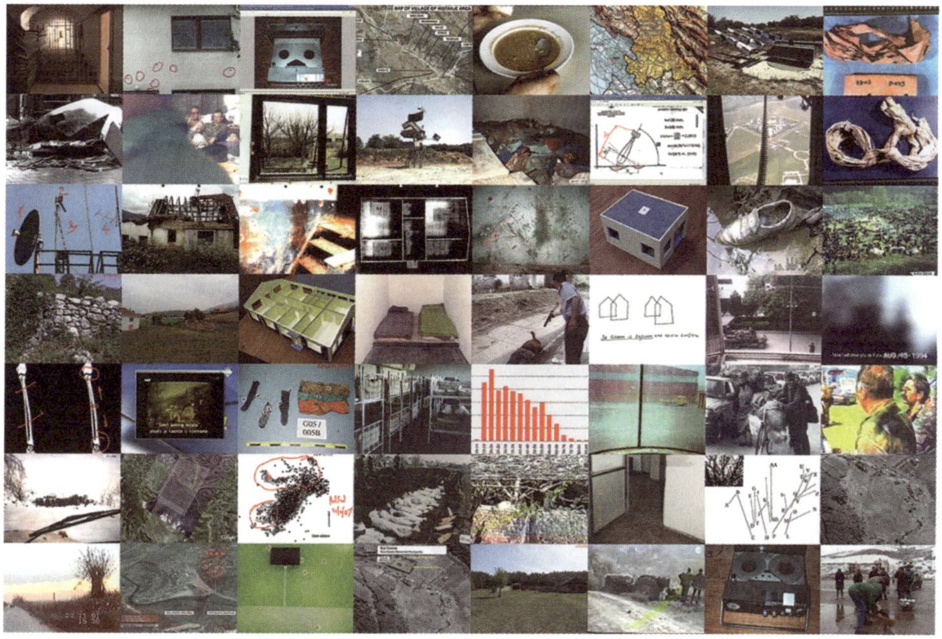

Figure 1.6
ICTY Court Records. Source: ICTY Court Records

of the court, moving in and out of different trial proceedings in various states of transformation. At every juncture in the administrative circuits of the Tribunal and its prosecutions, there is much "evidence" to suggest that evidential materials are not only carrying information related to a potential war crime (photographs of destroyed buildings, videos of hate speech, maps of military strategy, models of concentration camps, X-rays of bullet-ravaged bodies), but are themselves also registering and aggregating the protocols of the court. It is precisely these operations of extraneous registration that designate a condition of *material witnessing*. Because legal practices within a criminal case are heavily reliant upon the rhetorical potential of objects to assist the judiciary in making or disputing truth claims, the methods, which enable such forms of narration, are relatively legible, even to the layperson. Inasmuch as witnesses and experts do play a central role in testifying to events, the power of objects to help build a case by acting as visual aids, conferring authority, and substantiating the claims of specialists, is noteworthy. This artistic research, which continues, resulted in a series of photographic and video installations that documented the ways in which evidence itself was effectively put on trial.[32]

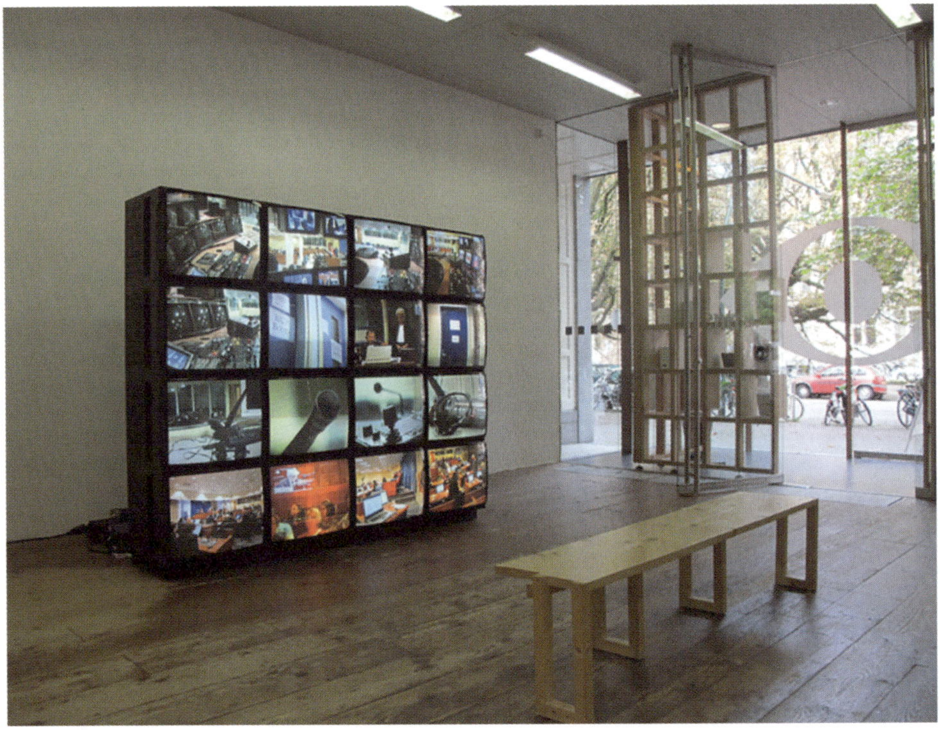

Figure 1.7
Installation view, *Evidence on Trial*, Sequence: Translation Errors, Susan Schuppli. *See you in The Hague* exhibition program curated by Brigitte van der Sande, 2014. Photo credit: Stroom Den Haag.

However, the mere fact that materials capture and archive eventful processes within their substratum, or harbor information as metadata, does not convert such entities into *de facto material witnesses* capable of testifying before the tribunals of history. Matter becomes a *material witness* only when the complex histories entangled within objects are unfolded, transformed into legible formats, and offered up for public consideration and debate. Without this dimension of public discourse (here I concur with Derrida, who maintains that witnessing, properly speaking, must take place within its appropriate public forums) artifacts cannot fully attain the status of the witness but remain virtual, carrying their archives of encrypted data into the future as mere latent potential. The conventions surrounding which public forums are able to confer legitimacy upon the speech acts of things, and which agreed-upon standards will permit material evidence to stand up to the scrutinies of the various frameworks that evaluate and pass judgment upon them, will of course be continually queried and critiqued in the case studies that follow. Nonetheless it is the communal feature of witnessing, whereby materials become the objects of public contestation over what claims can be made in their name, that is at stake here. Inasmuch as a given artifact might bear witness to the specific historical conditions out of which it emerged, it is of course influenced by many contemporary externalities such as procedural norms, financial resources, structural inequalities, political agendas, etc., that manage and even police its discursive and practical relevance. It is therefore also the admission or refusal of certain "matters" into the spaces of public discourse that converts them into a *material witness*, whether by entering into preexisting forums or, alternatively, by resisting and/or creating new ones. This is the complex feature of double agency that is being taken up.

The somewhat subversive nature of this dual condition proves useful, in that a dispute over a particular piece of evidence and its significance—juridical or otherwise—may well furnish evidence *of* and thus insight *into* practices that are willfully opposed to granting it any legitimacy. It may even cancel its probative value as evidence. Extensive examination of the Court Records of the ICTY has underscored the degree to which this is in fact the case, as the vast majority of its archival holdings are consigned to the status of visual aids, and do not assume the proper legal status of evidence in their own right. To be clear: if the *material witness* is indeed to function as an operative concept, then it is not a question of merely exposing the discursive practices and forensic procedures that produce the conditions of intelligibility whereby only legal matter attains its legitimating force, and thus capacity to testify. That would grant, as Barad cautions, "excessive power" to juridical and technoscientific apparatuses in determining what constitutes the *event* of evidence.[33] The point is to push at the limits of these institutional forums and disciplinary formations in order to question their authority and radicalize what matters as evidence, and who and what counts as a *material witness*.

The initial provocation that triggered the project was, in fact, a brief comment made by Stengers, who admonished scientists who came to their subjects with their hypothesis well in hand, and sought merely to test its validity, and thus confirm or deny their initial premise: "I'm beginning to suspect that a large part of the research has been done with the ulterior motive of imposing an answer on it. … If only we were content to let the material speak!"[34] Researchers, she argued, must accept "the possibility that it is not man but the material that 'asks' the questions, that has a story to tell, which one has to learn to unravel."[35] I propose a somewhat more potent reading of Stengers in which the material not only has the power to make and bear witness to history, but also brazenly speaks back. The more-than-human plaintiffs and witnesses that will be called upon to testify throughout this book might seem better positioned to narrate the object-world with the transparent objectivity and disinterest so cherished by the court than their arguably more subjective human counterparts. However, their implicatedness within the complex infrastructures and processes that convert material inscriptions and informatic dispositions into evidential entities that can be held accountable to the events they record troubles any possibility that the *material witness* could remain untouched by external forces or prejudicial arrangements. The whole point is to investigate the entanglements of materials at multiple scales of reality in order to activate their narrative potential as politicizing agents. Whether film footage contaminated by a lethal dose of radiation; a massacre video processed by incorrect compression codecs; a nature documentary turned camcorder alibi for a war crime; before and after satellite images that disclose signs of grave tampering; a telephonic transmission of an accidental napalm bombing remixed by inclement weather; an audiotape that archives 18½ minutes of crooked silence; an oil film whose shimmering iridescence masks a deep water horror of gushing hydrocarbons; dust particles that reveal trace evidence of destroyed architecture and pulverized human remains; or a decapitated grove of palms that bears the scars of a brutal civil war, *history* and, by extension, *politics* are registered at these junctures of ontological reckoning. In disclosing and publicly testifying to these deliberate events and accidental encounters, the *material witness* makes "evident" the very conditions and practices that convert such eventful materials into matters of evidence.

Evidence

The cases that will be brought before you arise primarily out of situations of political violence and legal contestation, even if conventional armed conflict is not their attributing source, and juridical accountability does not necessarily follow. This is because the various *material witnesses* that I analyze and present may require regime change before they can be called upon to testify legally. This is relevant for the ongoing situation in Sri Lanka discussed in chapter 10, "Burden of Proof," with regard to mobile phone footage documenting alleged war crimes on the part of the State against its minority Tamil population. Or they may be elusive witnesses whose legal status is held in abeyance until such time as an appropriate forensic technique might be brought to bear upon them. Chapter 4, "Hearsay," grapples with just such a sonic artifact: an 18½-minute gap in Watergate Tape 342 that is presumed to be an act of clumsy erasure by then US President Richard Nixon. Although this machinic silence is widely determined to have resulted from political malfeasance, and is thus sequestered in the vaults of the National Archives and Records Administration, its magnetic remainder has been the source of much conjecture and legal speculation. The *material witness* in the case of the missing 18½ minutes was divulged, not by the content-rich conversations left on tape, but by their absence: a series of noisy clicks and hisses that combined to produce a void in the historical record/recording. Indeed, the burden of evidential proof—direct evidence indicting a party with the commission of a crime—might in fact be missing altogether, either because the evidence no longer exists wholly or in part by the time the trial takes place, or because it has been lost or damaged. When this occurs, the missing evidence might be supplemented by other forms of corroborating evidence or reanimated for the court through witness recollection, or even forensic reconstruction. For example, ICTY testimony regarding the repurposing of the Omarska mine complex in Bosnia and Herzegovina as a Serb-run concentration camp during the Balkan wars of the 1990s was largely conducted using a scale model as an aid to help survivors remember their experiences and to spatially locate the movements and activities of guards and prisoners within the site.

Often direct evidence is missing or will have been discarded simply because its evidential value was not recognized at the time it was produced. The heavy storage requirements of automated video capture systems such as CCTV require the frequent deletion of files to free up space. Predigital CCTV systems, such as that used at HM Prison Maze/Long Kesh, also functioned by continuous looped recording. Likewise, owners of older video technologies (camcorders and VCRs) would frequently recycle previously recorded material because fresh tapes were rarely on hand just when they were needed. This was the technical dilemma with the Izbica massacre video, as I understand it from speaking with a local witness who was there at the time Loshi documented the massacre, and whom I later met on site when filming in Izbica, Kosovo, in 2013. Repeated audio and video capture using the same storage medium can also result in hysteresis or remanence, a technical condition discussed by Matthew G. Kirschenbaum in *Mechanisms* whereby residual traces from previous recordings telegraph through a magnetic medium to create an intermediary that carries trace evidence originating from different events.[36] It is important to note that within analog domains erasure of content is only ever achieved through the activity of re-recording over extant material: erasure must in these situations always be understood as an act of addition that includes the new as well as carrying micro-traces of past events. Such overinscription, whereby previous information comes to haunt subsequent recordings, is a hallmark of the *material witness*, allowing me to conjure the complex layered histories encrypted in images and sounds. Although such informatic supplements can help to narrate the deep time of media objects, this ghosting challenges the evidential integrity of material proofs as univocal and unsullied technical witnesses, which can in turn provoke

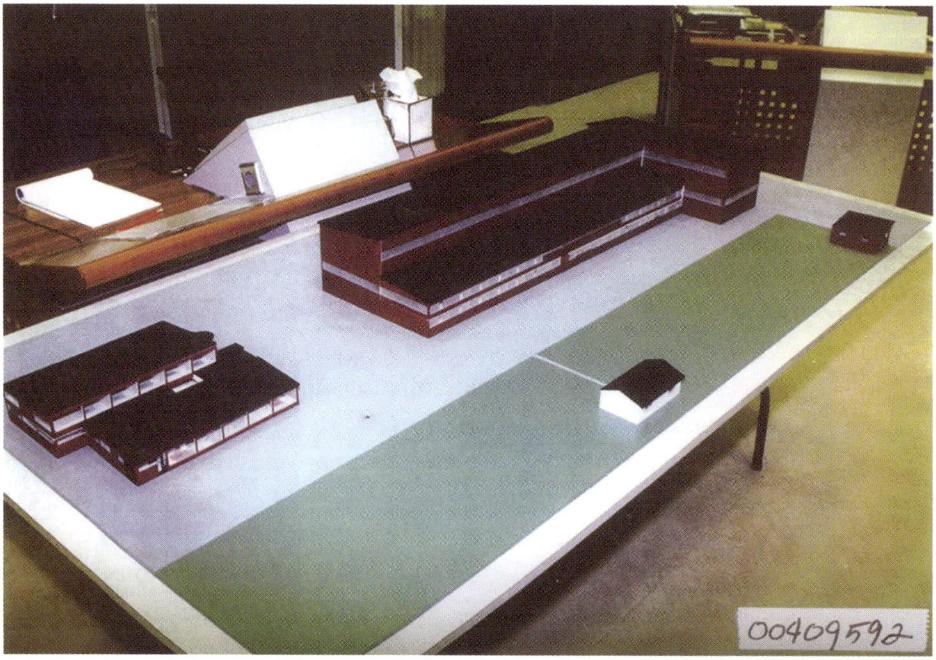

Figure 1.8
The Omarska Camp Model (0400-9592) presented during legal proceedings IT-99-36: Brdjanin. Source: ICTY Court Records.

legal uncertainties requiring further testing by forensic experts. As is the situation with many of the media artifacts discussed in this book, the burden of evidential proof concerning allegations of serious crimes or of tragic events falls, more often than not, upon the documentary claims of impoverished images and defective media:[37] that is to say, media shot or recorded under hazardous conditions or at great personal risk during times of conflict and war. Such visual shortcomings can also be attributed to the soft images produced by security cameras and remote sensing systems whose outputs are disadvantaged by their own technical limitations or by restrictions put in place by state intelligence agencies that downgrade commercial satellite resolution to maintain their military advantage. Nor are defective media necessarily diminished in quality. Hi-res images that have been subject to various forms of postproduction editing may also be considered penurious because their probative value is reduced. My usage of the terms impoverished image and defective media refers therefore not only to their aesthetic attributes and technical drawbacks, but also to their incapacitated juridical condition as convincing agents of truth.

Novel investigative methods that can relink information to shed light upon events may also be utilized to produce corroborating evidence when none seems to exist. The realization that legal evidence can be willfully manufactured is no longer the radical proposition it once was when patent models and photographic evidence first entered into nineteenth-century courtrooms. Accepting fabricated proofs as proxies for real world events required a transformation in the ways that the "legal mind" came to both recognize and "naturalize" material substitutions as persuasive new forms of evidence.[38] Forensic Architecture's work with Amnesty International on its "Black Friday" Rafah report (2015) into the last Gaza War and investigation into the Syrian torture prison Saydnaya (2017) are exemplary for their innovative production of evidentiary materials. In the Rafah report, scattered bits and pieces of media are aggregated to map events across shifting scales in order that they can bear sufficient legal witness to human rights abuses and violations of International Humanitarian Law (IHL).[39] In order to produce a three-dimensional reconstruction of Saydnaya, the team worked with the acoustic memories of "earwitnesses" (former detainees) to determine the spatial properties of the prison and model its architecture.[40]

Several cases explored in this book focus on *material witnesses* that are the unintentional by-products of an event, and although the information they disclose is perhaps too conjectural to matter legally except as forms of circumstantial evidence, they do offer opportunities for speculative research and proposition-making. Chapters 6, "Damages," and 5, "Motion to Strike," examine acoustic phenomena that have arisen from situations of aerial warfare whose emergence is not necessarily a purposeful attribute of such violence but, rather, a feature in its complex unfolding. "Damages" explores the operations of the Muirhead picture transmitter that sent the iconic image of Kim Phúc—a young South Vietnamese girl fleeing an erroneous napalm attack—from Saigon to New York via land and submarine wire communications, mixing extraneous noise into its telephonic file transfer along the way. Reports of radio chatter in the airwaves over Vietnam were frequent amongst fighter pilots in the 1970s, as was signal interference due to inclement weather. It is thus entirely plausible that the radio transmission of many images relayed during the war might also have carried trace evidence of this congested soundscape in their rematerialized form as photographic prints. This speculation is supported by the degraded quality of *Accidental Napalm* as it originally appeared on the cover of the *New York Times* on June 9, 1972, which has subsequently been replaced in our cultural imagination by the pristine Pulitzer Prize-winning print pulled later from the original 35mm negative.

"Motion to Strike" offers a much more recent account of a sonically induced *material witness* to a human rights violation: one that concerns the unrelenting 150 kHz emissions produced by armed combat drones as they survey the Tochi valley in the Federally Administered Tribal Area of Pakistan in search of targets. This acoustic condition results from a mixture of engine and propeller noise and has led to a dramatic rise in the occurrence of depression, anxiety, and fear, as well as a reorganization of daily life in the region, thus overturning the well-rehearsed political claims of minimal and contained damage to civilians living under the lethal conditions of the US-led drone war. At present these low droning frequencies are not regarded as instruments of sonic warfare, and are therefore not subject to legal determinations under the tenets of IHL as constitutive of forms of disproportional harm or, indeed, the collective punishment of a civilian population. However, attending to the sonic register of drone warfare and taking into account the collateral effects of a surveillance regime that can unleash a deadly force at any moment—quite literally out of the blue—opens up the analysis to a broader consideration of the diffuse and aggregate nature of such violence; one that a juridical analysis organized around direct strikes and casualty figures necessarily forecloses. In this context the material in question—sound—exposes the limits of the law and raises questions around what gets to count as evidence of wrongdoing in the War on Terror. It is in taking seriously the consequential nature of all matter, regardless of its determinate source or legal status, that the concept of the *material witness* becomes fully operational.

Temporal and spatial factors also determine the admissibility and validity of evidence. For example, the materials tendered might be subject to statute of limitations laws or be the result of aggregate actions conducted over many years by multiple actors. In the case of climate crimes, evidence could well be distributed across numerous geographies and therefore not meet the legal burden of direct causality as is often the challenge in prosecuting the perpetrators of environmental hazards and pollution, especially given that corporations operate by proxy through their subsidiaries. My analysis of celluloid film stock damaged by atmospheric radiation detailed in chapter 3, "Hostile Witness," led me to the unique case of caesium-137, an isotope distinguished by its radiological fingerprint and decay rate of 60 years. The alarming discovery of caesium-137 at the Forsmark nuclear power plant in Sweden on April 28, 1986 offers a rare counternarrative in the history of environmental pollution wherein cause and effect could be demonstrably relinked despite the spatial dispersion and temporal duration of contaminants. Radioactive isotopes found in the environs of the Swedish plant were irrefutably proven to have originated in the Soviet Union with the catastrophic meltdown of Chernobyl's Reactor Unit 4 two days earlier. A trail of atmospheric evidence carried aloft from the USSR across Belarus and Poland had rained its contaminants upon Sweden, where it was absorbed into surface and ground water, biota and soil. Yet the legal trial to determine responsibility for the accident took place one year later, and focused exclusively on the activities of six of its presiding staff rather than on senior decision-makers within the Politburo or, more importantly, upon the widespread and long-term impacts of radiation exposure. The six accused were sentenced to terms of imprisonment from five to ten years. While the direct legal fallout from Chernobyl remained narrow in its prosecutorial scope, resulting in a handful of convictions and the drafting of a convention on the early notification of a nuclear accident by the International Atomic Energy Agency, its enduring implications for international law are vast, and signal the first substantive call for the establishment of a transnational tribunal specifically for the prosecution of environmental crimes, the provisions of Nuremberg (which considered the destruction of environmental property as crimes against humanity in a few select cases) notwithstanding.[41]

Although The Hague Convention of 1907 respecting the Laws and Customs of War on Land has a provision for environmental protection, and was utilized during the Nuremberg Military Tribunal in several cases citing the wanton destruction of property as well as pillage, its prosecutorial force was hindered by the doctrine of military necessity.[42] In 2014 an innovative legal strategy was mounted by the Republic of the Marshall Islands in the International Court of Justice (ICJ) claiming that the "health and lives of its citizens have been destroyed by the dozens of nuclear tests conducted along its territory between 1946 and 1958."[43] This legal action was organized not around the payment of compensatory damages, or the meting out of punishment for past deeds, but a future-oriented claim toward environmental protection and biological well-being, one which posited that the principle of nuclear disarmament was by now sufficiently well established within international law to be considered customary law. "The Marshall Islands argues nuclear weapons states have failed to carry out good-faith negotiations towards nuclear disarmament, as required under the nuclear non-proliferation treaty, signed in 1968 and in force since 1970."[44] Of the nine atomic states against which this charge was filed, only the UK, Pakistan, and India have agreed to participate in preliminary proceedings. While this represents a significant legal move on the part of a very small Pacific Island nation to address the damaging and long-term consequence of nuclear weapons testing on its people and habitats, once again evidence of sustained nuclear contamination has had to take a very circuitous journey toward litigation, this time enlisting the practice of customary law and expanding its reach to include nuclear disarmament as one of its global norms, all the while knowing that such legal action is likely futile in the face of policies of deterrence that are increasingly being bolstered by the nuclear missives of North Korea.

Some 29 years after Chernobyl, caesium-137 reappeared in the coastal waters of Canada's western shores. Once again, the contaminants could have come from only one source: the meltdown at the Fukushima Daiichi Power Plant, which occurred on March 11, 2011, when a magnitude-9 earthquake and tsunami wreaked havoc on Japan's Honshu Island. While Chernobyl's fallout would eventually spread across extensive tracts of arable land throughout Europe, Fukushima's contamination seems to have traveled further still: crossing some 7,600 kilometers through the vast microbial channels of the Pacific over a period of four years. This causal connection between Japan and Canada could be established because the decay rate of caesium-137, with its half-life of 30 years, eliminated all other potential sources of contamination, including radionuclides produced by atomic testing in the Pacific Proving Grounds during the period 1945–1962. In spite of the radical temporality and global circulation of such nuclear materials, caesium-137 offers a compelling example of direct evidence, one that is an entirely predictable consequence of a radiological event, whether that of fallout resulting from atomic testing or an accidental release of contaminants due to reactor failure.

In my "Closing Arguments" I argue for a more expansive understanding of media and its evidentiary capacities through an analysis of the shifting visual scales of the Deepwater Horizon oil spill that began on April 20, 2010: a case which included earth observation satellites that monitored the slick's progress toward the coast, citizen initiatives such as Public Lab's DIY oil spill mapping project, and real-time underwater video streams that documented the gushing plume. I suggest not only that the event was distributed across multiple media platforms, but that the iridescent oil film, which crept across the surface of the Gulf of Mexico, was itself a mediatic agent comprised of hydrocarbon atoms interacting with water. The spectral effects returned to us by an oil slick are brought about by the play of reflected light waves moving through the mirrored molecular planes of an oil film crafted by the toxicological chemistry of nature. With this final example the *material witness* becomes the new media produced by the event as well as the media apparatus that now records evidence of the disaster. This case returns us to the origins of this project and the insights made possible by the radioactive contamination of Vladimir Shevchenko's Chernobyl documentary *Chronicle of Difficult Weeks* from 1986, in which radiation converted his film from an aesthetic representation of the event to an ontological capture of the real such that the film stock was both a material expression of the accident and the very means by which it could be represented. Additionally, the case of the Deepwater Horizon is legally notable because of an extraordinary lawsuit filed in the Constitutional Court of Ecuador on behalf of the rights of nature under the principle of universal jurisdiction against British Petroleum (BP), a transnational corporation headquartered in the United Kingdom. "We the plaintiffs invoke the principle of universal jurisdiction to request that this collegiate body authorize Magistrate Nina Pacari to carry out this act of recognition of one of the subjects most overlooked in history and whose rights have been most violated: nature or Pachamama."[45] The evidence—damaged nature—became both *material witness* and legal plaintiff.

In contrast to the scale of material reorderings, brought about by global warming and ecological disasters discussed in chapters 2, "Discovery," and 11, "Failure to Appear," with respect to the rise of new forms of evidence and new modes of data capture, the majority of media materials I explore tend to be modest in scale and duration. Yet despite their diminutive stature and limited temporality they are implicated in complex, multivalent events in which they forcefully "speak" back to history. Accordingly, the discussions that follow concern themselves not with a generalized material politics but with unique encounters between matters and events out of which a heterogeneous and distinctive form of material evidence was produced. Reading politics out of the technical strata of matter is not new, and a long history of media's complicities in the production of violence precedes my arguments. For example, the ID-2 Polaroid instant camera system used for making double-faced ID cards had a built-in "boost button" for enhancing darker skin tones, and was discovered to have been sold to South Africa's Apartheid regime by a secondary distributor (Frank and Hirsch) for making their infamous race passbooks.[46] Today, racial profiling—from healthcare determinations and credit scoring to predictive policing—is embedded in software tools.[47] However, it is important to signal that the evidential materials of my case studies cannot be reduced to standing in for mediatic matter in general, but must be understood as historically conditional: defined not simply by the coming together of certain matters and events, but by the ways in which a specific event and a certain form of media capture have combined to create an evidential artifact. It is their coming together that matters, not merely the fact of their existence.[48] This specificity retains its productive value as evidence moves into consensus-making forums such as courts and conventions that are characterized by generally accepted norms, policies, and agreements.

Furthermore, the selection of case studies and range of materials investigated within this book has been determined because each offers a unique opportunity for exploring the evidential capacity of a particular aesthetic arrangement of matter in which properties and processes combine to express themselves as sensible events that render the political visible. This is also the means by which, as philosopher Jacques Rancière might put it, what is held in common between the spaces and discourses of public witnessing is revealed and the political, as that which exposes and disrupts this consensual order, is activated.[49] In directing my forensic labors and imagination to the expressive singularity of a given piece of evidence, and tracking it through the discursive networks in which it gains its juridical or institutional traction, a conjunctive space is opened up between entities and events that enables even minor forms of material evidence to gather and testify on behalf of much larger political processes. This is a denaturalizing procedure that brings into perceptibility that which is neither self-evident, nor determined by judgments based upon existing standards and frameworks. It is a practice of invention and speculative thinking that builds new alliances as stakeholders gather around disputed objects and contested entities. The momentum of *Material Witness* must therefore be understood as an intervention within the general field of New Materialism in which the transformations of matter into "things that matter" remains crucial, but is undertaken with the specific aim of radicalizing the political relationships that such matter maintains to acts of witnessing and forms of testimony.

From the capture of radioactive contamination by celluloid film stock, the multiple translations of binary code into a satellite image, to the trapping of ever greater concentrations of black-carbon deposits within Arctic snow, when entities, including computational objects, are subject to external processes that bring about their structural reordering they produce an "informed material" in the sense that their internal composition becomes progressively enriched by information.[50] These are the moments when things are modified through direct contact; supplemented by extraneous information; or transformed through their handling and processing. Analog or physical entities do this rather well, in that they tend to offer up the visible proofs that can attest to their willful or accidental modification, and thus also the prospect of reading a contingent politics back out of their material condition. Such is obviously the case with the ghostly screen burn that inaugurates this book, or the Deepwater Horizon oil spill with which I conclude, both of which are treated in broad conceptual strokes as visual mediums that harbor and disclose information. On the other hand, digital objects seem immune to such ontological transformations, as any incoming information is subject to immediate recalculation, producing a new value—a difference of degree—but not a difference in kind. Software does have a history, but a digital bit does not carry a signifying history within itself. The computational archive appears at the level of its coding sequences as digital artifacts only when, for example, a programmer leaves trace evidence indicating that an application has been altered, or when the use of successive conversion algorithms results in data remanence.[51] Whereas analog media—whether a filmic negative or crystalline sheets of glacial ice—produces artifacts that physically transform over time as incoming information imprints itself directly within its material strata; an attribute that allows it to archive multiple superimpositions while still retaining the expressive singularity of each successive layering. Yet conceptualizing all recomposed matter or recoded objects as informationally enriched is strategically useful for my purposes, because it forces a rethinking of the normative distinction between the analog and the digital in which information is regarded as belonging to the purview of data, and properties are those which define physical matter.

This reconceptualization of information as a different kind of matter, which emerges out of physics and the life sciences, regards information as possessing many of the same attributes that have traditionally been assigned to biological organisms and material systems. In her critical work on digital capitalism and affective labor, sociologist Patricia Ticineto Clough has argued that "In these sciences, information is understood as a capacity of matter to self-form and to engage in self-measurement; information is itself, along with matter and energy, presumed to be physical."[52] This is not to suggest that the mathematics of self-modification and machine learning that governs the functioning of computational objects and algorithmic decision-making would be legible to us in ways that are comparable to how we might observe such adaptations in the physical world. However, fundamental concepts such as feedback, whereby external processes combine to amplify or diminish the overall state of a system, are operative across disciplines. Within climate science the modulation of outputs based on changes to inputs is known as "climate forcing," and functions in much the same way that cybernetic and computational feedback loops work toward equilibrium.[53] Scientifically speaking, all natural phenomena are increasingly studied as information systems that are productive of datasets, whether the method of measurement derives from ice cores or a thermometer. Proceeding from the conception of the informatic as proper to both analog [physical] and digital [intangible] entities enables aspects of this broader project—material *as* witness—to engage with computationally derived evidence, even when acts of recoding take place within the realm of abstraction, far beyond the thresholds of human perception. Rendering the *material witness* sensible within the microarchitectures of metadata requires that we work back—forensically—through all the nodes and points of data capture, compression, and conversion, including the computational object's transmissional relays with other networks and categories of assembly. This is why the notion of informational enrichment is so helpful—because it presupposes a new conception of materiality derived out of calculation and transcoding: a provocation for thinking materiality differently, for thinking the digital analogically.

Media Forensics

In taking seriously the contention that even nonorganic entities can manifest novel forms of agency, and that matter is expressive of changes that can narrate a history, we align ourselves with a forensic paradigm; one that I was closely involved with as Senior Research Fellow and Project Coordinator of Forensic Architecture, and with which I now work as an affiliated artist-researcher. The research project continues today as an agency that brings different modes of investigation together in order to analyze violations of human rights as they are generated by and within complex configurations of spatialized matter. Whether these violations are transmitted by urban infrastructure damage and border regimes, disclosed by the geophysics of a site such as a mass grave returned to vegetation, or reside within the pixelated mesh of satellite resolution, the interaction between spaces and objects is understood as offering up corroborating and at times even direct evidence of significant human rights abuses and war crimes. Propelled by specific questions with regard to the development of a legal file or to advance social justice and public advocacy, the Forensic Architecture team synthesizes data gathered from a wide range of sources in order to map and model a sequence of events in relationship to a perceived violation or alleged crime. Once this data is compiled and cross-referenced it is further composited to produce various reports, videos, animations, and online platforms that make legible the multiple forces at play within the constitutive spaces of violence. Through these kinds of technical and aesthetic intercessions, spatial products are transformed into evidential proofs and entered into forums of international law and human rights. Because of the unique sensibility that these aggregate forms of spatial evidence embody, new protocols governing, for example, admissibility standards or more imaginative legal infrastructures might be required to supplement existing ones. Indeed, the forum does not always precede the things that are brought before it; sometimes it must also be invented, as Forensic Architecture enjoins. If the admission, presentation, and contestation of evidence mediated by institutional forums and their disciplinary procedures guides a primary trajectory of this book, the other is directed toward the forensic analysis of media evidence itself.

Standard Operating Procedure, a 2008 documentary film directed by Errol Morris, offers a concise example of the investigative role that media forensics played in determining culpability for prisoner abuse at Abu Ghraib.[54] The film explores the central role of photography in the torture and defilement of Iraqi detainees at Abu Ghraib prison in 2004 by US personnel, both as a technical practice out of which discrete image objects emerged—the scandalous photos of the hooded man and naked human pyramid—and as a social technology that produced a series of image events, which brought US military actors, Iraqi prisoners, and digital technologies into new political configurations organized by various forms of coercive power. A pivotal scene occurs early on in the documentary when Brent Pack, an Army Special Agent in the Criminal Investigation Division, takes us through the laborious process of correcting time codes

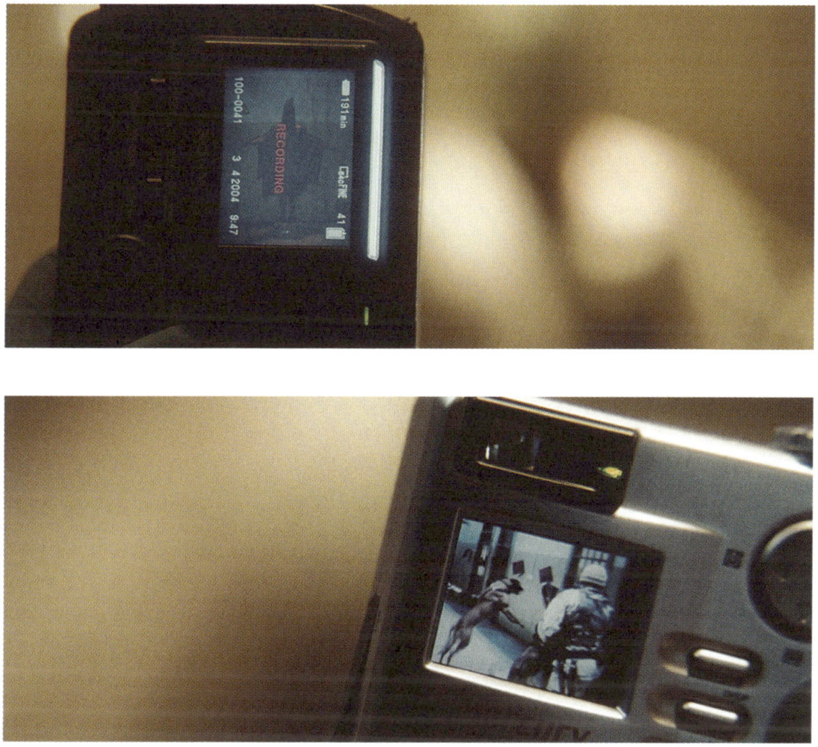

Figure 1.9
Standard Operating Procedure, Errol Morris, 2008, documentary film, 58 minutes. Courtesy: Errol Morris.

for the thousands of images taken at Abu Ghraib in order to generate a timeline of events that corresponds with the prison's logbooks. He did this so that the jury of ten soldiers participating in the trial at the Fort Hood military base could see when every incident began and ended, and how much time had elapsed between [photographic] events.[55] Despite being repeatedly copied, burned to CDs, and shared between various users, the metadata encoded in each image file remained intact. By matching similar frames across multiple cameras shooting at different resolutions, each of which registered a different date and time stamp, he was able to produce a synchronized account that located victims and perpetrators within the various temporal strata of Abu Ghraib. Today, GPS-enabled mobile phones have solved this key challenge for human rights investigators, as date and time are accurately encoded within the file structure of metadata, eliminating the need for painstaking manual date/time recalibration, as was the case in 2004.[56] Reorganizing this massive image dump into a legible sequence of events through the forensic analysis of metadata was crucial to constructing the legal brief, transforming seemingly random acts of aberrant behavior—the oft-repeated theory of a "few bad apples"—into a systematic, intentional, and repeated practice of prisoner abuse. As Pack remarks in the film, "The pictures spoke a thousand words but unless you know what day and time they were talking [about] you wouldn't know what the story was."[57] While 11 soldiers were found guilty of various offenses, and Brigadier General Janis Karpinski, who had oversight of all Iraqi detention facilities, was reprimanded and demoted, no criminal charges were ever leveled at leaders higher up the chain of command or, indeed, at any private military contractors who are also documented as having participated in prison abuse. The forensic reckoning of the images taken at Abu Ghraib revealed the timeline of events but also served to open up the case to broader questions around the tacit role of the Bush administration's "torture memos" drafted in 2002, which laid out arguments for preventing US officials from being charged with war crimes for prisoner detention and interrogation. While the preceding account demonstrates how metadata was utilized to create a timeline that would help to clarify the scope of prisoner abuse at Abu Ghraib, and thus aid in determining culpability, the disturbing visual content of the images was of paramount significance in establishing the event's attendant moral and political frameworks. As Errol Morris himself asked: "Is it possible for a photograph to change the world?"[58] Although metadata played an expedient role in reassembling the evidential archive, questions of accountability were decisively representational in their formulation as prosecutions and convictions were directed almost entirely toward those who were caught on camera. There was little political will on the part of the administration to delve beneath the surface of images, or to expand their frame and analyze their enabling conditions.

Another, very different example of the limits of representation is also linked to 9/11, and offers an even more challenging image of the violated body. At the time of the attacks on the Twin Towers in New York, much was said about the ways in which the smoke and dust clouds momentarily obliterated the human dimensions of the tragedy as Lower Manhattan was shrouded in an incendiary fog that defied all technical attempts at peering directly into the scene of the crime.[59] Instead our collective global gaze was transfixed by images of the transmutation of glass and steel into a kind of cosmic dust. Trapped and possibly interred within the architectural remains of the Twin Towers were the bodies of more than 2,780 people who had vanished from view, disappearing quite literally into thin air. For what the micro-spheres of dust carried were not simply the material remains of the destroyed towers but the entirety of the buildings' contents, including human occupants. The bodies of the more than 2,780 were not

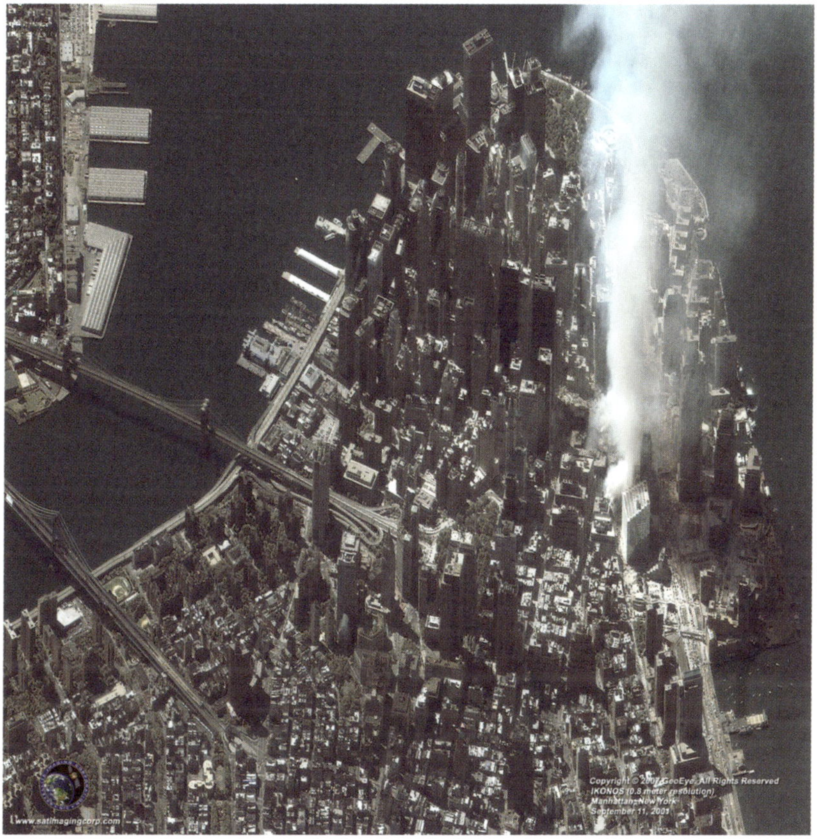

Figure 1.10
Space Imaging's IKONOS one-meter-resolution satellite image taken at 11:43 AM EDT on September 12, 2001. Courtesy: IKONOS.

missing in the images of billowing dust that we witnessed repeatedly during those first few days after the tragedy, but were emphatically present within each specimen of dust at 1.3 parts per 100.[60]

In the aftermath of recovery, rescue workers who had dug through the tons of hazardous rubble with their hands and rudimentary tools began to develop respiratory problems in the form of a dry and persistent cough. Within six months, elevators and air ventilators in buildings adjacent to the World Trade Center continuously began to fail.[61] The dust had not simply settled, but had entered into the lungs of rescue workers and local inhabitants as well as into the mechanical systems of nearby buildings.[62] As uneasy as the thought of such unwitting acts of ingestion might be, most common

Table 1 - Tabulation of WTC dust data.

Materials	Count	Percent of Total
Fiber Glass/Rock Wool	1615	45.1
Asbestos	5	Trace*
Synthetic Fibers	72	2.0
Human Remains	47	1.3
Natural Fibers	49	1.4
Paper Fibers	74	2.1
Ceiling Tiles	73	2.0
Mica Flakes	76	2.1
Plaster/Concrete Calcite, Dolomite, Gypsum	1138	31.8
Paint Smears & Chips	18	Trace
Metal Flakes	19	Trace
Wood Fragments	20	Trace
Foam Fragments	6	Trace
Charred Wood & Debris	257	7.1
Plastic Fragments	5	Trace
Perlite	8	Trace
Drug Fragments	12	Trace
Glass Fragment	50	1.4
Unknowns	40	1.1
Totals	**3584**	**100%**

*Less than 1%.

Figure 1.11
Tabulation of World Trade Center dust data. Courtesy: Nicholas Petraco.

dust specimens actually contain a high percentage of exfoliated human skin tissue and human hair along with many other natural and synthetic fibers, particles, emissions, and pollutants. Our bodies are constantly processing the sloughed-off excess and waste produced by our contact with other species or by the frictions occurring between different specimens. And we in turn deposit minute trace evidence of our passage through space and in time wherever we move and whenever we make contact with another surface. Dust, writes Steven Connor, is "both a terminal and a mediate matter."[63] Dust scrambles the material signals of objects and events, transmitting complex information from one space to another. Edmond Locard, the French criminologist credited with laying the foundations of forensic science, developed his famous postulate that "every contact leaves a trace" through his analysis of dust. His principle of exchange asserts that in any encounter between bodies, objects, materials, and spaces, certain residual traces are traded. These points of contact between entities can be mapped scientifically to link the distribution of bodies and objects within space. In the *Analysis of Dust Traces* (1930) Locard discussed the nature and composition of dust, noting that what is key to an understanding of dust is that it is "an accumulation of debris in a state of pulverization," whether derived from organic or inorganic entities.[64] Contrary to the popular image of dust as an expanding material surface, dust specimens are technically forms of "impure matter" that aggregate materials from different objects within themselves. As a compound substance in which radically heterogeneous entities are entangled, dust is the forensic media *par excellence* because each materially discrete particle can be individually studied and traced back to the particular circumstances out of which it came. For Locard, dust specimens were "the mute witnesses, sure and faithful, of all our movements and of all our encounters."[65]

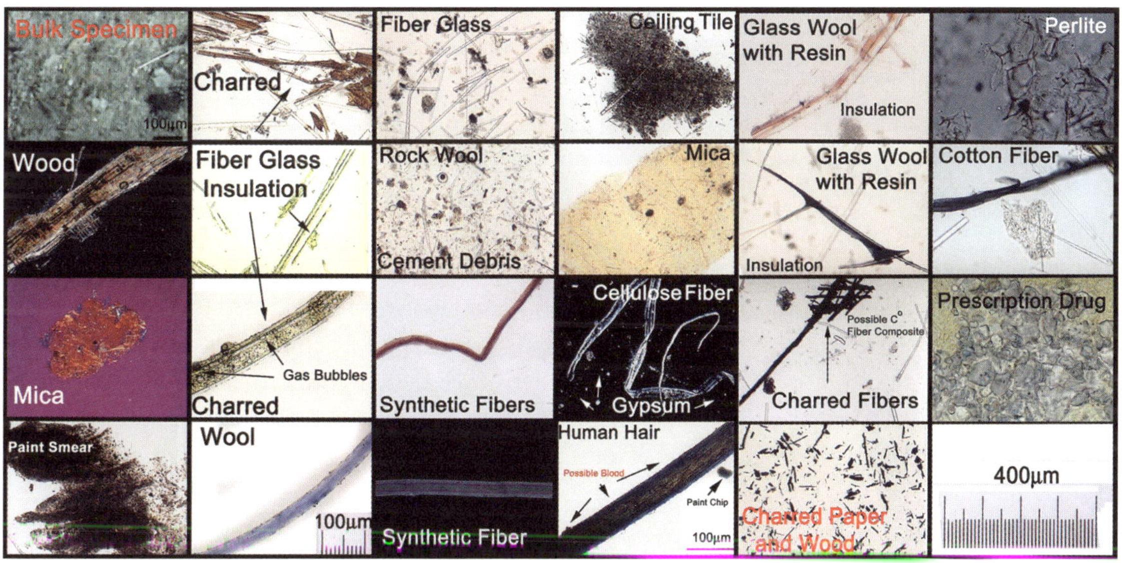

Figure 1.12

Macroscopically, each bulk specimen appeared somewhat like recently erupted volcanic ash. Tiny aliquots of bulk specimens were studied with a polarized light microscope (PLM). These initial PLM studies revealed that each bulk sample was composed of a myriad of materials. It appeared that all the materials composing the buildings and all of the buildings' contents were literally pulverized by the collapse of the Twin Towers. Courtesy: Nicholas Petraco.

Trace evidence of asbestos, revealed through the forensic analysis of WTC dust by means of polarized light microscopy, also retroactively links the material debris of 9/11, including the missing bodies of 2,780 people, to the fractious policies of the Environmental Protection Agency (EPA) and its 1973 prohibition on asbestos use. Subsequent postmortem debates within the scientific community around the collapsed Twin Towers have queried whether the greater fire-retardant capacities of asbestos would have resulted in fewer casualties had its banned usage not occurred midway through construction of the fortieth floor of the North Tower. The decision to subject dust particles to forensic examination inadvertently shed light on this and other issues, even though the investigation was prompted by the rise in respiratory problems amongst survivors and rescue workers. And while the information extracted out of these microscopic images of dust functioned to provide technical and medical insight into the direct consequences of the attacks, it also contributed to bringing other information vectors into the arena of public discourse, including the history of EPA decisions, many of which preceded the specific events of 9/11. These two examples—the presence of human remains and asbestos—drawn from the forensic analysis of WTC dust begin to suggest how the complex histories that accrue in matter might be decrypted and yield significant information in defiance or in excess of that which appears self-evident within the representational field of the image, even though it would ultimately be technical images produced by means of a polarized light microscope that enabled this forensic analysis.

Material Witness is thus concerned not directly with matters of documentation and representation, but with events that are captured by different media formats and transmitted by different forms of technology. Media and mediation provide essential terms of reference for engaging with the nonhuman entities and machinic ecologies that comprise this book, even when they are not themselves derived out of conventional media materials such as those identified with a photographic negative or binary code. Whether the consequence of deliberate action, the by-product of an activity, or even the result of an accidental encounter, the *material witnesses* that I investigate are all characterized by the manner in which they manage the regimes of intelligibility that enable us to perceive contested orders of knowledge and their corresponding truth claims. Consequently the political and affective register of such events never operates solely at the level of representation—the content displayed in an image or a sound file—but is also enacted at the structural level of an entity's technical organization: when, for example, pure data is captured by satellite sensors, transformed into binary code, assigned pixel values, mathematically adjusted, composited to produce a digital image, saved in a standardized file format, and transmitted to recombine with other circuits of technical and social assembly. The micropolitics of the *material witness* is expressed at all the points of contact between the various networks of information processing, transmission, and storage, which are also thresholds of potential transformation, whether we view these processes as antagonistic or productive to the overall functioning of the system. Politics is understood in this context as an attunement toward change regardless of the scale of events or degree of significance accorded to such alterations. It is constituted by a difference between states that can serve to reform and possibly even radicalize the existing rhetorical and discursive frameworks into which objects or entities have been historically placed or conventionally embedded. While transformations are an expression of the productive capacity of matter (signaling their informed condition and political explication), within a juridical context processes that bring about change in the ontological state of something, or trouble the integrity of a digital file's source code, advance legal concerns. This is why the burden of proof imposed upon material evidence is subject to intense custodial strictures and best practices that aim to discipline its entropic inclinations or guard against external interference. In order for materials, including digital media, to have any legal traction as evidence, approved procedures that guarantee the integrity of their material condition (chain of custody) or standardize their processing from grain to pixel (audit trails) are required to secure their legal determination as evidence. Yet materials that come out of conflict zones are often produced or secured under extremely perilous conditions that thwart such demands. Accusations of genocide and war crimes may be archived by media materials whose status is in dispute not only at the level of representation—information contained within the frame or file—but also at the level of processing, where corrupt data or informatic inconsistencies can immediately raise legal challenges. Nonetheless, these might be the only evidential materials that prosecutors have at their disposal to support an indictment. For example, corroborating video evidence proving that Croatian shelling on November 9, 1993 destroyed the Ottoman-era Mostar Bridge in Bosnia was thrown into doubt when forensic media analysis demonstrated that the tape in question had been spliced and reedited, thus nullifying its apparent truth claims.[66]

Online content, too, may be met with similar legal misgivings when it comes to determining its probative value. While social media platforms have dramatically increased the reach of citizen journalism, much of this user-generated material has been edited, captioned, copied, and recirculated. Although this is standard practice, such modifications, regardless of degree, may be sufficient grounds for dismissing the probity of online or uploaded media as a source of potential legal evidence unless corroborated by other sources. In my discussion of the amateur video documenting the massacre at Izbica, Kosovo (see p. 190) the damaged condition of the tape serves to

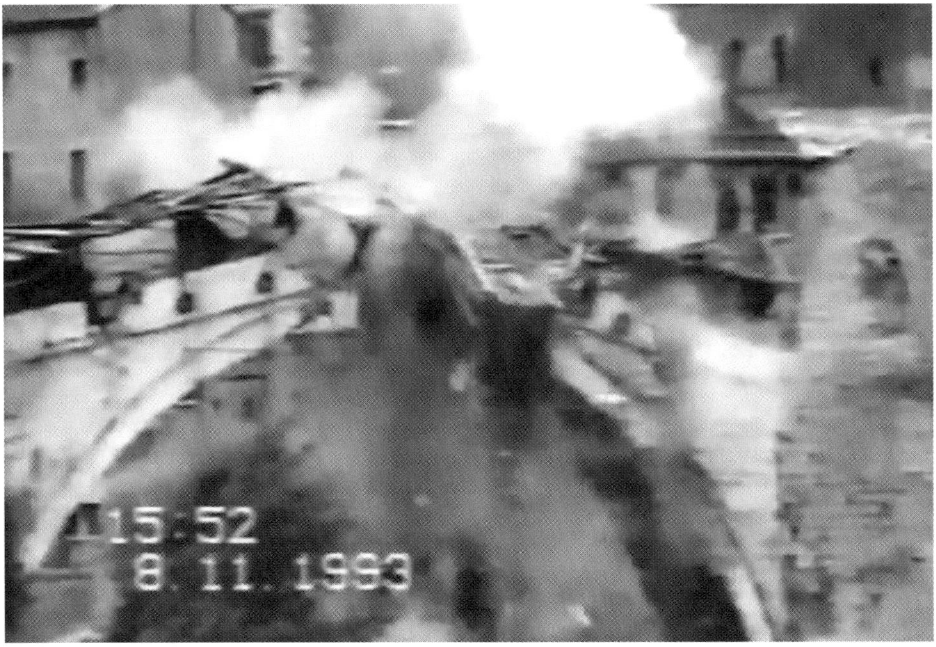

Figure 1.13
Video still from the Stari Most Bridge bombing footage, 1993. Source: Real War Films.

highlight the tension between the expressive capacities of materials to summon the inchoate violence of war and the perjurious potential that such compromised media might face in court. Forcing wholeness and clarity from such distressed materials can, I believe, violate events anew, whereas accepting their flawed conditions as symptomatic of the dangerous conditions under which they were secured can aid in expanding their testimonial reach.

A cultural conception of forensics might unfold electronic defects into a metareflection on the precarious role of witnessing during times of conflict, and thus position technical impurities as ethically productive and evidential of a moral truth, whereas a scientific approach to forensics needs to shore up legal probity by limiting interpretative accounts. Taking my cues from Felman's work, I maintain that impoverished forms of media can animate their defects as an affective supplement that operates in access of the testimonial demands produced by the conventions of legal speech. Damaged materials are generative insofar as they permit further analysis of the destructive forces at play, but are not to be treated as totemic or elegiac matter by the researcher or forensic analyst. This is an important distinction that I try to make throughout, as the lure of the defect must be countered by technical precision and rigorous critical assessment. In the chapters that follow I chart the appearance of a *material witness* that arises out of filmic emulsion, magnetic particles, photochemicals, metal oxides, and polluted environments, as well as from the dematerialized realms of audio frequencies, radio transmissions, atmospheric conditions, digital encodings, and electromagnetic activity. I track these entities in order to explore the ways in which matter archives and refracts the complex histories of violence in which it is implicated and, by extension, examine the condition of informed materiality that renders its politics visible. The productive role that forensics plays in this research is, as I have already suggested, not solely that of an investigative probe directed toward uncovering the true reality traces and absolute histories archived by matter, as might be the case with the deductive practices of forensic science. Rather, its role is that of highlighting what new understandings of matter might be required—its structural recodings and aesthetic assemblages—in order for the *material witness* to overcome its purely legal designation or metaphoric expression, and function as an operative concept in its own right: material *as* witness.

2 DISCOVERY

Caesium-137

"I didn't discover anything, I just happened to be there"—Cliff Robinson.[1]

In the early morning of Monday April 28, 1986, Cliff Robinson was about to begin his shift at the Forsmark nuclear power plant on the eastern coast of Sweden. When he tried to enter the plant he immediately set off its radiation detector, signaling the dangerous presence of radioactive contamination. After several repeated attempts, its warnings were finally silenced. He had not yet been in the controlled area of the plant that day, so he assumed that the alarm was faulty and needed some minor adjustments. Robinson was employed as a chemist at Forsmark, one of Sweden's largest nuclear power plants located a couple of hours north of Stockholm, on the country's east coast. His job was to monitor radioactivity throughout the power plant. When he completed his rounds that morning, he was astonished to see a growing queue of workers waiting at the detector. At every attempt to pass, the alarm would emit its seemingly temperamental caution: "No one could get through because the alarm kept going off."[2] Realizing that something much more serious might be happening, Robinson grabbed a shoe worn by one of the waiting workers and placed it on the germanium detector in the lab. "Then, I saw a sight that I will never forget, the shoe was highly contaminated. I could see this spectrum rising up very quickly. And it was just amazing, because there were many radioactive elements there that we normally didn't see in the cooling water at Forsmark. I remember vaguely that I had some idea that perhaps a nuclear bomb had been exploded somewhere."[3]

The contaminated soles of the engineer's shoes functioned much like a radioautograph or nuclear contact print in which the direct capture of radiation by objects is used to measure the gradient levels of radioactivity present in the environment. After alerting his superiors, Robinson was asked to inspect the plant's chimneys to determine whether a radiation leak was coming from Forsmark. By 11:00 a.m., widespread

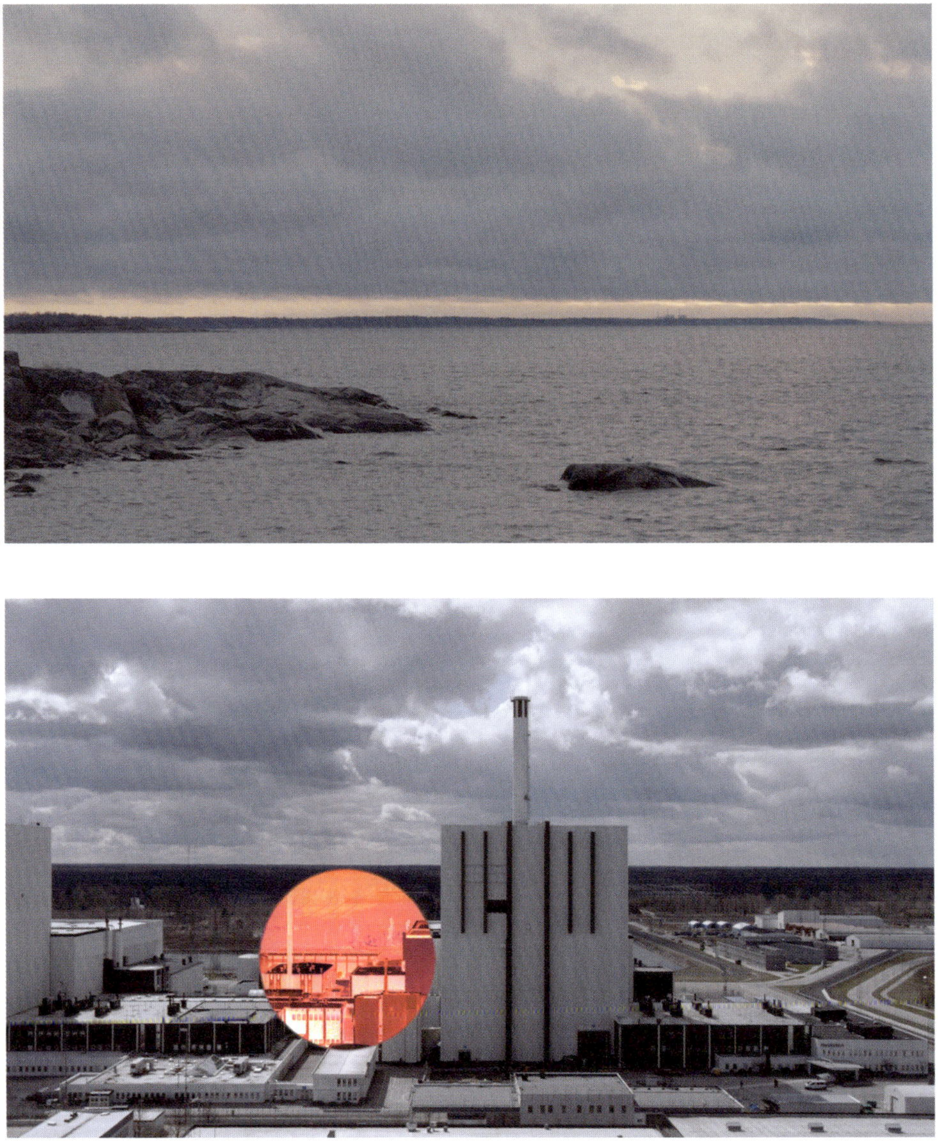

Figure 2.1
Forsmark Nuclear Power Plant, *Trace Evidence*, Susan Schuppli, 2016, HD video, color with four-channel sound, 53 minutes.

alarms sounded an evacuation order for the entire plant. Only key personnel involved in safety procedures remained behind; Robinson was one of those who stayed to monitor for radioactivity.[4] "Nothing indicated any malfunction or problem at Forsmark. It was just that the surroundings were very heavily contaminated."[5] Testing of all three of the reactor blocks came back clean, suggesting that the source of the leak must be coming from outside of the plant itself, a fact corroborated by the engineer who must have picked up the contamination on his shoes while walking around outside. Unbeknownst to Robinson and his colleagues, a dangerous wind had blown through the area over the weekend, raining its contaminants throughout the environs of the plant and beyond.

When the Swedish Radiation Safety Authority received notification from Forsmark later that morning reporting unusually high levels of radiation despite no evidence of any breakdown at the plant, concerns that an atmospheric release of radioactive isotopes had taken place somewhere else were immediately raised: a Cold War anxiety that conjured the specter of nuclear annihilation. Soon other Swedish plants also reported extremely high levels of radiation in their environs. Baffled, the Authority began plotting incoming reports of contamination in Sweden, cross-referencing them with reactor locations throughout the broader region. Several Soviet nuclear power plants, including Chernobyl, emerged as a probable source. Initial speculation pointed to a Russian plant close to the Swedish border, as the scale of the accident would have to have been massive if radioactive isotopes originating from as far away as the Ukraine were to have produced the levels of contamination reported in Scandinavia.[6] Eventually, direct evidence in the form of a radiological fingerprint—caesium-137—would corroborate the growing suspicion that the contamination discovered at Forsmark could only have come from outside Sweden.

Caesium-137 is an artificial radioactive isotope or radionuclide that results from anthropogenic activities manufactured either by a nuclear reactor or by the detonation of an atomic bomb. It occurs spontaneously when much heavier elements, such as uranium and plutonium, absorb neutrons and undergo fission. Caesium-137 has a half-life of 30.17 years and emits beta particles and gamma rays when it decays to barium-137m, which then decays to nonradioactive barium.[7] Although chemical testing at Forsmark revealed the presence of a radioactive isotope not native to those produced by its reactor, nor indeed by any of Sweden's other operational power plants, communiqués with Moscow resulted in an unequivocal "no" when Swedish diplomats inquired whether a nuclear accident might have taken place anywhere on its soil. Only when Sweden threatened to file an official alert with the International Atomic Energy Agency did the Soviet Union admit privately that there had been some sort of incident at Chernobyl.

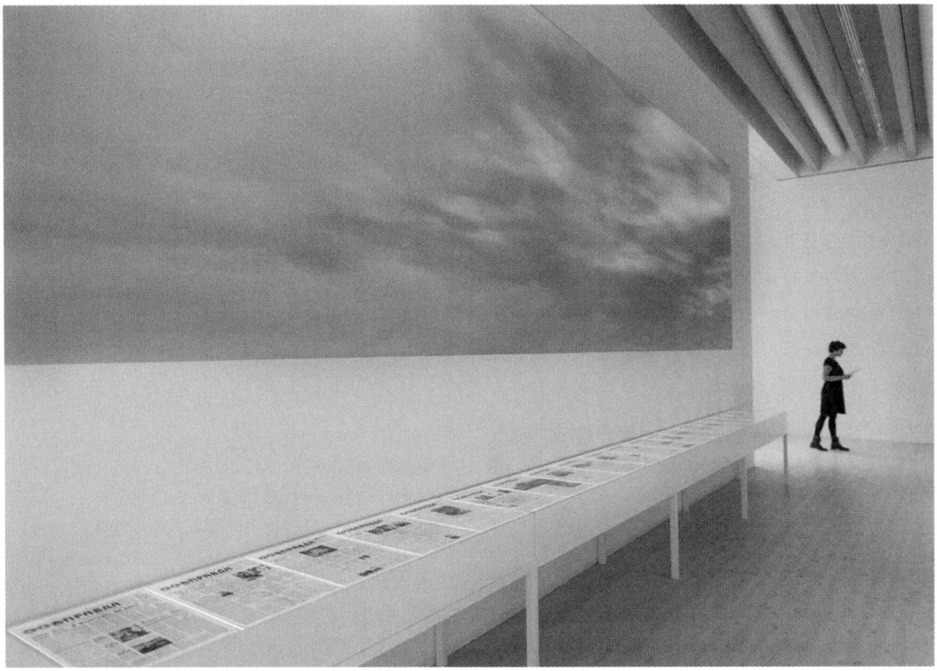

Figure 2.2
Installation view, *Delay Decay*, Susan Schuppli, 20 *Pravda* newspaper covers April 26–May 15, 1986, and HD video. Bildmuseet, Umeå, Sweden, 2016. Photo credit: Mikael Lundgren.

By noon on Monday, 42 percent of Forsmark's area residents had heard about events at the plant; by the same evening 66 percent had been informed.[8] In Pripyat, the city adjacent to Chernobyl, preparations were underway for May Day celebrations, so no public announcement was made as to the extent of the radiological disaster that lurked directly within their midst. In the crucial period immediately following the explosion at Reactor Unit 4, silence on the part of the Soviet State would prove fatal, as emergency measures such as the distribution of iodine tablets, which can absorb and neutralize radioactive isotopes, were not implemented. The *material witness* that would first come to testify publicly to the accident at Chernobyl was not to be found in the vicinity of the reactor but was located more than 1,100 kilometers away from the scene of the crime.

Microfiche v. Database

Today, any database search engine will return the nuclear accident at Chernobyl when the date April 26, 1986 is input into its search parameters, whereas a microfiche review of Soviet newspapers *Pravda* and *Izvestia* as well as other international papers from the same period reveals a time lag of 19 days before the fact registered publicly that a major nuclear accident had taken place. Although an orbiting American KH-11 photographic intelligence satellite took images of the reactor explosion, and scientists and meteorologists outside of the Soviet Union recorded extraordinarily high levels of radioactivity within days of the meltdown, this information was not publicly acknowledged as pertaining to Chernobyl for almost three weeks, because Mikhail Gorbachev and the Central Committee effectively withheld news of the disaster.[9] Safeguarding the State's reputation and its technical mastery over nuclear power suggested a willful indifference to human life, except as sacrificial.[10] Only on April 29, in response to growing rumors outside of the Soviet Union that "something had happened at Chernobyl," did Gorbachev finally deign to place a series of discrete notifications with five Soviet news agencies, indicating that a minor incident had occurred at Chernobyl. "An accident occurred at the nuclear plant in Chernobyl. One of the reactors had been damaged. Measures have been taken. A governmental commission is inquiring."[11] In reality the accident at Chernobyl was massive, releasing higher levels of radioactive contaminants into the environment than any preceding radiological event, including the detonation of two atomic bombs over Hiroshima and Nagasaki in 1945, the fallout from atmospheric nuclear weapons testing in the years 1952–1963, the explosion at the Mayak plutonium production and reprocessing facility in 1957, or the partial reactor core meltdown at Three Mile Island in 1979. By minimizing the gravity of the situation, delaying reports that a substantial nuclear explosion had taken place, and downplaying the potential for contamination, a tragedy of far greater consequences ensued. For those living in the adjacent city of Pripyat, this time lag would prove fatal as cells metastasized, seeding their malignancy throughout the zone.

In the basement of a deserted corner of a university library in Canada sits an abandoned fleet of aging and rather unwieldy machines known as microfiche viewers. In the summer of 2005, at the time I first began researching the accident at Chernobyl, I decided to use these machines in order to find the actual printed cover pages of global newspapers from the day of the accident onward. Newspapers are useful devices for reading events in their situated temporal contexts, in that they bring the news of the day into direct juxtaposition with other contemporaneous stories. The front page in particular features all of the events that are regarded as most newsworthy, as well as those that are presumed to be of specific pertinence to its readership, whereas the logic of search engine queries is to return events through an aggregation of connecting links that have been established over time by communities of users. What these two technical interfaces reveal are two different orders of legibility and two different ways of indexing time: the newspaper, which is organized hierarchically and thematically, ranking stories in order of their immediate significance to that specific date, resulting in a transversal field of information out of which a given event might come to one's attention; and the browser, which is a process of filtering that extracts a singularity already preselected by the user through the parameters of their key word search, but has no necessary *a priori* relationship to the specific date of their online search.

Only by scouring each small spool of microfiche film in the library's periodical and newspaper collection to see what newsworthy items had made it to the front page did I finally come to realize that Chernobyl never happened on April 26, 1986—at least, not by any publicly reported accounts. I might add that the library in which I worked had an extensive microfiche collection that included many Soviet as well as other foreign-language newspapers. Mine was not a mediatic discovery akin to Jean Baudrillard's infamous declaration that the first Gulf War never happened due to the hyperreality of an image world that overcodes the real to such an extent that it eventually surpasses it and, in so doing, effectively annuls it. No, my microfiche findings pointed quite literally to the fact that there seemed to be no public record of the nuclear accident having ever taken place on that day nor, indeed, on any of the following days. This realization spurred me into examining each spool of film subsequent to April 26 until I finally came across a substantial printed reference to the catastrophic events at Chernobyl 19 days later on the cover of *Pravda*. On the evening of May 14, 1986, President Gorbachev appeared on State television with the belated words "we have been struck by disaster," and then again as the lead story on the front pages of Russian newspapers the following day.

While the obviously tragic consequences of this delay go without saying, it was the process of carefully scrutinizing each reel of microfiche that enabled me to fully grasp the political implications of this time lag, and how it too was a *material witness* that could assist me in better understanding the events of Chernobyl. This conceptual revelation would never have been available to me had I relied solely upon digital database search engines that had retroactively corrected the timeline and erased the gap in the historical record. Throughout this book, many examples are discussed in which a break or breach in recording media offers a unique vantage point from which to grasp the political stakes of an event; an absence or lapse that functions as a form of compelling evidence in its own right, and whose testimonial capacity is productive of the forensic operations of imagination that allow for critical conjecture and sober speculation. This is not to suggest that the gap is merely a space for projective or fictive rumination but, rather, that its very presence is significant enough to warrant our investigative attention. In particular, the temporal disjunction of 19 days raised the epistemic question:

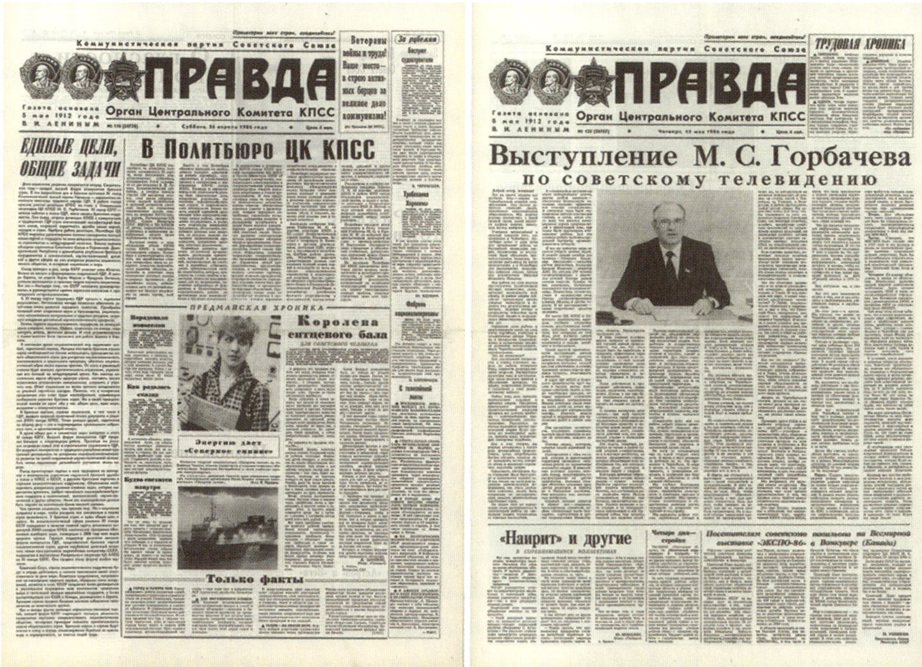
Пролетарии всех стран, соединяйтесь!
Коммунистическая партия Советского Союза
ПРАВДА
Орган Центрального Комитета КПСС
Газета основана 5 мая 1912 года В. И. ЛЕНИНЫМ
ЕДИНЫЕ ЦЕЛИ, ОБЩИЕ ЗАДАЧИ
В ПОЛИТБЮРО ЦК КПСС
ПРЕДМАЙСКАЯ ХРОНИКА
Королева ситцевого бала
Только факты

Пролетарии всех стран, соединяйтесь!
Коммунистическая партия Советского Союза
ПРАВДА
Орган Центрального Комитета КПСС
Газета основана 5 мая 1912 года В. И. ЛЕНИНЫМ
ТРУДОВАЯ ХРОНИКА
Выступление М. С. Горбачева
по советскому телевидению
«Наирит» и другие
Посетителям советского павильона на Всемирной выставке «ЭКСПО-86» в Ванкувере (Канада)

Figure 2.3
Cover of *Pravda* newspaper, April 26, 1986, day of the Chernobyl nuclear accident; and cover of *Pravda* newspaper, May 15, 1986. Nineteen days after the accident at Chernobyl, President Mikhail Gorbachev made a television address to the Soviet people. Courtesy: National Gallery, St. Petersburg, Russia.

when did the "event" of Chernobyl actually take place? On April 26, the day the reactor core exploded, or on May 14, when the accident entered into public discourse?

Despite this interval in public disclosure and its concomitant disclosure of the State's political priorities, an immense release of airborne radioactive contaminants was already being carried from the USSR across Poland to settle throughout northern Sweden, where it was absorbed into surface water, ground water, biota, and soil.[12] Contrary to the home-grown chemistry of Forsmark's radioactive outputs, Chernobyl had unleashed billions of becquerels of radioactive material in the form of strontium, plutonium, iodine, and in particular caesium-137, creating a trail of atmospheric evidence that would eventually lead scientists to the crime scene at Chernobyl.[13] Whether carried aloft by the wind or set adrift in the ocean's currents, this radioactive isotope is distinguished by its anthropogenic origins, solubility in water, and decay rate of 60 years. These characteristics set it apart from other naturally occurring radiological elements

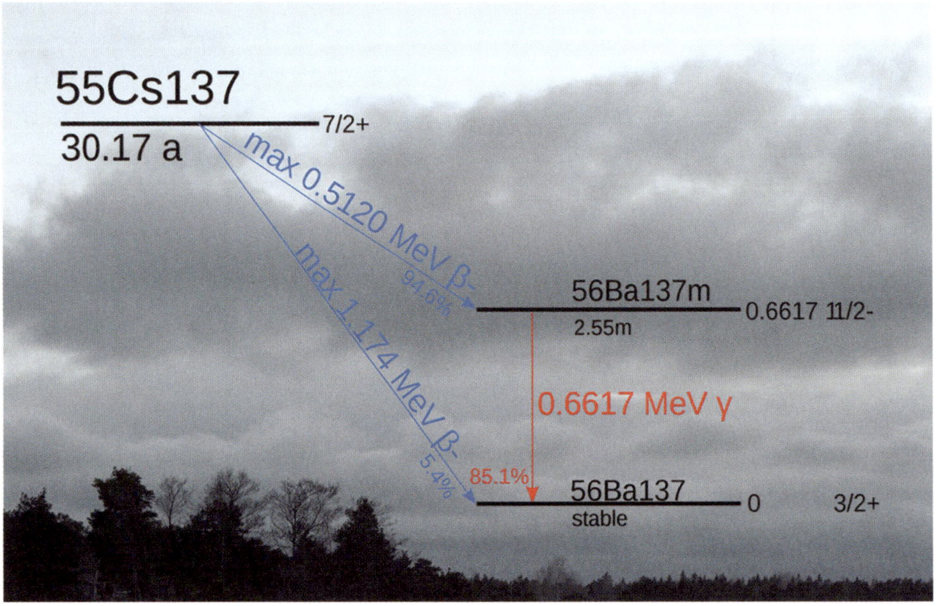

Figure 2.4
Caesium-137, *Trace Evidence*, Susan Schuppli, 2016, HD video, color with four-channel sound, 53 minutes.

and allow for its relatively easy detection as it moves through different environments until such time that its nuclear bounty will have sufficiently decayed or achieved it half-life, and thus also a change in state.

Witch's Brew

On page 4 of an Inter-Office Memorandum dated December 17, 1945 to Norris Bradbury, who followed J. Robert Oppenheimer as the Director of Los Alamos National Laboratory, nuclear physicist Henry W. Newson raised concerns about conducting atomic weapons tests in an ocean environment. According to Newson, "the water near a recent surface explosion will be a witch's brew, and this will be true to a lesser extent for the other tests. There will probably be enough plutonium near the surface to poison the combined armed forces of the United States at their highest wartime strength."[14]

On February 19, 2015, water samples taken off the coast of Ucluelet, a historically indigenous community located on Vancouver Island along the coast of one of Canada's most extraordinary expanses of marine biodiversity, revealed trace amounts of

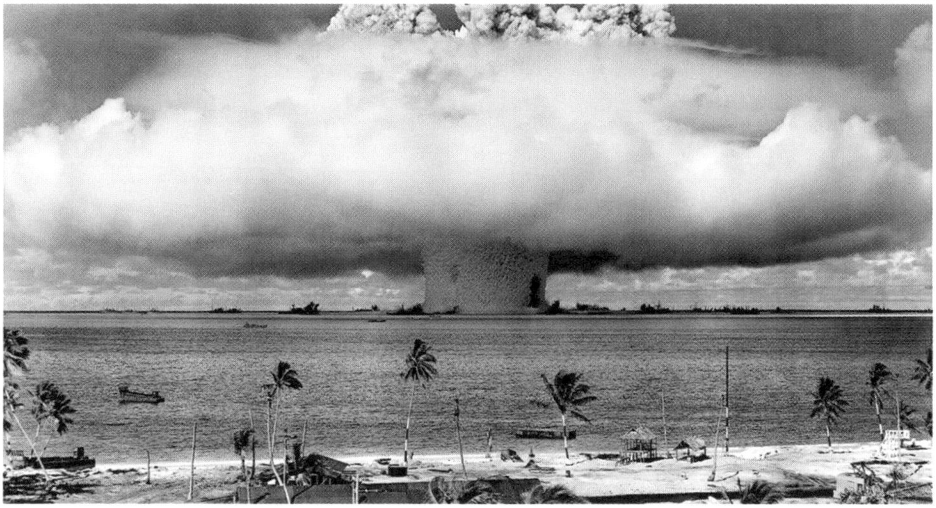

Figure 2.5
Baker explosion, Operation Crossroads, Bikini Atoll, Marshall Islands, July 25, 1946. United States Department of Defense. Source: Library of Congress.

the radioactive isotopes caesium-134 and caesium-137. For scientists from Woods Hole Oceanographic Institution who tested the samples, these radionuclides could only have come from one source: the Fukushima Daiichi Nuclear Power Station. Four years earlier, on March 11, 2011, a tsunami and earthquake wreaked havoc on the eastern shores of Japan's Honshu Island, destroying the plant's emergency cooling generators and permanently devastating its coastal communities. Reports indicating that the radioactive plume had arrived at the outermost reaches of the Canadian continental shelf first surfaced in 2013, with samplings of caesium-134 (which has a half-life of only two years) providing unequivocal evidence that the contaminants must have originated in Japan. While Chernobyl's fallout would eventually spread across extensive tracts of arable land in Europe, Fukushima's contamination seems to have traveled further still, crossing some 7,600 kilometers through the vast microbial channels of the Pacific propelled by the powerful force of the Kuroshio Current.

According to disclosures made by the Tokyo Electric Power Company (TEPCO), the company that owns Fukushima Daiichi, at least two trillion becquerels of radioactive material were released into the ocean between August 2013 and May 2014 alone. Water samples taken off the coast of Japan in the immediate aftermath of the accident registered dramatically elevated levels of radioactive isotopes. Five years later, levels still have not returned to their baseline recorded in the 1980s, when the world's oceans

INTER-OFFICE MEMORANDUM

DATE 17 December, 1945

TO: Mr. N. E. Bradbury

FROM: Henry W. Newson

SUBJECT: Possible Difficulties in Naval Tests

Radiation Slick:

Since we now know very little about the probable distribution of fission products in sea water, we must estimate their distribution pessimistically. Let us assume that all the fission products are captured by water warmed by the bomb explosion (under water) and are carried to the surface and spread uniformly. If no self absorption occurs, we will have a situation similar to the Trinity crater. Rough calculations made on the basis of the plutonium recovery there indicate that the crates captured 1% of the fission products. To maintain our pessimistic outlook, let us consider the seriously contaminated area increased by a factor of ten. This gives us a region about a half mile in radius which would irradiate a man at about $10^5 \frac{R}{h}$ a few hours after the shot if he should cross the region at uniform speed along its diameter. This is 10^7 times the tolerance level. If mixing occurred so that the fission products were uniformly distributed in a layer one meter thick, the dosage rate would decrease by a factor of ten (based on formulas by Morrison in Chap. V of The Chicago Handbook), and mixing to a greater depth would decrease the effects in proportion to the depth. Thus, uniform mixing to a depth of

7

1000 m (nearly to the bottom) would reduce the radiation level to $10\frac{R}{hr}$. This level is still too high for any kind of sustained activity, and the assumptions are no longer very pessimistic since it has been assumed that the surface water is no more contaminated than that at a depth. Induced radioactivities such as 30 min Cl and 14 hr Na may make the situation appreciably worse for times not long after the shot.

While it is unsafe to assume that water will not rise to the surface, it is quite possible that clean water will be carried in by wind or current. The thickness of this layer to give full protection need be only 2 or 3 meters for protection factors of 10^4 and 10^6 respectively. The same reductions might be obtained by 8 or 12 inches of steel.

Unless it can be shown fairly conclusively that none of the contaminated water will reach the surface, difficulty may be anticipated in boarding and inspecting test ships which have not been sunk by the explosion. The test ships should be so disposed as to take every possible advantage of wind and current which might wash at least the top layer of contaminated water away from them.

The same difficulty is far more likely in the case of a surface explosion. Here the ball of fire will roll over the sea to a radius comparable to that at Trinity and the fission

-2-

8

products will undoubtedly be spread even farther by the large waves generated by the explosion. As was pointed out before, surface mixing will not reduce the dosage by a great deal. If the ball of fire should actually touch a test ship, and that ship survive, it might not be possible to board it for days. Paint melted by the radiation would be an excellent collector of fission products delivered either by the ball of fire or a dust cloud.

If the bomb were dropped from a plane, no very important deposit of fission products would occur if it exploded 1000 feet or more in the air (Japanese experience). However, should the ball of fire touch ships or water, the same effects could be expected on a lesser scale.

Induced radioactivity will in general be much less of a nuisance than fission products. Its effect may predominate for a high drop but it will be much less serious than fission products are in the other types of test. Furthermore, it may be predicted fairly accurately from a few simple experiments. The activation of the steel bulls of ships will probably cause trouble for no more than 24 hours. A piece of reinforcement iron taken from the base of the Trinity tower showed no activity about three weeks after the shot. The 2.4 hour manganese activity is by far the most prominent effect in iron bombarded by slow neutron. The most intense fast reaction induced periods are even shorter.

The air and surface explosions will certainly give rise to clouds of fission products which are definitely dangerous. (Witness the hasty retreat from N 10,000 at Trinity.) This should be handled by careful study of the wind at all altitudes. No observer or any other human being should be alee of the explosion. In addition, only fast vessels should be near so that they may outrun a sudden shift of the cloud. Planes <u>with sealed cabins</u> should be able to maneuver rather freely over the whole region.

The water near a recent surface explosion will be a witch's brew, and this will be true to a lesser extent for the other tests. There will probably be enough plutonium near the surface to poison the combined armed forces of the United States at their highest wartime strength. The fission products will be worse. The probable number of fish casulaties, in addition to those caused by the explosion, can probably be calculated when more is known about the probable mixing conditions and the fish population. Considerable study of this general problem has been made in connection with the Hanford and Clinton Plants.

<u>Effects of the Actual Explosion:</u>

The protection of personnel from the effects of the actual explosion is relatively simple. We know from the Japanese experience that an unprotected man two miles from the bomb is fairly safe from all effects except the flying debris of flimsy structures. Special precautions could shorten this distance, but the uninvestigated effects - water shock, waves, unfavorable distribution of radioactivity, etc. - would make any such procedure foolhardy. Unless there are very compelling reasons, no man should be within five miles of the explosion, and the bulk of the personnel should be much farther. However, it might be well to populate the test ships which seem likely to survive the explosion with experimental animals. This would be a considerable undertaking if the results of the experiment were to simulate the effect of radiations on the crew.

The protection of experimental equipment located on test ships, particularly photographic plates, will be very difficult, and special calculations will be necessary for each case.

HWN:cl Henry W. Newson

cc: N. E. Bradbury
Roger S. Warner, Jr.
John Williams

-5-

11

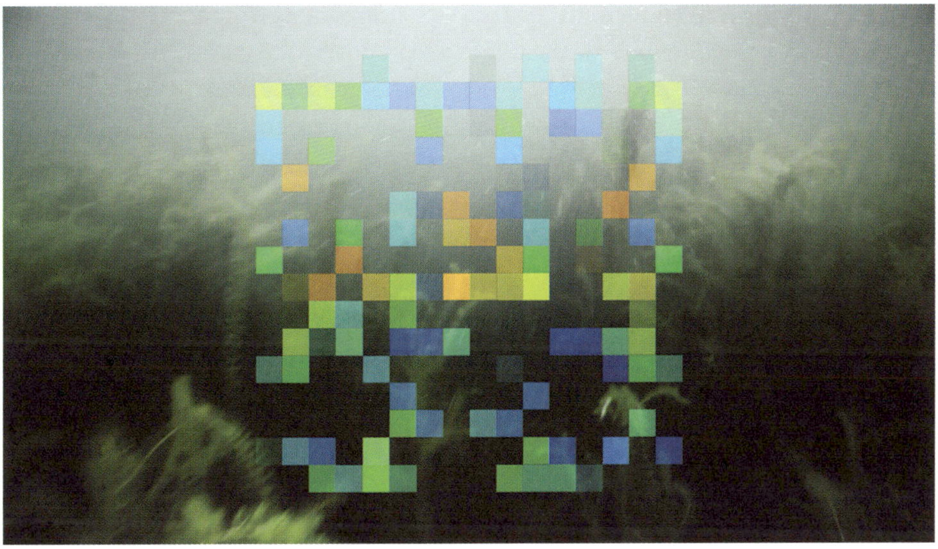

Figure 2.6
Trace Evidence, Susan Schuppli, 2016, HD video, color with four-channel sound, 53 minutes.

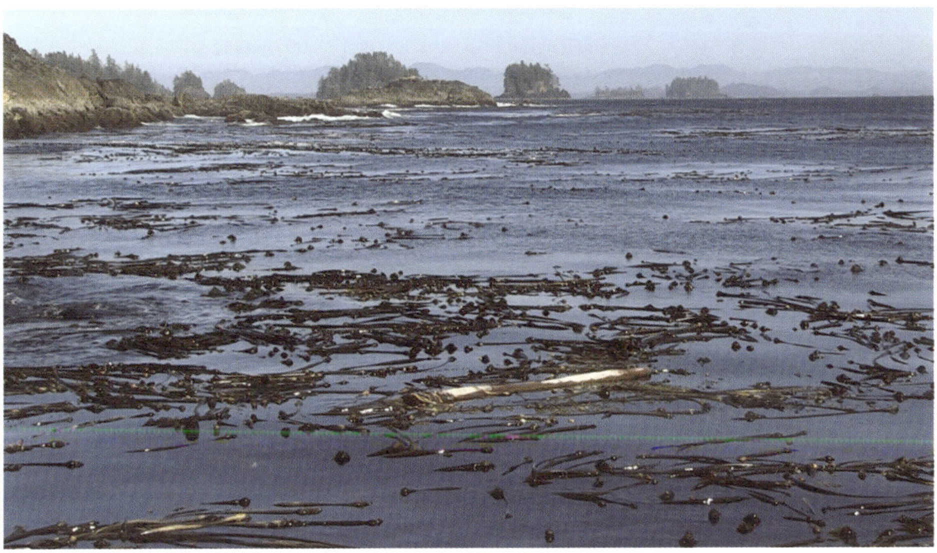

Figure 2.7
Ucluelet coast, British Columbia, Canada, *Trace Evidence*, Susan Schuppli, 2016, HD video, color with four-channel sound, 53 minutes.

were contending with fallout from the legacy of atmospheric weapons testing. "Levels today off Japan are thousands of times lower than during the peak releases in 2011," said scientist Ken Buesseler (Woods Hole Oceanographic Institution), who was involved in testing water samples from Ucluelet, "but we are not seeing the steady decrease we would expect to see off Fukushima if all sources had stopped; rather, we are finding values are still elevated, which confirms that there is continued release from the plant."[15] Although Fisheries and Oceans Canada recorded levels that were in an order of magnitude nearly six times higher in the coastal waters of Ucluelet than typical rates found throughout the Pacific Ocean, the increased presence of radioactive isotopes is not considered dangerous to human health, given the annual dosage we already receive from exposure to natural background radiation. "The levels the group [concerned Ucluelet residents and scientists from Woods Hole] detected are extremely low. For example, swimming in the Vancouver Island water every day for a year would provide a dose of radiation less than a thousand times smaller than a single dental X-ray, Woods Hole said."[16] However, as Buesseler notes: "Radioactivity can be dangerous, and we should be carefully monitoring the oceans after what is certainly the largest accidental release of radioactive contaminants to the oceans in history."[17] Today, irradiated debris and contaminants are still being discharged into the coastal waters off Japan's eastern shore as TEPCO continues a program of intermittent release into the Pacific. The controversial decision to discharge 580 barrels (777,000 metric tonnes) of tritium-tainted water that had been injected into the power station to cool its damaged reactors has been halted (as of July 17, 2017) due to public disputes as to its potential health hazards and a struggling fish industry.

Within environmental justice work, establishing the incontrovertible relationship between cause and effect has proven a difficult legal challenge. The spatial dispersal of contaminants and temporal latency of their material and biological effects, which may take years, even decades, to emerge, has allowed global climate change actors and states to operate with virtual impunity. But the nuclear event is not like other complex nonlinear events, nor does it behave like other toxic events. Despite its radical and covert nature, the unique signature of radioactive isotopes allows its traces to be forensically tracked back to their source, thus reconnecting the evidential links that global systems of circulation have seemingly pulled apart.[18] Studying the pathways of fallout from radioactivity has in fact been essential for understanding the dispersal and accumulation of other environmental contaminants and pollutants. In *Silent Spring* (1962), the work that is credited with launching the environmental movement, marine biologist Rachel Carson traces the indiscriminate use of chemical poisons on ecosystems, focusing her analysis on pesticide use, and in particular on DDT. While she did not set out to address the behavior of isotopic contaminants on the natural world, her study turned to strontium-90 because no information on the dispersal and accumulation of pesticides existed in the 1960s.

> Although research on the dissemination of fallout expanded rapidly, until about 1960 non-radioactive toxic substances could not be studied widely in nature because either no detection methods existed for highly diluted chemicals or they were overly tedious or expensive. Thus, models of the dispersion and accumulation patterns of radioactive fallout isotopes provided the basis for our understanding of pathways of persistent chemicals in the environment.[19]

In a strange turn of events, the genocidal violence unleashed over Japan with the dropping of two atomic bombs would yield the scientific basis for the coming discourse on ecocide. It has also been suggested by naturalist Ralph H. Lutts that the impact of Carson's work and its widespread acceptance by the American public, which played a significant role in mobilizing private as well as public and government initiatives, occurred, not least, because people were already attuned to the threat of a deadly stealth agent that could move through bodies and environments alike: namely, the nuclear which, by 1962, had been the subject of almost two decades of debate around the consequences of atomic weapons testing and radioactive fallout, albeit a fear on the part of Americans that was primarily directed toward Soviet activities. As Lutts puts it: "She [Carson] was sounding an alarm about a kind of pollution that was invisible to the senses; could be transported great distances, perhaps globally; could accumulate over time in body tissues; could produce chronic as well as acute poisoning; and could result in cancer, birth defects and genetic mutations that may not become evident until years or decades after exposure."[20] Despite this intertwined legacy between the study of isotopic fallout as an expression of not only nuclear anxiety but also ecological crisis, the productive conceptual labor of nuclear forensics, which is the contemporary field responsible for investigating and tracking nuclear materials (including their potential enrichment) back to their source, has yet, in my opinion, to become a force for enacting or, indeed, imagining new forms of environmental accountability. Instead, their efforts are almost entirely directed toward trafficking and security, and only exceptionally toward the evidential effects of a nuclear accident.

There is no denying that the radioactive contaminants discovered at a great distance in the boreal forests of Sweden or in the frigid waters off the Pacific Northwest are directly attributable to the accidents at Chernobyl and Fukushima Daiichi respectively. And whilst their discovery certainly functions as a form of *material witnessing* in which entities—lichens or the ocean—register evidence of external events, what is much more difficult to ascertain is whether the future occurrences of certain types of health-related effects might be directly attributable to these events, or are just statistical anomalies.

Establishing direct cause related to the emergence of latent consequences becomes even more challenging when contaminants form a part of environmental cycles that moves across territorial scales and between migratory species to enter food supply chains. Notable examples include the Chernobyl cycle between lichen, which absorbs radionuclides directly from the air, reindeer, whose winter diet consists primarily of lichen, and the health of indigenous Sámi, whose food supply relies heavily upon reindeer meat. Or the migratory cycle of Pacific Bluefin tuna which spawn for two years off the coastal waters of Japan before heading toward the feeding grounds of California, where they are eventually caught. In the toxicological aftermath of Fukushima Daiichi, concentrations of caesium-134 in Bluefin tuna were ten times higher than previously recorded.[21]

Without legal proof of direct causality there can be no finding of "criminal liability" and therefore little to no restitution, nor accountability for the long-term impacts that such toxicity might yield. The strategy of the Marshall Islands to focus their legal action prospectively toward global nuclear disarmament, rather than on compensation for past damages despite elevated levels of cancers related to radiation exposure, offers a case in point. Their decision may have been guided by the legal response to Chernobyl, given the limited number of casualties that are officially acknowledged as pertaining to the events of 1986.[22] This is why the dual nature of the *material witness*

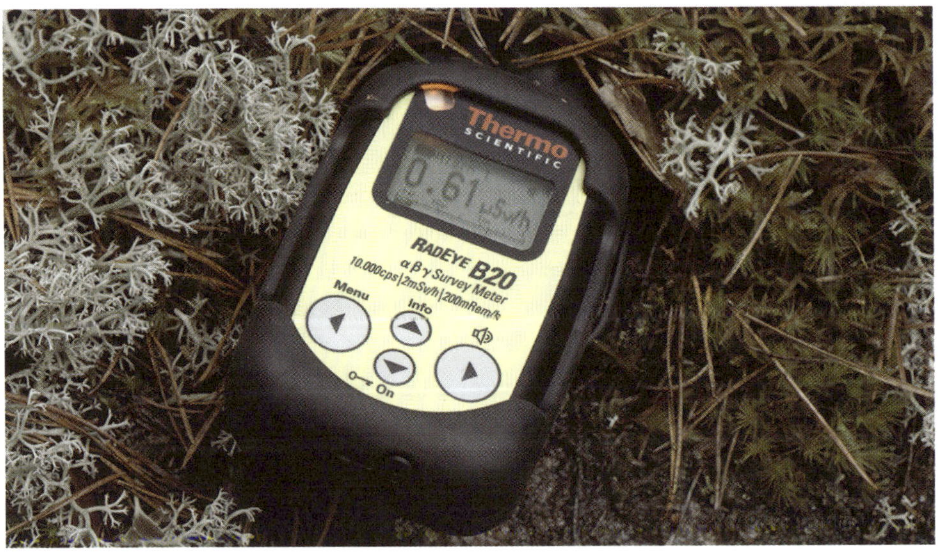

Figure 2.8
Radioactive lichen (0.61 mSv), *Trace Evidence*, Susan Schuppli, 2016, HD video, color with four-channel sound, 53 minutes.

FF083 B-WIRE 25-JUN-86 14:45

E/W -- SWEDEN LAUNCHES FOOD SURVEY TO MEASURE RADIATION
(WITH FF-558)

STOCKHOLM, JUNE 25, REUTER -- SWEDEN TODAY LAUNCHED A SURVEY TO MEASURE RADIATION LEVELS IN FOOD FOR SALE IN SHOPS AND MARKETS, THE NATIONAL RADIATION PROTECTION INSTITUTE SAID.

SCIENTISTS AT THE INSTITUTE AND WITH THE NATIONAL FOOD ADMINISTRATION WILL ANALYSE SAMPLES OF FOOD BOUGHT IN THE MAJOR CITIES AND AREAS OF THE COUNTRY WORST AFFECTED BY FALL-OUT AFTER THE CHERNOBYL NUCLEAR DISASTER, AN INSTITUTE SPOKESMAN SAID.

HE SAID THE AIM OF THE SURVEY, WHICH WOULD CONTINUE FOR SEVERAL MONTHS, WAS TO MEASURE THE AVERAGE LEVELS OF RADIATION CONSUMED BY SWEDES. MILK AND POTATOES, HE ADDED, WOULD BE PARTICULAR TARGETS FOR THE STUDY.

SOME FARMERS IN NORTHERN AND EASTERN SWEDEN ARE STILL KEEPING LIVESTOCK INDOORS BECAUSE OF HIGH RADIATION LEVELS IN GRAZING LAND AND THERE IS STILL WIDESPREAD UNEASE OVER THE AMOUNT OF RADIOACTIVITY IN WILDLIFE.

A TROUT CAUGHT YESTERDAY IN A REMOTE LAKE IN NORTHERN SWEDEN WAS ANALYSED AND WAS FOUND TO CONTAIN SOME 16 TIMES THE ACCEPTED LEVEL OF RADIOACTIVE CAESIUM, NEWSPAPERS REPORTED TODAY.

THE NATURE CONSERVATION COUNCIL HAS ALSO RECOMMENDED THAT CERTAIN TYPES OF HUNTING THIS SUMMER SHOULD BE KEPT TO A MINIMUM.

THE COUNCIL SAID THAT WOODCOCK SHOULD NOT BE HUNTED IN THE WORST AFFECTED AREAS FOR FEAR OF HIGH RADIATION LEVELS.

THE RECOMMENDATION CAME AFTER SPECIMEN BIRDS WERE ANALYSED AND FOUND TO CONTAIN UNACCEPTABLY HIGH AMOUNTS OF CAESIUM, THE COUNCIL ADDED.

THE SUMMER REINDEER CULL HAS ALREADY BEEN BANNED IN NORTHERN SWEDEN, ALTHOUGH OFFICIALS HAVE SAID THAT THE MAIN AUTUMN SLAUGHTER OF REINDEER AND THE ENORMOUSLY POPULAR ELK HUNT, ALSO IN THE AUTUMN, ARE UNLIKELY TO BE AFFECTED.

THE CONSERVATION COUNCIL HAS ALSO ASKED FOR GOVERNMENT MONEY FOR A STUDY OF THE EFFECTS WHICH FALL-OUT FROM THE STRICKEN SOVIET REACTOR HAS HAD ON SWEDISH FORESTS.

THE COUNCIL SAID THAT THE STUDY "WOULD PINPOINT HOW CAESIUM WAS TRANSPORTED, STORED AND CONTAINED IN PLANTS AND TREES, AND HOW ANIMALS, PARTICULARLY ELKS, ARE AFFECTED."

SWEDEN WAS ONE OF THE COUNTRIES WORST AFFECTED BY FALL-OUT FROM CHERNOBYL REACTOR, AND PUBLIC OPINION POLLS SHOW THAT SWEDES ARE STILL UNEASY ABOUT LEVELS OF RADIOACTIVITY IN FOOD AND WILDLIFE.

LA/

as that which discloses evidence of an event as well as that which provides insight into the event of evidence is crucial. The discovery of radionuclides in Sweden and Canada unfolded evidence of contamination into a much larger set of public and scientific debates around the continued risks associated with the production and use of nuclear energy, especially today, when alternate forms of renewable energy are much more viable. It also served to galvanize concern around the long-term disposal of nuclear waste, whether stored in purpose-built facilities or sequestered in geological repositories. In a recent interview I conduced with nuclear physicist John Rowat, he made the point that although Forsmark is building a repository for low- and intermediate-level waste that currently sits at 50 meters below the Baltic Sea, in 5,000 years it will be up at the Earth's surface because of glacial rebound, so it will not be undersea or under seal forever.[23]

In Nuu-chah-nulth or Nootka, the language spoken in the Pacific Northwest, Ucluelet translates as "people of the safe harbor."

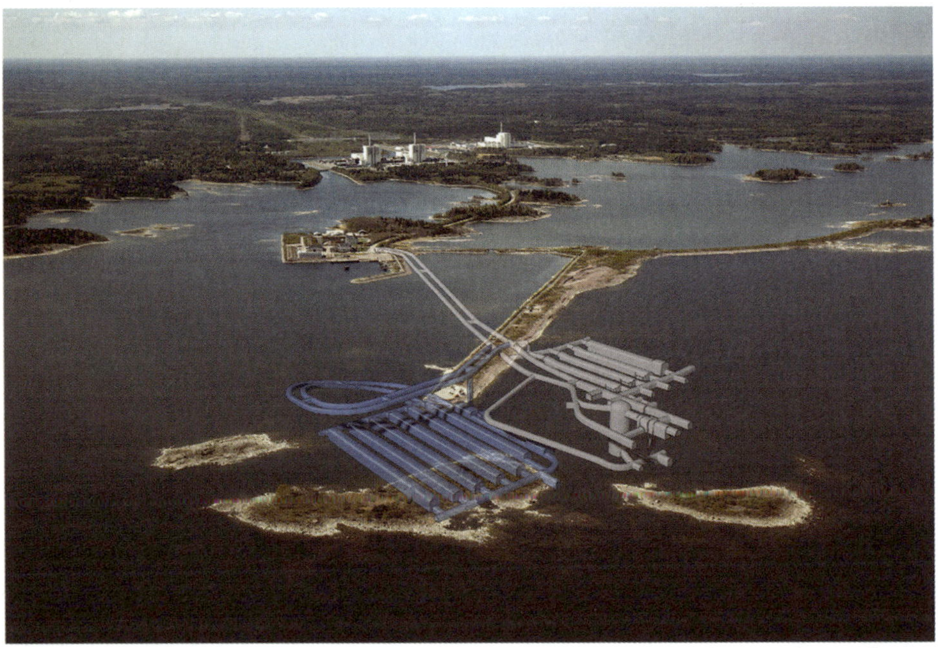

Figure 2.9
Excavated from a granite formation approximately 50 meters underground, the Final Repository for Short-Lived Radioactive Waste (SFR) at Forsmark is a permanent storage facility for low- and intermediate-level short-lived radioactive waste. The superimposed graphics depict the further extensions planned by the Swedish Nuclear Fuel and Waste Management Company (SKB) into the bedrock under the Baltic Sea. Photo credit: Lasse Modin.

3 HOSTILE WITNESS

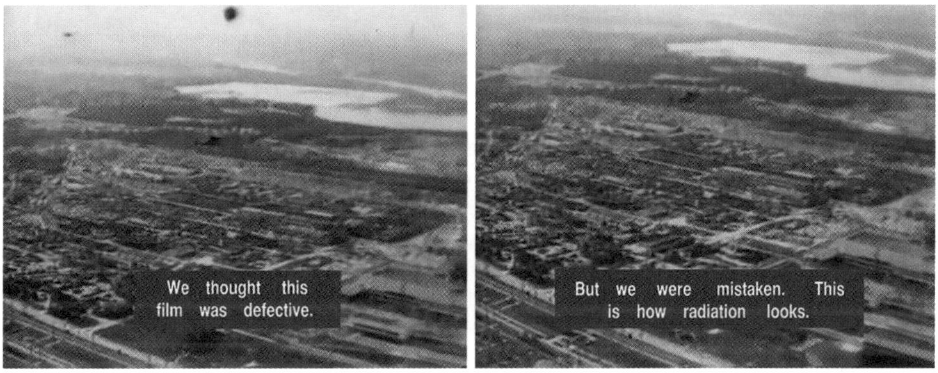

Figure 3.1
Film stills from *Chernobyl: Chronicle of Difficult Weeks*, Vladimir Shevchenko, 1986, 54 minutes. Source: The Glasnost Film Festival.

Dangerous Emissions

Three days after the explosion and meltdown of Chernobyl's Nuclear Reactor Unit 4 on April 26, 1986, Soviet filmmaker Vladimir Shevchenko was granted permission to fly over the 30-square-kilometer site known as the Exclusion Zone.[1] His assignment was to document the cleanup operations being carried out by Ukrainian workers and volunteers, most of whom would eventually succumb to the extraordinarily high levels of radiation they were exposed to while trying to contain the disaster. When Shevchenko's 35mm footage was later developed, he noticed that a portion of the film was heavily pockmarked and carried extraneous static interference and noise. Thinking initially that the film stock used had been defective, Shevchenko eventually realized that what he had captured on film was the image and sound of radioactivity itself. Upon

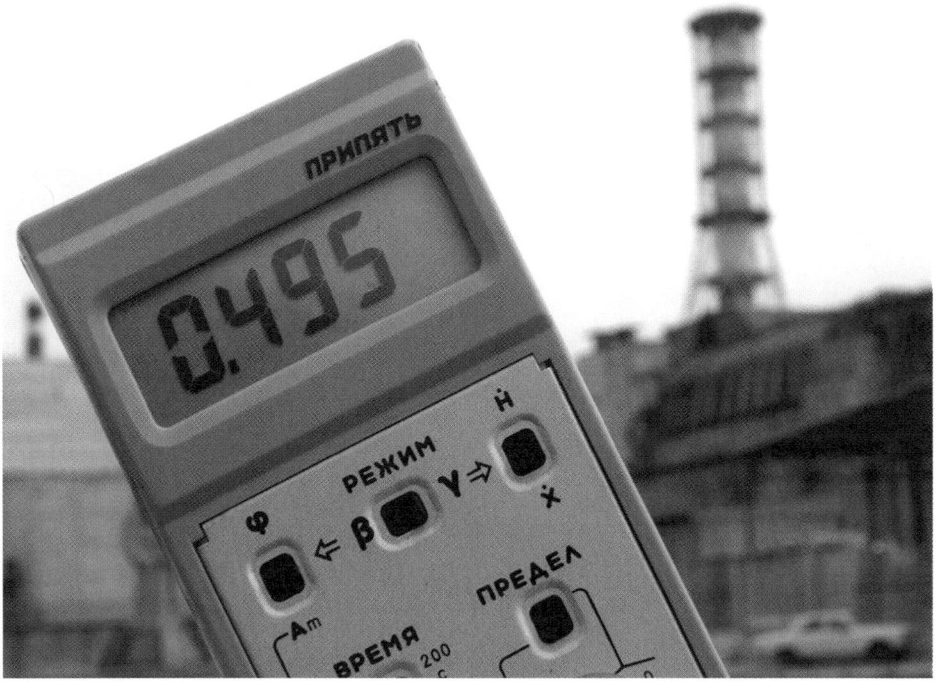

Figure 3.2
Reactor Unit 4 Chernobyl, April 23, 2016. Photo credit: Pyotr Sivkov. Source: TASS.

projection, small flares of light momentarily ignite the surface of the film. Sparking and crackling, they conjure a pyrotechnics of ghostly defects that are the consequence of decaying radioactive particles moving through the exterior casing of Shevchenko's 35mm Konvas camera to activate the emulsive properties of the film.[2] What we are witness to, in this fleeting energetic event, is the radiological conversion of a somewhat pedestrian account of the disaster into the most dangerous film in the world.

> Radiation is a fatal invisible foe. One that even penetrates steel plating. It has no odor, nor color. But it has a voice. Here it is. We thought this film was defective. But we were mistaken. This is how radiation looks. This shot was taken when we were allowed a 30-second glimpse from the armored troop-carrier. On that April night the first men passed here—without protection or stop-watches, aware of the danger, as soldiers performing a great feat. Our camera was loaded with black-and-white film. This is why the events of the first weeks will be black and white, the colors of disaster.[3]

Although Shevchenko's film, *Chernobyl: Chronicle of Difficult Weeks*, provides us with an intimate view into the space of disaster, its pictorial mediation allows us to remain at a safe and objective distance from the hazard. However, the sudden distortion of the documentary's sound and image flows by the Geiger-like interference of radiation displaces our initial confidence in its representational status as a fixed historical index, inaugurating, instead, a sense of dread that what we are witnessing on film is in fact the unholy representation of the real: an amorphous and evil contagion that continues to release its lethal discharges into the present and future yet to come. The contaminated film footage thus complicates the conventional partitioning of time by hurling us unwittingly back into the contact zone of the event—not merely as viewers but also as witnesses to an event whose time has not yet passed. Even when I am watching a safe VHS copy of this film, I am reminded of the transgressive agency of the nuclear to contravene the material borders that traditionally maintain the integrity between human and nonhuman entities, between bodies and images, between past and present. Given what we already know about the radical chemistry and anarchic temporality of nuclear materials, it is impossible to fully distance ourselves from this fallout on film, regardless of how far removed we believe ourselves to be from the event in both space and time, bearing in mind that the radiological composition of Earth was forever altered on July 16, 1945, with the Trinity test.

Detonating the first nuclear weapon altered the planet's baseline levels of ionizing radiation irrevocably as newly created isotopes such as caesium-134 and 137 began to supplement naturally occurring cosmic and terrestrial radiation. Although caesium-137 first appeared in the early solar system through processes of natural nuclear fission, more than 1.7 billion years would pass before it reappeared on Earth in any detectable amount—on December 2, 1942, as a result of a nuclear chain reaction produced by the first-ever human-made nuclear reactor, the Chicago Pile-1, built under the supervision of physicist Enrico Fermi. Applying Gayatri Chakravorty Spivak's conception of "planetarity" to the militarization of extraterritorial and extraterrestrial space, Elizabeth DeLoughrey makes the crucial point that in the decades that immediately followed Fermi's experiment, "humanity began to significantly change the global radiation environment by testing nuclear weapons in the atmosphere. By the early 1960s, there was no place on Earth where the signature of atmospheric nuclear testing could not be found in soil, water and even polar ice."[4] By extension, Shevchenko's contaminated film, whether the original 35mm print or its VHS copy, signals an intensification of an already increasingly "unnatural" radiological world where anthropogenic contamination would become omnipresent. The interference that we observe within the image field of *Chronicle of Difficult Weeks* is a tacit reminder that the nuclear always operates in excess of containment and is thus ontologically predisposed to breaching imposed limits, whether they are film frames, reactor units, or remote test sites. Although radiation is effectively everywhere, events around Chernobyl unfolded in such a way as to negate the scale and extent of the accident, and even initially to deny that it ever happened. As one Polish protestor would scrawl months later on his placard, in an antinuclear demonstration held after the USSR reluctantly admitted that an incident had occurred in the Ukraine: "Chernobyl is everywhere—except in the East."

The irradiated image matter of Shevchenko's documentary offers a paradigmatic account of a *material witness* in which trace evidence of an external event—the nuclear accident at Chernobyl—is registered directly by changes in the material composition of the artifact, producing a condition of informational enrichment that opens up the artifact to further analysis and critical reflection.[5] Material changes index new informatic conjunctions that multiply their potential connections with other events. In nondigital matter this expresses itself through processes of sedimentation and topological inscription, or even in deep material reconfigurations and alchemical exchanges. But as the introduction to this book makes clear, the specific informational value of this change is open to contestation. In the case of Shevchenko's defective film stock, there can be no dispute that the radioactive isotopes released into the atmosphere by the reactor meltdown—at a magnitude 400 times greater than that of the atomic bomb over Hiroshima—were the source of the film's contamination, and thus offered compelling evidence as to the scale and migrating nature of the disaster. Indeed, subsequent radiation readings also confirmed that all of his film equipment, including his Konvas and cherished Arriflex cameras, had been severely exposed, thus requiring their immediate decommissioning and disposal.[6] Shevchenko himself died less than a year later, in March 1987. This compromised footage also provides insight into the event of evidence—the disclosures that disputed materials evince as stakeholders gather around them to assess their particular relevance or exercise jurisdiction over them—which I have insisted is a necessary attribute that distinguishes the *material witness* from other processes of material registration. In this case, however, it was not quite that straightforward.

The public contexts in which Chernobyl's contaminants would come to feature as evidence that a major nuclear accident had occurred largely took place outside of the Soviet Union, as we saw in chapter 2. In the political aftermath of the tragedy at Chernobyl, the failure to inform its citizens served to expose the hubris of the Soviet State, which hid the disaster from the public, acted far too slowly in disclosing and managing the risk, covered up negligence in the reactor's operational procedures, and ultimately exposed millions to unnecessary poisoning, especially as the contaminating winds blew northwest across the Ukrainian border into Belarus, and onward into Poland and Sweden. Today, an estimated 3.5 million Ukrainians are still plagued with maladies linked to Chernobyl; many of them have received little or no compensation for their suffering. The situation in Belarus, recipient of 70 percent of Chernobyl's airborne contaminants, is even grimmer.[7] As we also saw in chapter 2, activities were underway for May Day celebrations throughout the USSR; Soviet officials felt that it would dampen festive spirits if news of the nuclear meltdown and potential health hazards were publicized during this period. As a result, atmospheric molecules carrying ionizing radiation entered into the respiratory systems of thousands of unsuspecting hosts. Children, it turned out, were the most susceptible to this migrating airborne malevolence. Radiation affects cells in the thyroid gland above all, which in young people are in an active state of duplication or growth. Consequently, irradiated cells were turned out at unprecedented metabolic rates, spawning, in turn, statistically abnormal increases in the incidents of thyroid tumors among children.

A subsequent legal trial was organized entirely around procedural failings rather than the admission of any evidential artifacts of a material nature. In this regard, State silence around the various material expressions of nuclear contamination could more aptly be described as disclosing the management of the disaster as a "nonevent." If the *material witness*'s dual obligation is to act as a registration system that archives trace evidence of events as well as accounting for the appearance of such evidence within the contested spaces of public discourse, then the willful lack of public acknowledgment for 19 harrowing days could be said to constitute an event in and of itself. Silence, secrecy, and the withdrawal of the conventions of public speech need to be understood as modes of evidence-making in their own right, in that they yield temporal gaps or spaces of redaction in the historical record which resonate with investigative potential. Many of these kinds of omissions are variously explored and discussed throughout this book. Within this context of denial, Shevchenko's film is a *material witness*, and a "hostile" one at that, in both the literal and legal sense of the term. As a materially compromised artifact the film inadvertently offered up damaging testimony that was willfully antagonistic to the narratives of nuclear containment and crisis management that were being advanced by the State via their commissioning of the documentary, with its focus on cleanup operations. As the airborne malevolence of Chernobyl moved beyond the borders of the Ukraine in the days immediately following the accident, the failure of the State to discharge its civil obligations was an act of malfeasance; one in which political silence was eventually reconfigured as evidence of gross negligence, and rematerialized in the form of public protest and anger. Today Chernobyl is regarded as the political catalyst that led to the collapse of the Soviet Union on December 26, 1991.

Double Agency

Before examining the broader evidential insights that materialized out of events at Chernobyl, I wish to underscore the significance that the distinction between representation and the real holds out for all the cases being discussed in this book. This involves a certain engagement with key ideas from the history of photography—its photochemical past—that might seem less relevant when social media and online platforms have completely reconfigured image production and circulation, but are nonetheless crucial: specifically for understanding how the trace effects archived by different media formats are more than simply indices of past events, but are the means by which a politics of matter can be produced in the present, which might in turn corroborate other findings, and even be constitutive of circumstantial evidence. As I have already stressed, the *material witness* is concerned not only with the evidence of events at the level of representation—the depiction of actions in an image, or the intelligibility of speech in sound—but with all the nodes and points of data acquisition and translation that constitute the event of evidence. Representation is downplayed in this book in favor of a consideration of the ways in which the actuality of events is expressed materially through processes of asignification, thus radicalizing what we might consider to be an image or a sound. With respect to Shevchenko's damaged film stock, reconceptualizing the sudden emergence of radiation as a "capture of the real" rather than a continuation of the representational program of the documentary proposes a rethinking of the ontological nature of the image itself.

Film theorist André Bazin defined cinema as "change mummified" in his seminal 1960 essay "The Ontology of the Photographic Image," arguing that the dynamism of the living is best guaranteed by technologies of exact recording. Only photography and film, he argued, could convincingly preserve the real time of an event through their contractual purchase with stillness, the frozen instant, which enables perpetual replay and imaginary return.[8] Bazin developed this idea with reference to the complex Egyptian art of mummification. The burial practices of the ancient Egyptians, he suggests, sought to sustain the vital realism of the dead through strategies of aesthetic substitution and temporal delay: "To preserve artificially his bodily appearance is to snatch it from the flow of time, to stow it away neatly, so to speak, in the hold of life."[9] Photography and cinema liberated painting and sculpture from the burden of trying to elicit realism through approximations of liveliness derived from color and form. The "preservation of life," Bazin writes, could be cinematically extended and mechanically achieved through the animation of "representations of life." However, the irradiated sequence in *Chronicle of Difficult Weeks* performs its "liveliness" not through technical feats of illusion that would resurrect the dead, but by means of its extreme image substance: filmic matter that is still dangerously alive.

In Gilles Deleuze's later writings on cinema around the concept of the "time-image," he actually invokes radioactivity to describe a potency inherent to the temporal operations of certain image and sound events.[10] These are moments and memories from the past that interpenetrate the present and register their difference. Somewhat free-floating, like a dream sequence in a film or a hallucination, such recollection and recognition signs (as he also refers to them) have durational capacities because they emerge out of the reservoir of lived experience, out of our comprehension of past events to connect with but also trouble our contemporary encounters with images and objects: "It is as if the past surfaces in itself but in the shape of personalities which are independent, alienated, off-balance, in some sense embryonic, strangely active fossils, radioactive, inexplicable in the present where they surface, and all the more harmful and autonomous."[11]

On November 22, 1895, German physicist Wilhelm Konrad Röntgen exposed his wife's hand to a new form of electromagnetic radiation as it rested immobile on a photographic plate. These wavelengths, which we now call X-rays or Röntgen rays, could pass through the atmosphere and pierce the body from a distance to generate shadowy photographic renderings, or "ghost pictures," as they were referred to at the time. Indeed, it was the spectral power of the radiological—a seemingly divine light—composed of invisible electromagnetic emissions that could contravene corporeal boundaries to expose a skeletal interiority, which is said to have caused Anna Bertha Röntgen to shudder in mortal dread upon first viewing her own hand in the lifeless form of an X-ray. "Like a dream, this form of light moved through objects, erased boundaries between solid objects, crossing their internal and external borders"[12]—a conjunction between the agency of the nuclear and a transcendent metaphysics of spirit that still haunts the history of atomic energy today.[13] The X-ray confronted Anna Bertha Röntgen with an extraordinary time-image: a prospective view of her own body as already skeletal remains. It was an image of a kind that she had never in fact seen before, given that this was the first X-ray ever taken, but it was also an image she would never be able to see—herself as dead—and yet she immediately recognized it and understood its portentous nature. This is the force of the time-image: to unsettle the present, as well as defy its full integration into the establishing shots of objective reality.

The description of such image flows as radioactive fossils, however apt, is still a somewhat metaphoric attribution rather than a strictly material condition. The micro-explosions that Shevchenko witnessed upon first viewing his rushes were the result of radioactive decay, even though the prints that now circulate are far removed from direct contact with this original event. Yet the afterlives of these flickering images still manage to produce an affective charge, because through them we can recognize and access something of our nuclear present, which oftentimes seems off-limits to all but industry experts and regulatory agencies. In this regard, the time-image of radiation contamination that haunts this particular film sequence remains resolutely "real" despite its transfer to other analog and digital formats. Each time we see and hear the transitory traces of radioactivity come to life in *Chronicle of Difficult Weeks* we experience its felt effects in the present. This relay between cinematic time and the time of lived experience is a consequence of the double agency of nuclear matter, which is forcefully reanimated for us both by its reach into the past event from which it derives its ongoing momentum (emissions that will carry it into the far distant future) as well as by the uneasy reminder that such matter can never be fully contained within a frame, nor fixed at 24 frames per second, because there is no radiologically chaste condition that we can return to (especially not after 1945), no film substance to rewind and playback, only the dynamism of continuous change. Or—following Deleuze's characterization—these are cinematic materials for machining time in which the "paralysed, frozen, petrified instance" of the 35mm film frame becomes "embryonic," teeming with the hallucinogenic elixir of alchemical life.[14] To confront Shevchenko's documentary as a radioactive artifact and witness that is materially hostile is to collapse the distinction between representation and the real, form and content, signification and affect, such that these moving images enter into a feedback loop with the *actual* material residue of the world. This is not to celebrate the power of radiological transformation but to grasp its productive nature as always generative of material change, whether this is beneficial or antagonistic to the entities and bodies it moves through, as might be the case in nuclear medicine or, indeed, with mutating cancerous cells. Through its direct contact with Chernobyl's elemental chemistry, mediatic matter's ontological status as a fixed record and index of past events was converted into an inscriptive medium of ongoing exchange.

Experimental filmmakers have long paid a great deal of attention to the aesthetic impurities offered by scratches and unstable film chemistry, shifting our attention to these defects as the source of our visual mediation.[15] The works of filmmaker Bill Morrison and contemporary artists Christoph Keller and Filipa César are very suggestive of the *material witness* in this regard, yet the scratches and decay that are foregrounded in their film projects tend to function as representations—albeit abstractions—that interfere with the original image stream rather than independent events that are reworking the film's own ontology. Strangely enough, one of the decomposing silent films that Morrison found and used in the making of *Decasia* has now been identified as J. Farrell's *The Last Egyptian* (1914). This project, for which he salvaged and celebrated deteriorating film footage from the silent era, was recently selected for preservation by the National Film Registry. Somewhat ironically, an investigation into the aesthetics of filmic decay, and the disappearance of celluloid film more broadly, has itself now been subject to conservation efforts to arrest the dynamic changes that are the foundation of *Decasia*'s creative existence. In order for any photographic negative and filmic medium to enable the possibility of "eternal return," the stability of its chemistry and material integrity must be assiduously secured, and any external forces vigilantly guarded against. Egyptian processes of mummification, too, sought to stave off the vagaries of time in order to maintain the pretence of life. As long as the mummified corpse offered up a material resemblance that was sufficiently realistic, its program of extending life into the afterlife was ensured.[16] However, unlike the illusory campaign of the photograph, its success was measured not so much by the absolute preservation of its mummified remains but by the conviction of an imagination spurred on by the power of mimesis. Despite changes in the material strata of the object, the myth surrounding its auratic potential worked to assure its continuities with the past. While all celluloid film stock undergoes a certain degree of entropic deterioration over time, exposure to radiation not only dramatically accelerated this process, it also functioned as a recording device in its own right by directly archiving the toxicological event that the cinematic apparatus had merely set out to document. Liveliness, in Shevchenko's documentary, was captured not in service to the preservation of life—the principle of the mummy complex—but as an unintentional consequence of a radiologically in-formed cinema whose material existence was still terrifyingly alive.

Covert Operations

Radiation, whether in its harmful ionizing form or its benign nonionizing state, defies easy visualization because its high frequency and short energetic wavelengths appear at the far end of the electromagnetic spectrum, well beyond those light waves that are visible to humans; a condition explored more fully in chapter 11, "Failure to Appear," which deals with the portable Gamma Camera invented by Toshiba to locate contamination at Fukushima Daiichi and its environs. Yet contrary to the covert operations of alpha, beta, and gamma rays, the radiological bursts and stammers captured by Shevchenko's film do actually result in the production of a new "image" that breaks its filmic continuity with what came before it on the reel. Arguably, this emergence is more akin to a kind of planetary medium if we remember that background radiation envelops us all. It both is and isn't strictly speaking an image of radiation, even if Shevchenko declares: "We thought this film was defective. But we were mistaken. This is how radiation looks." Nor does the sparking and crackling that arises out of this scene inaugurate the classic Barthesian "reality effect," in which the apparent realism of the image secures its veracity as a "natural" substitute despite the intercession of a mechanical contrivance. This conviction in the naturalism of the image, it was claimed, permits the photographic or filmic event to stand in as an agent of objective truth that points to an existence directly beyond the strictures of the frame. Image and event in this formulation are incontrovertibly linked, while occupying different spatial orders. Rather than merely confirming the existence of an external radiological reality, the film's direct isotopic capture produced a dangerous index internal to the image, one that also intensified the emergence of a new kind of image event in excess of representation.

While my references to Bazin as well as Barthes are obviously dated with respect to contemporary media theorizations, we still traffic in much of the groundwork laid out by such photographic thinking, especially in the domains of investigative journalism and law, which are two of the disciplines that I brush up against consistently. These are forums in which images often play an instrumental role as agents of the "real" for making public claims. Forensic Architecture's approach to building a dynamic field of interacting points of view, camera angles, and time scales—an architectural image complex—offers a unique alternative method for thinking images as always multiple. Even Rosalind Krauss, writing almost 40 years ago, considered the indexical operations of the photograph as much more materially entangled than merely signaling a cartographic relationship between reality and its various modes of recording: "For photography is an imprint or transfer of the real; it is a photochemically processed trace causally connected to that thing in the world to which it refers in a manner parallel to that of fingerprints or footprints or the rings of water that cold glasses leave on tables. The photograph is thus generically distinct from painting or sculpture or drawing. On the family tree of images it is closer to palm prints, death masks, the Shroud of Turin, or the tracks of gulls on beaches. For technically and semiologically speaking, drawings and paintings are icons, while photographs are indexes."[17] Throughout the cases presented in this book, representations of violent events captured by cameras and sensors *do* play a role in my analysis, but my insistence on the artifactual residue that many of these forms of media accrue as they move through various contexts and forums over, sometimes, many years needs also be understood as an actual event. Sometimes these traces become legally evidential in disclosing additional information about events that prosecutors can utilize to forward their cases or reopen a file; these are the material traces and digital artifacts that bring forensic experts onto the scene. At other times their value is perhaps more generative in spurring our forensic imagination to open up new lines of inquiry and produce new political assemblages.

It is worth noting that Shevchenko's archival recording of the Chernobyl disaster exists today, that is to say posthumously, only because it was captured by analog means. The extremely high levels of radiation within the Zone would have immediately erased any digital video data, which is always stored magnetically. It is not possible to archive the nuclear with digital technology if the hard drives used for data storage encounter high levels of radiation. In general, analog storage mediums, such as film stock, photographic negatives, and magnetic audiotape, are particularly receptive to registering external events because their surfaces allow them to archive trace evidence through direct contact or exposure. Walter Benjamin's discussion of the auratic capture of external events made possible by the lengthy exposure times demanded by nascent photographic practices is provocatively congruent here as a kind of precursor to the *material witness*. Because of the poor light sensitivity of early salt and silver solutions, inordinately long exposures were required if any likeness was to appear. For Benjamin, the temporal darkness out of which an image struggled to assert its presence meant that the surface of the photographic plate was saturated with the aggregate history of the subject's environment—thus establishing its aura.[18] The digital, while not impervious to noise and interference, must by definition recalculate and absorb this intruder data into its coding chains, whereas the deviance of radiological interference within analog domains sits side by side with the "proper" subjects of inscription, since there is no mechanism for reintegrating such extraneous information.

Soviet Defectors

In an uncanny premonition of things to come, *Stalker* (released in 1980), the final film shot by Andrei Tarkovsky in the Soviet Union, stakes out the apocalyptic terrain that would become the Exclusion Zone of Chernobyl a full six years prior to the actual meltdown of the reactor core. Tarkovsky's cinematic treatment of the Zone was itself drawn from rumors of an explosion at the Mayak nuclear waste facility near Chelyabinsk in 1957, which was said to have created a vast ecological nightmare. Although the industrial accident at Mayak took place prior to the production of *Stalker* in 1979, the Soviet government's denial that it ever happened effectively erased it from history as an actual event with real consequences. But of course, thousands could intuit that something dangerous had happened in the vicinity—not by way of any direct or established knowledge of the incident, but by means of its corporeal effects: physico-chemical changes in bodily matter. As was the case with Chernobyl, Soviet leadership concealed evidence of the accident and played down reports of human casualties. But unlike the time lag that attended Chernobyl, official confirmation of the chemical fallout from Chelyabinsk was made public only in 1989—32 years after the damaged landscape first testified to the presence of radionuclides in its water table and agricultural produce. Shevchenko actually borrowed elements from *Stalker*'s score in creating his sound design.[19]

Tarkovsky's science-fiction epic is also materially intertwined with Shevchenko's documentary through the tale of defective film stock that afflicted both productions. As the story goes, Tarkovsky's German producer supplied him with a new kind of Kodak stock, but then "disaster struck" when the artesian well water required for the film's processing ran dry due to a malfunction at Mosfilm. Not only is his film stock prospectively entangled with the heavy-water chronicles of Shevchenko's documentary yet to come, but the technical breakdown at the preeminent Russian film studio gestures toward future technological failings that will contribute to the accident at the Chernobyl nuclear power plant. Apparently *Stalker*'s exposed materials languished in an unprocessed state for 17 days (unbeknownst to Tarkovsky) as its filmic matter rapidly deteriorated. "In a word, the whole material for the first part ended up on the scrap heap."

> The review of the ruined footage ended in a scandal. Tarkovsky, Rerberg, the Strugatskys, and Tarkovsky's wife Larissa were all sitting in the projection room. Suddenly one of the Strugatskys turned towards Rerberg and asked naively: "Gosha, and how come I can't see anything here?" Rerberg, always considering himself beyond reproach in everything he did, turned to Strugatsky and said: "And you just be quiet, you are no Dostoievsky either!" Tarkovsky was beside himself with anger. But one can understand Rerberg. Imagine what it means for a cameraman to see the entire material turning up defective![20]

This narrative of defect exemplifies Paul Virilio's contention that there is no "accidental catastrophe" of a technical nature, which subsequently reveals an unattended error, programing glitch, or series of mishaps leading up to the improbable event. Failure is always-already engineered into the design process as technology's virtual double—its evil twin—the accident invented simultaneously with the invention, even though chance still has an important role to play in creating the necessary conditions for its emergence.[21] However, when circumstances conspire, accidents can happen, but as both Deleuze and Virilio note, they do not happen accidentally. Deleuze actually makes a specific distinction between the event and the accident. He regards the former—the event—as an ideal having an "eternal truth" whose time, unlike that of the accident, is never simply the present that brought the disaster into existence. There are no accidental events for Deleuze but, rather, events that problematize accidents and define their conditions. Nuclear energy was the event that problematized the accident at Chernobyl and established a radiological relay that would connect it to Fukushima Daiichi 25 years later, as well retroactively to the blast at the Mayak plutonium production and reprocessing facility in Siberia that took place in 1957.

When Chernobyl's reactor core went supercritical, what resulted was not something entirely unexpected but, rather, a statistical inevitability in the form of a major nuclear accident. According to Virilio, Chernobyl was an accident lying in wait, one that was invented when the power station was first conceived.[22] The potential failure of technical objects is an inevitable by-product of their invention and use, not merely the consequence of some safety procedure gone wrong, or even the outcome of a natural disaster. However, one cannot say that the events of Chernobyl were simply "invented" on April 26, 1986, when its operating staff made a series of grave mistakes, or were the result of the inferior design of the RBMK graphite-moderated light-water reactor. Many prior factors contributed to this accident, not the least of which was the invention of the technology itself and the risks that attend any use of atomic energy. "The odds of a meltdown [at Chernobyl] are one in 10,000 years," boasted Vitali Sklyarov, Minister of Power and Electrification for Soviet Ukraine.[23] Standard maintenance protocols are processes not for preventing but for minimizing the magnitude of the error dimension that one can expect with any technical system. Backup systems and software recovery programs exist not because of the unlikelihood of a fatal error, but because hard-drive failure can be calculated as a statistically probable event. The virtual is always real. Nuclear disasters do not happen by mistake, they are designed as one of the many possible consequences of harnessing nuclear energy. This is why the powerful myth of a fail-safe system still requires a series of backup operations and contingency plans, just in case that unthinkable future event does arrive.

While inventions are generally understood as coming about through processes of experimentation, or even fortuitous luck, an invention can also provoke new modes of witnessing that can bring some previously hidden or unobserved reality into public perception. In the case of Chernobyl it was the distance traveled by caesium-137 combined with elevated readings of radioactive contamination throughout the environment of the Forsmark Nuclear Power Plant in Sweden that first invented the Soviet disaster as considerable. Later it would be the act of encasing the reactor in a colossal concrete and steel shelter that would further acknowledge the gravity and scope of the accident.[24] Its public recognition as catastrophic would require acts of signification equal in scale to the cataclysmic dimensions of the tragedy itself. Gorbachev understood this implicitly when he issued his first press release reporting minor damage at the Chernobyl plant site. To acknowledge the immensity of the disaster would also be to reinvent it as such—as calamitous and massive. This would in turn require a reciprocal response of similarly dramatic proportions on the part of the Soviet Union; an admission that would trigger accusations of culpability in equal measure, a direction the Central Committee was reluctant to take for fear of reprisals. The State finally acquiesced to widespread pressure, both domestically and internationally, to launch a legal investigation into the chain of events that had led to the gravest nuclear accident ever. One year later, a modest trial was held in the Exclusion Zone. Six power plant employees were tried and charged with technical misconduct and incompetence.

Yet as the more recent accident at the Fukushima Daiichi Power Station also powerfully recalls, efforts to control short- or long-term risk are ultimately a calculation that amortizes the contingencies of the future against the known perils of the past. Internal events—leaks, explosions, and fires—are much easier to plan for than dangerous events that might erupt out of unknown scenarios coming from the distant future. The design and engineering of nuclear reactors is organized by the conviction that one can manage risks, whether brought about by natural disaster or the result of human error, through careful planning and preparation, and with tightly controlled regulatory mechanisms. And while reactors are not expected to operate beyond 60 years, the extreme temporality of their by-products—spent nuclear fuel—requires a design strategy that can guarantee containment of hazardous waste into the far distant future: that is, for up to 10,000 years, the date at which most anthropogenic radioactive isotopes will have fully decayed and discharged their lethal latency. Nuclear waste storage thus assumes the inevitability of change over millennia, whereas nuclear reactor design assumes the improbability of a highly unlikely event occurring during its working life. Such was the risk calculus that brought about the events at Chernobyl.

Five months after the accident, Reactor Unit 4 was itself entombed within a metal-clad structure ominously called the Sarcophagus.[25] It is a burial chamber for the many workers and volunteers who died while trying to quell the fire and seal off escaping contaminants, as well as a form of architectural embalmment aimed at preserving its radioactive contents. Few other human-made structures, save the pyramid complex at Giza, had previously attempted a similar feat, which was to shield the material remains of the past against the volatility of unknown future events. Today it literally is a death trap, and a decaying one at that, whose critical breach will be not the result of tomb raiders but an act of vandalism perpetrated by the very radioactive materials that it houses. When the core melted, its uranium seeped into the sand bedding below, temporarily petrifying its radioisotopes in a silica bond. Now these solid forms have largely disintegrated, creating a subterranean reserve of radioactive materials that loom in wait of its atmospheric release. Given the failing state of the Sarcophagus, the unleashing of its evil spirits may happen sooner rather than later. What it guards through containment is also that which it guards against: the virulent reanimation of its airborne radioactive particles. "Nuclear materials," writes Peter C. van Wyck in *Danger Signs*, "stand in relation to their containment only very imperfectly—there is always leakage."[26] Retracing the narrative arc that led from the first self-sustaining nuclear chain reaction set off by Enrico Fermi in 1942 to the harnessing of nuclear energy always throws us unwittingly back into the dark malignancy of Chernobyl, in whose lethal dust clouds Fukushima Daiichi already lurked. The bursts of radiant energy fixed by Shevchenko's film are therefore not the residual traces of a past that has come to haunt future media recordings in the telegraphic manner that sound and image ghosts typically appear within analog regimes, but the spectral forces of the future past archived by the continuous present. The film registers both the "this was" of the past—the initial accident—as well as the "this is still to come" in the future—the ongoing event of contamination.

Courting Disaster

In 1989, during one of the many public demonstrations demanding State accountability for what was widely regarded as an improvised "show trial" blaming the nuclear disaster at Chernobyl solely upon its presiding staff, protestors carried a banner calling for "A Nuremberg Trial for Chernobyl." A of number Ukrainian flags raised in public defiance and anger toward the Soviet State were also prominent. Prior to the establishment of the International Criminal Tribunals for the former Yugoslavia and Rwanda in the 1990s, and the International Criminal Court in 2002, Nuremberg exemplified the legal model for putting a state on trial. The demand made by the protestors called for a new trial that would challenge the Soviet Union's impunity with regard to its tacit role in bringing about the world's worst nuclear accident as well as in misleading the public afterward. By deliberately downplaying the severity and scale of radioactive pollutants released into the atmosphere, especially during the initial period of the accident when more precautionary measures might have been taken, the death toll was multiplied exponentially. Today the official number of victims attributed to Chernobyl is still calculated at just 50, and represents only those directly killed at the time of the explosion and during cleanup operations in the immediate weeks following the meltdown. The ongoing debates as to how many actually died or will die from Chernobyl-related cancers remains in considerable dispute, with International Atomic Energy Agency (IAEA)

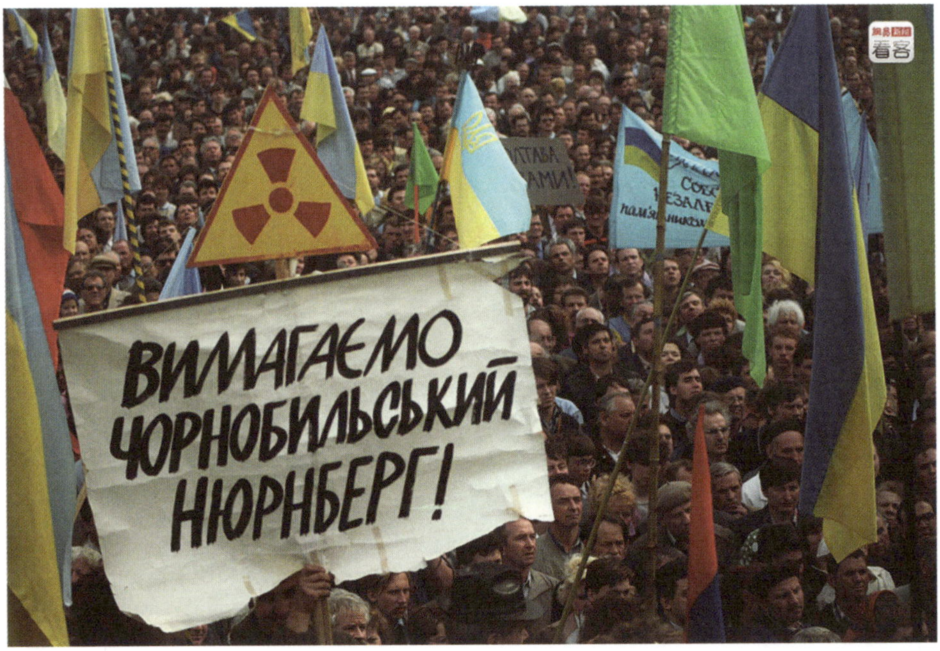

Figure 3.3
A demonstration on August 1, 1989, with protestors carrying the national flags of Belarus, Ukraine, and Russia. The central banner demands "A Nuremberg Trial for Chernobyl." Photo credit: Igor Kostin. Source: Sygma/Corbis.

estimates controversially pegged toward the lower end of the spectrum, at around 4,000, whereas Greenpeace projections reach as high as 270,000 potential victims.[27]

"A Nuremberg Trial for Chernobyl" also makes an implicit but forceful request that the administrative archive of the State be cross-examined and made to speak. Paperwork, it was believed, would provide the corroborating evidence that the Soviet Union was directly responsible for the series of events that led to the devastating accident in the Ukraine on April 26, 1986: from the awarding of government contracts; misguided decisions to reduce construction costs; lax implementation of safety procedures; to the infrequency and limited scope of technical inspections.

Radioactive Show Trial

Two years earlier, in July 1987, a derelict cultural center in the vicinity of Chernobyl was repurposed as a makeshift courtroom, its theatrical seating and elevated proscenium a

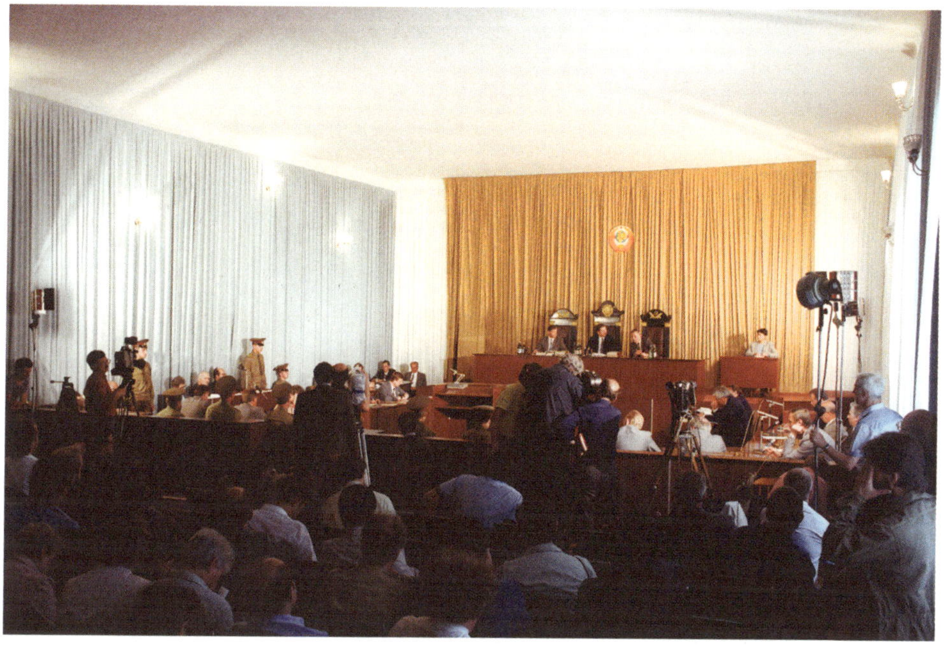

Figure 3.4
Location of the trial in the repurposed Chernobyl House of Culture, July 1, 1987. Photo credit: Igor Kostin. Source: Sygma/Corbis.

legal readymade for staging a trial over the defining crisis of the late twentieth century. Soviet law at the time mandated that all legal proceedings be conducted in direct proximity to the scene of the crime—a criterion that would prove strategically useful to the State in controlling access to and coverage of the hearings. Accordingly, the Chernobyl Trial took place just 18 kilometers southeast of the failed reactor site; within the 30-square-kilometer radius of the Exclusion Zone that marks the limits of a radioactive territory still considered too dangerous to support prolonged exposure. Although the trial was officially open to the public, permission to enter the Zone was granted only by special authorization. In an unassuming civic building—the Chernobyl House of Culture—the trial of six employees accused of irresponsibility, abuse of power, and violating safety procedures at the plant was conducted over a period of 18 days.[28] The defendants were charged under Article 220 of the Ukrainian Criminal Code for violating the safety procedures of an industrial site, leading to death or other grave consequences. Only a handful of domestic and foreign journalists were granted limited access to the reading of the indictment and delivery of the verdict. The remaining 16

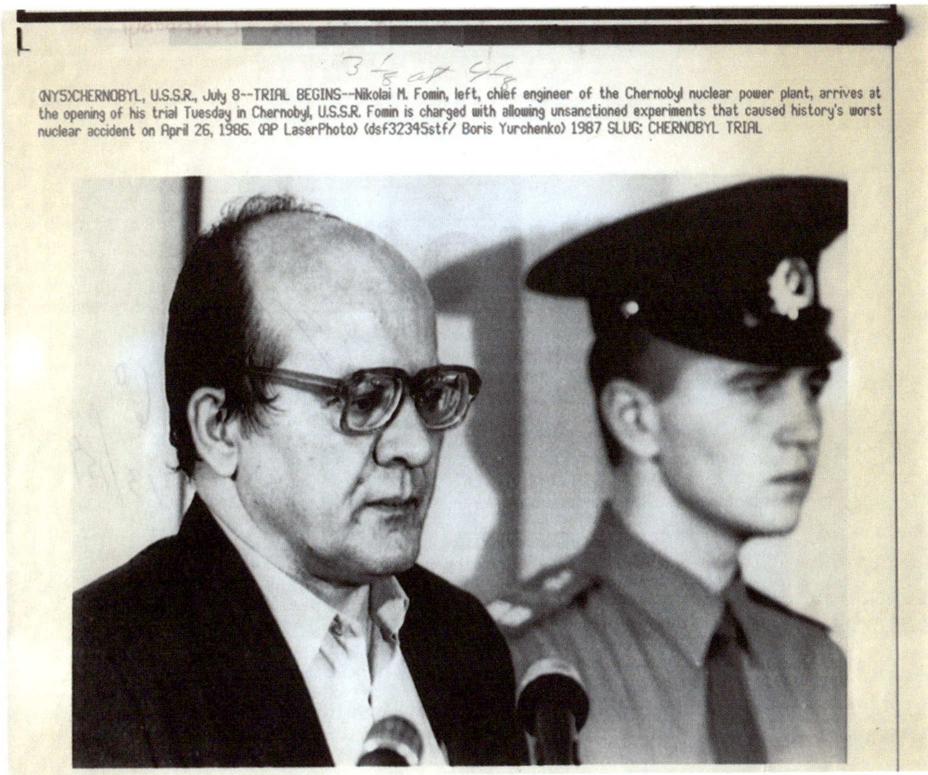

Figure 3.5
Nikolai M. Fomin (left), chief engineer of the Chernobyl nuclear power plant, arrives at the opening of his trial in Chernobyl on July 8, 1987. Collection of the author.

sessions were carried out under a media blackout, with local press and television consigned to reporting on the July heat wave and progress of the local harvest. Without the presence of the press as a public witness, proceedings of the trial remain sketchy. My own research relies upon accounts given by Chernobyl Nuclear Power Plant (ChNPP) personnel who numbered amongst the 60 attendees who followed the trial over the course of two-and-a-half weeks.

The court also decided that only personnel present at the time of the explosion and reactor meltdown would be indicted, so neither the company, RBMK (Reaktor Bolshoy Moshchnosti Kanalnyy) that designed and built the nuclear reactor, nor the experts who developed the plant's accident protocols, were called to account for their decisions. To highlight the degree to which the Chernobyl Trial was politically compromised, it is worth noting that the group of forensic technical experts commissioned by the court to investigate the accident included representatives from RBMK, the same firm that had overseen the construction of the power plant and made the strategic decision to reduce costs in key areas of reactor safety. Rather than being punished for their negligence, the company was subsequently awarded the cleanup contract. In an effort to maximize their profits and reduce building costs, RBMK had modified the nuclear power plant's design so that the reactor was positioned outside the reinforced leak-tight compartment. This decision would ultimately lead to the massive release of airborne radioactive isotopes, which under other circumstances would have been substantially curtailed at 3 to 5 percent instead of at 80 percent. In an ironic twist, funds saved by RBMK's maneuvering would now be redirected toward cleanup operations. It took a criminal clerk two hours to read the indictment and charges drafted by government lawyer Yuri Shadrin and Raymond Brize, a member of the Supreme Court of the USSR, who headed the Panel of Presiding Judges. Forty witnesses, nine complainants, and two victims were called to testify. On July 29, 1987, the verdict was delivered. Six personnel from the Chernobyl Nuclear Power Plant were to be sentenced to terms of imprisonment ranging from five to ten years. According to TASS, the official news agency of the Soviet Union:

> Viktor Brukhanov, the former plant director, received the maximum penalty of "ten years' deprivation of freedom." He was found guilty of gross violation of safety rules and criminal negligence. Singled out as the chief culprit in the world's worst atomic energy accident, Brukhanov also received a five-year sentence for abuse of power, to run concurrently with the ten-year sentence. The former chief engineer, Nikolai Fomin, and his deputy, Anatoly Dyatlov, each received ten-year sentences for their roles in the accident. Boris Rogozhkin, shift chief at the plant's fourth reactor where the explosion and fire took place, was given five years "in an ordinary corrective labor camp." The reactor chief engineer, Alexander Kovalenko, received three years. Senior engineer Yuri Laushkin will serve two years in a similar labor camp.[29]

Employees who disagreed with the legal scapegoating of their colleagues were summarily discharged; those who had died on site or later in hospital were not in a position to defend themselves and were thus "magnanimously forgiven" for their presumed misdeeds in bringing about the disaster.[30] In my "Opening Statements," I argued that the pubic dimension of witnessing is crucial for conferring legitimacy on acts of testimony and evidence-making. However, in this radioactive show trial neither the evidence presented in court nor the complete transcripts of the legal proceedings have, to my knowledge, ever been made available for subsequent scrutiny.

Because of the technical findings of the forensic experts, the court limited legal responsibility to the presiding staff, not the State or its representatives. Charges under international law for any damages sustained by another state were largely averted, and the potential financial burden to care for the future ill health of the many thousands who were exposed to Chernobyl's radiation was minimized. As lawyer Victoria Riess Hartke has argued, procedures for proving state liability for damages incurred through exposure to radiation contamination is a complex process.[31] If, for example, Belarus, which received the brunt of Chernobyl's lethal emissions, were to file a legal action, it, as the injured State (which at the time was still part of the USSR), would have to prove that the Soviet State was directly responsible for the accident. Liability, in the Chernobyl Trial, was legally determined to be entirely personal; therefore responsibility was imputed to six individuals, not to State actors such as RBMK. Holding the trial within the environs of the plant and limiting responsibility exclusively to plant workers was akin to the belief that cleanup efforts during the first few days after the accident would somehow be able to quell the migration of radioactive particles and suppress its attendant political fallout: a fantasy of nuclear containment that ultimately proved untenable.

Evidence of malfeasance on the part of the Soviet Union would ultimately be disputed not within legal forums but through a distributed network of stakeholders comprised of survivors, concerned citizens, antinuclear campaigners, doctors and healthcare workers, scientific researchers, scholars and teachers, writers and artists. This remains the case today, with the widest public debates around the use of nuclear energy taking place within the forums of civil society. Even with the resurgence in antinuclear activism post-Fukushima, and an increasingly informed public, there are no international forums that can take substantive political action. The IAEA, a self-declared "Atoms for Peace and Development" organization founded within the United Nations in 1957, with jurisdiction for overseeing and monitoring the safe use of nuclear energy, has, in effect, a pronuclear position. "A petition with more than 150,000 signatures was delivered to the United Nations earlier this November [in 2013 with regard to Fukushima], calling for the world to take action. But who?" asks Harvey Wasserman, a nuclear researcher.[32] According to protocol, the UN will refer their petition to the International Atomic Energy Agency, but it has a mandate to promote nuclear power. Article II of the IAEA Statute cites its objectives as follows: "The Agency shall seek to accelerate and enlarge the contribution of atomic energy to peace, health and prosperity throughout the world. It shall ensure, so far as it is able, that assistance provided by it or at its request or under its supervision or control is not used in such a way as to further any military purpose."[33]

When I presented preliminary findings around my research into Shevchenko's film at a conference in Japan on July 17, 2007, the lecture room at the University

 Атомная энергия — электроэн.

FF063 B-WIRE 27-JUN-86 10:02
EAST -- NUCLEAR POWER: NOW AN EAST BLOC DEBATE

LONDON, JUNE 27 (SPECIAL) -- THE LONDON TIMES HAS AN ARTICLE BY ROGER BOYES IN WARSAW WHICH READS AS FOLLOWS:

TWO MONTHS AFTER THE CHERNOBYL DISASTER, SOVIET BLOC COUNTRIES ARE REAFFIRMING THEIR FAITH IN NUCLEAR POWER AND ARE PLANNING A NEW GENERATION OF 1,000 MEGAWATT REACTORS. BUT A DEBATE HAS AT LAST EMERGED IN THE FORM OF SMALL DEMONSTRATIONS, MASS PETITIONS, AND SCIENTISTS EXPRESSING UNEASE.

AT A DEMONSTRATION IN CRACOW EARLIER THIS MONTH A YOUNG POLE HELD A PLACARD ON WHICH WAS SCRAWLED: "CHERNOBYL IS EVERYWHERE -- EXCEPT IN THE EAST". MANY OF THE DEMONSTRATIONS SINCE CHERNOBYL -- MOTHERS WALKING WITH PUSHCHAIRS THROUGH THE STREETS OF WROCLAW IN POLISH SILESIA, CZECH STUDENTS WHO HAVE BEEN PRINTING THEIR OWN PROTEST POSTCARDS -- ARE NOT SO MUCH ANTI-NUCLEAR AS ANTI-CENSORSHIP. THE PEOPLE WANT INFORMATION ABOUT CHERNOBYL AND A DEBATE ON EVERY ASPECT OF NUCLEAR ENERGY.

THERE ARE, OF COURSE, COMMITTED ANTI-NUCLEAR GROUPS, FOR EXAMPLE EAST GERMAN CHURCH GROUPS INFLUENCED BY THE SUCCESS OF THE GREENS IN WEST GERMANY. AN EAST BERLIN PARISH WROTE TO THE GOVERNMENT RECENTLY SAYING IT BELIEVED THE RISKS INVOLVED IN NUCLEAR POWER WERE TOO GREAT AND DEMANDING THE IMMEDIATE CLOSURE OF ALL NUCLEAR REACTORS.

AS IN THE WEST, THESE PROTESTERS ARE ALSO OPPOSED TO MISSILES AND HAVE THEIR OWN INTERNAL PROBLEMS OF IDEOLOGY AND STRATEGY. HUNGARIAN ENVIRONMENTALISTS, SUPPORTED BY WEST GERMAN AND AUSTRIAN PROTESTERS, HAVE BEEN DEMONSTRATING AGAINST THE CONSTRUCTION OF A HUGE HYDRO-ELECTRIC DAM ON THE CZECHOSLOVAK-HUNGARIAN BORDER. UNTIL CHERNOBYL, THE HUNGARIANS WERE ARGUING THAT AN ATOMIC POWER PLANT WOULD BE A MORE ATTRACTIVE ALTERNATIVE TO THE DAM. SINCE CHERNOBYL AN OPINION POLL CONDUCTED BY THE AUTHORITIES IN NORTH-EASTERN POLAND, WHICH WAS AFFECTED BY RADIOACTIVITY, SHOWED THAT MOST PEOPLE WERE UNHAPPY ABOUT THE LACK OF INFORMATION THOUGH POLISH OFFICIALS WERE REMARKABLY FRANK ABOUT RADIATION LEVELS.

THE GENERAL UNREST PUTS SOME PRESSURE, EVEN ON CLOSED COMMUNIST SYSTEMS, TO EXPLAIN AND DEFEND. ALMOST 3,000 RESIDENTS OF BIALYSTOK IN EASTERN POLAND DEMANDED THAT WORK BE STOPPED ON POLAND'S FIRST NUCLEAR PLANT AT ZARNOWIEC NEAR THE BALTIC COAST. IN A PUBLISHED REPLY THE GOVERNMENT SAID THAT SHORTAGES OF COAL, OIL AND GAS MEANT THAT NUCLEAR POWER WAS ESSENTIAL, ADDING THAT THE PLANNED PRESSURIZED WATER REACTORS WERE SAFER THAN THAT AT CHERNOBYL.

THE FACT THAT POLAND AND HUNGARY ARE IN THE EARLY STAGES OF NUCLEAR POWER DEVELOPMENT PRESENTS POSSIBLE ADVANTAGES FOR BOTH SIDES. THE POLISH AUTHORITIES CAN ARGUE THAT CHERNOBYL IS PARTLY THE RESULT OF THE SOVIET UNION'S EARLY NUCLEAR EXPANSION AND THAT, AS A NEWCOMER, POLAND CAN EXPLOIT THE LATEST DEVELOPMENTS IN NUCLEAR ENGINEERING AND SAFETY. BUT EAST EUROPEAN ENVIRONMENTAL GROUPS MAY TAKE ADVANTAGE OF THE EXISTING LAWS -- FOR EXAMPLE OVER THE SITING OF NUCLEAR PLANTS -- TO SLOW DOWN THE NUCLEAR PROGRAMME. THERE IS ALSO THE PROBLEM OF NUCLEAR WASTE, WHICH WILL BE TAKEN FROM EASTERN EUROPE TO THE SOVIET UNION FOR REPROCESSING. SOME EAST EUROPEAN GREENS SAY THAT THE SECURITY OF THESE CROSS-BORDER TRANSPORTATIONS NEEDS TO BE SCRUTINIZED.

AMONG SOVIET BLOC COUNTRIES THE SOVIET UNION HAS THE GREATEST NUCLEAR CAPACITY, WITH 85 REACTORS IN USE OR UNDER CONSTRUCTION. CZECHOSLOVAKIA FOLLOWS, WITH 13 REACTORS AND EAST GERMANY WITH 11. IN CZECHOSLOVAKIA, WHICH HAS ITS OWN URANIUM DEPOSITS, NUCLEAR PLANTS ACCOUNT FOR 15 PER CENT OF ENERGY PRODUCTION, WITH PLANS TO INCREASE THIS TO 60 PER CENT OVER THE NEXT 15 YEARS -- A COMMITMENT IT IS UNLIKELY TO ABANDON. NON-ALIGNED YUGOSLAVIA IS THE ONLY EAST EUROPEAN COUNTRY SERIOUSLY TO CONSIDER HALTING ITS NUCLEAR PROGRAMME. THIS MONTH DEPUTY HEADS OF SOVIET BLOC COUNTRIES WILL MEET IN EAST BERLIN TO DISCUSS CHERNOBYL, BUT ARE LIKELY TO CONFINE THE TALKS TO SAFETY ASPECTS SUCH AS AN EARLY WARNING SYSTEM AND SOVIET PROPOSALS FOR AN INTERNATIONAL COMPENSATION LAW FOR NUCLEAR ACCIDENTS.

EVEN SO, SOVIET BLOC COUNTRIES ARE BEGINNING TO BE FORCED INTO THE OPEN IN NUCLEAR ISSUES. AD/

of Tokyo suddenly began to shake. As I was speaking, an earthquake of magnitude 6.8 was violently tearing apart the landscape around Niigata, resulting in a series of malfunctions—leaks, burst pipes, and fires—at the Kashiwazaki-Kariwa Nuclear Power Plant. Subsequent technical studies discovered that the plant had "accidentally" been constructed directly on top of an active seismic fault. Experiencing the tremors of this radiological event directly as it was unfolding signaled the uncanny entanglement between the epistemological matter of my research and the very ontological ground upon which these ideas momentarily trembled. It was as if the actions of the future—Fukushima Daiichi—had colluded with the past—Chernobyl—to bring about this dramatic turn of events.

4 HEARSAY

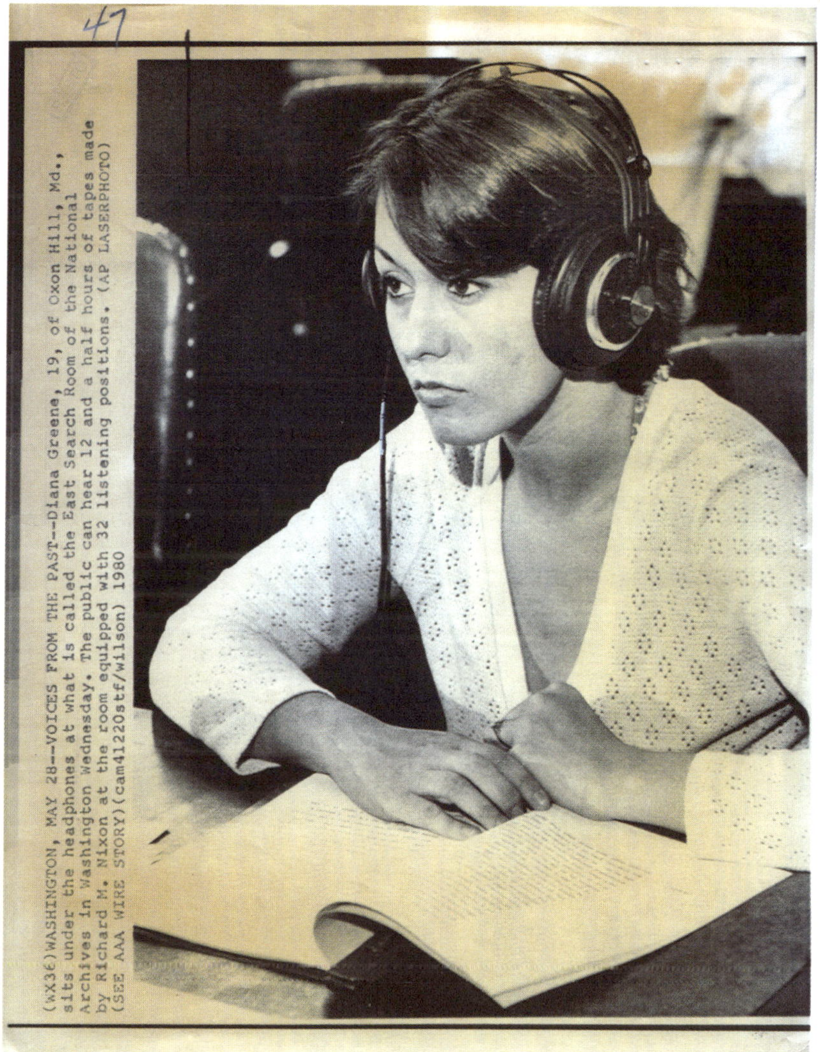

Figure 4.1

VOICES FROM THE PAST—Diana Greene, 19, of Oxon Hill, Md., sits under the headphones at what is called the East Search Room of the National Archives in Washington Wednesday. The public can hear 12 and a half hours of tapes made by Richard M. Nixon at the room equipped with 32 listening positions, May 28, 1980. Collection of the author.

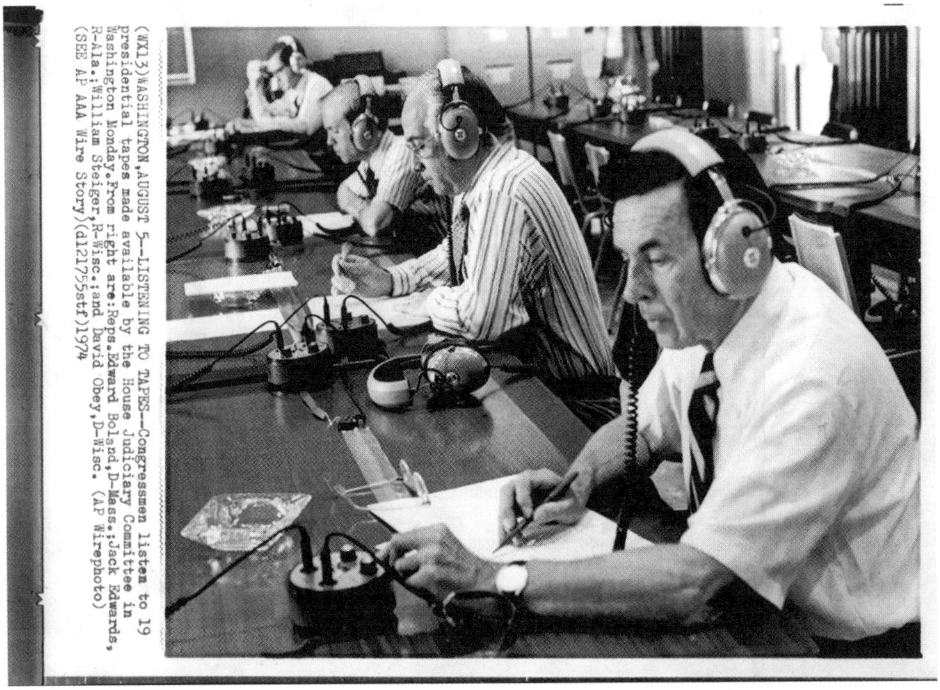

Figure 4.2
LISTENING TO TAPES—Congressmen listen to 19 presidential tapes made available by the House Judiciary Committee in Washington Monday. From right are: Reps. Edward Boland, D-Mass.; Jack Edwards, R-Ala.; Willaim Steiger, R-Wisc.; and David Obey.; D-Wisc., August 5, 1974. Collection of the author.

WHITE HOUSE TAPES 3RD CHRONOLOGICAL RELEASE JANUARY 1972-JUNE 1972

On Thursday 28 February 2002, the US National Archives released 494 hours of Nixon White House Tapes. In one rather shocking tape recorded in the Executive Office Building in Washington on 25 April 1972, then-National Security Adviser Henry Kissinger presents President Richard Nixon with various strategies aimed at intensifying the war in Vietnam including the destruction of power plants and flood barriers. Nixon had become increasingly worried that further losses in Vietnam would seriously jeopardize his bid for reelection.

Nixon dismisses Kissinger's suggestions with the cavalier comment: "I'd rather use the nuclear bomb."

"That, I think, would just be too much," replies Kissinger.

But Nixon rebukes him again: "The nuclear bomb. Does that bother you? I just want you to think big."

In the months that followed the war reached levels of violence not seen since 1968.

At a later stage in the same taped conversation Nixon reproaches Kissinger for being overly preoccupied with concerns for civilian casualties.

"I don't give a damn," Nixon says, "I don't care."

* *

In another provocative conversation recorded on 12 June 1972, Nixon discusses the war in Vietnam again, but this time with his White-house chief of staff HR Haldeman. Their conversation is directed toward a photograph of a young Vietnamese girl and several other children running in terror from a napalm attack; an image which had just been published on the cover of the *New York Times* three days earlier too much domestic outrage at American actions in Vietnam.

Nixon can be heard questioning the veracity photograph: "I'm wondering if that was fixed?"

Haldeman replies: "Could have been."

Press "Play" to Begin

At some point during the evening of June 20, 1972, a conversation between two men was secretly taped on a Sony TC-800B reel-to-reel voice recorder. This innocuous machine uses 0.5mm tape and was set to run at the irregular speed of $^{15}/_{16}$ IPS—or half the rate of a standard tape recorder. In keeping with this low-fidelity recording mode, the tiny lavalier microphones that picked up this particular conversation were cheap and unevenly distributed throughout the space. The result was a tape of degraded sound quality, produced under deficient recording conditions.[1]

Fast-forward to 1973: An entire nation is now magnetized by the play of forces around a single reel of 0.5mm tape. Tape 342, as it is officially referred to, is but one of a sprawling archive of approximately 3,700 hours of audio recordings taped surreptitiously by the late American President Richard Nixon over a period of several years. Known as the "Nixon White House Tapes," these recordings detail conversations between the President, his staff, and visitors to the White House and Camp David. Of the many thousands of audiotapes confiscated from the Oval Office, Tape 342 remains by far the most

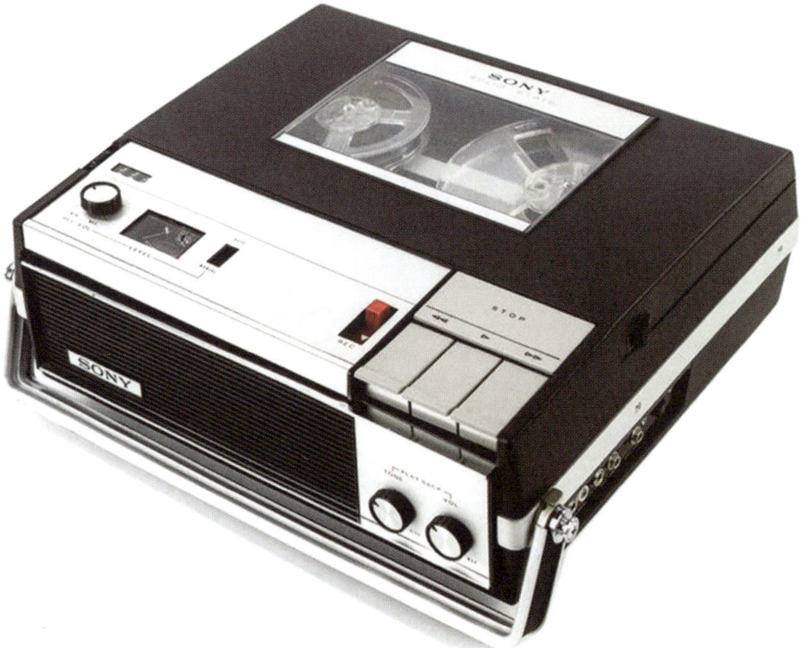

Figure 4.3
Sony TC-800B reel-to-reel voice recorder. Source: unknown.

infamous—not because of the shocking information it contains, but precisely because of its absence: an 18½-minute gap in the 6 hours 21 minutes 26 seconds of recorded material. A residual silence that is still haunted by the specter of a man who refused to speak on the grounds that such testimony might be self-incriminatory. In pleading executive privilege, Nixon chose not to fill in the void and enable the playback of history. The tape gap occurs during a rambling conversation between Nixon and White House Chief of Staff H. R. Haldeman just three days after the break-in at Democratic National Committee Headquarters in the Watergate Hotel. The timing of their discussion, with its suspicious erasure midstream, has led many to speculate that the tape must have contained highly damning information. The American Bill of Rights, under the aegis of the Fifth Amendment, gives individuals the right not to speak on the grounds that such speech may implicate them in activities that are punishable by law; it does *not*, however, allow one to take back or "erase" something already spoken. Ultimately a machined silence of 18½ minutes would convert nonevidence into such compelling and incriminatory proof of the willful destruction of material evidence that moves toward Presidential impeachment were, in part, activated.

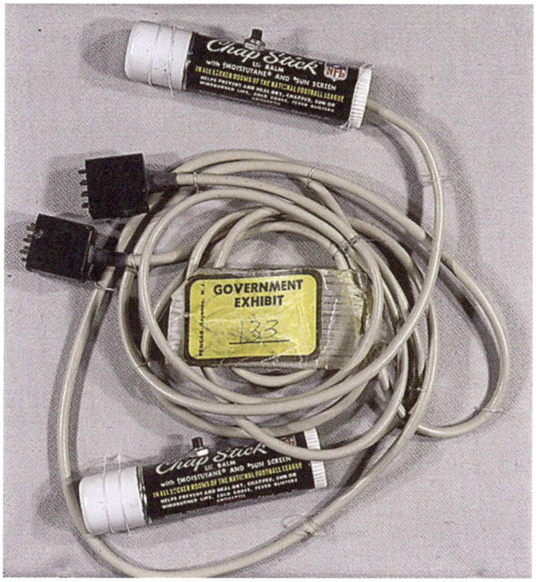

Figure 4.4
Government Exhibit 133—Chapstick tubes with hidden microphones. Source: US National Archives and Records Administration.

A BRIEF HISTORY OF THE WHITE HOUSE TAPING SYSTEM

In February 1971, the United State Secret Service (USSS), at the request of the President, installed listening devices in the White House. They placed seven microphones in the Oval Office: five in the President's desk, and one on each side of the fireplace. They placed two microphones in the Cabinet Room under the table near the President's chair. The Secret Service technicians wired all devices to central mixers which were then connected to recorders in an old locker room in the White House basement.

In April 1971, the Secret Service technicians installed four microphones in the President's office in the EOB. These microphones were located in the President's desk and wires led to a mixer and recorders in an adjoining room. The Secret Service also tapped the telephones in the Oval Office, in the President's EOB office, and in the Lincoln Sitting Room. These telephone conversations were recorded by tapping the telephone lines from the White House switchboard and relaying the conversations to recorders in a closet in the basement of the residence.

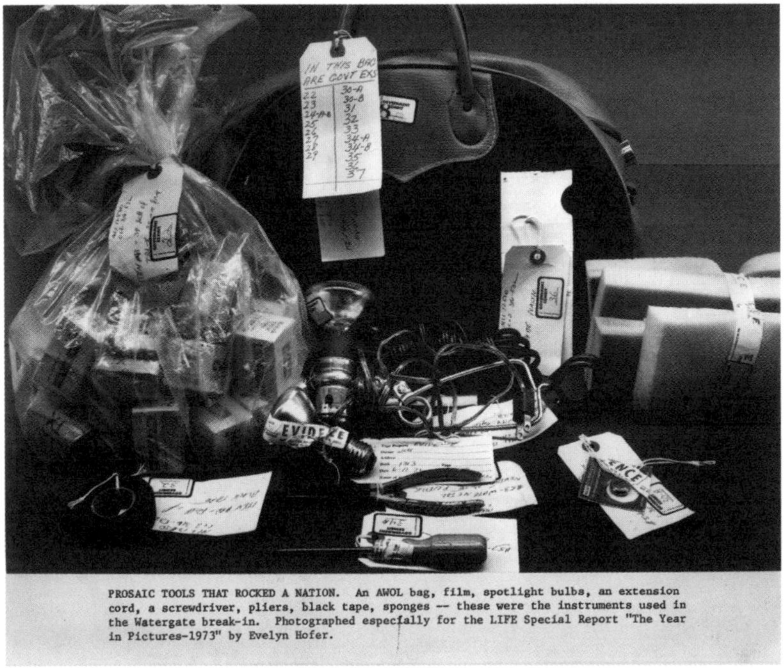

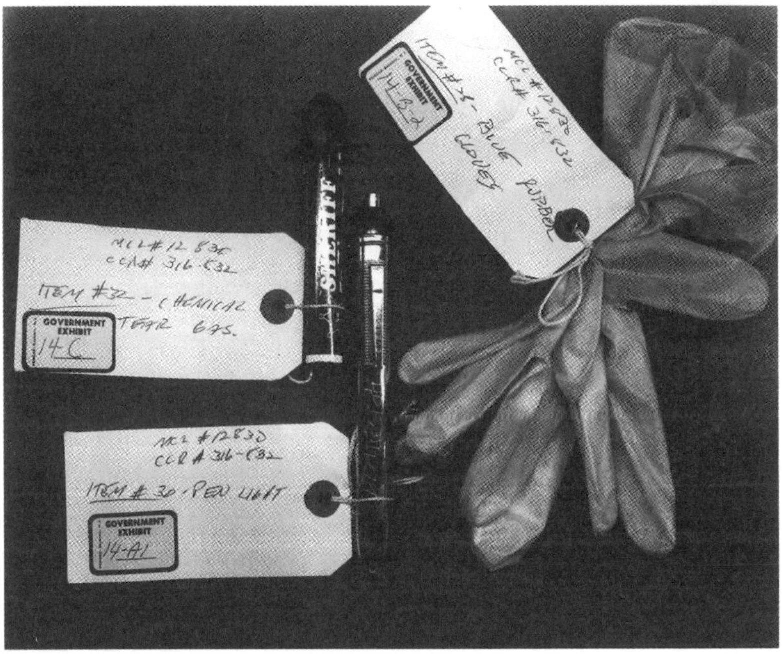

Figure 4.5

PROSAIC TOOLS THAT ROCKED A NATION. An AWOL bag, film, spotlight bulbs, an extension cord, a screwdriver, pliers, black tape, sponges—these were the instrumen s used in the Watergate break-in. Photographed especially for the LIFE special Report "the Year in Pictures—1973" by Evelyn Hofer. Collection of the author.

Finally, in May 1972, the Secret Service set up a taping system in the President's study in Aspen Lodge at Camp David. There were three separate recording systems put in place. A single microphone recorded conversations taking place in the study. The President's telephone on the President's desk was tapped as was the telephone on the study table.

This was a secret taping system maintained by the Secret Service. Only President Nixon, H. R. Haldeman, and a few of the President's close personal assistants knew the system existed. One of its key features was that the recording equipment in the Oval Office, the EOB office, at Camp David, and on the telephones was sound activated, operating without a conscious decision by the President to record a specific conversations. Most participants were unaware that their conversations were being recorded. The system was tied to the Presidential Locator System and would only activate if the President were present in the room. It was designed to continue recording for fifteen to thirty seconds after the President left the room.

The Cabinet Room recording system operated somewhat differently. It was a manual rather than a sound activated system. It was activated by Alexander Butterfield, a Special Assistant to the President who managed the President's activities in the West Wing of the White House. Butterfield activated the system from a switch on his desk (although the Secret Service also placed on/off switches on either side of the President's chair at the Cabinet Room table). When Butterfield inadvertently left the system "on," the tape recorders captured nonhistorical conversations as well as hours of room noise.[2]

February 16, 1971. Deputy Assistant Alexander Butterfield briefed Nixon on the newly installed taping system.

Nixon: How does it work in here? . . . The system stays off, no? It's working?

Butterfield: You're wearing the locator right now and you're in the office. . . . It depends on voice activation—

Nixon: Right.

Butterfield: —so you don't have to turn it on and off.

Nixon: Oh, this is good. Is there any chance to get two? You see, the purpose of this is to have the whole thing on the file—

Butterfield: Yes, sir.

Nixon: —for professional reasons. . . . This is totally for, basically, to be put in the file. In my file. I don't want it in your file or [Chief of Staff] Bob [Haldeman]'s or anybody else's. My file. . . .

Butterfield: I think it's gonna be a very fine system.

Knowledge of the White House taping system, which was installed by the Secret Service in 1971, first came to the public's attention during the testimony of former presidential aide Alexander Butterfield before the Senate Watergate Committee in July 1973. And although all recordings by Nixon stopped shortly thereafter, the actual equipment was not removed from the Oval Office until after the disgraced President left office on August 9, 1974.[3]

> Less than a week following Butterfield's revelation, Nixon ordered an end to White House taping. Shortly afterward, the Senate committee, Special Prosecutor Cox, and Judge Sirica ordered relevant tapes be turned over. Nixon refused, claiming executive privilege. By August the matter was in court. Nixon addressed the nation on August 15, 1973, explaining to the people why confidential conversations between the president and his advisors should not be made a matter of public record. Lawyers for the Watergate committee and Special Prosecutor's office argued that conversations dealing with matters of potential illegality should not be suppressed by claims of executive privilege.[4]

During the initial stages of the Watergate investigation, the existence of the White House taping system was not known; therefore Nixon's refusal to speak on the grounds that such testimony might incriminate him marked his body as the initial locus of silence. With the revelation of the recording system and the existence of the vast tape archive, the US Circuit Court of Appeals in Washington ruled that Nixon must turn all of the tapes over to Presiding Judge John Sirica. He refused to comply with this court order. Instead, Nixon countered with an offer to provide edited transcripts of the tapes. Public criticism mounted, including calls for his impeachment. Eventually Nixon relented and agreed to surrender the missing tapes, although the White House always claimed that certain tapes subject to the subpoena did not actually exist.[5] As the Grand Jury proceedings unfolded, silence subsequently shifted from the aphasiac body of the President to the absence of the subpoenaed tapes and, upon their recovery, to the 18½-minute gap in Tape 342 itself.

Through this series of juridical displacements, silence was reconfigured as the very means by which material artifacts could begin to speak for themselves. Although Nixon would continue to maintain his resolute silence, the tapes, including the gap, would now testify in his place. Once evidentiary silence was relocated to the tapes, Nixon's live testimony became largely irrelevant, as he was already literally on the record. Changing definitions of silence were thus central to shaping both the public perception of Watergate and the ways in which the prosecution developed their legal arguments. Crucially, a series of clicking noises distributed throughout the 18½-minute tape gap offered circumstantial evidence that a process of clumsy erasure had occurred, raising the possibility that this breach in the historical record was the consequence of a deliberate act. Controlling the discourse around silence proved to be a decisive strategy in turning the tide against Nixon in favor of the opposition. Yet to this day, the 18½-minute tape gap is still regarded as *the* singular piece of missing evidence that could render an unequivocal verdict, despite the subsequent conversation recorded on June 23,1974, that led to allegations of criminal conspiracy and Nixon's resignation.[6]

Stretching the Truth

> Next to a man's wife, his secretary is the most important person in his career. She has to understand every detail of his job; to have unquestioning loyalty and absolute discretion. On every count Rose measures up. I'm a lucky man.
> —Richard Nixon, 1957[7]

> Woods was a stand-up woman and an ideal secretary. She could decipher Nixon's handwriting, she was very discreet, and she was a formidable gatekeeper who knew who should get access to the president, and who shouldn't.
> —John Dean, former White House counsel[8]

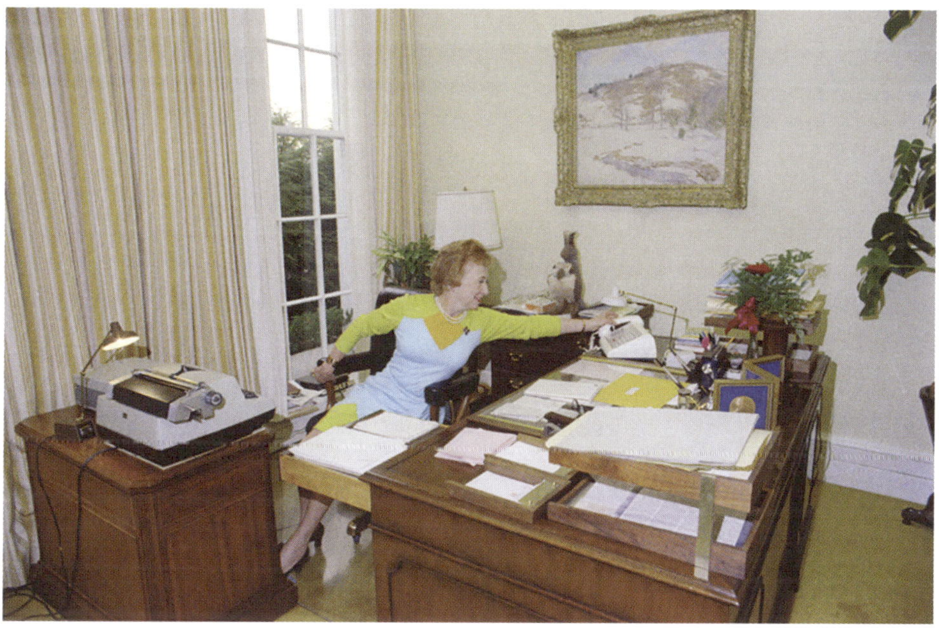

Figure 4.6
Rose Mary Woods demonstrating how she may have erased Tape 342. December 1973. Photo #E1874-16A. Source: US National Archives and Records Administration.

When news of the tape's potential tampering was made public, Nixon's personal secretary, Rose Mary Woods (1917–2005), made two rather contradictory public statements. In her court testimony of November 8, 1973, she asserted her secretarial competency, flatly denying ever making any clumsy transcription errors when handling the tape recorder. "The buttons said on and off, forward and backward. I caught on to that fairly fast. I don't think I'm so stupid as to erase what's on a tape."[9] However, a month later, under cross-examination in a federal courtroom, she told a rather confused story of how she might after all have made "a terrible mistake" and been partially responsible for the glitch. Woods claimed that while she had been transcribing and typing the conversations of June 20, 1972, the telephone suddenly rang, causing her to press the wrong pedal on her foot-controlled Uher 5000 tape recorder, which she was using for purposes of playback, resulting in the erasure. Summoned by the imperative ringing of the phone, summoned to testify in court, Rose Mary Woods was called to explain both her own actions and, ultimately, the actions of her boss. In reenacting her testimony for Judge John Sirica, Woods tried to demonstrate how she inadvertently erased the tape by pressing the foot pedal while simultaneously typing and reaching across her desk to answer the phone. It was a highly contorted and unconvincing performance that would come to be called the "Rose Mary Stretch," one that also "stretched" the gullibility of the court.

I maintain that this was not a reenactment of a past event but, rather, the first time this particular testimonial had ever been performed. The "Rose Mary Stretch" was an original act, probably coerced, which aimed to deliberately mislead the court through the theatrical production of false evidence. Rather than providing corroborative proof to substantiate her retroactive culpability in the erasure of the tape, the reenactment became, in effect, part of the criminal deeds surrounding the activities of the Nixon White House. In recanting her testimony Woods took a dangerous gamble, as she now opened herself up to charges of perjury, obstruction of justice, and—perhaps most damaging for Nixon—the possibility that she could potentially be called as a witness for the prosecution. When audio experts later examined Tape 342, they concluded that the RECORD/STOP/RECORD button had actually been pressed five to nine times: anomalies that Watergate prosecutor Leon Jaworski insisted could come about only through the manual operation of the Uher's controls. The materials told a different story, one that refuted the loyal secretary's half-hearted admission of guilt. A nonhuman *material witness* was now made to appear on the stand, one that disclosed the holes or gaps in Wood's own fraudulent testimony.

> Magnetic signatures that we have measured directly on the tape show that the buzzing sounds were put on the tape in the process of erasing and re-recording at least five, and perhaps as

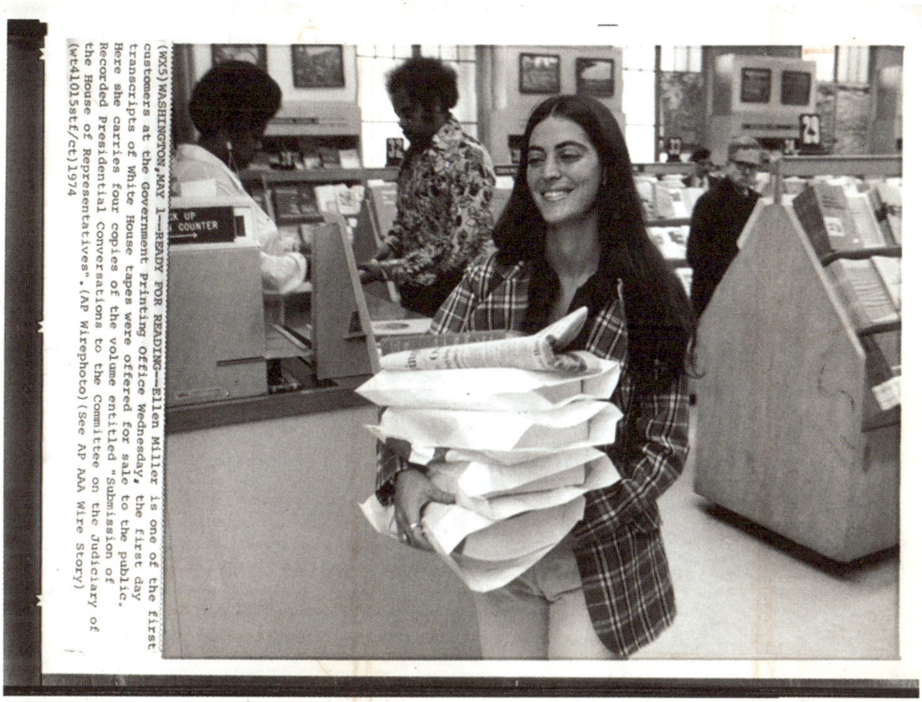

Figure 4.7
READY FOR READING—Ellen Miller is one of the first customers at the Government Printing Office Wednesday, the first day transcripts of White House tapes were offered for sale to the public. Here she carries four copies of the volume entitled "Submission of Recorded Presidential Conversations to the Committee on the Judiciary of the House of Representatives." May 1, 1974. Collection of the author.

> many as nine, separate and contiguous segments. Hand operation of keyboard controls on the Uher 5000 recorder was involved in starting and again in stopping the recording of each segment. The magnetic signatures observed on the tape show conclusively that the 18.5-minute section could not have been produced by any single, continuous operation. Further, whether the footpedal was used or not, the recording controls must have been operated by hand in the making of each segment.[10]

Nixon himself was involved in a previous case of political "machination" concerning technologies of inscription in relation to the trial of Alger Hiss, who was accused of spying for the Soviets. A fledgling congressman at the time, Nixon tried to prove that Hiss, a State Department official, was guilty of perjury: "The typewriters are always the key. We built one in the Hiss case." By this he meant that the prosecution team knowingly fabricated evidence by duplicating State Department documents on a typewriter, which they then alleged Hiss had copied on his wife Priscilla's Woodstock typewriter. Nixon's assertion that the typewriter "was the key witness in the case" would eventually prove to be true, albeit a hostile one. The serial number of the Woodstock typewriter confirmed that it was acquired long before the one used by the State Department had even been built. A mechanical witness would ultimately corroborate Hiss's testimony that the charge of perjury as to the falsified documents was trumped up. Once again, technical matter machined a different verdict.[11]

Etymologically speaking, the secretary is the "keeper of secrets." In managing the space of the administrative archive she becomes a kind of essential recording device that encodes the incoming transmissions of the patriarchal order: speech acts performed and recorded in the specialized domains proper to the masculine subject—the inner sanctum of the Oval Office—outside of her own feminine jurisdiction of the secretarial pool. Was Rose Mary Woods a mere conduit for the voices of others: a device for channeling the audio dispatches that would broadcast Nixon into history? Unable to answer for herself as a self-sufficient subject, the secretary finds herself transmitting clandestine communiqués, which she faithfully records but of which she mustn't speak. The secretary, when called to testify before the tribunal of history, discovers that her hands are literally tied to the typewriter and her ears plugged by the tape recorder. And so she transforms her secretarial proficiency into a story of incompetence. She becomes a scapegoat. She takes the fall. In late November 1973 Rose Mary Woods hired her own lawyer, Charles Rhyne.

Even with the testimony of Nixon's secretary now in tatters, the Prosecution was not content to let the gap stand merely as circumstantial evidence pointing to a possible crime. They sought direct evidence of Nixon's knowing involvement in the Watergate burglary. And so in December of 1973, Tape 342 was escorted by six fully armed US Marshals to the Federal Scientific Corporation in Harlem for testing. There, the tape was met by another six court-appointed technical experts—an Advisory Panel of engineers and electronics specialists—entrusted with the forensic mission of reviving the tape and bringing its latent speech acts back to life. Together these experts carried out over 200 hours of testing using spectrum and waveform analyses with digital signal processing equipment, an emerging technology at that time. They also conducted optical inspections of the distribution of magnetic particles on the tape in the hopes of revealing visible patterns that might be indicative of specific configurations of speech. This was accomplished by washing its surface with a solution containing ferrite particles that would align themselves spatially in accordance with any residual magnetism left on the tape. Yet even after this extensive barrage of tests, Tape 342 maintained its stubborn silence.

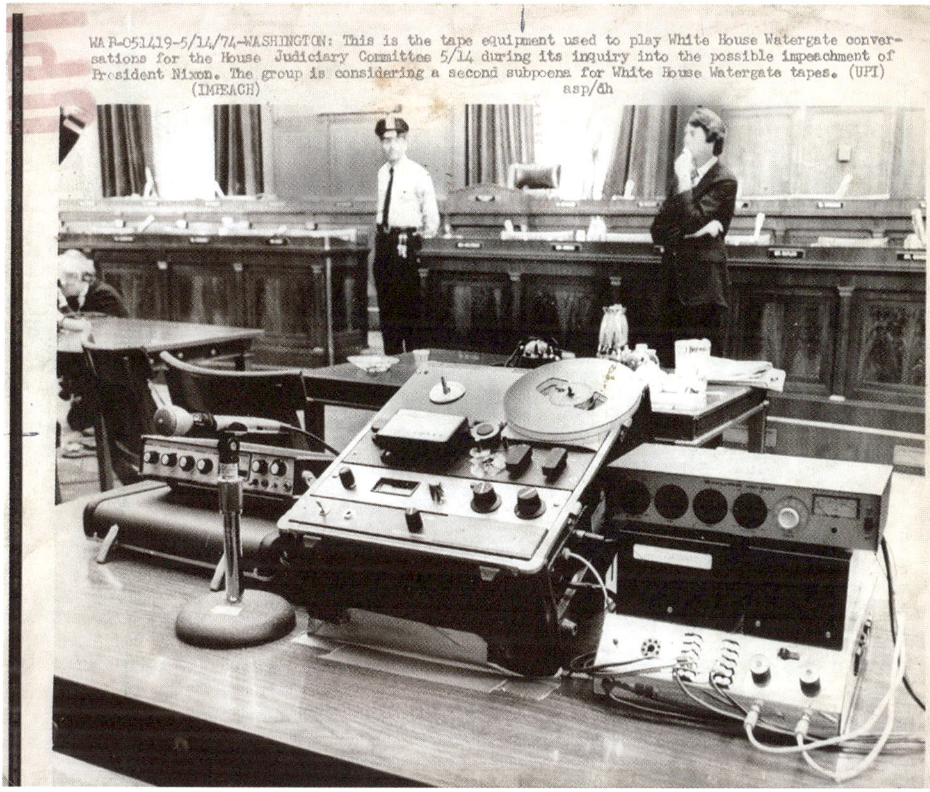

Figure 4.8
This is the tape equipment used to play White House Watergate conversations for the House Judiciary Committee during its inquiry into the possible impeachment of President Nixon. The group is considering a second subpoena for White House Watergate tapes. May 14, 1974. Collection of the author.

Forensic Futures

Although the tape defied all technical efforts at conjuring its sound ghosts, it was considered a singularly important historical artifact; one that might harbor trace evidence testifying to Nixon's criminality in the Watergate break-in. Fear of disturbing the magnetic particles that still clung to the 18½-minute gap meant that after its initial playback and testing, Tape 342 was placed under permanent seal and deposited in the vaults of the US National Archives and Records Administration (NARA) located in College Park, Maryland. There the tape has lain undisturbed for over 40 years, stored at precisely

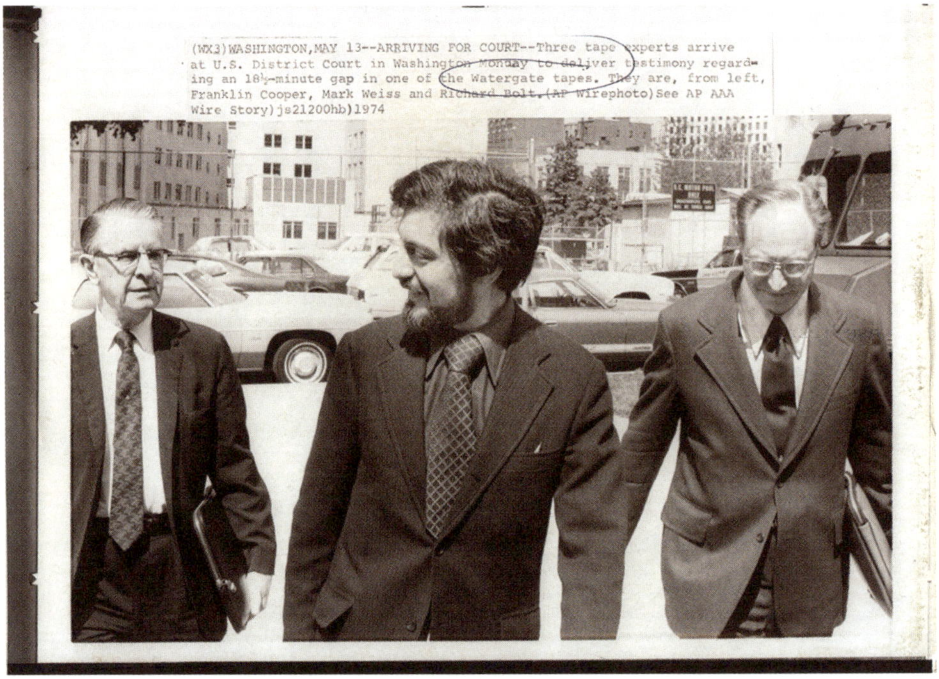

Figure 4.9
ARRIVING FOR COURT—Three tape experts arrive at US District Court in Washington Monday to deliver testimony regarding an 18½-minute gap in one of the Watergate tapes. They are, from left, Franklin Cooper, Mark Weiss, and Richard Bolt. May 13, 1974. Collection of the author.

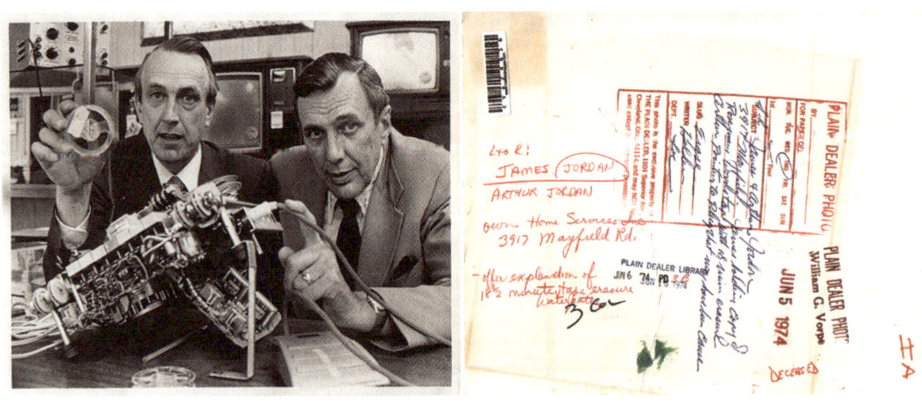

Figure 4.10
James and Arthur Jordon 3917 Mayfield. James holding copy of Rosemary (sp.) Woods tape with 18 mins. erasure. Arthur pointing to plug that may have been cause, June 5, 1974. Collection of the author.

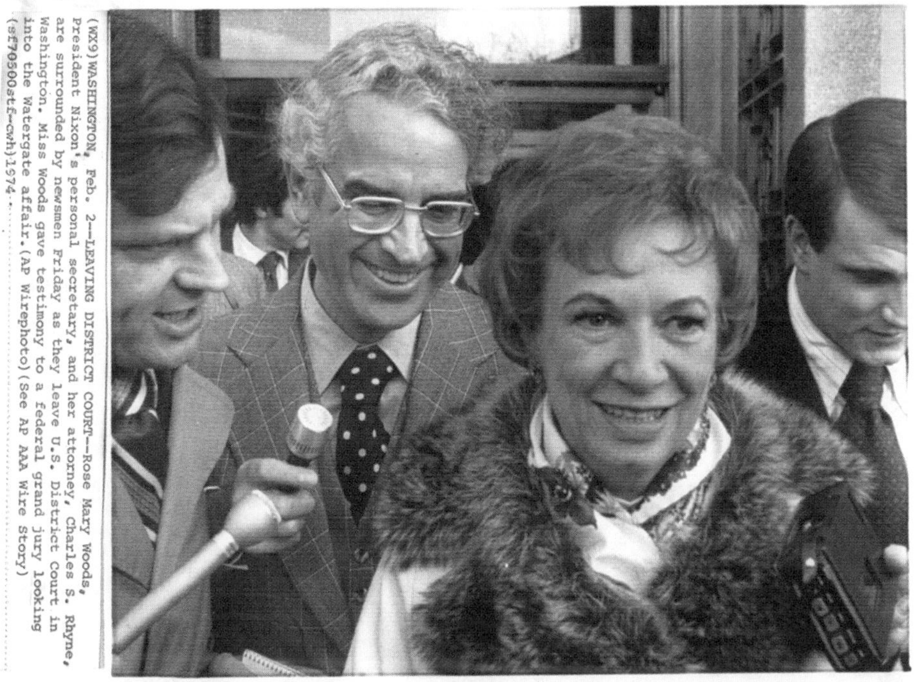

Figure 4.11
LEAVING DISTRICT COURT—Rose Mary Woods, President Nixon's personal secretary, and her attorney, Charles S. Rhyne, are surrounded by newsmen Friday as they leave U.S. District Court in Washington. Miss Woods gave testimony to a federal grand jury looking into the Watergate affair. February 2, 1974. Collection of the author.

65 degrees Fahrenheit and 40 percent relative humidity, waiting like a somnambulant bride for that moment when the kiss of technological progress will reawaken it. Moreover, the tape waits for an explicitly forensic caress that will not only revivify it but also restore its capacity to speak. The archive leverages the partial erasure of Tape 342 against the projected forensics of the future, wagering that further developments in technology will eventually restore its lost speech acts.

But in listening to the 18½ minutes of silence, it becomes immediately apparent that the tape is far from mute. It is fully resonant with acoustic buzz, granularity, and noise, having been enriched through processes of attempted erasure—RECORD/STOP/RECORD—albeit with information that diverges from intelligible patterns of human speech. Qualified researchers who have had access to copies of Tape 342 describe the 18½-minute interval as follows: "At the point of the first erasure, the muffled

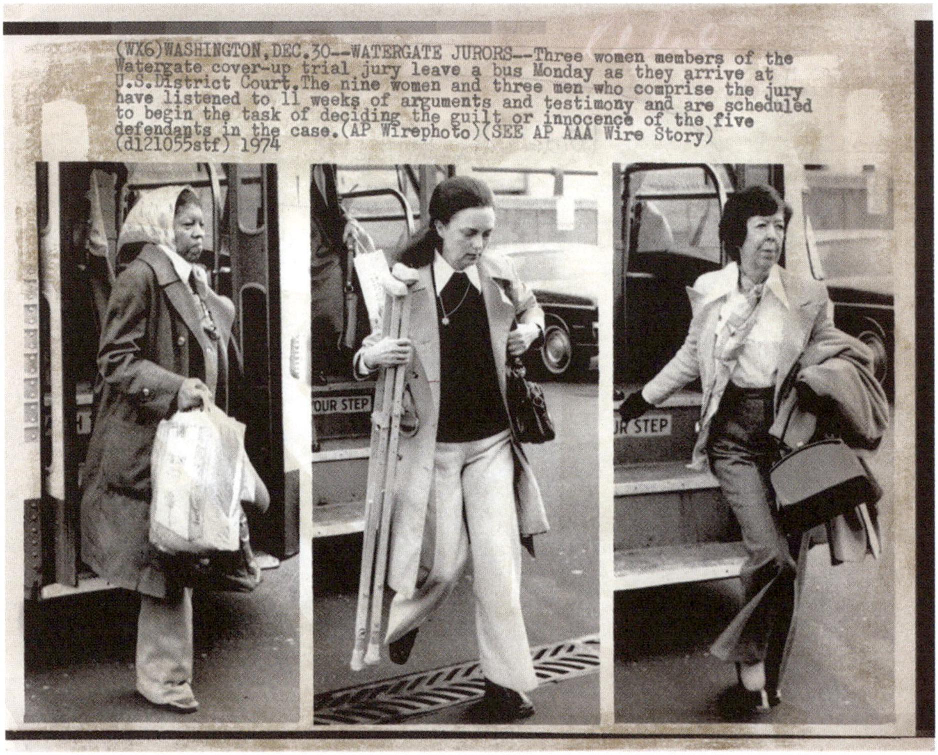

Figure 4.12
WATERGATE JURORS—Three women members of the Watergate cover-up trial jury leave a bus Monday as they arrive at U.S. District Court. The nine women and three men who comprise the jury have listened to 11 weeks of arguments and testimony and are scheduled to begin the task of deciding the guilt or innocence of the five defendants in the case, December 30, 1974. Collection of the author.

conversation is suddenly replaced by a buzzing noise, presumably the sound of a 60-cycle hum leaking from the power grid as interpreted by a high-grain microphone input circuit. Throughout the gap, the buzz occasionally drops in volume, but never is there any discernible speech."[12] This acoustic impurity recalls the oral impurity of the man himself (Nixon was notorious for his foul mouth) and his steadfast refusal to explain his silence and fill the void. And yet, what could the decoding of this affective silence give us that would be more resonant with meaning than its current status as designating all possible meanings?

When a tape is "erased" the erase head scatters magnetic particles, scrambling the recorded content. This phenomenon does not actually result in the removal of

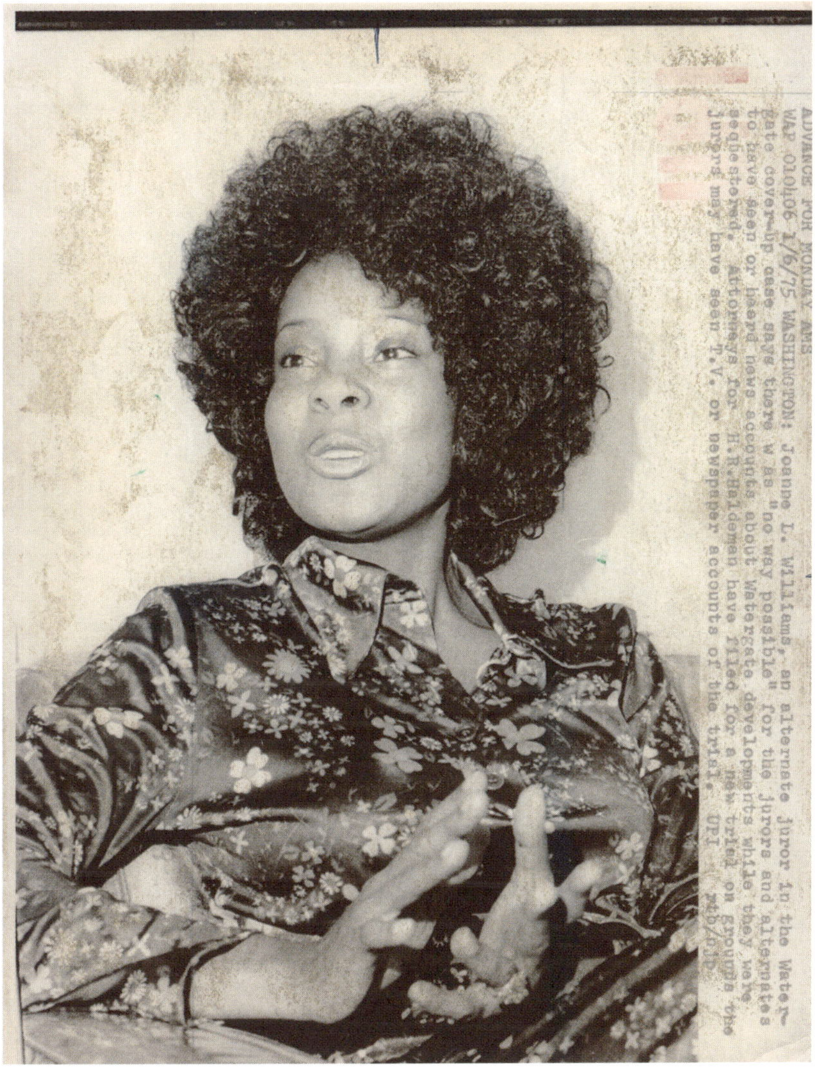

Figure 4.13
Joanne L. Williams, an alternate juror in the Watergate cover-up case, says there was "no way possible" for the jurors and alternates to have seen or heard the news accounts of Watergate developments while they were sequestered. Attorneys for H. R. Haldeman have filed for a new trial on the grounds the jurors may have seen T.V. or newspaper accounts of the trial, January 6, 1975. Collection of the author.

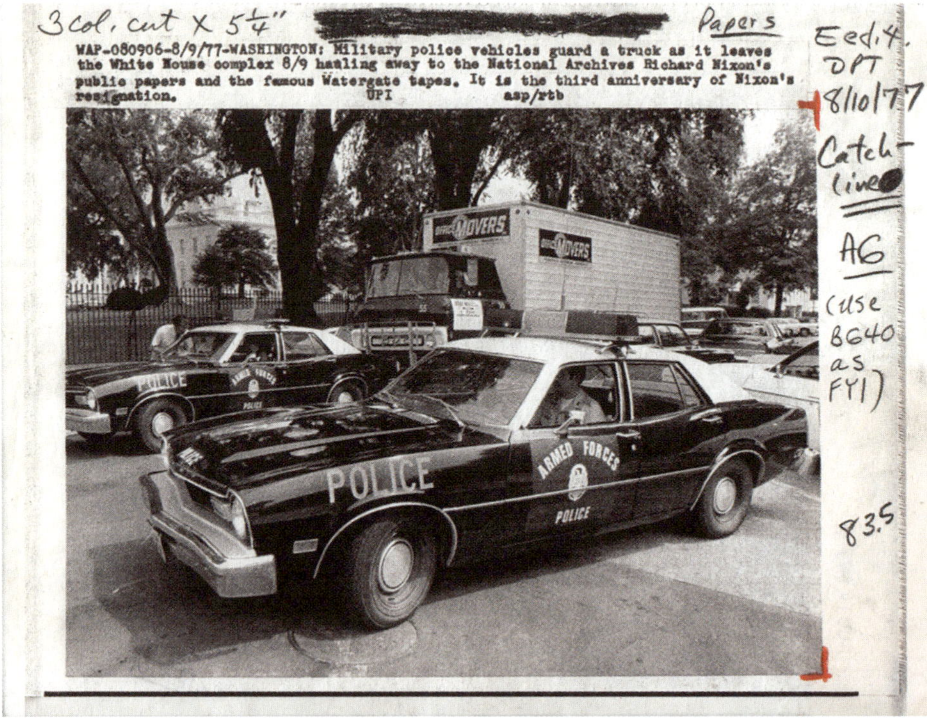

Figure 4.14
Military police vehicles guard a truck as it leaves the White House complex 8/9 hauling away to the National Archives Richard Nixon's public papers and the famous Watergate tapes. It is the third anniversary of Nixon's resignation, August 9, 1977. Collection of the author.

particles, but radically reorients them through demagnetization. The original recorded voice still clings to the tape, but is ventriloquized by its machinic deterritorialization into a field of new magnetic potential. The more the tape is rewound and replayed, the more mobile or animated its particles become. In their migration across the surface toward the outer edges of the tape, these particles carry artifactual traces of previous recordings, producing a kind of veil of latent noise. But this imperfect erasure should not be viewed negatively as an act of subterfuge; rather, it is one of the means that the machine has at its disposal to create new sounds and new meanings. "[T]he very absence of meaning in pure noise," says political and social theorist Jacques Attali, "frees the listener's imagination [because it] un-channels auditory sensations."[13] The absence of specific meaning in noise, for Attali, becomes the placeholder for all *possible* meanings because it creates an open field for exploration—spurring our forensic

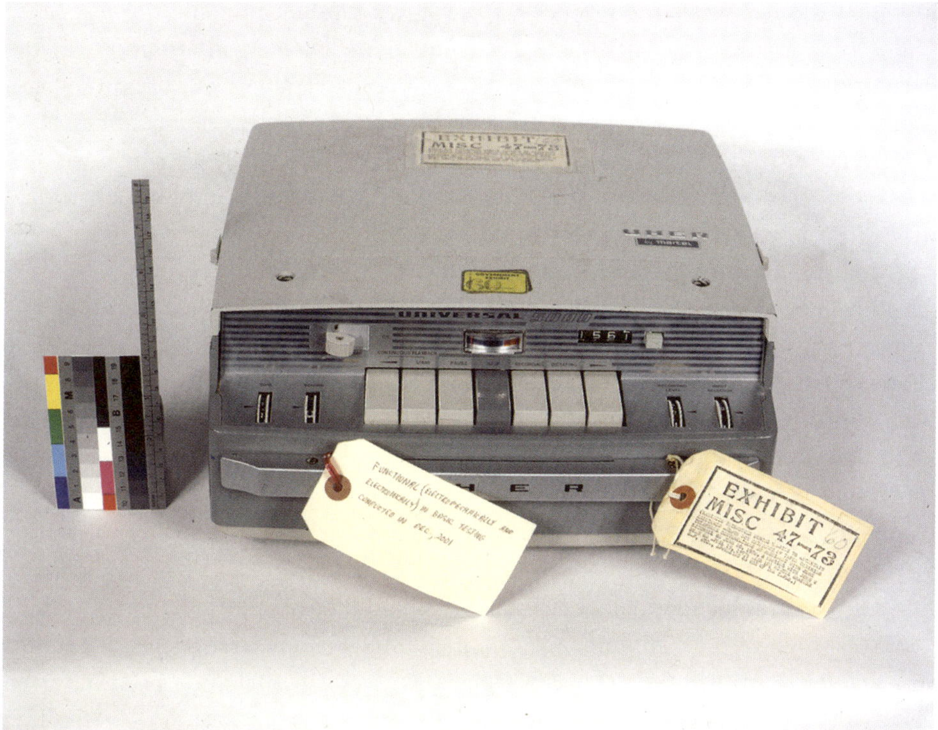

Figure 4.15

Record Group 21: Records of District Courts of the United States; U.S. District Court for the District of Columbia; Watergate-Related Cases; Miscellaneous Case 47-73 (In Re Subpoena Duces Tecum Issued to Richard M. Nixon for Production of Tapes, Etc.); Government Exhibit Number 60: Uher 5000 Reel-to-Reel Tape Recorder. Source: US National Archives and Records Administration.

imagination into action. The concern for the fragility of Tape 342 and recovery of its latent speech acts has of necessity limited the number of times it has been played back. To date, proposed restoration techniques have all relied upon methods of digital enhancement that still require the tape's actual transit through the mechanical components of a machine. This physical encounter between artifact and apparatus is highly problematic for NARA, as each successive playback of the tape alters the relative spatial distribution of its magnetic particles ever so slightly. Repetition thus engenders transformation and difference, actively resurfacing the topological features of the tape with each rewind and playback.

Such repetition is also a form of returning that conjures forth what media theorist Janne Vanhanen calls "sound-ghosts," or the memory effects of magnetic recording in which the technical inscription of a previous recording mysteriously reappears. "Ghosts in machines always appear as malfunctions, glitches, interruptions in the normal flow of things. Something unexpected appears seemingly out of nothing and from nowhere. Through a malfunction, a glitch, we get a fleeting glimpse of an alien intelligence at work."[14] This "sound effect" was first reported in 1947, when two new kinds of tapes were introduced with varying degrees of coercivity (resistance to demagnetization), but also results from errant microns located at the edge of a recorded track which have escaped full erasure and come to haunt subsequent recordings. The latter phenomenon, also known as "hysteresis" or "remanence," is what Vanhanen has called the "ghostly unpresence of gaps in recorded time." Alexander Haig, the White House Chief of Staff (1973–1974) who replaced Haldeman, actually suggested that the Nixon tape gap was the result of "some sinister force."[15] The refusal to replay Tape 342 emphasizes NARA's conviction that Nixon's sound ghost will appear not through the repeat performances of the tape, but through the exorcisms of new forensic techniques.

One such proposed strategy for recuperating the missing audio involves the use of filters for discerning potential speech fragments and tones. If aperiodic signals can be detected within the 18½-minute tape gap, they could be indicative of speech patterns that register at particular frequencies. Once a word or a partial voice-print has been extracted, then it is possible to use this as a kind of baseline for measuring and locating other areas of the tape that exhibit similar "frequency characteristics."[16] Another, more advanced technology is second-harmonic magneto-resistive microscopy (SH-MRM), a form of digital forensics used for purposes of audio authentication that works optically, by scanning magnetic tape to create a map of its sonic features. Rather than actually making physical contact with such a fragile artifact, sensors move back and forth across its surface—line by line—slowly generating a topographic image of the tape's magnetic field over millions of points. "The mapped data can then be plugged into an imaging program. If enough data is recovered, investigators can rebuild the original signal."[17] SH-MRM has apparently been used to recover sound from damaged flight data recorders. "The SH-MRM technique is exacting; two inches of cassette tape can take an hour to scan. If you're passing a half-inch-wide tape over a 1-micron-wide head," said David Pappas of the National Institute of Standards and Technology (NIST), "you have to scan it about 12,000 times to realize the full resolution."[18] Visualization technologies such as SH-MRM would also allow scientists to scan Tape 342 for any residual fingerprints, which would confirm who physically handled the media. "Pappas considered applying SH-MRM to the Nixon tape gap, but after September 11, the NIST lab has been focused almost exclusively on homeland security projects."[19]

Nonetheless, NARA still faithfully ministers against the material challenges that might jeopardize Tape 342's technological and historical revivification. The tape's ability to endure the entropic pressures of time positions it as a witness to history, entrusted with the complicated task of bringing the past back to life in the future, while the inevitable forces of material deterioration—random drift of magnetic particles and machinic decomposition—also offer warning that its testimony will necessarily be compromised by its years in solitary confinement. As such any rescue operation, therefore, is an enterprise predicated entirely upon risk: the risk that the tape may be irrevocably damaged during such invasive forensic procedures, and the even greater risk that any recovered speech might actually change our understanding of the past, and thus challenge accepted historical narratives. The uncertainty that this intercession by the future heralds is one in which the tape's potential capacity to rewrite the past and reframe the present is founded upon the very movement of difference that philosopher Elizabeth Grosz insists is fundamental to the emergence of the new. "In seeking an open-ended future [one acknowledges] the capacity of any future eruption, any event, any reading, to rewrite, resignify, reframe the present, to accept the role that the accidental, chance, or the undetermined plays in the unfolding of time."[20] Even NARA has no *a priori* insight into how its artifactual holdings will be rhetorically reconfigured in the future by its users, despite its considerable efforts to arrest their physical change.

In 2001 the National Archives reconvened a scientific panel to evaluate whether forensic audio technology had advanced sufficiently to consider unsealing Tape 342 and submitting it to a new barrage of tests. Several "proof-of-concept exercises" were conducted using test reels recorded on the original Nixon-era tape recorders over a period of two years. "Five individuals or companies participated in the tests which consisted of two test tapes recorded on an original Nixon White House Sony 800B tape recorder, then erased on Rose Mary Woods' UHER 5000."[21] To date, all such proof-of-concept exercises have failed. A few years ago I decided to track down these test tapes and contacted Paul Ginsberg, a forensic audio expert whose employer Federal Scientific had participated in the 2001 Watergate trial. Ginsberg reminded me that Tape 342 had never been unsealed for the purposes of testing, and that while NARA had made test reels using the original tape recorders, it had not in fact employed Tape 342, or a copy, for this purpose. In order to assess the relative success of any procedure's capacity to recover audio material from the test tape, and thus guarantee the outcome of applying the same technique to Tape 342, NARA would have had to know exactly what information was already recorded on the tape prior to its erasure and subsequent testing. This precluded them from using the unknown audio content from the 18½-minute gap, since the objective was to determine the feasibility of applying new forensic methods. I have always wondered what audio tracks NARA used in preparing their test tapes. Was it Nixon musing over the possibility of using the atomic bomb in Vietnam, or questioning the veracity of photograph depicting a young girl fleeing a napalm attack? Chief Archivist John W. Carlin conceded the failure of this most recent round of testing, but held on to the possibility that future attempts would solve the enigma at the heart of their historical collection. "I am fully satisfied that we have explored all of the avenues to attempt to recover the sound on this tape. The candidates were highly qualified and used the latest technology in their pursuit. We will continue to preserve the tape in the hopes that later generations can try again to recover this vital piece of our history."[22]

In reading through the NARA press releases as they relate to Tape 342, it is clear that the history of the tape is largely a story still waiting to be written, and is therefore intimately conjoined with teleological accounts of technological development. If the rhetorical pledge of NARA is to rescue Tape 342 from its state of solitary confinement, Jacques Derrida reminds us that "the question of the future" will always remain open, that the full significance of the tape will not be understood even at the moment when its gag order is lifted—the moment of its revelation.[23] Accordingly, the historical relevance of the 18½-minute tape gap will always be endlessly deferred as its contextual anchors shift. Likewise for Michel Foucault, the archive is not the repository to which artifacts and documents are consigned in order that they might settle and collect dust; on the contrary, it is a site of regeneration that refuses the inclination toward torpor through the sustained "miracle" of potential "resurrection."[24] The remainder of this chapter is devoted to conceptually extracting Tape 342 from the deathly contagion of *le mal d'archive* with a view to establishing its "silent" bounty as a kind of "vibrant matter": a term developed by Jane Bennett to account for the vitality and political force of nonhuman agents.[25] This strategic gesture acknowledges that Tape 342 already "speaks" in many complex ways, and that Nixon's act of "erasure," rather than destroying the sonic transmissions of the tape, radically reinvented it, renewing its orality so that it now speaks a kind of machinic glossolalia.

4′33″ v. 18′30″

Throughout John Cage's extensive writings on silence, particularly after his legendary visit to the anechoic chamber at Harvard University, he insists upon the impossibility of complete silence. As the story goes, Cage was perplexed to hear two sounds in the anechoic chamber, which as a vacuum should have been soundless. When he queried this residual sound, he learned that he was in fact hearing the interior sounds of his own body: "the low sound of his blood circulating, and the high-pitched sound of his nervous system in operation."[26] Cage thus theorized silence as "always-sound," which is a state of sonic contingency not attached to specific acts of amplification but, rather, a continuous unfolding across entities. Sound theorist Douglas Kahn suggests that this crucial experience of the anechoic chamber inaugurated a fundamental shift in Cage's thinking about the capacities of technology to access events beyond the thresholds of natural human perception, prompting him to conceptualize a sonic continuum between the covert chatterings of his own body and the soundful reverberations of all matter.[27] As Cage emphasized: "Within each object, of course a lively molecular process is in operation. But if we are to hear it, we must isolate the object in a special chamber."[28] He was convinced that if we deployed the appropriate technology we would be able to discern the acoustic resonances of matter at the subatomic level, recording the particulate vibrations of protons, electrons, and neurons within atoms. His conceptual project to "interpolate sound back onto the seemingly intransigent silence of objects" is supported by the physics of quantum mechanics, in that all subatomic particles actually have wave properties, including those of frequency (rate of vibration) and wavelength (distance between successive wave crests).[29] "If silence was actually sound then all matter too must be audible, given the proper technology to detect the soundful activities at the level of subatomic vibrations. Matter is dissolved as technology denies inaudibility and forbids silence."[30]

Cage's innovation was to overturn the dualism that "opposed silence to sound" and replace it with an extensive set of scalar operations that involved *all* possible sounds, including those microsounds that exist beyond the frequency range of human hearing. His theorizations of silence "as all sounds which we don't intend" links his work of this period to the concurrent developments in information theory advanced by Claude Shannon in 1948, which overturned a similar opposition between noise and information. For each possible state in the transmission of a signal, said Shannon, there will be a set of probabilities that assign it relative degrees of entropy. According to his theory, there is an entropic condition for the signal's source, its input and output channels as well as its noise quotient. Consequently entropy is no longer equated exclusively with noise, as it was in the formulations of Shannon's contemporary Norbert Wiener, but is conceived as a dynamic dimension of all facets of signal relay. Rather than being detrimental to the flow of information within a system, noise is now regarded as an essential condition for the emergence of legibility and pattern. Attali developed his related conception of noise as always conditionally legible to the specific context in which it appears. What is noisy interference in one radio broadcast may be the affective acoustic relay of a thunderstorm in another. "Noise, then, does not exist in itself, but only in relation to the system within which it is inscribed: emitter, transmitter, receiver."[31] Governed by operations of difference, intelligibility sets itself against the backdrop of disorder or nonpattern as its very constitutive force. The contingency of noise creates new meanings. Shannon's ideas forwarded a positive understanding of noise as information, a kind of always-noise that finds its expressive corollary in Cage's notion of always-sound, as well as in the notion of informational enrichment discussed at various points throughout this book. If noise becomes information and silence becomes sound, then the 18½-minute transmission of microsignals—clicks, hisses, and buzzing—becomes an extension of the political event rather than an enigmatic rupture. Accordingly, NARA's archives provide the background noise, the 3,700 hours of audio recordings produced by Nixon, against which the singularity of Tape 342 and its 18½ minutes of silence may be discerned, but to which it is still indelibly sutured.

Situated Hearing

The impression that technical recordings offer a faithful inscription of an original auditory event is countered by an understanding of how sound recording devices work. In actuality, no technology is able to produce an exact copy of an occurrence in the real world; we merely suspend our disbelief and edit out those incidents or "noises" that interfere with our experience of mimetic authenticity. Bernard Stiegler, in a conversation with Derrida called "Phonographies," argues that the technologies of "exactitude" used to record and transmit sound produce an authenticity effect for acoustic materials that is akin to the "scandalous effect" described by Roland Barthes to account for photography's testimonial capacity: "The Photograph does not call up the past (nothing Proustian in a photograph). The effect it produces upon me is not to restore what has been abolished (by time, by distance) but to attest that I what I saw has indeed existed."[32] Although this Barthesian reality effect can never "guarantee the authenticity of what is captured," it is able, claims Stiegler, to "elicit *an* authentification effect for the person who looks" at the photograph or listens to the audio emanating from a phonograph, a radio transmission, a tape recorder, an mp3 player, or a streaming platform, bestowing a sensation of this-actually-was.[33] Despite the immediacy and convincing nature of this encounter, the relationship between the recorded event and the act of listening is itself further contracted to the specific acoustic conditions of playback, whether this is online, in an archive, a courtroom, an art gallery, or elsewhere. Listening is always inflected with the properties of its immediate environmental context, laying down an additional ambient track that conjoins with the recorded event to trigger different experiential registers, and even actualize different narrative possibilities.

Musicologist Rich Altman stresses that variations in the spatial positioning of the hearing ear can script entirely different acoustic accounts of the same recorded event, so that what the recording actually consists of is not the sound event *per se* but a recording or "record" of a situated mode of hearing.[34] Even at the moment when the recording is made, extraneous information has already combined with the recording process (ambient acoustic phenomena and technical aspects relating to the quality of the recording medium, the spatial distribution of the microphones, etc.), creating a heterogeneous acoustic materiality. No microphone, says Altman, can produce a faithful sound recording, because it always carries some trace of the recoding process, overlaid onto the sound event. Certainly the mediocre lavalier microphones used by Nixon in his White House recordings are a case in point. I have had difficulty making out the conversations that bracket the 18½-minute gap on Tape 342 due to the exceptionally poor quality of the recordings. Altman writes: "Far from arresting and innocently capturing a particular narrative, the recording process simply extends and complicates that narrative."[35] Even if we could recover the 18½ minutes of erased audio material on the Nixon tape, its fidelity to the originary sound event would be entirely conditional, producing at best a partial voice-print, as every recorded sound is recorded at least twice over: first by the specific circumstances of its recording, and then again by the particularities of its reproduction and the vagaries of the playback situation. However, the situational information captured by the recording technology can provide additional insight that might prove evidentially significant. This is one of the many ways in which the acoustic properties of matter can be figured as *material witnesses* to external events.

A clear example of how this extraneous inscription of noise might prove legally useful is offered by the 50Hz emissions produced by the electrical grid in the UK, an example brought to my attention by artist and "private ear" Lawrence Abu Hamdan. Since 2005, the Metropolitan Police have been continuously recording the sound of the national electrical grid in their south London forensic laboratory. When electricity is supplied by the grid it produces an inaudible 50Hz hum known as the "mains frequency," which is subject to microfluctuations and surges at various points throughout the day. These minute changes are, in effect, acoustic fingerprints that can be mapped to produce a comprehensive timestamp for the entire country on any given day. "Any digital recording made anywhere near an electrical power source, be it plug socket, light or pylon, will pick up this noise and it will be embedded throughout the audio."[36] When, for example, a phone call is made at a specific time on a particular day, it cannot be attributed to any other day or time because of the unique acoustic properties produced by the mains frequency during the period of the call. Using a process called electric network frequency (ENF) analysis, forensic audio specialists can determine if digital recordings of any kind made since 2005 have been edited, tampered with, or are original. "Comparing the unique pattern of the frequencies on an audio recording with a database that has been logging these changes for 24 hours a day, 365 days a year provides a digital watermark: a date and time stamp on the recording."[37] Being able to ascertain the authenticity and spatiotemporal attributes of any digital audio recording has provided the judiciary with new forms of probative evidence based, not on the spoken content of a given recording, but rather upon a form of incidental noise or ambience embedded in the file.[38]

All recorded audio, therefore, performs a kind of double take that constitutes it as both more than and other to the original event of sonification. In registering evidence of external conditions, whether that of the environment in which the recording was made or of the technology itself, such acoustic materials offer up a kind of sonic plenitude that can be forensically analyzed to furnish supplementary information to the representational histories captured by media. Historically, the mimetic arts were criticized for their lack of liveness and resolute muteness, doomed to merely repeat their prescripted narratives. In "Plato's Pharmacy," Derrida discusses the ancient Greeks' condemnation of the imitative arts of poetry and painting, as forms of recording that are impotent to answer for themselves. Socrates, in comparing a piece of writing (*graphema*) to a painting (*zographema*), states that these arts "stand before us as though they were alive, but if you question them they maintain a majestic silence."[39] By extension, the Platonic critique of mnemonic technologies suggests that Tape 342 could never speak for itself, that is to say, testify on its own accord. It could merely be rewound and played back again. Yet throughout this book it is recorded materials that forcefully speak back and challenge accepted truths. Mimesis is fixated upon resemblance—the appearance of things as natural analogs—whereas *Material Witness* is concerned with the recodings of matter that can activate political imaginaries beyond the realm of representation. Understood as such, the missing 18½ minutes does not preserve its stubborn silence through its contracted state of resemblance to an originary incident or accident, but returns the recorded event to the listener as a multilingual object that can speak through time.

Sony TC-800B v. Uher 5000

The act of erasure, like the concept of silence, is a technical misnomer that is immediately overturned through a basic observation of the functioning of a tape recorder, which reveals only six buttons: PLAY, STOP, PAUSE, REWIND, FAST-FORWARD, and

RECORD.[40] The most important button is missing. In fact, not only is it missing, it has never even existed. The ERASE button is a mechanical delusion, yet numerous accounts of the 18½-minute tape gap have referred to its existence.[41] The technical organization of an analog tape recorder *does* consist of something called an erase head over which the tape glides each time the record button is activated. Alternating positive and negative fields emitted by the erase head reformat the tape in efforts to minimize the amount of telegraphy or carryover of acoustic information into subsequent recordings. Immediately upon passing over this erase head the winding tape makes contact with the record head, which reassembles its electromagnetic particles and reinscribes it with a kind of soundless sound. Only a bulk eraser with a large AC magnet operating at the frequency level of a high-voltage power line can actually cancel all extant tape noise. In short, it is virtually impossible to erase an analog tape. Even the digital, which allows for the deletion of a track, is still acquiescent to processes of deep-data recovery. "Erasing" is thus only ever achieved as an abstraction, a by-product of the act of recording. Consequently, erasing must be reconceptualized as an additive, not subtractive, process; something that produces a surfeit of information, albeit of a different order that is perhaps analogous to the 50Hz hum of the mains. In fact, the Advisory Panel on White House Tapes who submitted their report into the technical investigation of Tape 342 to Judge Sirica on May 31, 1974, determined that the source of the buzz throughout the 18½-minute gap probably came from the electrical grid: "The buzz sound probably originated in electrical noise on the electric power line that powered the recorder. Any speech sounds previously recorded on this section of the tape were erased in conjunction with the recording process, as is normal in recorders of this kind."[42] Philosopher Henri Bergson contends that there is always more in nothing than in something: "In the idea of disorder there is already the idea of order, plus its negation, plus the motive for the negation when we encounter an order that is not the one we expected."[43] When something does not perform as expected we perceive it as lack, states Bergson, but this lack is not implicit in the thing itself, rather, it is a projection of deficiency onto the thing as the absence of what interests us.

Although Tape 342 was recorded on Nixon's Sony TC-800B, the Advisory Panel to Judge Sirica (1974) concluded that Wood's Uher 5000 had been used to produce the actual 18½-minute "erasure" in Tape 342.[44] This makes sense, given that the Oval Office microphones were wired to central mixers connected to a Sony tape recorder stored in a locker room of the White House basement, whereas the Uher sat beside Woods's desk and would have been the most accessible tape recorder to Nixon. The likelihood that any latent vocalizations might be conserved by the tape was increased with this machinic displacement. As Ginsberg notes: "A crack in the erase head, a dust mote on the tape or heads, slack in the tape at start-up, head misalignment" would have compromised efforts at masking the presumably incriminatory information captured on tape.[45] "A decade ago, this wouldn't have mattered. But today's digital tools can help make something out of what sounds like nothing."[46]

Archival conservation of Tape 342 has focused on maintaining its overall stability, and in particular on preserving the integrity of the remaining iron oxide particles that are distributed along the length of the 18½-minute "silent" segment of the tape. Because the magnetic layer of a tape is extremely fragile, it is bonded to a smooth plastic substrate that provides it with tensile strength and flexibility so that it can easily conform to the tape heads of a variety of machines. During the recording process the tape travels across the record head of the machine, where a small gap interrupts the magnetic circuit of the head (made up of a high-permeability core and signal coil). As the current passes through the signal coil, it concentrates its electrical field at the small gap over which the tape is moving. "The signal changes in amplitude from one instant to the next, so that each element of the tape as it passes the gap 'sees' and remembers a different amplitude and polarity of magnetization, becoming magnetized in a pattern."[47] After recording, the tape's surface is marked by areas of discrete magnetization of varying depth and direction that can now be converted into electrical waves—sound—by a playback system.

Determining the tape speed of the recording is normally governed by qualitative considerations which take into account the density of the material, its bits or wavelengths per mm. Nixon's decision (or that of the Secret Service) to run his machines at less than their optimal setting ($^{15}/_{16}$ IPS—half the standard rate) increased the available recording time of the tapes but decreased their audio fidelity. Analog audio recorders such as the Sony TC-800B reel-to-reel voice recorder must drive the tape at a steady speed with short-term variations of not more than 25 percent in order to produce coherent voice recordings. A precision roller called a capstan is used to smooth out irregularities deriving from the mechanical workings of the recorder (rollers, belts, gears, motors, reels) as the tape winds its way through the machine. Apparently less precision is acceptable in lower-cost recorders such as that used by Nixon, but any unsteadiness in the capstan process will result in fluctuations: a phenomenon called "wow and flutter" which superimposes additional sounds into the recording process, thereby extending the point already made by Altman. The incongruity of speeds could prove to be a useful factor in Tape 342's restoration, although the degraded quality of the original voice recordings that resulted from this deviation might further obfuscate the intelligibility of any recovered data.

Another important factor that affects the quality of any analog recording is that of AC or high-frequency biasing, a technique for removing distortion. High-frequency biasing introduces residual or additional magnetization into the recording process, superimposing positive and negative charges between the tape's passage from erase to record heads, which in turn cancel out errant signal peaks, leaving the tape in a stable neutral condition.[48] All of these technical features—tape speed, wow and flutter, capstan precision, high-frequency biasing—impact upon the recording process and are thus also sites of potential transformation that will further complicate NARA's salvage operations. To this end, NARA's specialized expertise has been enlisted in preserving and recuperating the sound event—a voice and nothing more—whereas the technical expressions of its machinic processes have been largely ignored, relegated to the ignominy of noise and interference; something to be eliminated rather than ministered to in its own right.[49] Despite NARA's archival vigilance, the passage of time will inevitably change the material integrity of the tape even in its protracted state of suspended animation, as well as our evaluation of the consequential nature of the tape gap's existence.

Case of the Missing 18½ Minutes

Whether or not Tape 342 will corroborate Nixon's criminality is clearly not my abiding concern here; there is more than enough evidence, including the "smoking gun" conversation recorded three days after his discussion with Haldeman, to be able to declare the case closed in this regard. Rather than offering a space for the retrospective replenishment of recuperated speech, the 18½-minute tape gap is a transition that designates the interval between the actual and the virtual, between what was said and what might be said in the future. Only the digital, with its comprehensive program of microacoustic scanning along with other yet-to-be-invented processes, might eventually retrieve sufficient data for restoring traces of human speech. However, emphasizing the promissory note of technology to resurrect the media artifact for us at some future date disavows its present status as already enunciatory: rich in information. Asserting the tape's contractual purchase with the past, as well as with the future yet to come, must not negate its immanent potential to "speak" to the many contexts through which it continues to move as a political artifact.

The case [study] of the missing 18½ minutes is ultimately a kind of "tape cut-up" that aims to reorganize the narrative field by splicing the historical event of the tape into our contemporary political landscape.[50] Might the active intercession of the gap, in this sense, be affirmative in opening up the tape to a consideration of other political voids from redaction, secret courts, extraordinary renditions, black ops, and dark sites, or is its use value only of historical significance? With the rise of WikiLeaks and the Edward Snowden revelations of 2013, the scale of political malfeasance has no doubt changed the public optics around what counts as a notable clandestine act. Tampering with a White House tape recorder seems perhaps less criminal than the current scope of hacking and data scraping. With global telecommunications providers and European states tacitly cooperating with the National Security Agency's (NSA) program of mass domestic surveillance, the motivation for recovering Tape 342's evidentiary truths may have finally abated. Yet what connects these paradigmatic cases of the shadow state is that they are all are marked by what cultural theorist Clare Birchall has called the productive labor of the secret, which works not to hide but to expose the aporia at the heart of democratic politics. This is also the considerable labor that the *material witness* performs in disclosing the event of evidence. Its efforts are not enlisted for the purposes of unveiling the lie or, indeed, discovering an absolute truth encoded in magnetic matter but, rather, for revealing the machinations of institutional processes that have become powerfully operative in scripting our new myths. In her discussion of the aesthetics of the secret, Birchall argues: "a direct look at the politics of secrecy and the value of the secret at a geopolitical level has had an oddly depoliticising, perhaps even obfuscating, effect."[51] She goes on to suggest that "we might be better able to form a radical political response to the 'Snowden event' by situating the secret 'itself' within a distributive regime and imagining what collectivities and subjectivities the secret makes available (rather than those that it closes down)."[52] From my point of view, this is the generative work that an exploration of the missing 18½ minutes of Watergate Tape 342 can enable; something that this chapter only gestures toward at present in its attempt to read magnetic matter against the grain of representation. Rather than simply declaring the case closed, and thus consigning it to the chronicles of a history charted by one solitary man and his cadre of loyal staff, the secret keeps the political question open as an event that is distributed across actors and institutions as well as across time. The secret challenges the limit conditions of what might be known at any given moment and, ideally, pries open the horizon of political change. Curator Steven Lam made a related point in his essay for the exhibition "For Reasons of State" at The Kitchen, New York (Whitney ISP, 2008), for which I created a photographic installation called "Stretch" based upon my research into the 18½-minute tape gap. "Despite the current regime of secrecy and opacity, artistic production provides a way to speculate and materialize the hidden and the unknown. If the secret impedes and blocks democratic deliberation, these practices mirror processes of declassification, offering methods in discussing a form of politics beyond evidence."[53] I take this to mean a form of doing politics beyond the self-evident nature of things, or a politics that is not organized around an instrumental relationship to evidence whereby actions can be galvanized only by the unequivocal proof of wrongdoing. The gap is an intervention into the field of representation that challenges the contractual relationship between recognition and action: the belief that one must have full knowledge in order to respond.[54] Understanding how to act ethically in a world of unknowns and secrets remains a fundamental challenge.

While the National Archives' commitment to investigating the magnetic remainder of the tape and unlocking its secrets is tied to its conviction of technology's progressive futurity, the tape gap's status as mute has already been extensively undone by the sheer volume of speculation around what kind of lurid data lurks within; musings that far exceed what any one man can actually say in 18½ minutes. Likewise the actual machinic utterances that the tape gap already emits, as well as those that it will continue to transmit as it reels off toward an uncertain future, can surely activate many more imaginative registers. In comparison with the array of possibilities that the gap in the tape invites for thinking about how evidential materials govern the changing conditions of truth, the recovery of intelligible speech seems a rather pedantic objective that may serve only to control the limits of historical discourse. For many, the very existence of the tape gap has already rendered an unequivocal verdict of guilty. But for those inclined toward a speculative mode of forensics organized by the reassembly of matter, the mystery of the missing 18½ minutes is not entirely an open-and-shut case. In creating a temporal breach within the extended voice recordings registered on tape, the gap encourages its virtual magnetic polarities to reach out beyond the formal limitations of what might have been said within a period of 18½ minutes to link with other potential information vectors, producing new narrative conjunctions and political reverberations. To some degree the tape gap was always-already there, already prefigured within the virtual archives of the machine, prior to the Secret Service ever having placed the reels of tape into the Sony TC-800B and pressed RECORD. The very fact of a tape recorder is affirmation that an "erasure" of some kind—deliberate or accidental—will occur at some point, which will in turn attach itself to a localized event. My task as a researcher has been to probe the intercession produced by this particular gap—the acoustic evidence of the event, as well as the political and juridical event of evidence. Should NARA succeed in discovering a technology that will be able to repair the tape—and, by extension, history—such a process will never fully erase the many conjectures and contestations already recorded by the evidential emergence of the gap. Ultimately, the material power of 18½ minutes of noisy silence is to assert the productive agency of the gap as that which shifts our attention away from the foreground—the act of speech—to the background—the field of noise which is also its enabling condition, and that which constitutes the broader field of causal relations out of which any single event can emerge. In making this focal shift we also reorganize the vantage point and scale of our politics: an incitement, certainly, for investigating the many gaps in our "recorded" histories, but also a provocation to listening itself: one that demands an aesthetic engagement with the situated material politics of noise such that what is seemingly "missing" is rendered fully present through other channels of perception.

Stop, Rewind, and Press "Record" Again

5 MOTION TO STRIKE

Honey Bee v. Assassin Bug

> "These drones hover over our heads constantly and one can always hear the buzzing, mosquito-like sound they make."
>
> "The constant noise from drones has driven many villagers to insanity. When I hear a loud noise now, I am very frightened that a drone strike is happening and I live in this constant fear."
>
> —Survivors of a drone strike in Datta Khel, FATA Pakistan, March 17, 2011[1]

While the value of noise in chapter 4 functions to highlight a material politics of sound organized not by direct recourse to human speech but as a machinic expression of an array of acoustic technologies, in the following case "noise" is analyzed as an indirect consequence of the use of a weapons technology—drone warfare—but one whose social effects ultimately serve to weaponize sound itself. Likewise, the legal discussion that ensues turns not on an investigation of artifactual (tape) noise as cipher or index of potential wrongdoing (the intentional violence done to recorded sound through erasure) but, rather, on the affective emanations of noise as a form of harm, deliberate or otherwise, that raises a tangle of related legal questions and arguments.

The origin of the term "drone" that is frequently used to describe unmanned aerial vehicles is actually a reference to the graphic resemblance they bear to the male honey bee or drone bee and not, as is commonly assumed, to the buzzing insect-like sound emitted by their whirring propellers. Early pilotless planes were frequently painted with black stripping along their fuselage, hence their visual designation as drones. Such radio-controlled aircraft were first employed as targets for training antiaircraft gun crews during World War II, but eventually their primary use was directed toward aerial

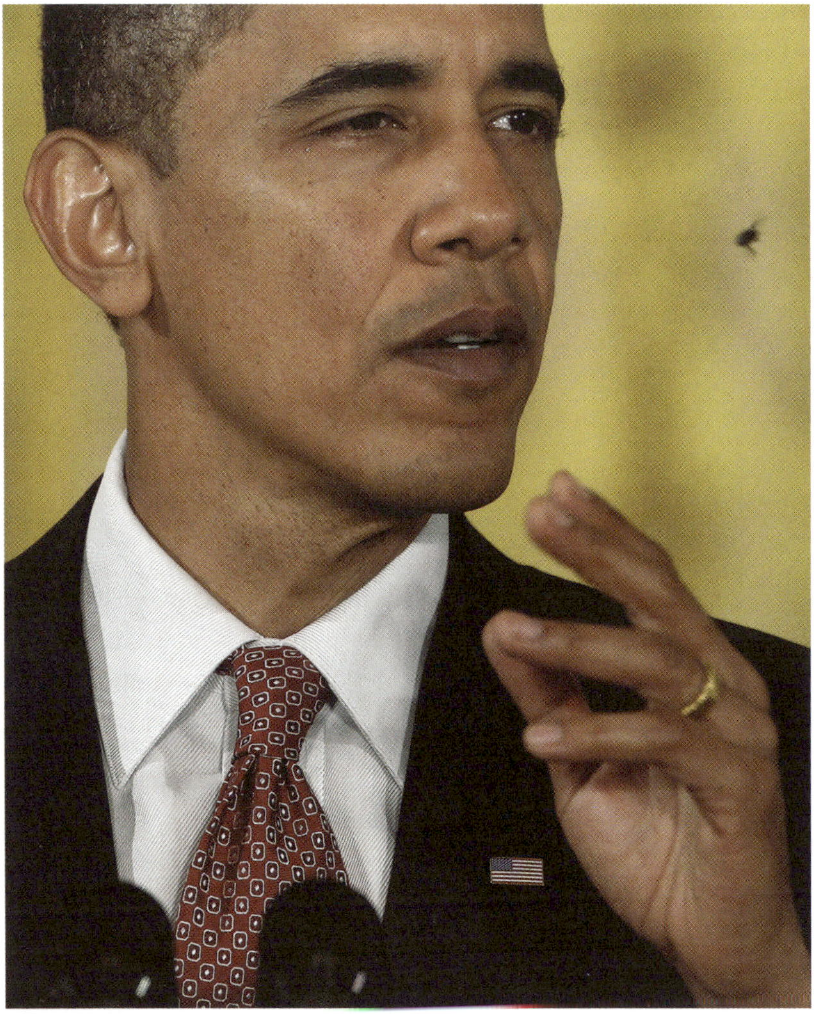

Figure 5.1
President Obama speaks on implementation of new health care reform, June 22, 2010. Photo credit: Win McNamee. Source: Getty Images.

reconnaissance and scientific data collection. Cloud-penetrating drones (unmanned B-17s) flew extensive missions during Operation Crossroads in 1946, recording and gathering atmospheric data from the fallout of underwater nuclear weapons testing conducted at Bikini Atoll in the Marshall Islands. Contemporary drone warfare is indebted to the legacies of both remote-controlled targeting and surveillance. These parallel military developments find their technical convergence in today's armed combat drones and are used extensively in the global war on terror or, as British photographer Edmund Clark more aptly puts it, in the global "war *of* terror."[2] While this case study explores the evidentiary role of sound, as do others in this book, in this case the sonic regime is the very means by which a certain violation is produced rather than the acoustic artifact offered up for criminal investigation.

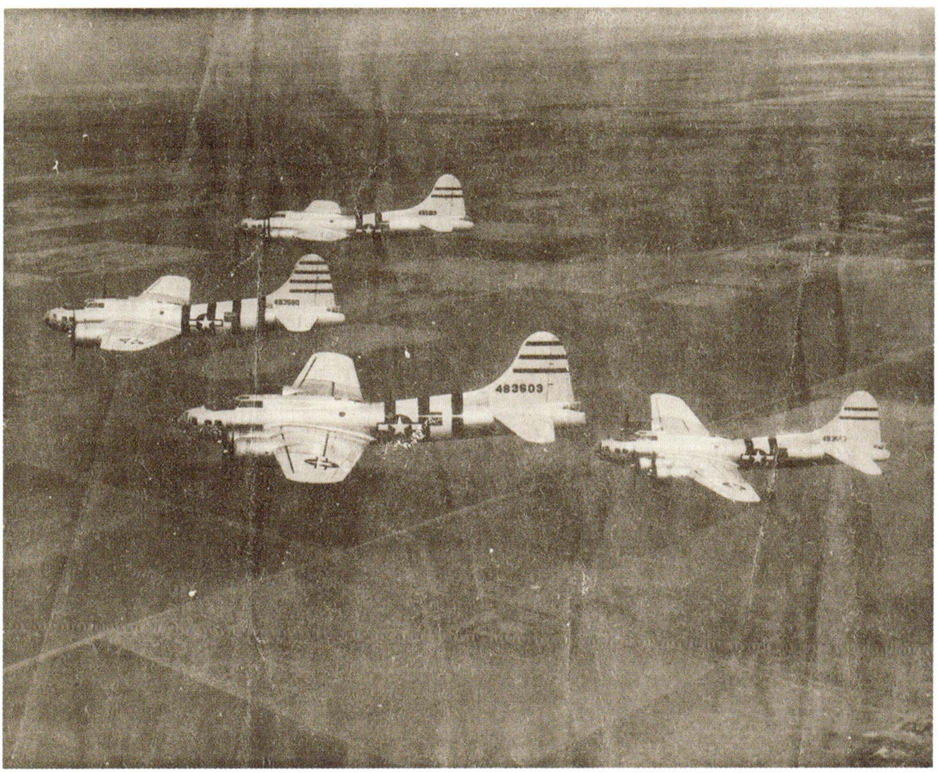

Figure 5.2

They've [drones] been clay pigeons in gunnery practice, bombed Jap and German targets, and brought back data from the heart of Bikini's cloud. Uncle Sam's radio-controlled planes have missions in mind never remotely guessed at by Jules Verne. *Planes without Pilots*, 1946. Source: A.A.F. Drone Unit, Air Instrumentation and Test Requirement Unit.

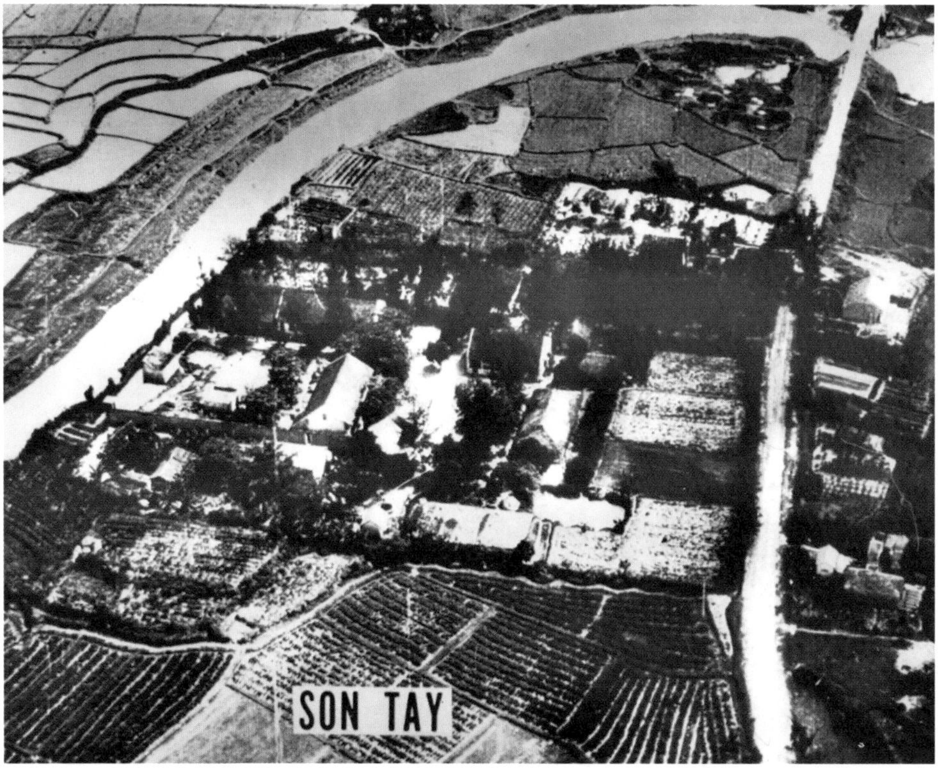

Figure 5.3
US Military reconnaissance photograph of a prisoner of war camp near the city of Son Tay in North Vietnam. Aerial photos of the camp were taken by Ryan Lightning Bug reconnaissance drones from 1969 to 1970. Source: US Air Force.

When US antiterror strategies shifted from secret prisons and detention camps to targeted assassination under the Obama Administration in 2009, Predator and Reaper drones came to saturate airspace over the Federally Administered Tribal Areas (FATA) of Northwest Pakistan.[3] These armed combat drones troll the geographies of FATA in search of targets whose names emerge out of the "disposition matrix" or "kill list" compiled from the aggregation of metadata and presented weekly at the White House.[4] Former director of the NSA and CIA General Michael Hayden once made the chilling admission: "We kill people based on metadata."[5] Guided by the Obama Presidency's conviction that the war on terror could be won by "out-computing" its enemies, and preempting terrorist threats using predictive software and machine learning, a new generation of remote-controlled drones became a permanent feature of the skies along the Afghan border, their ubiquitous presence signaled by low-frequency emissions of 150 kHz.

Various organizations, most notably the Bureau of Investigative Journalism (BIJ) based in the UK, try to maintain comprehensive datasets as to reported casualties (both fatalities and injuries) from drone strikes in Pakistan and elsewhere; however, these numbers do not begin to represent the injurious nature of what it means to live under the constant sonic presence of drone sorties. And while the male honey bee from whence the term "drone" is mistakenly thought to have originated is a harmless and stingless descendant from the Apoidea family of the Insecta class whose main role is to assist in species reproduction, the drones deployed in contemporary military operations are lethal. In combining aerial reconnaissance missions with the capacities for a deadly airborne assault, today's drones are surely no longer the conceptual offspring of the Apoidea line but, rather, the predatory descendants of the Reduviid family—that of assassin bugs.

Sorties v. Strikes

Fatalities due to drone strikes, although extremely difficult to confirm definitively in many areas of the world where they occur (most notably in Pakistan, Afghanistan, Yemen, Gaza, and Somalia), do offer up statistics that confer a degree of empirical irrefutability.[6] Upward of 40 people were killed in a drone strike on a Tribal Jirga (assembly) held on March 17, 2011, in the village of Datta Khel, North Waziristan. While the actual death toll ranged from 42 to 53, with an additional 14 injured, there is no doubt that a large number of civilians died from the Hellfire missiles fired by a US drone that day.[7] While I do not wish to diminish the scale of this deadly event, far greater numbers are psychologically affected by the relentless drone surveillance that takes place throughout this region. As Mohammad Kausar succinctly expressed it: "They are like a mosquito. Even when you don't see them, you can hear them, you know they are there."[8] Acoustic noise has become a kind of omnipresent threat—a low sonic violence—whereby invisible frequencies are converted into states of anxiety, depression, and fear. The daily lived terror of a deadly attack from a remote-controlled assassin that one cannot so much see as hear is difficult to quantify and convert into the kinds of graphs and statistics required for producing an evidential basis upon which a legal claim might be advanced, or even a human rights campaign. The diffuse and deleterious violence of this by-product of drone surveillance raises further challenges for statisticians who are increasingly faced with accounting for the collateral effects of conflict as they bear upon issues not just of food production, water supply and treatment, and other aspects of infrastructure damage linked to mortality, but also upon vulnerabilities related to mental health. "The sound alone gives us psychological grief," said Kaleemullah Mehsud, a man in his thirties from Waziristan, who spoke to *Agence France-Presse* in Peshawar.[9]

The absence of a comprehensive analysis of the effects of drone emissions within the public record is notable especially given their chronic, albeit not specifically fatal, impact upon civilian populations in regions such as FATA. Yet this research, which focused primarily on FATA, came about through my observation of incidental but repeated comments made by witnesses as to the fear they experienced when hearing the presence of drones overhead. I accessed this information via witness statements taken by lawyers representing the families of drone strike victims, a first-person interview, and written reports. One of the primary problems that I faced in trying to understand the impact of drone surveillance was in ascertaining specific aspects of their operations and presence throughout FATA. How often did drones fly overhead, how many were dispatched at a time, and at what altitude? All these factors would combine to create a highly specific stratum of noise. Some of my answers came via military regulations (permissible flying altitudes vary between countries) or from reading the autobiographical accounts of military personnel who described their experiences, while others needed to be inferred from datasets sourced from other contexts. For example, General McChrystal discusses the drone flying formations they (Joint Special Operations) used in Iraq to track various targets, including the "pancake stack" of nine drones employed over high-value target Abu Musab al-Zarqawi's compound in Hibhib, Iraq.[10] Calculating the approximate ratio between the number of missions or sorties flown to those that resulted in a strike would help me determine the degree to which communities were subjected to drone flyovers in key areas of FATA, and thus the degree to which they might experience the sound and intensity of drone presence. This was crucial but nonexistent information or, at the very least, classified US data. While drone strikes are recorded and now made public, numbers concerning the much more frequent missions conducted for purposes of surveillance and intelligence-gathering are not included in these public records. Investigative journalist Chris Woods, who headed the Drone Warfare project at BIJ at the time that I conducted this research, and who now leads Airwars, a journalist-led transparency project monitoring the coalition air war against ISIS, helped me come up with working figures from data of drone sorties collected by the British in Afghanistan.

If one were to extrapolate from this data, which indicates that for every 30 armed drone sorties flown in Afghanistan only one actual strike results, then the approximate number of drone sorties in FATA during the Obama years (2009–June 2013) could have reached a possible 9,500 if the ratio of sorties to strikes remained somewhat similar.[11] This staggering figure must be further underscored by the fact that these sorties were not short missions that entered sovereign Pakistani airspace in search of targets to head directly back to their Kandahar airbase in southern Afghanistan. On the contrary, these were extended sorties that tracked moving vehicles, loitered over villages and towns, and targeted adversaries for up to four days at a time without returning to refuel. The current generation of hunter-killer Reaper drones carries nearly two metric tonnes of fuel in addition to an equal payload of equipment, allowing it to stay airborne for around 42 hours, or 14 when fully loaded with munitions. A quick calculation puts the figure of Obama-era drone hours flown over FATA, a relatively small geographical region of 27,220 square kilometers, at between 133,000 and 399,000 hours if flight patterns were somewhat analogous to those in Afghanistan. Plans are currently underway to increase these capacities dramatically, so that in the future non-hydrocarbon-reliant UAVs (unmanned aerial vehicles) may allow drones to scour inaccessible regions of the globe for months on end without refueling. Furthermore, the density of armed drone surveillance is much higher in North Waziristan's main towns of Miranshah and Mir Ali, where nearly round-the-clock drone emissions from sorties are being observed. These rarely reported figures documenting the hours that drones spend cruising the skies of FATA would provide an altogether different dimension of the War on Terror and its extended impacts upon civilian life on the ground if such flight logs were made public. Another witness declaration: "I have actually heard drones fly day and night and during the day have also seen them. At night, they were very loud, a kind of roar, as they flew much lower than during the day. Sometimes there were breaks of one hour, but then they came back."[12]

Sound v. Vision

I began this discussion with a brief clarification that the etymological namesake of the drone was inherited through a visual schema rather than by acoustic filiation, as is most often presumed.[13] This etymological confusion, with its reordering of vision and sound, is folded into the very political reorganization of drone warfare today, with its attendant claims around the minimal impact of unmanned aerial violence upon civilian life. Drone vision is arguably precise, but drone sonics are vague and diffused, producing a difference in both degree and kind of injury. Near-continuous drone surveillance in towns such as Miranshah and Mir Ali has created a background stratum of noise that is an indelible feature of these environments. Yet the sonic dimension of such remote-controlled warfare has received only scant attention in comparison to contemporary theorizations around the lethal vision of drone technology. This deficit persists, in spite of the fact that accounts of the sonic features of drone sorties are a consistent component of witness testimony. Whilst the targeting accuracy of Predator and Reaper drones is conjoined to their ability to send almost instantaneous information back to operators who observe terrestrial life in FATA on screens sometimes thousands of kilometers away, their sonic impact is dispersed across village populations, ranging in volume from debilitating to benign depending upon the aerial proximity of the drone and the varying acoustic properties and contours of the landscape below that absorbs and refracts sound waves differently.[14] The low frequencies of a drone sortie are thus independent of an actual decision to strike. However, the deafening blast and kinetic impact of a Hellfire missile has been known to cause permanent hearing damage and loss. Another witness who survived a drone strike: "I also suffer from a hearing problem because the sound when the missile landed was so loud. … I will never forget the sound the missile made when it was fired on the building where we were meeting. It was a very loud and severe sound."[15] The objective of visual surveillance is directed toward a vertical event—a laser-guided missile strike—whereas the by-product of drone vision manifests itself as a horizontal distribution of acoustic emissions at varying intensities of amplification, resulting in psychological distress more than physical injuries. However, when a Hellfire missile attack suddenly emerges out of this atmospheric "drone," it temporarily reorganizes the fields of vision and sound as the impact is converted into a penetrating acoustic singularity and the visual field redistributed through the violent disarticulation of bodies and buildings that merge figure with ground.

Current acoustic research into reducing the noise footprint of unmanned aerial vehicles in order to increase their stealth capacities as they engage in low-altitude surveillance and military missions might well contribute to an overall reduction in noise generation by drones. This is not to say that their impact upon civilian life will necessarily be diminished, rather that the role of sound as source of anxiety and fear may lessen.[16] Minimizing a UAV's sound emissions would also safeguard against its own operational noise being fed back into its acoustic sensors, and thus aid in differentiating between various external sounds, including those currently being produced by the drone itself. Drones use a combination of infrared and radar sensors to enhance their situational awareness and perimeter defense against other small low-flying aircraft and antiaircraft missiles. Despite these advanced detection systems, numerous collisions have taken place between drones and other aircraft in the increasingly congested airspace over the Afghanistan–Pakistan border region, such as the August 2012 incident in which a drone struck a C-130 cargo plane, forcing an emergency landing.[17] Consequently, efforts to control the noise generated by drones has become part of a specialist field of aero-acoustics that tries to identify, measure, and classify the acoustic signal propagation characteristics of propeller aircraft in real time using digital signal processing hardware and advanced computational algorithms.[18] Because drones are engineered into highly integrated technological systems, it is extremely difficult to separate and classify the various noise-producing components that comprise their overall acoustic outputs. As sound waves radiate away from the drone they also interact with meteorological phenomena in the air, producing new "mixed" frequencies. This further complicates the task of assigning a definitive acoustic signature to a given model, as the identification and classification of drone sound is registered by detection devices and microphones external to the machine that are generally located on the ground. As research and development in aero-acoustics progresses to silence the drone, will a reduction in noise lessen the anxiety and distress that populations in FATA now experience living under drones, or will the prospect of an omnipresent and lethal payload that one can neither see nor hear induce an even greater degree of fear and trauma?

Earwitness

Human rights investigators and legal practitioners, with generally limited resources and restricted access to eye and ear witnesses, need quite rightly to focus on the lethal outcomes of actual drone strikes—numbers killed or wounded. This means that public accounts detailing the impact of drone activity in a region such as FATA are disproportionately rare when it comes to reporting on the daily lived experiences of drone surveillance. The coauthored 2012 Stanford and New York University report "Living Under Drones: Death, Injury, and Trauma to Civilians from US Drone Practices in Pakistan" offers a significant effort to correct this imbalance by examining the broader impact of US drone operations in the area.[19] The report, based upon witness accounts, is populated with citations as to the debilitating effects of living with the constant sound of drones buzzing overhead, from mental health concerns to impacts upon the social activities of communities.

> One man described the reaction to the sound of the drones as "a wave of terror" coming over the community. "Children, grown-up people, women, they are terrified. ... They scream in terror." Interviewees described the experience of living under constant surveillance as harrowing. In the words of one interviewee: "God knows whether they'll strike us again or not. But they're always surveying us, they're always over us, and you never know when they're going to strike and attack.[20]

Within the broader thesis of the *Material Witness*, how is it that a process of transmission—the 150kHz emissions that trouble the skies of FATA—might be reconceptualized as registering the presence of external events, and even bearing witness to such histories? Certainly there is no trace that is directly carried by the frequency, only the latency of a future violence that it both signals and brings into perceptibility as a felt effect. If, as the many ear-witness statements recount, the sound alone operates as a trigger to bring about recursive experiences of stress, anxiety, and even terror, can one argue that the specific acoustic properties of the sound are a kind of technical archive that is capable of carrying residual effects of previous events—the deadly consequences of a Hellfire missile strike? Conventional wisdom would have it that the sound is merely a signifier of a potential threat that repeated exposure, with its sometimes deadly consequences, has conditioned as to its particular lethal meaning, whereas I am arguing that this knowledge as to the specific implications that such an aerial frequency yields to those living under drones can itself be understood as a form of material knowledge that is situated within the particular geopolitical context of FATA. Sound waves carry the evidential quotient of prior events in the form of acoustic energies that can be identified and mapped onto an archive of lived experiences of violence, which they are also capable of reactualizing. When these low-frequency emissions combine with physical matter, they vibrate the tympanic membrane of the ear, so that hearing becomes a kind of barometer for reading the atmospheric pressure of drone surveillance on the body public.

However, inasmuch as earwitness testimony contains repeated references to the distressing acoustic conditions of life under drones, these observations are largely anecdotal and have yet to make their way into the legal analysis of US drone strike practices in Pakistan. Until there is a comprehensive study undertaken that charts this acoustic phenomenon, it is unlikely that the implications of chronic drone sonics will be integrated into the legal framework of International Humanitarian Law (IHL) as it bears most tellingly upon the issue of a collective punishment inflicted upon a civilian population. Encouragingly, conversations with lawyers at Reprieve, a legal rights organization in the UK that advocates on behalf of drone strike victims, informed me (now several years ago) that work to map the increased use of antidepressants in FATA is slowly being undertaken. This information could prove very useful in helping to determine the collateral effects of drone warfare, including its psychological dimensions, even if establishing direct causal links between drone emissions and depression will be difficult to advance with legal certainty.

> Depression is really high in Waziristan, said doctor Muktar ul-Haq, head of the psychiatry department at the government-run Lady Reading Hospital in Peshawar, the largest city in the northwest. "There is uncertainty generally in Pakistan but particularly in this area. They are always apprehensive about the drones, about their lives," he said. While drone attacks do

> bring patients "episodically" for treatment, he says, residents in Waziristan complain of living in constant fear of drones that patrol in the skies above and the buzzing sound they say they emit.[21]

It is worth noting, however, that aircraft noise already has a quasi-legal status, and has been argued to be a willful agent of warfare even though the legal petition that brought forward this claim in Israel ultimately did not succeed. Municipalities with airports, too, are subject to bylaws that regulate the flight corridors of low-flying aircraft to minimize sound pollution or EPNdB (effective perceived noise decibels) caused by a plane's propulsion system and aerodynamic noise. There has also been related discussion around a request to the European Court of Human Rights to ban the use of the "Mosquito," an anti-loitering device that emits painful high-frequency pulses audible only to children and young people. Coincidentally, the technical term for repetitive drone surveillance over one dedicated area is also called "loitering." The UN Committee on the Rights of the Child (CRC) has "called on all governments to reconsider the Mosquito devices, insofar as they may violate the rights of children." While the Home Office and the EU Commission rejected this appeal on the grounds that there was "insufficient information to establish guidelines for safe exposure to high frequencies," the Association of Police Officers in the UK has refused to endorse the device due to a lack of "sound" evidence proving that short-term exposure to the Mosquito has no adverse health implications.[22] Whether local constabularies choose to use the Mosquito or other sonic devices in their arsenal is, however, up to them.[23] All this is to say: recommendations and regulations governing the use and extent of sound-producing technologies for purposes of domestic policing are already legally entangled, if not necessarily enforceable under law. Debates continue around what constitutes acceptable levels of exposure to sound before injuries are inflicted and permanent hearing damage is sustained.

Sonic Booms

For a period of five weeks following the abduction of Corporal Gilad Shalit on June 26, 2006, Israeli Air Force jets repeatedly flew low-altitude sorties over the Gaza Strip at night, generating a series of sonic booms. Questioned as to the use of such aggressive sounds to create an atmosphere of intimidation and fear, Prime Minister Ehud Olmert replied: "Thousands of residents in southern Israel live in fear and discomfort, so I gave instructions that nobody will sleep at night in the meantime in Gaza."[24] According to lawyers at B'Tselem, the Israeli Information Center for Human Rights in the Occupied Territories:

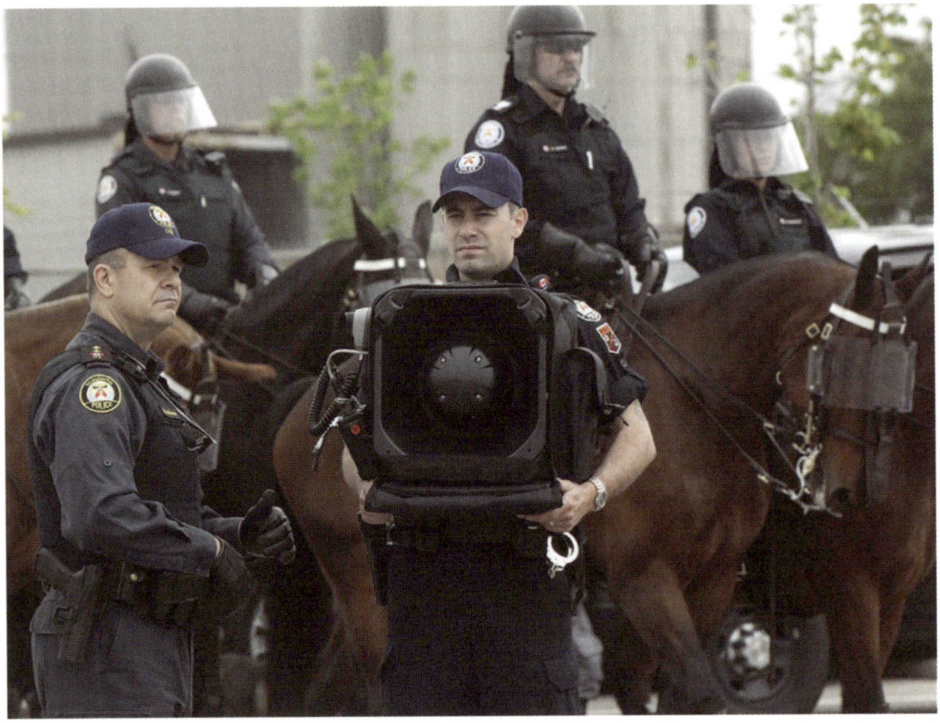

Figure 5.4
Insp. Gary Meissner, left, with Const. Paul Breeze, right, who is holding the LRAD-X 100 Acoustic Communication Device (also know as a sound cannon) during a demonstration prior to the G20 summit in Toronto in June 2010. Photo credit: Frank Gunn. Source: The Canadian Press.

> The use of sonic booms flagrantly breaches a number of provisions of International Humanitarian Law. The most significant provision is the prohibition on collective punishment. Article 33 of the Fourth Geneva Convention, which is intended to protect civilians in time of war, categorically states that: Collective penalties and likewise all measures of intimidation or of terrorism are prohibited. The Article also states that, "Reprisals against protected persons and their property are prohibited." Air Force supersonic sorties also breach the principle of distinction, a central pillar of humanitarian law, which forbids the warring sides to direct their attacks against civilians.[25]

In response to these nightly sorties, Physicians for Human Rights and the Gaza Community Mental Health Center filed a petition in the Israeli High Court claiming that the deployment of sonic booms as a terrorizing tactic was in violation of IHL, and therefore constituted an illegal act.[26] Their petition ultimately turned on the legal question of whether sound as an immaterial agent of violence constituted a weaponized entity for purposes of "attack." Air Force lawyers argued that the petitioners' claims were unfounded, since sonic booms had never been classified as an attack weapon; therefore their use, irrespective of the distress induced, was not accountable to the tenets of IHL governing proportionality and distinction. "As mentioned, the prohibitions and limitations of the laws of warfare, in classified operations, refer to 'Attack.' What is meant by the term 'attack' refers to acts of violence involving weapons used for/or against another target." The illegality of sonic booms as an instrument of collective punishment would have required a legal redefinition of sound as a weaponized technology—a reclassification rejected by the court. The Defense also maintained that "supersonic passes do not cause 'unnecessary suffering' of enemy fighters," another opinion informed by the framework of proportionality and distinction. The petitioners' claims as to the illegality of sonic booms were based, they argued, on the assumption that their use in Gaza was intentionally directed against its civilian population for the express purposes of intimidation and collective punishment: "This premise regarding the purpose of making supersonic passes is erroneous. And therefore any legal argument based on it is wrong."[27] Yet both the rejection of sound as constituting a form of assault, and of sonic booms as harmless, were flagrantly contradicted in the initial public statement made by the prime minister when he threatened Gaza with sleepless nights of fear as a reprisal. Historian David Suisman argues that the instrumental use of sonic booms for purposes of social control can be traced back to acoustic experimentation conducted on urban populations during Cold War, and thus is already deeply intertwined with the rise of the "modern national security state":

> Each sonic boom was, in effect, an assault, felt both as a social and political act and as a physiological, emotional experience. Through sound, the state touched people's bodies. It also entered their homes uninvited, penetrated the most intimate spaces of their lives, and damaged their property. Thus, sonic booms reverberated simultaneously in multiple registers—social, political, economic, legal, environmental, emotional, and psychological—and as they did, they created a new relation between state and citizen, connecting the affective and material experience of the soundscape to the political and economic will of the state.[28]

Sound Proofs

This case from Gaza raises a series of very urgent questions as to the weaponized dimension of sound that may also inform the kinds of legal claims that could be brought by drone strike survivors on behalf of victims and their families in Pakistan. How are we to understand the legal difference between the use of sound as an instrument of policing and control versus sound that is used as a weapon? If sound waves, due to their radiating nature, are unable to differentiate between a target or enemy combatant and a community of civilians, does the argument around intentionality still hold legally when the continued deployment of a given weapon has known effects that supersede the technology's intended use? At what point is a sound event, one that is the by-product of a specific military technology, deemed sufficiently harmful to count as collateral damage? If its side effects are known, does the continued use of the technology constitute a form of legal liability? Finally, can the constant threat signaled by the sound of drone sorties (irrespective of strikes) be considered a form of collective punishment as defined by Article 33 of the Fourth Geneva Convention? While in practice, sonic warfare actually has a long history that theorist Steve Goodman has elucidated in detail, now complemented by Martin J. Daughtry's 2015 book on Iraq, *Listening to War*, legal arguments still need to prove that the sound effects—psychological and physiological—of drone warfare are well known to health-care professionals, and are systematically being logged by human rights agencies.[29] In sum, these cases and the legal challenges they pose (despite their failures in court) begin to create the demand and conditions for conceptualizing new juridical tools whereby this kind of low-frequency violence and the many others that assume diffuse and invisible forms cannot simply be dismissed as incidental features of human technologies and activities.

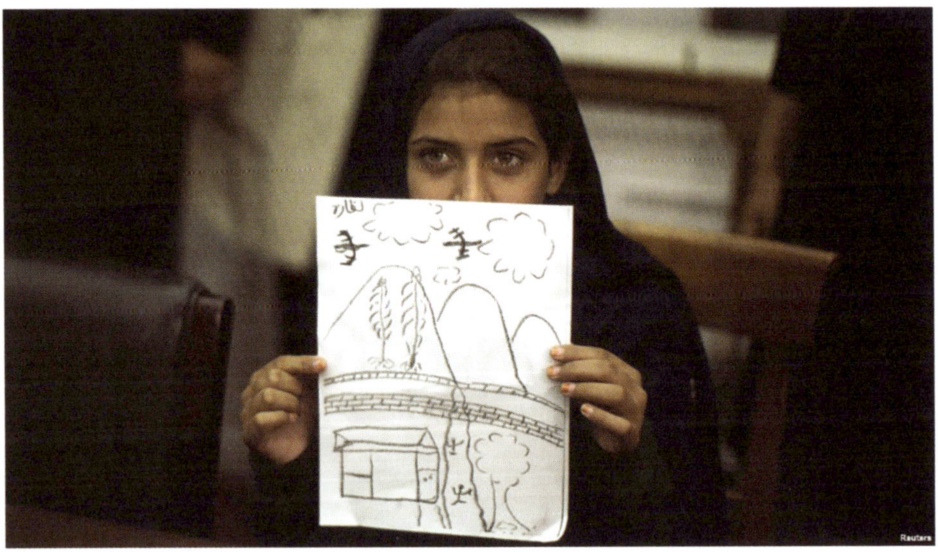

Figure 5.5
At a news conference in Washington on October 29, 2013, Nabila Rehman holds up a picture she drew depicting the US drone strike on her Pakistani village which killed her grandmother in 2012. Source: Reuters/RFE/RL.

The high-resolution sensors carried by drones that, in principle, permit laser-guided pinpoint accuracy underscore military and political claims that the use of armed drones dramatically lowers civilian casualties. In 2011, President Obama's chief counterterrorism adviser, John Brennan, even went so far as to publicly claim that "there hasn't been a single collateral [civilian] death in Pakistan since August 2010." Brennan's assertion, proven by BIJ to be false, contributes to the ethical arguments around robotic and remote-controlled warfare, which positions UAVs as "moral predators" immune from fatigue, stress, or undue concern for self-preservation, in marked contrast to ground troops, whose "unsound" decisions can lead to tragic consequences for civilians.[30] It could be argued that drones do minimize civilian fatalities over conventional weapons such as cluster bombs; however, the acoustic damage from drone sorties is by no means contained, and thus radically expands their zone of impact upon human populations, with varying consequences for individual mental health as well as for the social dynamics of communities. "Drones have been circling over Manzar Khel for two or three years now. They are all my children can think about and they cannot concentrate on their studies or play carefree like children should."[31] The sonic bleed of a circling drone that one cannot necessarily see, but can hear, is a constant reminder that a deadly strike may come at any time quite literally out of the blue. Zubair Rehman, a 13-year-old Pakistani boy who survived the drone strike that killed his grandmother and injured his sister, testified in Congress with these poignant words: "I no longer love blue skies. In fact I now prefer cloudy days when the drones don't fly. When the sky brightens and becomes blue, the drones return and so does the fear. Children don't play so often now, and have stopped going to school. Education isn't possible as long as the drones circle overhead."[32]

Unremitting drone surveillance has created a widespread culture of fearful apprehension, to the extent that the sound of loitering drones triggers mental and bodily responses indicative of post-traumatic stress disorder in advance of a drone strike having actually taken place. "Anxiety is best conceptualized as a future-oriented cognitive-affective-somatic state, the prominent feature being a sense of uncontrollability focused on possible future threat, danger, or other upcoming, potentially negative events"[33] A drone strike that lurks in the future but whose effects are experienced in the present finds its disconcerting inversion in the now-banned US policy of "signature strikes," which was designed to eliminate potential terrorist threats before they became actualized on a future date. In his documentary film *Dirty Wars* (2013), investigative reporter and filmmaker Jeremy Scahill went so far as to suggest that the 2011 targeted assassination of radicalized cleric Anwar Al-Awlaki's teenage son in Yemen (both were born in the US) was carried out not because the boy *was* a terrorist, but rather because of the terrorist he might one day become. Questioned about the drone strike that killed 16-year-old Abdulrahman Al-Awlaki, former White House Press Secretary and senior adviser to President Obama's reelection campaign Robert Gibbs made the flippant rejoinder that the boy should have "had a more responsible father." The spatial dispersion of drone sound brings the future into the present as a felt effect, whereas drone vision is directed toward staving off a future event through targeted assassination. Together they conjoin to produce a state of continuous violence for civilian life under drones, one that categorically overturns President Obama's most recent assertion that drone warfare is a "war waged proportionally, in last resort, and in self-defense."

Flyover

During a CNBC interview in 2009, a determined fly kept buzzing around the President. "Get out of here," warned Obama in irritation, yet the insect brazenly persisted. When it finally landed on his forearm, he struck, killing it instantly. "That was pretty impressive, wasn't it? I got the sucker."[34]

6 DAMAGES

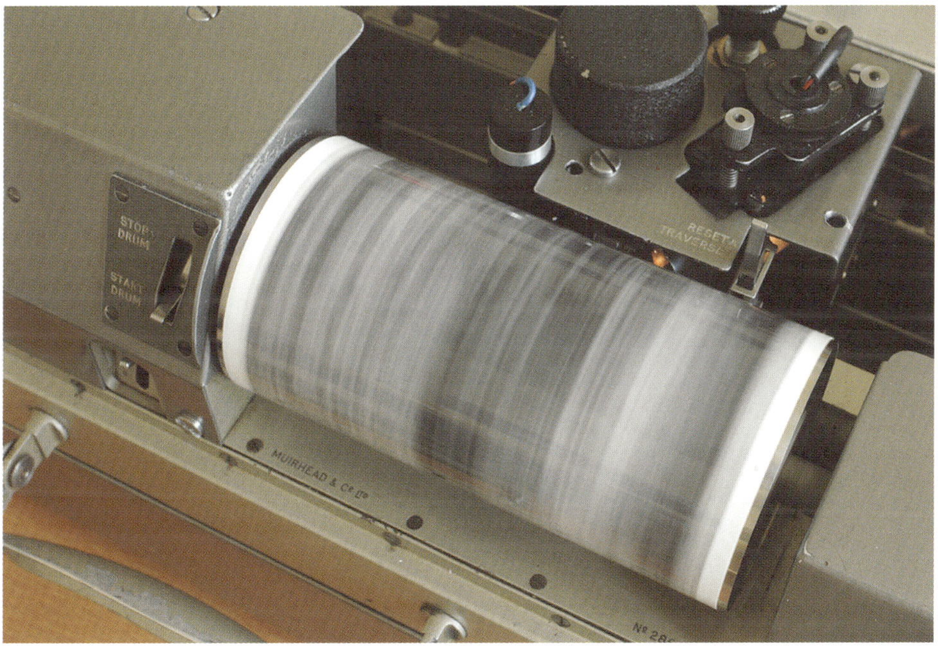

Figure 6.1
Muirhead Picture Transmitter in operation. Photo credit: Michael Ebert.

Signal Relays from Saigon

On June 8, 1972, the mechanical drum of a Muirhead K220 Picture Transmitter slowly rotated, scouring the surface of a 5-by-7-inch black-and-white photograph that had just been placed on its scanning drum. The machine's photoelectric cells were charged with the task of converting variations in the amount of light reflected by the print into a series of electronic pulses that could be transmitted, line by line, over a standard telephone relay system as radio waves. As the photograph revolved around the drum of the machine, the trace of another incandescence emerged: the residual glow of a napalm fireball that had just scorched the South Vietnamese village of Trang Bang, 30 miles northwest of Saigon. An air strike by two South Vietnamese Skyraiders from the South Vietnamese Army 25th Division had erroneously leveled the village in an attempt to dislodge a recent North Vietnamese roadblock on Route 1 near Trang Bang. During this action the 518 Squadron of the Vietnamese Air Force from Bien Hoa airbase near Saigon dropped explosives, white phosphorous bombs as well as napalm.[1] The anguish of Phan Thị Kim Phúc as she runs naked toward the camera of press corps photographer Huỳnh Công Út (Nick Ut) alongside other members of her family and villagers has been permanently seared into our collective cultural memory. "The girl was running, with her arms out. She was crying, 'Nong qua! Nong qua!' (Too hot! Too hot!). She had torn off all her clothes. When I saw she was burned, I dropped my camera beside the road. *I knew I had a good picture.* I got her into our van and took her and the family to the Cu Chi hospital."[2] In recalling this scene, Ut makes the prescient comment: "I knew I had a good picture." Yet, as this chapter will argue, such photo transmissions were subject to a sequence of technical translations that permitted extraneous information to enter at each point in the image event's conversion from captured sunlight to photographic grain into acoustic signals, resulting in the production of what might be considered damaged or "bad" pictures.

The image of Kim Phúc is one of the three most iconic and widely circulated photographs documenting the despair and violence of the Vietnam War, each of which garnered their respective photographers the coveted Pulitzer Prize for print journalism. The others are: Malcolm Browne's image of Buddhist monk Thích Quảng Đức's act of self-immolation in a busy Saigon intersection on June 16, 1963 (Đức was protesting the increased religious persecution by the American-backed regime of President Ngô Đình Diệm); and the shocking image of South Vietnamese General Nguyen Ngoc Loan executing a Viet Cong officer with a single shot to the head on February 1, 1968, taken by Eddie Adams. Although they are distinguished as singularly compelling images that crystallize the moral dimensions and political forces of the conflict, do

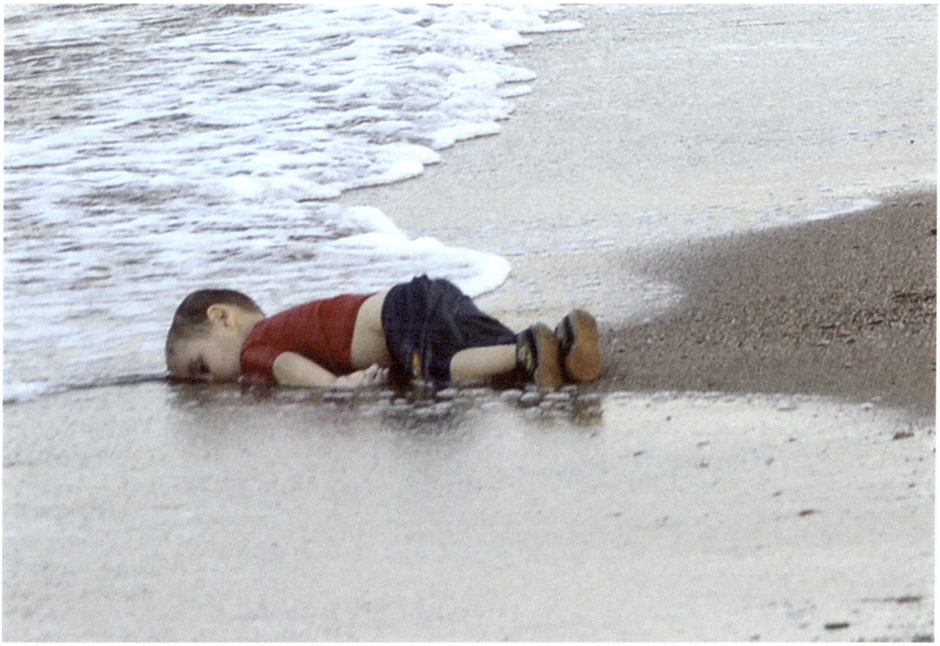

Figure 6.2
Aylan Kurdi, the drowned Syrian child who washed ashore in Turkey on September 2, 2015. Photo credit: Nilüfer Demir. Source: Dogan News Agency.

these photographs continue to operate as enduring visual proofs that can bear witness to the atrocities of the past, or does their iconic status intervene to moderate, and even cut, their affective flows? Has the proliferation of such crisis-bound images exhausted us by their empathic demands, or is our continued failure to act in the face of self-evident human misery the consequence of other forces and conditions? Today, similar examples can be drawn from across the shifting war zones of Syria and Iraq as fleeing refugees navigate the Mediterranean at great peril, or are left to suffer in the ruins of a city reduced to rubble.

The "sacrificial" image of Phúc provoked moral outrage in the US, and fueled public opposition to what was already an unpopular war. In developing a case study around this paradigmatic photograph, I am well aware of more recent theorizations that question the "putative power" of the image in the work of media theorists such as Thomas Keenan, who argues that disclosure of suffering is by no means contracted to the public sphere as a call to action or prompt for humanitarian intervention.[3] The "live" coverage of the genocidal violence that swept through Bosnia in the mid-1990s

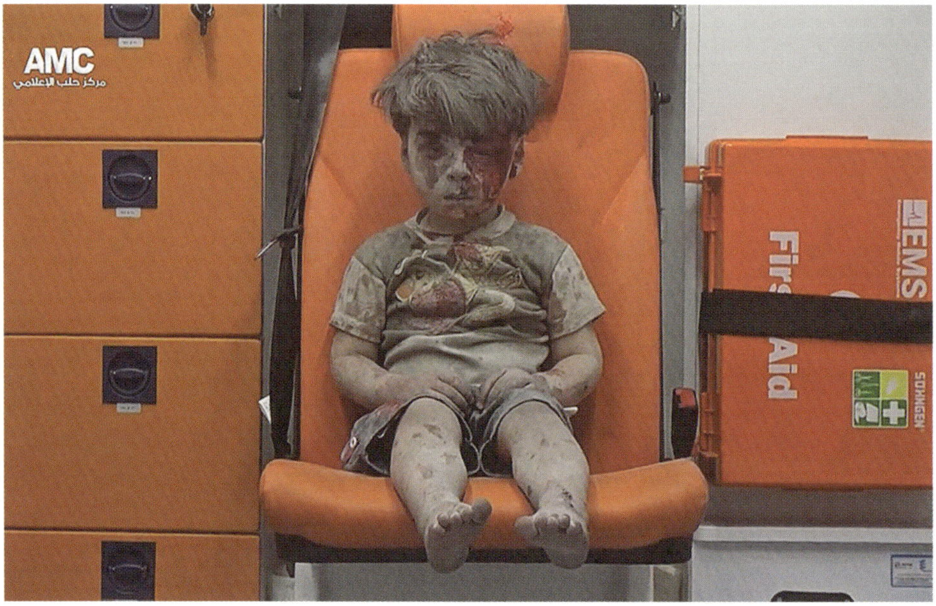

Figure 6.3
Video still of Omran Daqneesh, sitting in an ambulance after being pulled out of a building hit by a military airstrike in Aleppo on August 17, 2016. Source: Aleppo Media Center.

designates an infamous shift in screen theory as images brokered new alliances with perpetrators who committed atrocities in full view of TV cameras and crews, or indeed expressly for such cameras. Mass publicity had engendered indifference at best and willful disregard at worst. But Keenan's commentary is ultimately not an indictment of the potential of the image to act as a witness to a crime, but rather a concern that our faith in the Enlightenment concept of the public sphere might itself be misplaced.

> What is at stake is the program which expects that, as David Rieff puts it, "one more picture, or one more story, or one more correspondent's taped stand-up in front of a shelled, smoldering building would bring people around, would force them to stop shrugging their shoulders, or like the United Nations, blaming the victims"—one more picture would force something to happen—what if just that expectation about information and illumination was part of the problem?[4]

Keenan is questioning the "cherished" precept that knowledge is self-sufficient; that public disclosure of injustice—our collective confrontation with the truth of images streamed from contemporary conflict zones or, indeed, from urban contexts

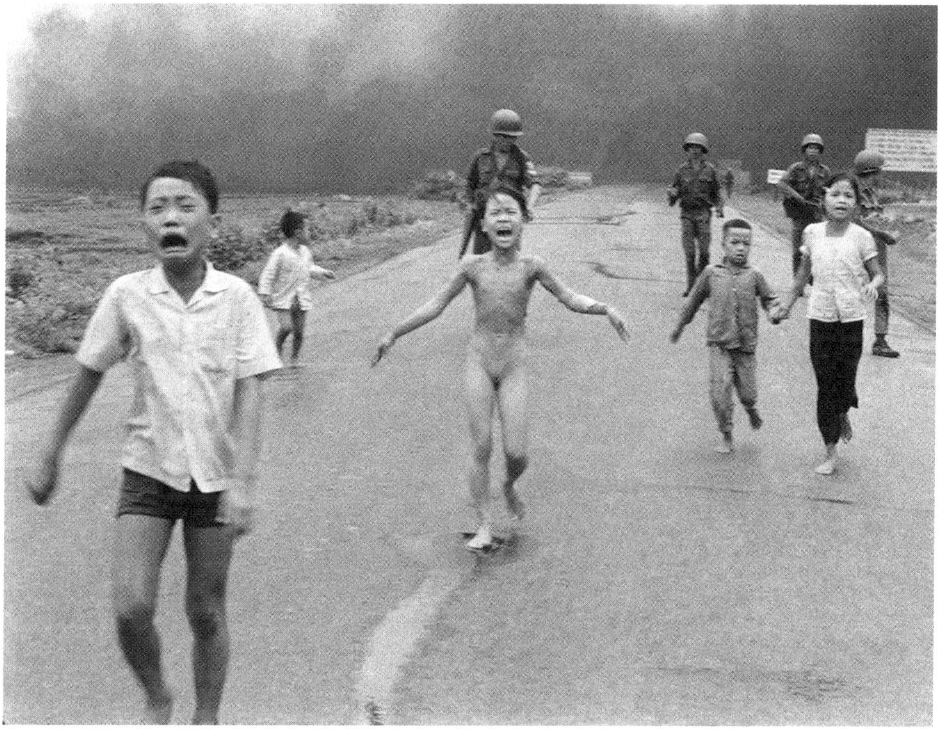

Figure 6.4
Accidental Napalm, image of Kim Phúc running from a napalm attack on June 8, 1972. Photo credit: Nick Ut. Source: AP/Press Association Images.

documenting the killing of unarmed black life—is wholly adequate for bringing about a transformative politics. But if, as he implies, our flawed faith in the cathartic power of the information that images yield has resulted in a kind of collective paralysis, should we be calling for a renewal of the concept of the public, or should we perhaps shift our attention from simply a concern for "making things public," which includes demands for accountability and transparency, to making things political?[5] That is to say: doing the considerable work that is required to establish links between images and events that operate across multiple scales, durations, and geographies: a strategy of cross-cutting between locations and temporalities that both enlarges the frame of reference and also reframes the iconic images that we have simply allocated to history. In suggesting that the live screen event is not naturally contracted to action by way of public exposure, Keenan uses the term "information" to refer to the rhetorical capacity of images to "out" wrongs: a choice that has direct, if unintended, stakes in the reflections I am presenting in this chapter *vis-à-vis* the informational enrichment of the image through its elaborated technical mediations.

Using a supplementary AM/FM converter, it took the Muirhead K220 Picture Transmitter exactly 14 minutes to transmit this record of the Vietnam War into history. "The radio conditions were favorable that day and the picture, along with three other photographs of the incident, reached the Tokyo photo bureau of the Associated Press. From Tokyo the radio signal coming from Saigon was auto-relayed on AP-controlled land and submarine wire communications circuits to New York and London, and from there to AP offices and newspapers around the world."[6] It was a transmission that would signal the infamy of an increasingly unpopular war to an American public in ways that only an image of a defenseless child seems able to fully enact. Images of children in situations of despair are particularly charged sites of symbolic transaction, as evidence of their extreme helplessness and dire muteness is forcefully reanimated by the media circuits in which their representations traffic to gain their political purchase and transfiguration into universalizing narratives. This produces an ethical struggle between images that "bruise the public eye"—pictures that confront viewers with the sheer visceral force of their representations—and the violence that is done to images through processes of mediation, which reduce embodied subjects to transactional objects.[7] Can photographs of distressed and dying children bestow on them the proper position of "personhood," as curator and critic Okwui Enwezor has asked in reference to another Pulitzer Prize-winning photograph of a desperate child, that of a struggling baby girl being preyed upon by a vulture during the Sudanese famine? Or will their "status," above all, be conditioned by their use value to the public discourses and institutions in which they acquire their traction and instrumental relevance?[8] These are some of the questions raised by Enwezor that this chapter seeks to unfold through an analysis that returns the technical operations of the picture transmitter, including its sonic materializations, to the image of Kim Phúc running from a napalm attack.

Eight Rolls of Kodak Film

By 1972, the year of Nick Ut's acclaimed photograph, almost all remaining American ground troops had been evacuated from Vietnam as peace talks resumed in Paris. Nonetheless, the American-led Air Force continued its bombing of Hanoi and various North Vietnamese targets such as Haiphong Harbor; all the while, Henry Kissinger, President Richard Nixon's then-Secretary of State, was secretly meeting with the North Vietnamese to negotiate a ceasefire. More than 388,000 metric tonnes of napalm were delivered over the course of the war, destroying and displacing untold thousands of people and incinerating 100,000 acres of Vietnam's forest ecologies.[9] On the day of the accidental napalm attack, Ut shot eight rolls of film using a German Leica camera manufactured in 1965, fitted with a Leitz wide-angle f/2 35mm Summicron lens. Whilst he was not the only photographer or journalist on the scene, it was decided that he would take the wounded girl to hospital prior to dropping off his film for development at the lab of the Saigon Associated Press Office. Network coverage of the war had substantially diminished, due in part to the closing of 11 Saigon-based newspapers in 1972 by the South Vietnamese Police, so competition between the remaining Saigon press bureaus (Associated Press and United Press International) was fierce. It was not without some reservations that Ut took time out of his filing deadline to find medical treatment for the girl in the city. Napalm is a flammable gasoline gel that burns at blistering temperatures of between 800 and 1,200 degrees Celsius, and clings to everything it comes into contact with. The attack left Kim Phúc with third-degree burns over 35 percent of her body, and led to 13 months of rehabilitation in a Saigon burn unit run by the Barsky Foundation, a children's medical relief agency.

Phúc survived the war, and in her teenage years she was rediscovered as the emblematic "girl in the picture" by the now-unified Socialist Republic of Vietnam, which regarded her as "living proof" of the carnage of imperialist intervention throughout Southeast Asia. Positioned as such, Phúc was frequently presented to foreign journalists eager to cover the aftermath of the war and report on the new socialist reality of Vietnam. In interviews she gave as an adult, Phúc maintains that she was victimized twice over: first by the West that caused her debilitating physical wounds (the South Vietnamese Air Force was controlled by US military strategy) and then by her own government, which inflicted emotional scars by using her as a *material witness* to war crimes committed against a civilian population. All the while her family was deliberately brutalized by ongoing poverty to prevent Phúc from defecting.[10] As long as she maintained her indexical relationship to that terrifying day in June, she would be of political and rhetorical use to the State. As the girl in the picture Phúc had become famous, a valuable resource far too precious to relinquish but also one whose photographic fate was sealed—permanently fixed through the chemistry of the image as well as by the ferocious chemistry of napalm whose toxic traces are recorded directly by her skin. Many years later, and now living in Toronto, Phúc was once again singled out by the lens of a camera, this time through a chance encounter with two British tabloid journalists who, in their moment of recognition, inflicted what Phúc equates to a kind of violent assault. "The accident of those two women [showing up] on the sidewalk," she lamented to Toan [her husband], "was like a bomb falling out of the sky."[11] Today

Phúc is an active advocate for the peace movement, but it is still the centrifugal force of that singular image taken in 1972 that secures her legitimacy to speak out on such matters: "I wanted to escape the picture because the more famous it got, the more it cost me my private life. It seemed to me that my picture would not let me go […] I realized that now that I have freedom and am in a free country, I can take control of that picture."[12] Unlike so many other victims of war depicted by photojournalists, Phúc did not remain nameless and voiceless.

Of the more than 240 negatives that Ut shot that day, three were selected for transmission and only one was singled out. In fact only 12 of these historic negatives still exist today, conserved within the AP archives, including Ut's prize-winning shot, which now circulates exclusively as a digital file. The originals are consigned to the vault in the hope that careful preservation will stave off the incursions of time that would enact further material violence upon the now historic violence preserved within the image.[13] Ut's iconic negative already carries a significant emulsive scar in the upper regions of the sky. The 240-plus exposures constitute a virtual archive from which any frame could have been selected and photographically printed, electronically scanned, and telephonically transmitted. As such, the remaining outtakes provide the background noise against which a singular artifact would emerge to achieve its emblematic status. But what was chosen, as worthy of record, is always the consequence of a deliberately selective process that reveals far more than any momentary capture induced by the snapping of the shutter. Horst Faas's decisive editorial choice, as head of AP's Saigon photo unit, provides us with a unique vantage point from which to consider the operations of this iconic photograph as it migrated through history. At the time of its publishing the photograph certainly catalyzed a series of transnational events—protests, discussions, controversies—with respect to the antiwar movement, US foreign policy, and increased North Vietnamese agitation and opposition to Western incursions into Southeast Asia.

Accidental Napalm finds its contemporary corollary within the digital image files flowing out of new war zones depicting civilian tragedies and a growing humanitarian crisis, exemplified by the images of Syrian children: Aylan Kurdi, whose lifeless body washed ashore in Turkey (2015) and Omran Daqneesh, who miraculously survived an airstrike in Aleppo (2016).[14] But recently, Ut's celebrated image ignited a somewhat different controversy when it was removed from social media accounts, including that of Norway's Prime Minister Erna Solberg, by the world's most powerful photo editor: Facebook—because of its depiction of child nudity. While Faas understood the power of Kim Phúc's photograph to speak directly to America's involvement in the war in Vietnam, and thus overrode AP's own prohibition against publishing images of naked

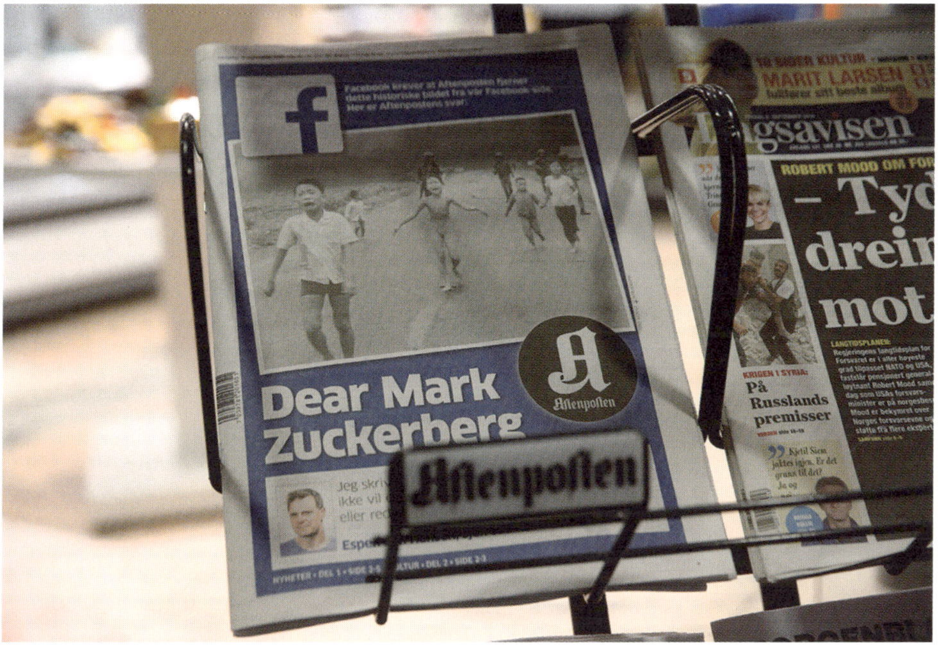

Figure 6.5
Cover of Norway's largest-circulation newspaper, *Aftenposten*, displayed in Oslo on Friday September 9, 2016. Editor-in-chief and CEO Espen Egil Hansen wrote an open letter to the founder and CEO of Facebook, Mark Zuckerberg, accusing him of threatening the freedom of speech and abusing power after deleting the iconic picture from the Vietnam War, taken by Associated Press photographer Nick Ut, of a young girl running from a napalm attack. Photo credit: Cornelius Pope. Source: AP/TT.

children, Facebook misconstrued the photograph as one that was gesturing toward child pornography.

> An image of a naked child would normally be presumed to violate our Community Standards, and in some countries might even qualify as child pornography. In this case, we recognize the history and global importance of this image in documenting a particular moment in time. Because of its status as an iconic image of historical importance, the value of permitting sharing outweighs the value of protecting the community by removal, so we have decided to reinstate the image on Facebook where we are aware it has been removed.[15]

In severing *Accidental Napalm* from its situated political context, the social media giant further disclosed its transition from a hosting site for user-generated content to a global news editor that actively and selectively makes and remakes the stories that we read. It also raised the specter of the company's outsourced "dirty" labor practices in which low-paid workers from desperately poor situations are contracted to view and screen all materials uploaded to Facebook by its users. Sarah T. Roberts, who researches the working environments of tech companies, says that these subcontracted services constitute some of "the most psychologically damaging digital work imaginable."[16] Content management decisions of Facebook posts are undertaken according to strict predetermined criteria, and at a relentless pace that would not allow any worker to reflect upon the contextual history of a given image even if they were aware of its particular relevance, nor indeed to bring their own judgment to bear upon the many horrific events they are forced to witness.

Muirhead K220 Picture Transmitter

The technical processing and transmission of what has become one of the most compelling images of the Vietnam War is detailed in the lengthy excerpt that follows. Given the manner in which digital images now appear in public seemingly unencumbered by the elaborate procedures and complex situations out of which they emerged, it is easy to overlook the extensive technical history that underwrites this analog photograph. With that in mind, what I wish to focus on in this chapter is not so much the politics of the war in Vietnam at the level of state actors, which implicitly brackets my discussion, but rather the micropolitical dimensions of image production that were conditioned by an aggregate field of causal relations operating across scales that would come to include human as well as nonhuman actors. Breaking apart the perceived chain of symmetries between translating practices that organize information as it moves from its eventful capture at the scene of a crime to its recomposition within a pictorial field challenges not only the cartographic claims central to photography's theoretical history as constituted by relations between the apparatus and photographic situation, but also the evidential capacities of images themselves. In these processes of informatic exchange, extraneous information or noise enters into the system at each nodal point in the image's emergence, whether analog or digital, and thus forces us to think about the event of photography as an expanded field of operative relationships. The following excerpt begins to make explicit the many technical variables and vagaries that were already in play prior to the photograph of Kim Phúc being placed on the scanning drum of the Muirhead K220 Picture Transmitter.

> Nick Ut's eight rolls of Kodak 400 ASA black and white films were developed in the lab of the Saigon AP office by the Japanese photographer Ishizaki Jackson, a known AP Tokyo news photographer at this time. The development solutions (Ilford Microfen developer and self-mixed fixative) were stored in large food jars. Since the temperatures of the chemicals were rarely

> below 30 degrees centigrade the processing time was relatively short and the film had to be slowly moved at all times, by hand, like slow motion laundering. The films were then dried in a special cabinet with hairdryers rigged up and switched in a way as not to damage the swelling emulsion.
>
> Nick and Ishizaki prepared a selection of eight 5 x 7 inch prints for the next "radio photo cast" at 5 PM—but an editor at the AP rejected the photo of Kim Phúc running down the road without clothing because it showed frontal nudity. Pictures of nudes of all ages and sexes, and especially frontal views were an absolute no-no at the Associated Press in 1972. While the argument went on in the AP bureau, writer Peter Arnett and Horst Faas, then head of the Saigon photo department, came back from an assignment. Horst argued by telex with the New York head-office that an exception must be made, with the compromise that no close-up of the girl Kim Phúc alone would be transmitted.
>
> AP had this equipment stationed next to the switchboard at the Saigon PTT's (Post and Telegraph) telephone exchange in Saigon. The radio conditions were favourable that day and the picture, along with three other photographs of the incident reached the Tokyo photo bureau of the Associated Press. From Tokyo the radio signal coming from Saigon was auto-relayed on AP controlled land and submarine wire communications circuits to New York and London, and from there to AP offices and newspapers around the world.[17]

During the Vietnam War, urgent news photos such as that taken by Ut were usually sent by shortwave radio transmitters, a process that was relatively expedient, taking on average only 12 minutes to scan and send each image. In translating an analog visual representation—a continuous tone photographic print—into quantitative acoustic data or electrical impulses, the Muirhead performed some of the fundamental operations that also govern the regime of the digital. It began by moving haptically across the photographic print as it rotated around the scanning drum of the transmitter, exploring its surface grain by grain while the syncopated firing of its photoelectric cells measured tonal variations to create an overall image map. By calculating the relative intensity of each grain's luminescence, and then calibrating the machine to send out a sequence of discrete audio signals that map the exact distribution, location, and gradient levels of the image's original data, the material properties of the photographic object were transformed into a set of mathematically derived calculations; a form of analog computation that converted image matter into signals rather than into code. World War II cryptographers spoke in similarly forensic terms when describing their meticulous accounts of decoding aerial reconnaissance photography, a process now largely assumed by adaptive image analysis software. These early cryptanalysts literally had to plunge into the depths of the photographic image, probing each variable grain that was suspended in the print's emulsion in order to bring particularities and patterns to the surface that could then be compared with earlier imagery of the same site. In *War in the Age of Intelligent Machines*, Manuel DeLanda described one such scene as follows:

"After 'resurfacing' from extracting data from an image, the photo-analyst must then organize that data into patterns from which further inferences and extrapolations can be made."[18] The photograph in these accounts becomes a subterranean geology comprised of silver halide crystals suspended in a gelatin bedrock that the cryptographer mines for information.

However, these forensic modes of image exploration and information extraction are not guided by reference to a bounding frame or the edge of a visual field; they therefore always risk a fall into the abyss, that is to say, into the space beyond representation: confusing the topographic coordinates of a territory internal to the image with the unknown volumetric space outside its structuring parameters. This misperception occurs when an image is pressed up so closely to our eyes, or to the optical receptors of a scanner, that we can never know with certainty when we will reach the edge of the print or the brink of image data. It is not insignificant that the Muirhead's scanning procedures always recovered more information than that specifically delimited by the frame. In automatically extending the boundary of the photograph (the area to be scanned) the machine ensured that the image was never inadvertently cut or cropped. This blurred the threshold between the representational space of the image and the abstract spatial conditions bordering the print. Not only did this increase the statistical possibility of extraneous information entering into the reassembly of its image data, but as an automated function of the machine, overscanning returned "uncertainty" to the translating procedure in that the machine was never entirely certain where the actual image began and ended.

Although the print introduced into the circuits of the Muirhead Picture Transmitter was, in photographic terms, an indexical image that bore direct witness to a real event, its transit through the mediating apparatuses of the camera, darkroom, transmitter, and printing press repeatedly decoded and recoded the image at the micro-scale of its technical assembly. Media theorist John Johnston, in borrowing and extending the concept of the "machinic" developed by Deleuze and Guattari, refers to this program of decoding and recoding as a form of "machinic vision" that "presupposes not only an environment of interacting machines and human-machine systems but a field of decoded perceptions that, whether or not produced by or issuing from these machines, assume their full intelligibility only in relation to them … machinic vision is not so much a simple seeing with or by machines—although it does presuppose this—as it is a decoded seeing, a becoming of perception in relation to machines that necessarily also involves a recoding."[19] The telephonic transmission of the image of Phúc required the conversion of vision into sound, a transmutation of the photographic body in which the ear/scanning drum of the transmitter sees what the camera's eye has already heard.

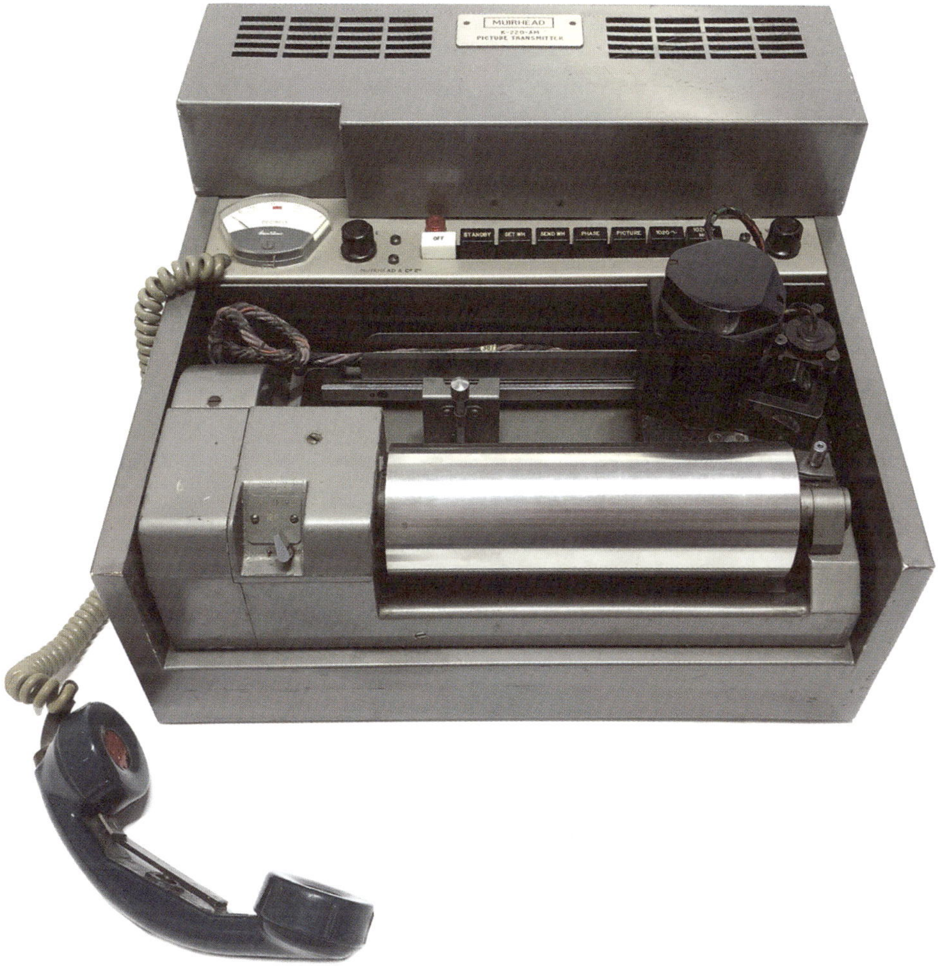

Figure 6.6
Muirhead K220 Picture Transmitter in the collection of the author. Photo credit: Susan Schuppli.

The picture transmitter is a paradigmatic machine in this regard, one that exemplifies corporeal confusion, but also gestures toward the program of digital convergence that would come to unite the technical operations of human sensing in contemporary media delivery systems such as augmented reality.[20] Ultimately, the photographic print that entered into the rotating scanning drum of the Muirhead K220 was not the same representation that exited via telephonic AP transmission, but an overencoded media object and supplement to the originary historic event it indexed. Moreover, the negative originally selected and printed by Ut and Jackson was already the product of a series of alchemical exchanges, beginning with the flesh of Phúc herself, which was radically transformed by the incendiary gel of napalm that continues to exert its influence deep within the subcutaneous layers of her body. Without open pores to modulate her internal temperature in areas of scarring, a seemingly alien force moves within that pushes at the body's frontiers, causing ongoing pain and swelling. At each point in the translation from the living body of Phúc, through the framing device of the camera, the exposure of the film's emulsive surface, the developing and printing of the photograph in the darkroom, and finally to its scanning, signal relay, and reassembly, minute variations and extraneous noise entered into the process, producing a surfeit of information that also multiplied its indexicality across the various domains of its transformation. Because the *material witness* is concerned not with representation *per se*, but with the registration of external events, the index is always assumed to be a distributed property of the media object, and so only ever functions as a form of inferential evidence, or a "partial print" signifying that something did indeed happen at that juncture in its processing. It has no comprehensive or totalizing role to play in our understanding of events. Media theorist Ariella Azoulay has made a related point in stressing that the photograph (properly conceived) can only ever register that "something happened" in a certain place, but cannot account for the complexity of conditions that enabled the emergence of such an image event.[21]

The transmissional regime of *Accidental Napalm* also complicates its iconic singularity, by opening up the picture to its material entanglement with the many other images that were sent by AP's equipment in the Saigon PTT at one time or another to be recomposited in New York. Unless it was cleaned continuously, the scanning drum of the transmitter would almost certainly have carried residual traces from previous transmissions. Given that the transit of each photographic print through the workings of the machine resulted in the deposition of minute paper fibers, speculation suggests that the accumulation of artifactual debris from each scan would eventually recombine with every subsequent image transmitted over time, thereby progressively enriching the informational quotient of all images that passed through the machine. The

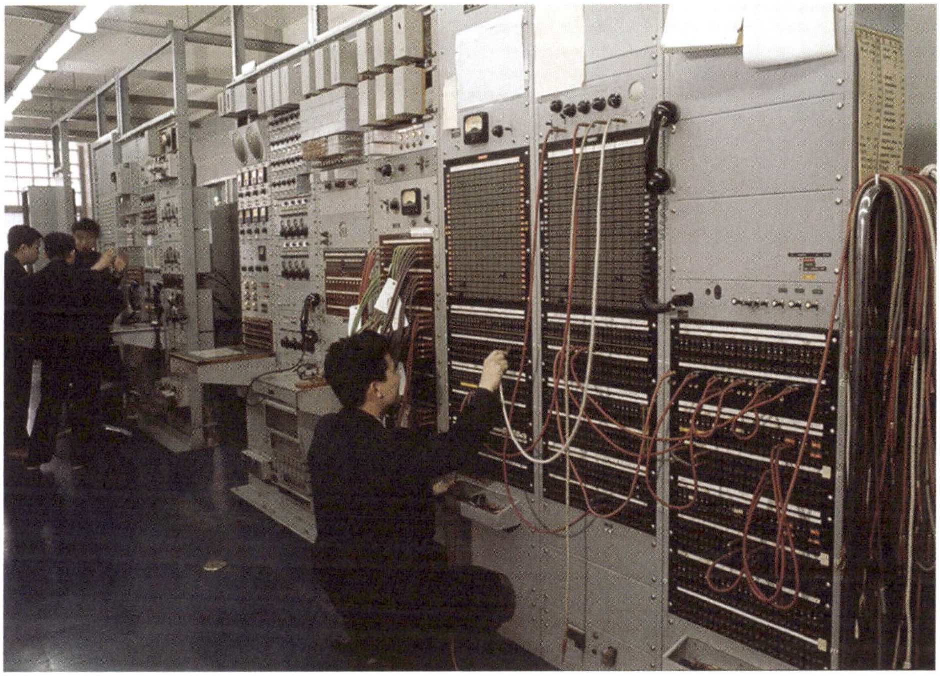

Figure 6.7
Vietnamese postal worker preparing to send photo by wire, Saigon Post Office, early 1970s. Source: Dateline-Saigon/AP Corporate Archives.

Muirhead was, in effect, transformed into a virtual transmitting device in which all of the conflict imagery that had already coiled around its scanning drum, as well as that which was yet to come, might eventually aggregate to express itself collectively. Freed from the indexical demand to account for events solely at the level of content, the recombinant image of *Accidental Napalm* should theoretically be able to forge relations of significance across scales of assembly from the interference patterns of extraneous events to the macro scale of culture.

Atmospheric Noise

The radio waves emitted by these early transmitting devices were subject to many unpredictable elements including the consistency of their fluctuating electronic current and, perhaps even more significantly, the stability of meteorological systems and relative degree of atmospheric noise. While the Muirhead Picture Transmitter was designed to reassemble its image data according to predetermined patterning sequences, the potential for signal relay complications due to interference from inclement weather, radio chatter, or overloaded telecommunications lines and cables was not infrequent. Consequently, the information sent was not necessarily contiguous with the information received. When atmospheric events feed physical phenomena such as electrical surges from storms back into the image-making process, they can interrupt the integrity of the radio transmission. Such tampering at the level of signal relay is a form of machinic deviance that introduces change into the dataset and can expresses itself within the technical reassembly of an image, albeit inflicting various degrees of damage from intangible to considerable. In chapter 4, "Hearsay," I briefly discussed the ways in which audio forensics is mapping the micromodulations of the electrical frequencies of the grid or mains hum here in the UK to produce a geolocatable timestamp for the entire country. The same principle is at work here, in that minute variations in electrical pulse would, in effect, become part of the image regime, and would thus recode each image at the level of signal relay. And while the introduction of such atmospheric noise would not be differentiated by the machine that eventually recomposited the image at the office of the *New York Times*, all photographs sent from Vietnam via picture transmitter were composite recordings of multiple inscriptive events. Paul Virilio quotes a US fighter pilot, Colonel Broughton, who experienced similar transmission difficulties in Vietnam as radio chatter and rough weather cluttered the airwaves, making communication highly unreliable and increasing the risk of payload miscalculations, often with tragic consequences.

> The radio chatter was really picking up about this time—in fact, it was so dense with all the Mig and Sam warnings and everyone shouting directions and commands that it was almost impossible to interpret what was going on. This is a real problem and once it starts, it just keeps getting worse and worse and is almost impossible to stop … you see something that you know you have to tell other people about in a desperate hurry to protect them and to protect yourself, and the temptation is to blurt out as quickly as possible without using the proper call sign. The result is that everyone in the air immediately gets a shot of confusion and wonders who is talking about whom … you have no idea where you are.[22]

Within the history of information theory, the work of mathematician and cryptographer Claude Shannon remains key. "For Shannon, the issue was not about communicating significance or meaning, but simply about optimizing the signal-to-noise ratio in message transmission. Shannon measured information as inversely proportional to the probability of a signal reaching its receiver, and its quality in this formulation is determined by message length, complexity, and signal integrity."[23] While he explicitly evacuated rhetorical content from transmission, Shannon conceded that the conditions governing the relay of information, its susceptibility to interference, actively contributed to its own refashioning. This case study and chapter argue that informatic transmission, which was achieved internally through the scanning procedures of the Muirhead and modified externally through atmospheric channels and radio frequencies, was at every moment subject to micromodulation. Attentiveness to the contingencies of transmission as consequential, as an index of the complex material entanglements that preside over the intelligibility of images such as *Accidental Napalm*, converts unforeseen events into the enabling conditions which give rise to the *material witness*. Fellow mathematician Norbert Wiener called such deviations in transmission "noise," which he regarded as detrimental to the probability function of message relay, and equated with entropy (a measure of randomness).[24] Wiener insisted that information control was necessary to maintaining the stability of signaling regimes, which were continually under threat by the disorderly conduct of noise. The more the flow of information could be controlled within a given system through feedback, the less entropy. For Shannon, on the other hand, everything coming through the channel was information, including noise.

According to Warren Weaver, who coauthored aspects of Shannon's information theory, mutations in the transmission of the message are not antagonistic but crucial if systems are to evolve in new directions. This idea is particularly relevant with respect to the informatic transmissions of the Muirhead and its capacity to machine new image events. "Mutations normally occur when some random event (for example, a burst of radiation or a coding error) disrupts an existing pattern and something else is put in its place instead. … The randomness to which the mutation testifies is implicit in the very idea of pattern, for only against the background of non-pattern can pattern emerge."[25] Gregory Bateson reworked these ideas two decades later in *Further Steps to an Ecology of Mind* (1972), arguing that the more unlikely or random the event, the more information it contains. For example, to say that it is raining in London is not as informationally rich as saying it is snowing in Saigon. The quantity of information a message contains is directly proportionate to the amount of difference it communicates.[26] This is called a "surprisal," and it holds out much expressive potential for my work, because it stresses the "anomalous" as the indicative locus of evidence.

When weather systems such as lightning storms, which result from the electrical discharge of electrons, enter into a technical feedback loop with the signal transmissions of the machine, they become coterminous with it. That is to say: a thundershower or other natural event could be regarded as a vital force in the generative recomposition of images coming out of the war zones of Vietnam, such as Ut's *Accidental Napalm*. And while evidence of these electrical mediations—atmospheric damage caused to picture files in transit—are imperceptible to the human eye when presented with the reconstituted image, the mere fact of their existence reminds us that information, just like biological life, is always subject to the dynamism of external events. In "The Task of the Translator," Walter Benjamin emphasizes the crucial role that translations play in the afterlives of works, stressing that *his* is an "unmetaphorical" attribution of the concept of life to nonbiological entities: "Even in times of narrowly prejudiced thought, there was an inkling that life was not limited to organic corporeality. [...] The concept of life is given its due only if everything that has a history of its own, and is not merely the setting for history, is credited with life."[27] Translations are transmissions of previous events as well as the means by which originals are sustained, modified, and supplemented in the present. The mistranslation of the historic significance of *Accidental Napalm* by Facebook, Inc. is part of the afterlife of the original image.

Despite being sent during the height of the rainy season, the "radio conditions were favourable that day," and atmospheric disturbances at a minimum. But had the weather been inclement on June 8, 1972, might I be writing about an altogether different photograph? Every day of war in Vietnam saw the production of thousands of photographic negatives from which an editor might select and scan only a few. Indeed, the material remainder of Ut's more than 239 negatives, most of which have now vanished, are also part of this virtual archive, a repository of potential witnesses lying in wait for that moment when they might yet be called forth to testify. Such a surplus prompts one to reflect upon the ways in which we might repoliticize the testimonial traces of images that are forgotten, lost, or were never selected for their transmission into history, and thus exist solely within the register of the virtual.[28] Although the sonic transmissions from Saigon to Tokyo were met with minimal interference from weather or congested air waves on that particular day, when the radio signals arrived in New York and were reassembled back into a photographic image and printed on the cover of the *New York Times*, the political atmosphere was immediately recharged.

Sound Effects

Accidental Napalm was received as a kind of collective body blow: an impact upon the retina of a viewing public that immediately rewired its carnal receptors. Eyes turned into angered speech further condemning the war, and ears into vision haunted by the silent screams of fleeing villagers amidst the sounds of dropping bombs. While the "aural trace" is generally weak within the register of the photographic, the auditory impacts of this image were equal to its powerful visuality.[29] It was as if the machine itself both saw and heard the horror of the attack, and channeled these reverberations

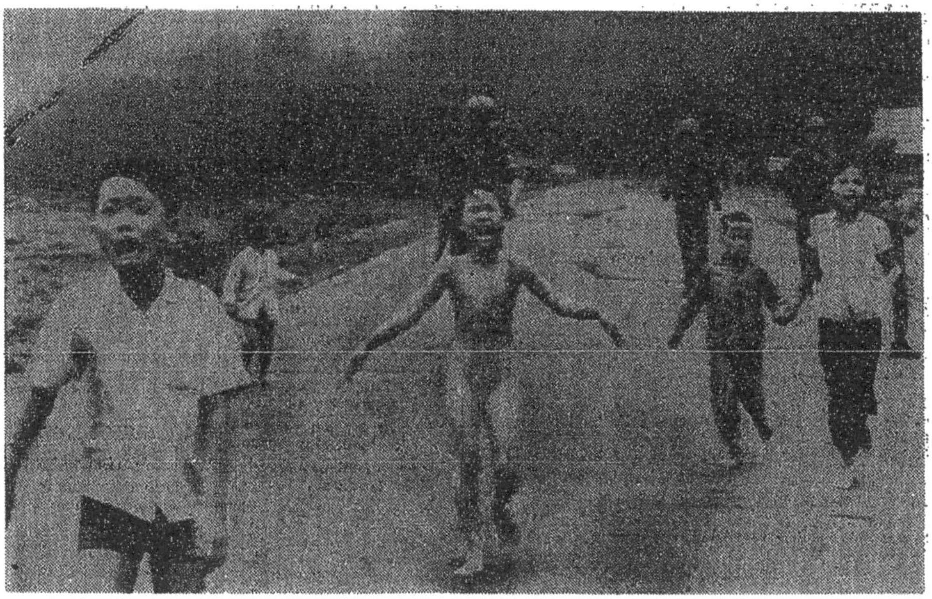

Associated Press

ACCIDENTAL NAPALM ATTACK: South Vietnamese children and soldiers fleeing Trangbang on Route 1 after a South Vietnamese Skyraider dropped bomb. The girl at center has torn off burning clothes. Details on Page 9.

Figure 6.8
Cover of the *New York Times*, June 9, 1972. Source: The New York Times.

through the transmitter into the body public. While sound is implicitly represented in the gaping open mouth of the little girl as she tries to flee the engulfing firestorm, her missing voice was repatriated by the Muirhead as the generative force by which the photograph was to achieve its public coherency—namely, through its telephonic relay as radio waves that would eventually recompose themselves into an image. The photograph of Phúc was converted into acoustic information, but this was not a process that would restore her original speech acts, her anguished cries, but rather a machinic deterritorialization that further accentuated the breach between the event and its electronic mediation. Yet the affective residue of Phúc's voice manages, in its photographic stillness, to register across different domains to generate the acoustic presence of terror. Somehow, newspaper readers around the world were able to access the sonic virtualities latent in the image and actualize them as felt sound effects within their own bodies, inducing a renewed consciousness upon which they, in turn, began to act. In *No Caption Needed*, authors Hariman and Lucaites have argued that this "iconic photo was capable of activating public conscience at the time because it provided an embodied transcription of important features of moral life, including pain, fragmentation, nodal relationships amongst strangers, betrayal, and trauma."[30] Even Nixon acknowledged the power of the photograph to incite public anger and fuel domestic opposition to the war. In an illicit tape recording made on June 12, 1972, but released publicly only on February 14, 2002, the President can be heard callously questioning the authenticity of a photograph of fleeing Vietnamese children burnt by napalm: "I'm wondering if that was fixed?" His White House Chief of Staff, H. R. Haldeman, replies: "Could have been."[31] While Nixon is obviously referring to the possibility of the image having been deliberately doctored, or the scene set up to produce an antiwar narrative, the photo was not in fact completely "fixed," as I have suggested. Through an understanding of the technical processing of the image, its muteness is transformed into a kind of noise that can reamplify our contemporary cultural imaginaries as concerns this now historic event. Because of the familiarity of Kim Phúc's image as a visual icon, the intensity of the sensation felt in 1972 as a bruising of the collective public eye is perhaps no longer fully operative, repetition having engendered a certain image ennui. If we are to tease any residual affect out of the image, we may need to activate its other virtualities, such as its technical origins in sound. This is the implicit ontological provocation raised by the Muirhead, which is after all a machine for scoring images and visualizing sounds, one that asks us to listen to the virtual compositions of the picture. Not a cancellation of the human voice that is contracted to the image but, rather, a "freeing" of sound, as Jacques Attali has suggested, that also allows it to prospectively entangle itself with other events. It is this activity of visual decoding and acoustic recoding of the image that also yields the possibilities for Phúc to renarrate her own story and slowly step out of the picture frame in which she has been imprisoned these past 40-plus years.

By contrast, documentary footage capturing the same napalm attack inserts the actual sound of the air strike directly into the visual field of the image, where it is experienced in its immediacy. The connection of documentary recordings to the virtual are, in this regard, very "weak," because their authority rests on their ability to fix the event indelibly in time and space, leaving little in the way of residual affects to be repotentialized in the future.[32] In the broadcast news coverage it is the screeching sounds of the falling bombs that dominate the image track. Here the voice of Phúc is not so much silent as rendered inaudible because of the massive sonic attack of exploding napalm. News of a possible air strike had been circulated in advance, and reporters were dutifully dispatched from Saigon to cover the unfolding action. As the first napalm flares ricocheted off the ground, creating bilious clouds of dense black smoke, a soldier with his camera turned toward the bombing is seen standing in the middle of the road in anticipation. Out of this smoldering inferno a group of Vietnamese villagers run

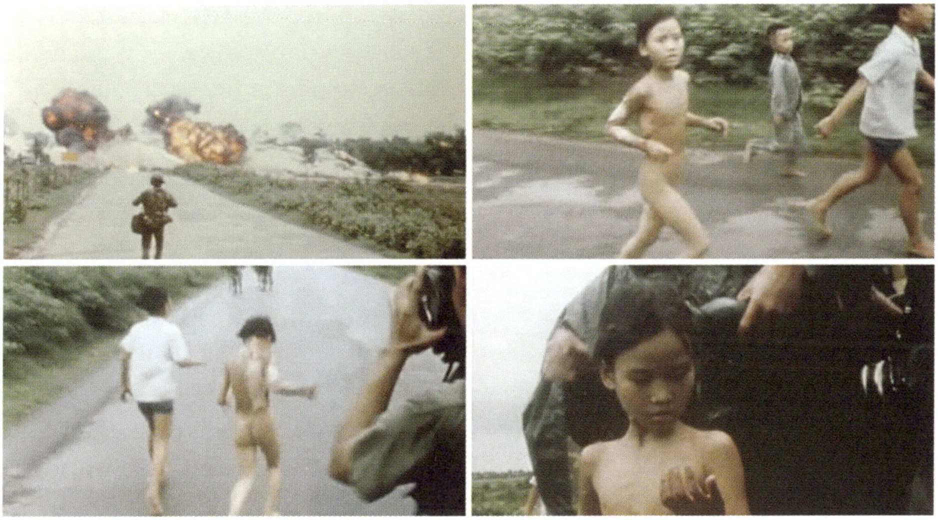

Figure 6.9
Film stills from the television broadcast of Kim Phúc and the accidental napalm bombing of June 8, 1972. From *Hearts and Minds*, Peter Davis, 1974, documentary film, 112 minutes. Source: BBS Productions.

screaming. One young girl is entirely naked, and as she passes the cameraman we can see ragged sections of her charred skin flaking off as she runs. Her eyes and those of the other fleeing children flicker briefly toward this photographer, indicating that they are aware of his curious presence, but then quickly return to the road in front of them as they continue to run. Eventually the girl comes to a stop, and two watching soldiers empty their canteens of water across her back to dowse the chemical burns.

This film footage makes explicit the various roles that the theater of operations known as war assigns to each of its actors in its diegetic unfolding. Even the victim, it suggests, has an *a priori* role to play. As if on cue, Phúc and the villagers emerge out of the exploding backdrop to run toward the waiting soldiers and a photographer, who is able to shoot a remarkable 240 frames, one of which will become singularly significant. Yet within the flow of moving images, the visceral charge of any single frame is diffused throughout the entire sequence. Because we are given access to the moments that both preceded and followed the iconic image event, the distilled emotions of the single black-and-white photograph are reframed as an extensive series of events, which includes the photographers who are on assignment doing their job. This perfunctory and predatory dimension of journalism—14 photographers waiting with their cameras directed toward an impending napalm attack—is perhaps as disturbing an evidential capture of the horrors of war as that of the unmediated terror of Kim Phúc herself. Moreover, in the photographic still, the subject is universalized—the girl in the picture—and the photographer is conspicuously missing from the scene, an absence that arguably intensifies the visual hold of the still image over the viewer. This transparency around the scene of image production stands in stark contrast to the broadcast news footage, which reveals the media infrastructure of conflict.

In the tradition of documentary photography, those on the threshold of death are always pictured in desperate need of the intercessions of an external agent that will relieve their anguish and attend to their dire conditions.[33] Ut's iconic photograph testifies to this perceived state of vulnerability, which is all the more poignant because it is located within the representation of a child who is already coded as defenseless. Only through photographic mediation, argues Enwezor, can these subjects seemingly be brought back from the brink of death, a situation that confers on the photographer the power of giving "life."[34] Yet, over the years, even those evidential dimensions that had initially ignited moral outrage with respect to US involvement in the war in Vietnam dissipated as the photograph transitioned from media circuits to art galleries. When I first discovered that the photograph of Kim Phúc, which had materialized in our collective consciousness in June 1972, was actually transmitted via radio waves, the image was forcefully reanimated for me in an entirely new way. Through the sonic register I was able to access the affective and virtual dimensions of an event that had long perished. Perhaps the mute acoustics of the photograph, with its pictured cries of anguish, should already have alerted me to its eventful genesis in sound.

Transmission Time

Throughout the period of writing up this case, I have confronted the question of relevance: specifically why these now well-rehearsed photographic artifacts should still matter, and what their significance might be for reflecting upon media operations today. An anachronistic and cumbersome machine like the Muirhead K220 Picture Transmitter seems, no doubt, like an object of mere historical curiosity rather than one that is prescient for our times. Indeed, what contemporary conjunction is opened up in the larger field of politics through careful consideration of this machine and its technical provocations? One way to respond to this question is by "staying with the temporal trouble" of the analog machine, as Donna Haraway might posit. Our present digital era entered into a feedback loop with its analog precursors at the constitutive moment when the Muirhead converted a continuous tone photograph into a series of discrete electrical impulses: a technical sleight of hand that not only anticipated contemporary digital systems but also gestured toward the immediacy with which such crisis-born images would be created and transmitted in the future. However, due to the extreme velocity and intensive computation of our contemporary digital devices, in which convergence creates the appearance that all relations are temporally synchronous and spatially contiguous, an important understanding of machinic processes as staging a series of translations between incommensurate entities and events appears to have been lost. Information seemingly performs itself as a closed circuit between transmission and event. "A photograph appears to be self-generated—as though it had created itself."[35] When photo theorist Abigail Solomon-Godeau made this remark in 1991, she had yet to confront the ways in which computational power would exacerbate this condition to eviscerate the temporality of the image. Increasingly, only the spinning animation of the "throbber" indicating background computer activity or the download progress bar gives us humans any access to time in these virtual domains. Yet near-instantaneous feedback between the image event and its public mediation complicates the time that may be needed for critical reflection. The immediacy of the digital can induce a reactive mode in which the procedures of "click and send" sometimes fire all too quickly, even though there are many examples where the quick turnaround time between information that is captured at the scene, distributed, analyzed, and recirculated has enabled investigative digital journalism to respond to a crisis in what is effectively real time.

Mine is not an attempt to privilege the time of human cognition as the sole means by which a material politics can be unfolded and made intelligible. Quite the contrary, as much work has been done to highlight the role of machinic processes throughout my case studies. Rather, it is an effort to develop a research methodology whereby we can consider the ontologies of input and output as progressively entangled across multiple temporal scales. This takes time. The Muirhead was to some degree a machine for delaying time, as each photographic object that entered its scanning drum to exit as a sound event was transmitted *over time*. Intervals are crucial for understanding how elongated temporalities might open up a much-needed space of reflection and conceptualization that seems to be largely unavailable to the regimen of temporal compression characteristic of contemporary computational processes, even though it is all relative to the specific entity for whom a certain timescale matters. Forensic Architecture's 2018 presentation at Tate Britain, "The Long Duration of a Split-Second," offers a useful example of the ways in which the contraction and expansion of time becomes a political act that one must learn to read.[36] The space of elongated transmission has certainly allowed me to work my materials forensically to probe the evidential encodings latent within the noisy image printed on the cover of the *New York Times*; an aesthetic condition which raises the real possibility that extraneous events might have folded themselves into its processing and transmission. Walter Benjamin's musings on the penetrating saturation of history into the image (the pure presence of the scene) by virtue of the elongated exposures required by early photographic techniques also come to mind here. Outmoded technologies like the Muirhead K220 Picture Transmitter playback histories in slow motion, allowing us to grasp the thresholds of their machinic processes. What the preceding discussion has tried to explicate are the distinctive attributes that characterize the Muirhead's operations, so that we can better understand the ways in which certain events come into being through the transmissional programs of technology. The Muirhead exposes the manner of these entanglements as a multiplicity of separate but aggregating processes, each of which is subject to its own unique temporal duration. Some events, such as my analysis, may come into being only long after the machines that captured, transmitted, and composed the initial event have disappeared into the twilight of their technical obsolescence, while others remain fully virtual, waiting to be rematerialized at some future date.

As "the girl in the picture," Kim Phúc seemed forever archived by her chemical exposures to the past, evidenced both by her painful scars that continue to recall the napalm attack and by the photographic embalmment that fixes her permanently within the image event. "Although the activity within the frame directs the action, the fact that this is a photograph—a 'static' image—means that time has stopped. The picture holds its experience of terror and uncompleted action for all time, while having the activity within the frame eternally repeat itself."[37] Rather than reducing her to a static representation that can only ever offer contingent historic testimony, shifting our attention to the processing of the machine, in particular its acoustic interface across global geographies, enables our forensic imagination to activate other narrative futures for the image. In doing so we begin to produce the conditions of renewal whereby Kim Phúc, too, might finally be released from her singular story.

7 TOXIC TORT

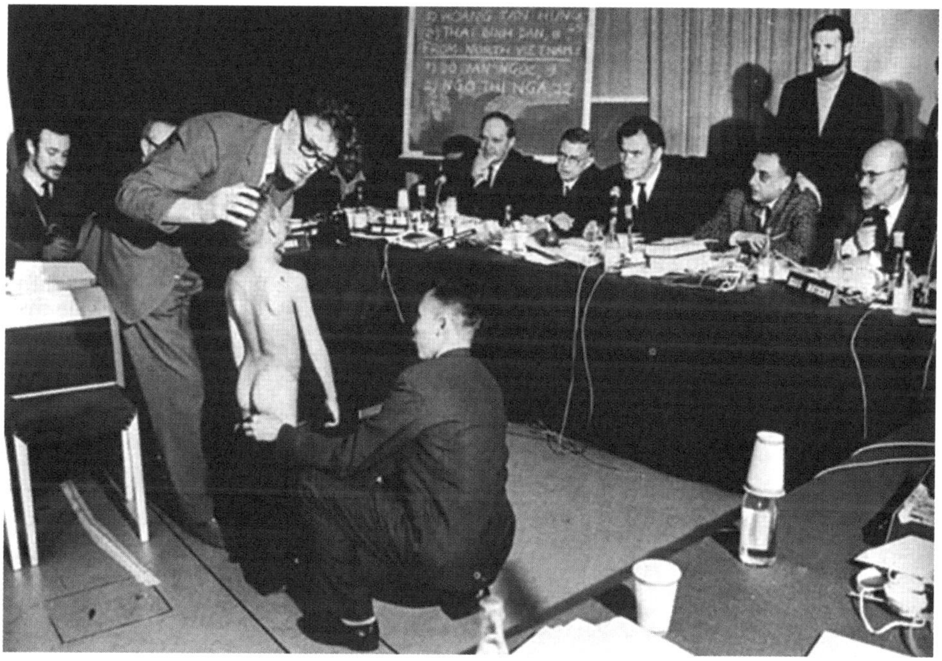

Figure 7.1
Nine-year-old DoVan Ngoc exhibits injuries from napalm in Vietnam to the Russell Tribunal in Stockholm, 1967. Photo credit: Carl-Adam Nycop.

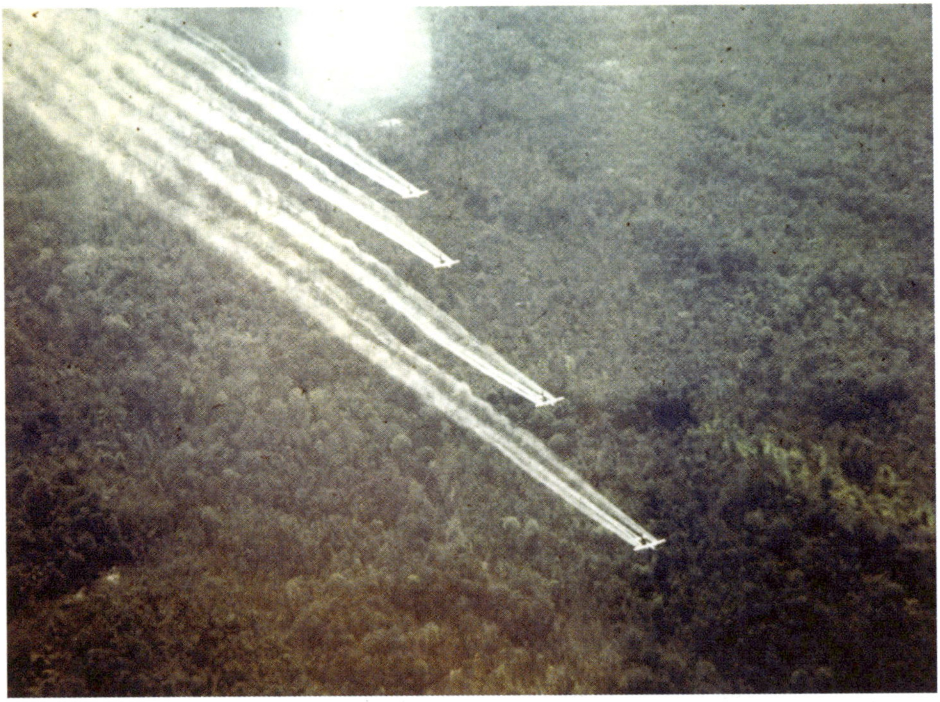

Figure 7.2
Defoliant spray run, part of Operation Ranch Hand, during the Vietnam War, by UC-123B Provider aircraft. Source: National Museum of the US Air Force photo 071002-F-1234P-022.

Verdicts on Vietnam

As a direct consequence of the Vietnam War, two unique forums emerged: the International War Crimes Tribunal (IWCT) convened by philosopher Bertrand Russell in 1966–1967 to determine whether the US was committing war crimes in Vietnam as part of their overall military strategy; and the Agent Orange Trial initiated by returning US Veterans in 1978 over adverse health effects which, they claimed, were caused by the widespread use of rainbow herbicides to defoliate forests hiding communist guerrilla fighters sympathetic to the National Liberation Front.[1] One was a nongovernmental tribunal modeled after Nuremberg, which had no legal standing but became a paradigmatic "moral architecture" for the emergence of subsequent Russell Tribunals, citizens' commissions, and a Permanent Peoples' Tribunal; the other was a new "legal genre" known as mass toxic tort litigation, in which personal harm resulting from contact with hazardous materials became collectivized as a civil action. Two mirror-like entities, each with its complex juridical entanglements. The Agent Orange Trial sought legal redress on behalf of American soldiers deployed to the warzones of Vietnam who had been exposed to harmful dioxins, but not for Vietnamese victims on the ground; whereas the IWCT, also known as the Russell or Stockholm Tribunal, was a paralegal experiment and court of conscience that investigated the atrocities committed against the civilian populations of Vietnam, on whose behalf they advocated. Criticisms were leveled at the Tribunal for its singular focus on the activities of Saigon and its allies, but as Lelio Basso, who sat on the Tribunal and set up the Permanent Peoples' Tribunal, emphasized in his concluding remarks: "Our serious evidence which we have accumulated, the testimonies which we brought to the knowledge of the public, the search for the truth we have together pursued, has, in the eyes of public opinion, legitimatized our existence."[2] My brief examination of the advent of these two parallel forums in the late 1960s and 1970s constitutes an important conceptual bridge within the project of *Material Witness* because they signal both the shift from trials to more activist models of accountability and the transition from war crimes to environmental crimes: genocide to ecocide.

The two sessions of the Russell Tribunal took place in Stockholm, Sweden, and Roskilde, Denmark, respectively. Although the US largely ignored the Tribunal, its 25 members were drawn from around the world and involved prominent peace campaigners and political activists including African-Americans James Baldwin, Alice Walker, and Stokely Carmichael. The findings of the Tribunal concluded that violations of human rights and transgressions of international law had been committed by the US against the civilian populations of Vietnam. Their moral authority to assert such a claim was established, in part, by a striking remark made by Judge Robert H. Jackson, Chief Prosecutor for the United States, as to the universality of the principles of Nuremberg: "If certain acts and violations of treaties are crimes, they are crimes whether the United States does them or whether Germany does them. We are not prepared to lay down a rule of criminal conduct against others which we would not be willing to have invoked against us."[3] These words are still a forceful reminder of the transgressions and abuses of power by state and corporate actors that have gone unchecked by legal processes, whose jurisdictional reach is limited or whose prosecutorial will is at times indifferent or partisan, several of which are explored in this book. This issue raises the repeated question: can the injustices of political violence, even when they are in direct violation of the rules of law, be fully met by the protocols of a judicial body, or do they require the production of different ethical arrangements such as those proposed by the Russell Tribunal? Likewise, when the legal threshold of criminal wrongdoing turns on questions of direct causality (*sine qua non* causation), can the dispersed nature of environmental contaminants produce sufficiently compelling juridical narratives that will result not only in restitution for plaintiffs, but substantive justice, or will it require the production of more proactive legal instruments?

The end of herbicidal warfare in Vietnam came about by domestic pressure from scientists who testified before the Senate Committee on Foreign Relations, arguing that the Geneva Protocol of 1925 prohibiting the use of chemical and biological methods of warfare must extend to the life worlds that support and sustain humans.[4] "The massively destructive effects of herbicidal warfare became known as 'ecocide,' so called by several academic scientists who protested herbicidal warfare beginning in 1964 and who ultimately won the right to inspect its effects in Vietnam six years later."[5] But the story did not end with the renunciation of herbicides as a weapon of war in 1975. The molecular latencies of chemicals used to defoliate over two million hectares of jungle would extend the horrors of the Vietnam War on multiple fronts for decades to come. In 2005, the Vietnam Association for Victims of Agent Orange/Dioxin filed a lawsuit in the Eastern District of New York against more than 30 chemical companies, including Dow Chemical and Monsanto, for "harms allegedly done to them and their land by the United States' use of Agent Orange and other herbicides during the Vietnam War from 1965 to 1971 and the South Vietnamese government's subsequent use of such herbicides until 1975.[6] They allege that the manufacturer-defendants are responsible under domestic tort law and under international law."[7] The case was dismissed, because prior to 1975 the use of such chemicals was not regarded as unlawful by the US; therefore the basis for making such a legal claim could not be argued as in violation of international law. In arriving at his ruling, the judge recognized the highly toxic nature of the herbicides sprayed in Vietnam, but did not find that their use met the legal definition of "chemical warfare." The Federal Court of Appeals in Manhattan likewise denied the appeal to reinstate the lawsuit in 2008, and the Supreme Court concurred one year later. Yet in Vietnam, 4.8 million people were exposed to dioxins (the highly toxic chemical compound mixed in Agent Orange which acts as an endocrine disruptor), causing 400,000 deaths and untold related illnesses. These rainbow herbicides, which were sprayed at 13 to 20 times the recommended concentrate for killing plants, remain in Vietnam's biotic systems and will take generations to disappear completely.

The judge who made the decision to dismiss this lawsuit was none other than Judge Jack B. Weinstein. As presiding judge in the earlier Agent Orange Trial, Weinstein had made the unorthodox decision to argue the veterans' class action on the basis of "causation," despite the inherent uncertainty that hampers abilities to link environmental toxins to changes in human health. In doing so, Weinstein shifted the Agent Orange Trial away from the pretrial discovery made by Judge Pratt, who had focused the first five years of legal proceedings on "government contract defense," a provision under US law that protects those awarded government contracts from corporate liability. The chemical companies supplying herbicides claimed that the array of cocktails mixed in Vietnam made it impossible to know which company's products were used in combination with any other, thus also making it impossible to establish lines of accountability between chemical contractors, their products, and allegations of chronic health conditions and death. Peter H. Schuck, Professor Emeritus of Law at Yale University, who has written extensively about the trial, notes that veterans themselves were "reluctant to cast aspersions on the government's conduct because by doing so they would be impugning their sense of loyalty to the country."[8]

As civil litigation, the mass toxic tort case, officially known as *In Re Agent Orange Product Liability Litigation*, had a notably different character than the 2005 criminal lawsuit argued within the framework of international law.[9] Although mass toxic tort litigation in the US began with asbestos and DES litigations, the Agent Orange Trial was by far the most complex and challenging in both scale and scope, folding more than 600 separate actions filed by more than 15,000 individuals into one class action. These consolidated actions represented more than 2.4 million veterans, their families (wives, children born and unborn), as well as soldiers from Australia and New Zealand who had fought in Vietnam, civilians, corporate defendants, and the government.[10] As Schuck highlights in his detailed analysis of the case, the indeterminacy that lies at the heart of such litigation raised fundamental epistemological questions around the constitution of "facts" and the role of the court in grappling with the behavior of chemical pollutants and their attendant politics of uncertainty as to human and environmental health.[11] As Sheila Jasanoff has argued in *Science at the Bar*, resolving complicated scientific questions in legal forums presents its own unique set of challenges, not least of which are the court's longstanding difficulties in staying abreast of scientific and technological developments (a dilemma addressed in research I conducted questioning the legality of automated decision-making in drone warfare).[12] The "toxic commons" that results from chemical contagions such as herbicide use is characterized by highly dynamic metabolic agents whose effects are distributed unequally, usually amongst the most disenfranchised, and thus tend to map onto existing socioeconomic pressures, and by perpetrators who, more often than not, are shielded by complex transnational subsidiary arrangements. Forensic Architecture has referred to the networked nature of such events as one of "field causality" in which the traditional burden of direct evidence or proof of direct causality no longer holds.[13] Schuck argues that our current legal system is woefully inadequate for addressing the consequences of new forms of harm arising from chemical disasters in which violations are dispersed across indeterminate actors and contexts: "Entirely different forms of proof, demanding new kinds of evidence and witnesses, are usually necessary. Different rules of procedures, evidence, and substantive law may be required. And if implemented, these new legal arrangements inevitably alter the roles and relationships of litigants, lawyers, trial judges, juries, appellate judges, research institutions, regulatory agencies, and other governmental organs in profound ways."[14]

Causation

The considerable problem of evidential proof in the Agent Orange Trial was that of demonstrating causality through the production of statistical correlations, many of which involved highly unpredictable carcinogens whose debilitating effects could take years to reveal themselves, and would ultimately fall prey to the maximal time allowed for legal proceedings to be initiated. In focusing the trial on "causation," Judge Weinstein made what is arguably a moral decision recognizing that the public would not be satisfied with a trial that turned on legal technicalities—government contract defense and the statute of limitations—adjudicated over by a judge. It must, however, be noted that Pratt's earlier decision to certify the case as a class action lawsuit was itself singularly pivotal. Weinstein believed that the experiences of returning veterans, and their sense of betrayal and anger, would only intensify and grow if there was no public-facing dimension on offer. As the dismissed 2005 case makes clear, the outrage over the dire consequences of the use of defoliants in Vietnam has not ceased but multiplied over the years, with Vietnamese victims and their families pursuing their own independent litigation. Diverging from Pratt's legal strategy (much to the consternation of the plaintiff's adversaries) also made it clear that Weinstein did not view the chemical companies as absolved from responsibility if they had manufactured and sold a product they knew to be harmful despite government protections. "It is not only a question of what you knew … in the case of a manufacturer but what you should have known."[15] Weinstein insisted that the litigation could be resolved with the active participation of the public in the form of a jury: a trial that would somehow also involve the government, despite its immunity under the Federal Tort Claims Act: forcing, in effect, lay citizens to adjudicate over complex scientific issues that he himself, as a judge, also understood only by means of limited self-erudition. "I don't want anybody to waste too much time telling me [this case] can't be tried by a jury. … This seems to me the kind of case where the community is going to have to be heard. They are going to tell the world what the answer is on all of these technical problems, whether they have a high school education or not."[16] With these decisions made, Weinstein decreed that jury selection would begin on May 7, 1984, a mere six-and-a-half months after taking responsibility for the case on October 21, 1983.

According to Schuck, on whose account I draw heavily, the Agent Orange Trial ultimately revealed itself as a "social problem" of multiple and competing actors rather than a strictly legal or technoscientific challenge. Weinstein himself acknowledged the difficulties that such litigation posed for the courts: "It is a political as well as a Court problem. It involves the Executive, the Veterans Administration and the Legislature, which has to appropriate a lot of money for veterans and their problems, if they are attributable to service."[17] Managing such a complex and prodigious case was a significant feature in its move toward settlement (Weinstein's actual desired outcome), and wrested control of the case out of the hands of the plaintiffs. In tort litigation the plaintiffs' lawyers are paid on a contingency fee, requiring them to raise more funds as the case progresses, whereas the legal fees of defendants are paid upfront. As Jasanoff put it, in the end veterans were no longer in charge of their own "legal destinies," a situation that she saw as having direct implications for future litigation concerning cases of mass exposure to toxic materials.

> Faced with critical financial shortages, the veterans might well have abandoned the case if they had not been assisted by a consortium of lawyers prepared to risk considerable amounts of money to keep the suit alive. But the result, paradoxically, was to create a "lawyer's case," in which the veterans' simple desire for justice took a distant second place to the financiers' interest in recouping their investment through a favorable settlement.[18]

The chemical companies eventually agreed to a negotiated out-of-court settlement awarding 180 million dollars to be directed toward veterans' medical expenses or compensation to families for deaths.[19] Although this sum was the largest of its time, it was modest given the number of plaintiffs represented by the class action. Most accounts suggest that the companies were prepared to offer a considerably larger sum, and faced the prospect of paying out billions of dollars had they gone to trial and the veterans won. As Deborah A. Stone asks: "Why then did the veterans accept the settlement, and why was the figure so low?[20] Weinstein feared that the case would drag on interminably, and that the sheer complexities of the veterans' case might not find ultimate favor with a jury who had to determine whether the plaintiffs' ill health was directly attributable to their exposure to Agent Orange. Nonetheless, in conceptually reorganizing the case so that its most vulnerable feature—causality born out of conditions of indeterminacy—produced its centrifugal force, Weinstein was able to move a mass toxic tort litigation closer toward achieving substantive justice on the part of the plaintiffs than the corrective measures to which tort law conventionally aspires. This dimension sets the Agent Orange Trial apart in my mind as a civil action in which the moral

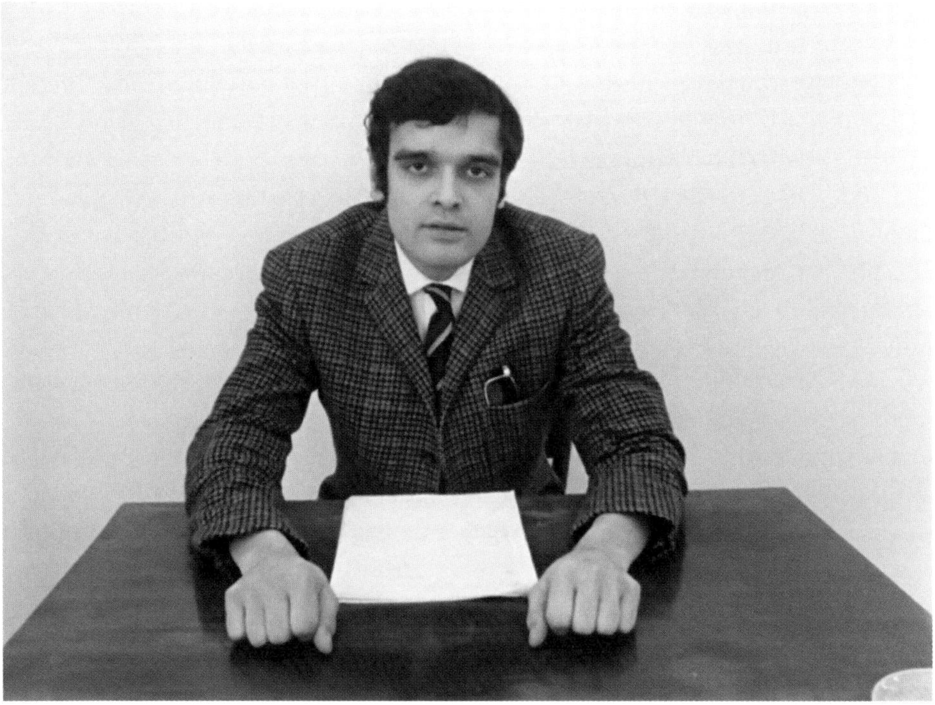

Figure 7.3
Reading testimony from the Russell Tribunal, opening scene, *Nicht löschbares Feuer / Inextinguishable Fire*, Harun Farocki, 1969, 16mm film transferred to video, 25 minutes. Courtesy: Harun Farocki GbR, Berlin.

register (victims' suffering and loss in the face of uncertainties created by environmental toxicity) rather than the protectionist stance of product liability litigation prevailed. Yet this did not resolve the issue of Vietnamese victims who were further wronged by the courts' reluctance to hear their criminal case.

Trial by Fire

> The image always occurs on the border between two force fields; its purpose is to testify to a certain alterity, and although the core is always there, something is always missing. The image is always both more and less than itself.
>
> —Serge Daney, *Libération*[21]

In 1969 the filmmaker and artist Harun Farocki made *Inextinguishable Fire*, a visual indictment of the use of chemical warfare in Vietnam. He began this agitprop documentary by reading a statement given before the International War Crimes Tribunal in Stockholm in which a young Vietnamese villager describes the incendiary effects of napalm bombing on his body and home. Under contract to the American government, the Dow Chemical Company manufactured both Agent Orange and Napalm B, for which its reputation as directly complicit in war crimes would be forever conjoined in the opinions of many. While Dow ceased the production of napalm in 1969, the US continued to use it throughout Vietnam well into 1973. With an unflinching demeanor devoid of affect, Farocki sets out to provide the viewer with an "image" that can testify to the ferocious heat of such an attack; but one from which they won't turn away nor shield their eyes: a confrontation with the military violence of Vietnam that he mediates in order that the "facts" of chemical warfare can be properly understood and denounced. Farocki narrates:

> My name is Thai Binh Danh. I am Vietnamese born in 1949.
>
> I want to report crimes that the United States imperialists committed against me and my village.
>
> On March 31, 1966 at 4p.m. As I was washing dishes, I heard planes approaching.
>
> I rushed to the underground shelter, but I was surprised by a napalm bomb exploding close to me.
>
> The flames and unbearable heat engulfed me and I lost consciousness.
>
> Napalm burned my face, both arms and both legs.
>
> My house was burned as well.
>
> I was unconscious for thirteen days then I awoke in a bed in an FLN hospital.
>
> How can we show you napalm in action?
>
> And how can we show you the injuries caused by napalm?
>
> If we show you pictures of napalm burns, you'll close your eyes.
>
> First you'll close your eyes to the pictures.
>
> Then you'll close your eyes to the memory.
>
> Then you'll close your eyes to the facts.
>
> Then you'll close your eyes to the entire context.
>
> If we show you a person with napalm burns we will hurt your feelings.
>
> If we hurt your feelings, you'll feel as if we tried napalm out on you, at your expense.
>
> We can give you only a hint of an idea of how napalm works.
>
> A cigarette burns at 400°C.
>
> Napalm burns at 3,000°C.
>
> If viewers want nothing to do with the effects of napalm then it is important to determine what they already have to do with the reasons for its use […]
>
> When napalm is burning it is too late to extinguish it.
>
> Napalm has to be protested where it is produced, in factories.

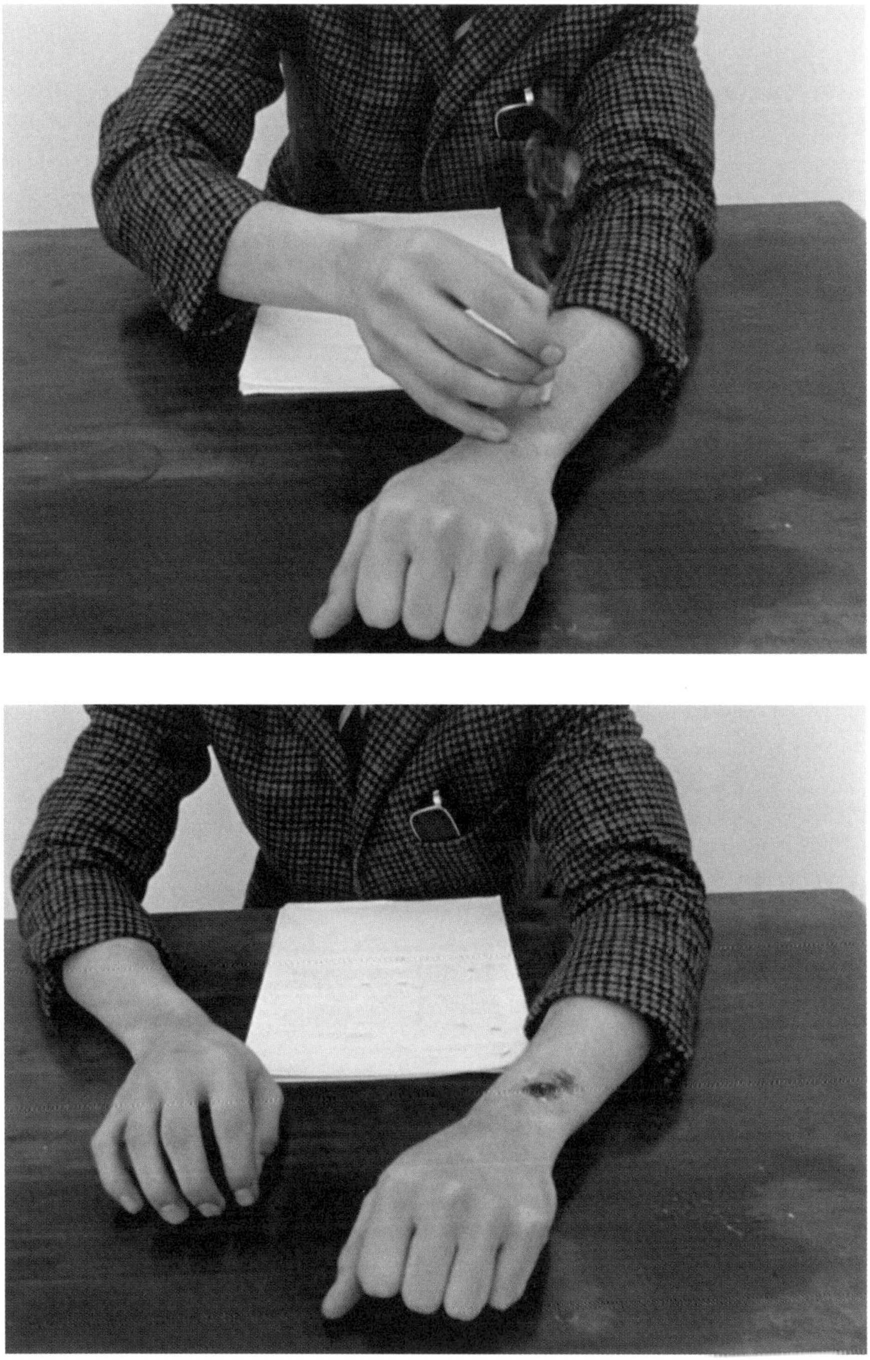

Figure 7.4

Burning his flesh with a cigarette. Film stills from *Nicht löschbares Feuer / Inextinguishable Fire*, Harun Farocki, 1969, 16mm film transferred to video, 25 minutes. Courtesy: Harun Farocki GbR, Berlin.

This pivotal scene at the beginning of the film is based on testimonies gathered by the Russell Tribunal, and tries to grapple with the condition of indeterminacy that besieges toxic tort litigation, and which I have signaled at various points throughout this book as challenging restitution for environmental crimes. Taking a smoldering cigarette, Farocki stubs it out on his forearm to produce a visceral sensate experience that might momentarily capture the comparative intensity of napalm scorching human flesh. The cigarette burn is an interscalar wound that allows Farocki to narrate the larger story of chemical warfare and imperial aggression. Historian Gabrielle Hecht, who researches uranium mining in Africa, has developed the concept of the "interscalar vehicle," which is a device for "treating scale reflexively, as both an analytic category and a political claim."[22] Rather than moving along a sliding scale from the particular to the planetary—zooming in and out—the interscalar manages incommensurate realities through the deployment of a kind of material proxy. In Hecht's case, a chunk of uranium ore extracted from one of Gabon's colonial mines allows her analysis to move from the geological processes of early Earth to enrichment facilities in 1970s France, and on to the global uranium trade today. As she puts it, the interscalar offers "a means of holding *the planet* and a *place on the planet* on the same analytic plane."[23] In Farocki's work, it is the heat transfer between flesh and fire that operates as such a device, allowing him to expand the frame of the film from Dow's laboratories in Midland, Michigan to the jungle canopies of Vietnam dosed with the chemistry of aerial warfare, a scene he conjures through archival and staged images of insecticide and herbicide use.

While Farocki's cigarette burn is not an accurate approximation for the searing fire of napalm, it does provide a way to understand an event whose magnitude might otherwise elude us. I have returned to this scene in Farocki's work time and time again to think about the conundrum posed by material effects whose spatial and temporal reach defies their easy grasp. On the one hand, we can use technical probes and sensors to render certain extensive events perceptible, such as the Gamma Camera I discuss at length in chapter 11, "Failure to Appear," or we can infer and project such realities on the basis of our knowledge of how certain systems work in combination with others. Climate scientists turn to proxies (modes of indirect measure) all the time, given that the study of the Earth's climate at the scale of its ancient history would otherwise be impossible. The tree ring offers an opportunity for extrapolation to the scale of temperature for an entire year. Artists often work with proxies as forms of scalar explication to dramatize events to which they have no direct access. Within law, corroboration secures particular forms of evidence as legally trustworthy, and thus operates as a kind of working proxy in relation to the overall facts of the case being established. The Russell Tribunal was itself an activist proxy for a war crimes tribunal that might one day take Judge Jackson's provocation seriously. However, the productive value of the interscalar, which in my mind builds upon notions of the proxy, is that, in addition to forging cognitive identifications, it also allows for affective relationships to be developed toward events, which might combine to activate a political response. Unlike the formal correspondence between proxies and the conditions they seek to express, the interscalar is not constituted by a singular correlation. "What makes something an interscalar vehicle is not its essence but its deployment and uptake, its potential to make political claims, craft social relationships, or simply open our imaginations."[24] This was surely part of Farocki's ambition with *Inextinguishable Fire*. In chapter 6, the transmissional process of a sound file dispatched from Saigon to New York via radio waves was my interscalar device for navigating the complex image of a napalm attack in Trang Bang: opening our ears to other histories of signal relay in order to unfold their many political registers. Invoking the interscalar is not to disavow the thesis of *Material Witness*, which has argued for an attentiveness to medium and material specificity, away from metaphorization and analogization, but is, rather, one of its operations: that of deployment and uptake. In this research project the interscalar is a *property* of the *material witness* that enables transversal connections to be made—retroactively potentializing them and prospectively activating them.

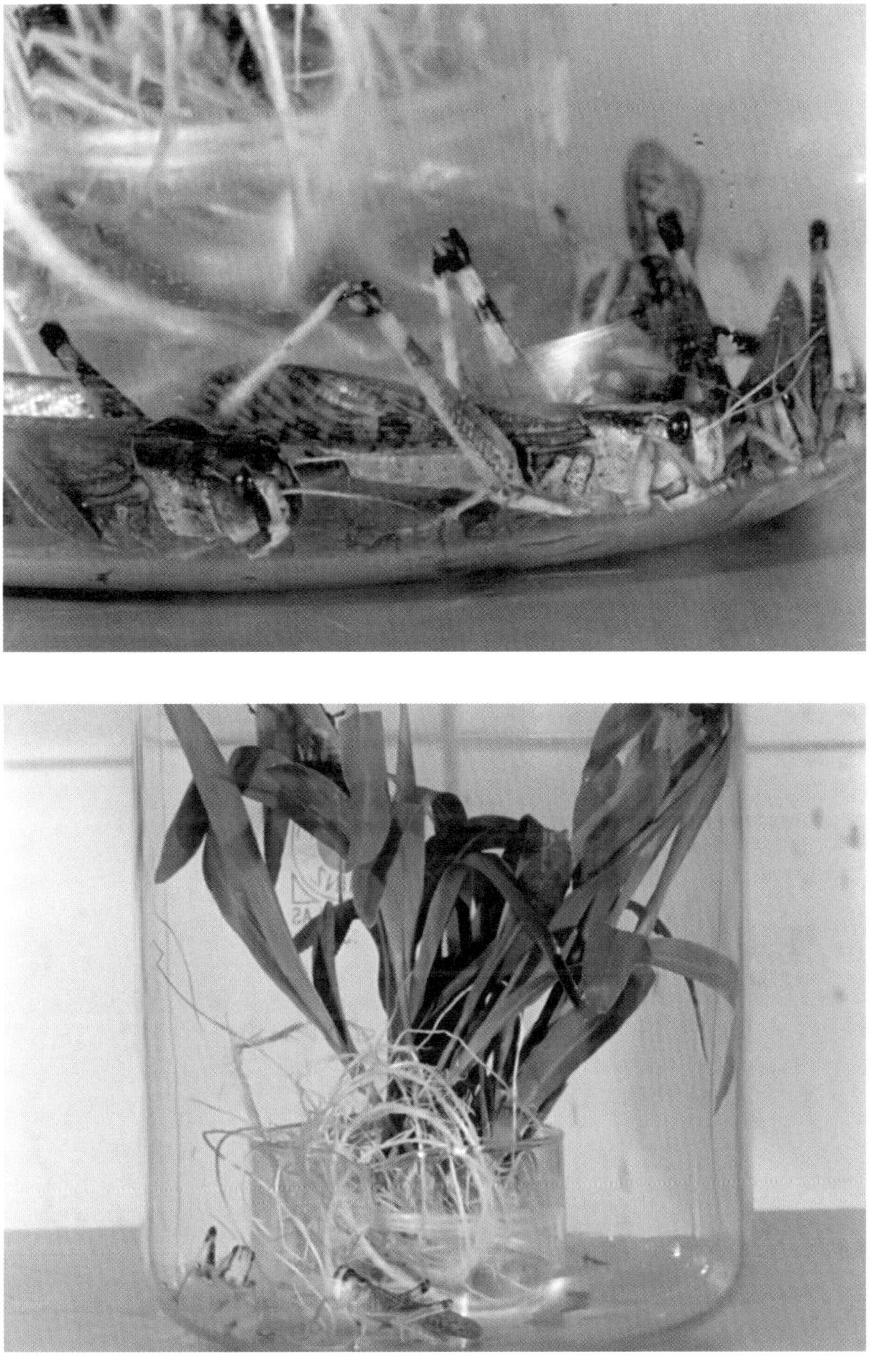

Figure 7.5
Insecticides and herbicides produced by the Dow Chemical Company that are used in the US, Europe, and Third World. Film stills from *Nicht löschbares Feuer / Inextinguishable Fire*, Harun Farocki, 1969, 16mm film transferred to video, 25 minutes. Courtesy: Harun Farocki GbR, Berlin.

8 CROSS-EXAMINATION

Izbica Massacre

As Serb forces advanced across northwest Kosovo in late March 1999, thousands of ethnic Albanians fled their homes to seek refuge in rural communities. Burned-out tractors and abandoned vehicles marked their westward procession. Upward of 10,000 flooded into Izbica, a small town in the municipality of Skenderaj, some 68 kilometers to the west of Prishtina. On March 27, Serb forces reached the outskirts of the village of Izbica and later that evening they struck, firing into the gathered masses as people tried to make their way across the fields and flee into the surrounding woods. Upward of 120 Kosovar Albanians were slaughtered by Serb forces that day in three execution sites. When word of the killings emerged, Liri Loshi, a doctor who had already left Izbica the night before the attack, made the fateful decision to go back and see whether the reports of an unfolding massacre were true. Many of Loshi's family members lived in Izbica, and it was with fearful apprehension that he returned home three days later. When he arrived, he was confronted by a scene of abject horror. Damaged bodies shot at close range littered the meadows, the newly born and elderly amongst them. The blood of victims saturated the ground where they had been brutally slain. Determined to provide the world with stark evidence of the atrocities being committed in Kosovo, Loshi set out to find a video camera.

> When I returned to Izbica, I saw the bodies lying at the place where they were executed. I stayed there for a very short time. It was dark, but I could see that my fears came true, that there was a large number of people, which had been calculated as about a hundred or over a hundred that had been killed.[1]

By the time of the Izbica massacre, war crimes prosecutions had already been underway for three years in The Hague, with the first indictments issued on March 22, 1996. Reports of grave wrongdoings in Bosnia and mounting pressure from the international community had prompted the UN Security Council to pass Resolution 827 on May 25,

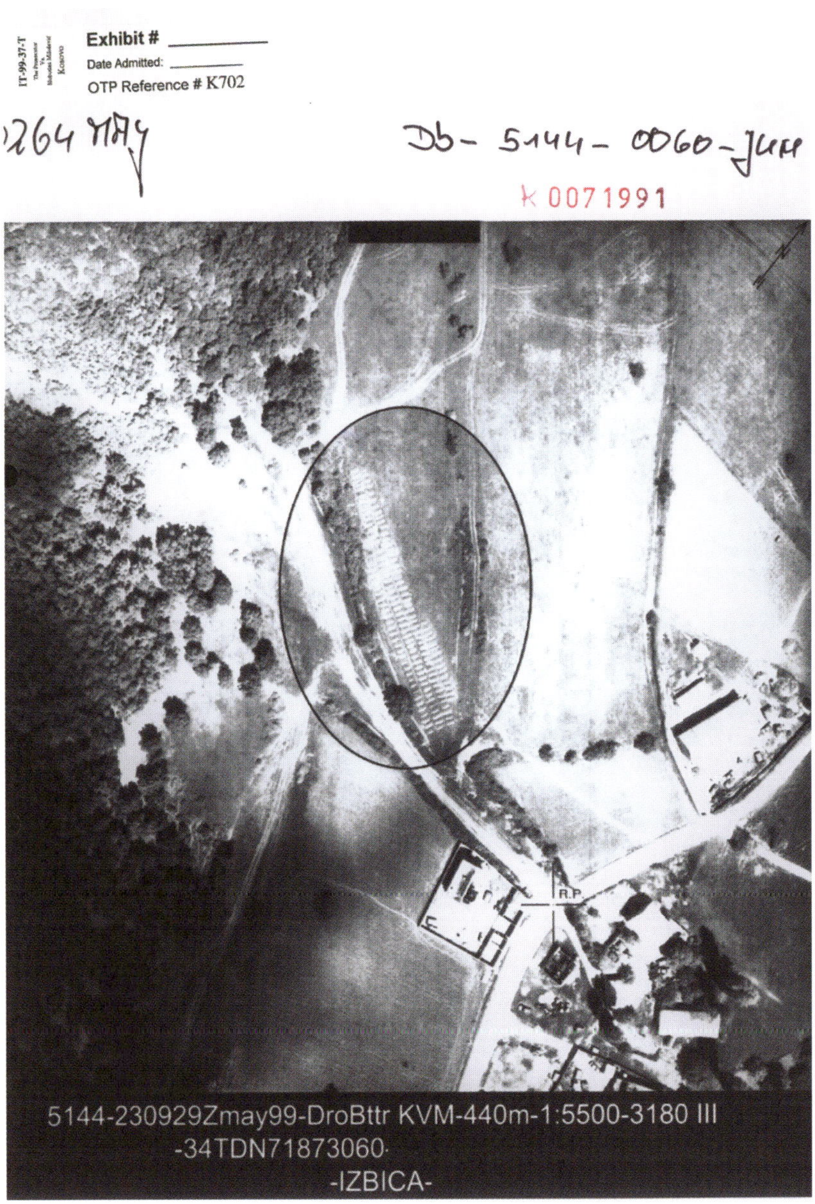

Figure 8.1
Aerial photograph of the grave site in Izbica. Source: unknown.

1993, establishing an International Tribunal for the Prosecution of Persons Responsible for Serious Violations of International Humanitarian Law Committed in the Territory of the Former Yugoslavia since 1991. This Tribunal, better known as the ICTY, was given specific prosecutorial jurisdiction over allegations of crimes against humanity committed in the region. Yet the continued violence in Kosovo was a blatant and deliberate act of defiance signaling the sense of impunity that still pervaded the Serbian leadership despite the prosecutions taking place in The Hague. As a fledgling legal body and temporary *ad hoc* institution, the ICTY was perceived in some quarters to be largely ineffectual in curtailing the violence raging across the Balkans, as few significant perpetrators had yet been brought to face charges in its early years.

The United Nations, along with most network media and human rights organizations, had already pulled out of Kosovo by March 1999; access to professional recording technology of any kind was therefore extremely limited. Availability of personal video equipment was even scarcer in the rural communities of Kosovo. In his search for a video camera, Loshi was eventually directed toward Sefedin Thaqi, a local schoolteacher, who had buried a camcorder in the ground along with other valuable possessions in an effort to hide them from looters. Thaqi agreed to help Loshi, and together they dug up the camera and set about filming evidence of the massacre. Working with Thaqi as the camera operator, Loshi systematically filmed each of the victims, taking long shots to establish the crime scene and scale of the killings as well as close-ups and details of injuries that would later assist with establishing cause of death and identification. As they labored throughout the day, some of Loshi's own family members were discovered amongst the victims in the eastern field. "Three generations of his family—a father, Selman, in his eighties; son, Jashar, about fifty-five; grandson, Sami, about twenty-five—were killed together."[2] Having secured the incriminatory evidence on tape, survivors of the massacre began to bury the dead, transferring the decomposing bodies from the meadow to a makeshift grave where, it was hoped, relatives would one day be able to return to give their loved ones a proper burial. Loshi also filmed this process over the two days it took to move the bodies, identify victims whenever possible, and note their burial location. The documentation of the internment and gravesite would provide a crucial piece of contested legal evidence in the years to come, although he did not realize it at the time.

A Tale of Two Tapes

With Serbian forces and Yugoslav nationalists on the rampage throughout Kosovo, the next challenge was trying to smuggle the videotape out of the region. Thaqi had an

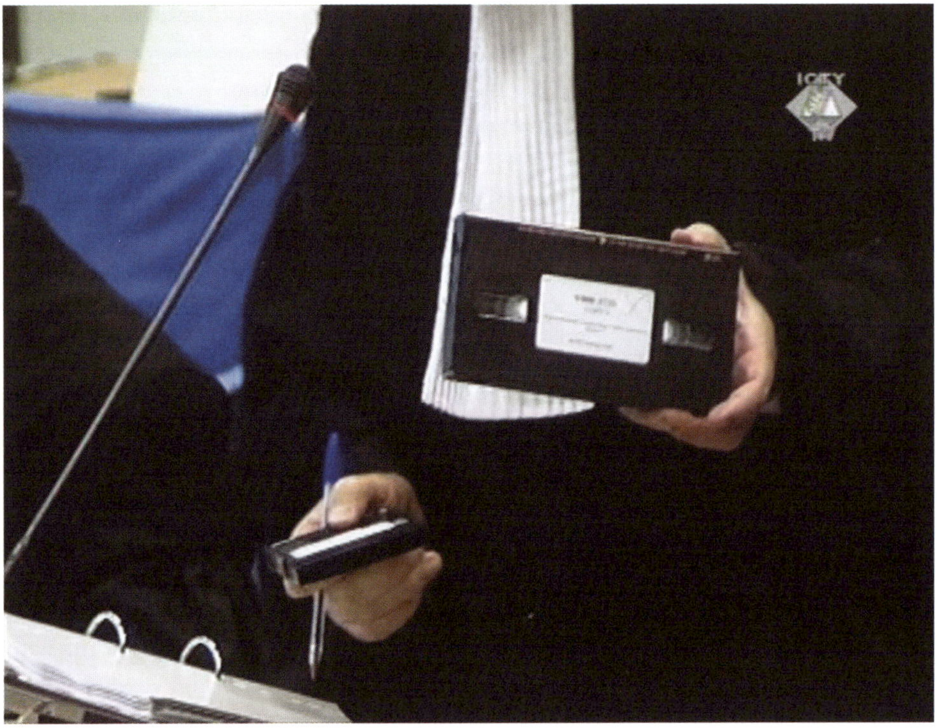

Figure 8.2
The Prosecutor of the Tribunal versus Slobodan Milošević, September 3, 2002. Source: ICTY Court Records.

electrical generator and used it to make a VHS copy of the smaller Hi-8 videotape (or mini DV), which he then passed on to Loshi. At this point the history of the two tapes becomes somewhat confusing. My understandings of this event of evidence are assembled directly from the extended ICTY transcripts produced during the times Loshi was called to testify in The Hague. From everything I have read, including interviews conducted with Loshi and transcripts of his court appearances from 2002 and 2006, Loshi took the VHS copy with him and attempted to leave Kosovo. He traveled at night, away from the convoys of refugees, fearing that he would be searched and the large VHS cassette would be discovered upon his person. Eventually his efforts to leave Kosovo with the tape proved futile; he gave up and returned to Izbica, where he stayed until May. Meanwhile Thaqi had fled Izbica and joined the procession of refugees heading toward the refugee camps set up along the Albanian border. Before leaving he once again hid his camera with the original Hi-8 video still inside. This camera, along with its precious video evidence, was stolen at some point and later recovered by Loshi with the assistance of the local chief of the KLA brigade, Shaban Dragaj. On May 3, Loshi attempted to leave Izbica once more and headed toward Montenegro, this time with both tapes in his possession. While *en route* he feared again that the size of the large-format VHS cassette would risk its disclosure and seizure; he therefore decided to safeguard it by leaving it with a man in the Istok Mountains. He continued his journey with Thaqi's smaller tape hidden on his person, and eventually made it across the border into Albania using false ID. He then journeyed on to Tirana, where he handed over the Hi-8 recording to ICTY investigator Tait-Harris on May 18, 1999.[3] Loshi would eventually return to retrieve the VHS copy, which he would keep in his possession for the duration of the war. The original videotape, along with its VHS copy, were entered into evidence during the ICTY war crimes prosecutions. The following excerpts from ICTY court transcripts highlight key aspects of Loshi's testimony and cross-examination regarding the filming and chain of custody of the videotape during the trial of former Yugoslav President Slobodan Milošević in 2002. They are included here to provide insight into the ways in which the video evidence functioned as a paradigmatic *material witness* around which a set of stakeholders gathered to arrive at a legal truth.

CASE NO. IT-02-54-T

THE PROSECUTOR OF THE TRIBUNAL AGAINST SLOBODAN MILOSEVIC

Witness for the prosecution Liri Loshi gives evidence before Senior Prosecutor Mr. Dirk Ryneveld, International Tribunal for the former Yugoslavia, Tuesday, September 3, 2002

Mr. Ryneveld: Your Honours, the witness describes in his statements how various villages in the area around Srbica were attacked by Serb forces on various dates in March 1999 and notes that by the 25th of March, thousands of refugees had assembled in an open field in Izbica. He heard about the massacre in Izbica by speaking to some of the women who were forced to leave.

The witness's statements indicate that on the 31st of March, 1999, he subsequently attended Izbica along with Sefedin Thaci and others, where he assisted in the recording of a videotape of the bodies found in the village of Izbica. The video camera was operated by Sefedin Thaci under instruction from Dr. Loshi.

The original videotape was apparently handed over by the witness to an investigator, Tait-Harris, of the ICTY while he was in Tirana, Albania, on the 18th of May, 1999.

The witness, in his statement, explains how the video was made and states that this tape was the original version and had not been edited, added to, or altered in any way.

The witness relates that the tape was filmed showing most of the bodies in the locations that they were found. The tape shows their faces, where possible, for identification purposes, together with the injuries on the bodies.

The tape also shows the size of the burial site and depicts three of the survivors re-enacting the massacre to illustrate what took place. The statement describes in detail what is shown on each relevant frame of the video, the name of the victim where known, and describes the clothing worn.

On the 22nd of May, 1999, in Tirana, Albania, the witness handed over to investigator Kevin Curtis a list detailing the names of the 127 people buried in Izbica which had been compiled with the assistance of Afrim Xhemajli.

Now, during the course of this evidence, the witness—we will also be asking to mark a videotape which bears a number V000-1733. From this videotape, still photographs were produced showing both the massacre scenes and the bodies. They are contained in the Izbica binder which has been made available to Your Honours and has been marked as an exhibit.

In addition, the Prosecution has now edited that tape to show approximately slightly less than four minutes out of Exhibit 1733, to show highlighted portions of the video.

I propose to show the witness this four-minute tape, and it shows four—and I'm now told actually five—scenes.

The first scene shows the first group of victims where they were found. And I pause here to say you've heard one witness who testified about that first group.

Then there is a short break in the film, purposely to separate the scenes, and we then see the second group of victims—and I pause here to say that you've also heard a witness who testified about being a survivor of that second group—followed by a brief view of the large meadow where the people had been assembled. You will then see the remnants—you will see the remnants of the tractors and the debris left behind.

The tape then pans to the third group of victims; and also at the very end, there's a very small segment of the actual burial site. All that is still within four minutes.

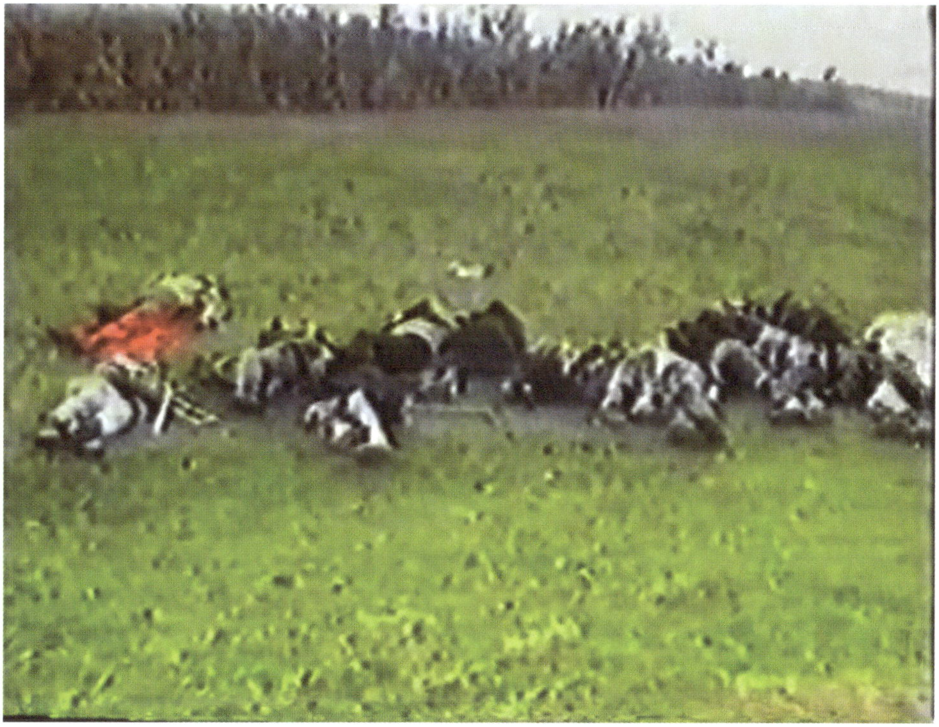

Figure 8.3
IT-02-54: Milošević [WMV] Videotape of Izbica Massacre (extracts). Document Type: Exhibit P308A. Date: 03/09/2002. By: Prosecution. Source: ICTY Court Records.

Now, Your Honours, I could play the tape here, but I think I will finish with the summary, if I may.[4]

Witness for the prosecution Liri Loshi cross-examined by Slobodan Milošević, International Tribunal for the former Yugoslavia, Tuesday, September 3, 2002

Mr. Milosevic [Interpretation]: Q. The question is: Did you, three days later when you went to Izbica, take with you a camera or, rather, did you arrange for this videotaping in order to document the event which you wished to document? Is that what you did?

The Witness [Liri Loshi]: A. The filming of the footage from the Izbica massacre was not done by me alone. It was myself with Sefedin Thaci and with the assistance of the civilian population and members of the Kosovo Liberation Army. This was not my—this was not an initiative of mine quite by chance.

At the same time, I was working as a reporter for the Kosovo television channel, and during all the time, I had my own camera with me. However, on the 26th of March, my camera had been burnt, as I have mentioned in my statement as well. It was burnt in a house of the village of Lecina, where I used to live.

And on the 30th of March, 1999, I did not have a camera when I went to the site of the event in Izbica. Therefore, we asked one of the villagers to provide a camera for us the next morning, and a friend of mine promised to bring one the next morning.

So by the next day, we found ourselves a camera and proceeded with the filming. This is the truth about the camera and the filming.[5]

Witness for the prosecution Liri Loshi gives evidence before Judge Richard George May, International Tribunal for the former Yugoslavia, Tuesday, September 3, 2002

Judge May: Q. All right. And after the 4th of April, when the tapes were—after a few days, when they were re-recorded, you said the tape was stolen, you asked the commander for help, and it was confiscated from the thieves.

Does that mean that the tapes were not in your possession or in the possession of the persons—the person who taped them all the time? Is that true?

The Witness [Liri Loshi]: A. The truth is that the tape was obtained in an unfair way by some irresponsible person, and I asked for the assistance of the main chief of the brigade, Shaban Dragaj, who made sure, after a conversation with those persons, to have the tape back within a very short time.

Meanwhile, as concerns the truth about the tape, it is true that this tape—I mean the original tape which I gave to the ICTY—was filmed with the camera of Sefedin Thaci while he himself was not present.

In the meantime, I had my own tape which on the 4th of April I recorded from this original tape into VHS. And I had that tape all the time.

But due to technical reasons, I left it somewhere in the mountains of Istok because it was very big, and I was thinking that there were chances that I could get caught by Serb forces and I didn't want the tape to be on me by then. And it was a wise thing to do to hide this tape.

So that's why I took the other one, in order to use it for information purposes. In the meantime, as I said, I left the tape in the

```
Istok mountains, and I then found it and brought it with me every-
where, and I've been carrying it with me everywhere I go all the
time.[6]
```

Groundwork of the Image

On a hazy morning in October 2013, Steffen Kraemer, Srdjan Hercigonja, and I made our own way to Izbica. Ours was a sobering journey, generated in part by a conviction that making contact with the site and its remaining residents might somehow counter the procedural operations of the court that had systematically deconstructed the massacre video and in the process, I felt, evacuated it of all affect. This impression was borne out by the recordings of the court sessions I had obtained, in which the tapes and Loshi's corroborating testimony were variously debated by prosecutors and defense counsels in the trials of Milošević and Milutinović, and related prosecutions such as that of Vlastimir Đorđević.[7] As the legal cross-examination of the video was played out across the months and years of the trials in which it featured, the scenes captured on tape were studied, interpretations assessed, chain of custody ascertained, exhibit numbers assigned, and so forth. This incommensurate relationship between the emotive charge of materials called forth to bear witness to war crimes and the perfunctory

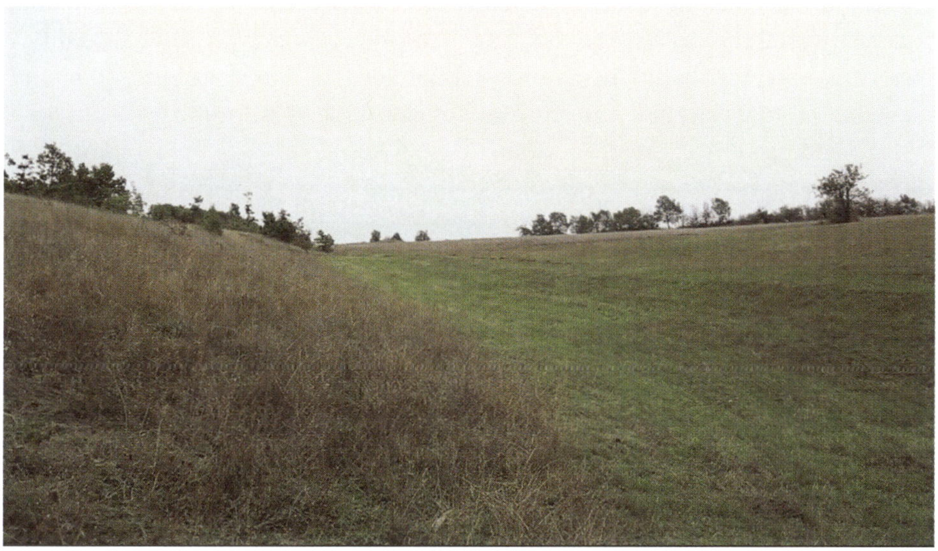

Figure 8.4
Site of the Izbica massacre in Kosovo. On location Izbica, 2013. Photo credit: Kraemer/Schuppli.

nature of their legal scrutiny is no doubt more difficult for a layperson to reconcile than for a legal practitioner who understands the exigencies of the system even if they are still personally disturbed by the materials they are asked to review. But even so, with years of legal experience in Canada behind him, ICTY Prosecutor Eliott Behar was still completely shaken when confronted with the visceral violence and shocking scale of the killings documented by Loshi's video. Paradoxically, this struggle between the evidence captured on tape and the ways in which in the massacre video starts to unfold the intricacies of the legal process, and thus also make legible evidence of the court's particular practices and structuring logic, is also the productive force that gives shape to the dual nature of the *material witness*. Behar describes his first encounter with the Izbica videotape as follows:

> My first direct look at mass killings in Kosovo came with this video footage, shot in the municipality of Skenderaj in the immediate aftermath of what became known as the Izbica massacre. The footage was captured by a man named Liri Loshi, who managed to sneak a tape out of the country while the war was still raging. One of my first tasks was to review and organize this footage, matching it to other evidence in the Dordevic case. I was given the coded electronic evidence numbers and after a couple of failed attempts to navigate the system 1 was able to pull the videotape and start watching them at my desk. From my work as a prosecutor in Canada I was used to seeing and dealing with the aftermath of violence, but the scale of this, the rawness of it, was something else altogether.[8]

I first traveled to Kosovo in 2011 with a group of researchers interested in examining the architectural aftermath of the conflict and the ways in which the cultural politics of preservation were scripting the new postwar narratives of normalization, and inscribing them into the emergent infrastructures of globalization throughout the Balkans.[9] When I returned to the Drenica region of central Kosovo in 2013, buildings still carried the scars of the "hurricane of violence" that had blown through this landscape in 1999.[10] But the crimes committed in the pastoral landscape of Izbica would not entirely reveal themselves through the visible remainders of war. Different modes of seeing would be required than that of my more tourist-like gaze from previous excursions. Walter Benjamin has characterized this attempt to attune ourselves to new perceptual modes of inquiry as a kind of self-educating vision whereby we learn to see or sense events that have dissolved into the shadowlands of history.[11] Using aerial imagery taken during the Balkan war and contemporary Google Earth screen grabs as a guide, the three of us eventually found the unmarked road that would lead us back to this tragic site of ethnic violence. As the residual haze that clung to the rolling hills slowly lifted, the rural features of Izbica became all the more remarkable—not for the horrific past that one might imagine they would somehow still manage to express, but for their apparent calm. A farmer ploughed his field with an aging tractor, and a dog growled at grazing cattle; there was little to see as we approached the meadow. This experience of returning to a site of extreme trauma and political violence to be confronted by a lack of visible evidence that something dreadful happened is a common enough experience, one that is often the result of a simple need for life to return to "normal." If history is to be invoked, it generally comes in the form of symbolic markers: ruins and memorials that designate the official geographies of loss. This is also the case at Izbica, where a series of gravestones carrying inscriptions that record ages ranging from one to ninety-three mark the dead. For the three of us, the meadow functioned as a kind of living filmic medium for summoning the past: a metabolic field of interacting processes, which we knew carried the materialized traces of victims in its soil.

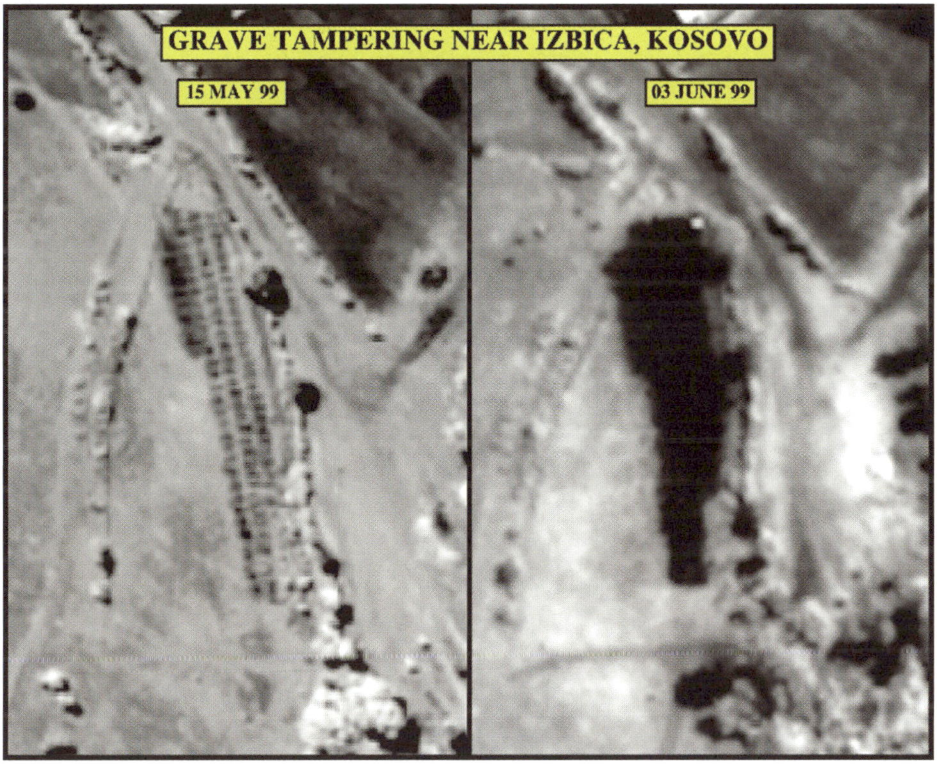

Figure 8.5
Aerial photograph showing grave tampering near Izbica, during the Kosovo War in 1999. Source: US Department of State.

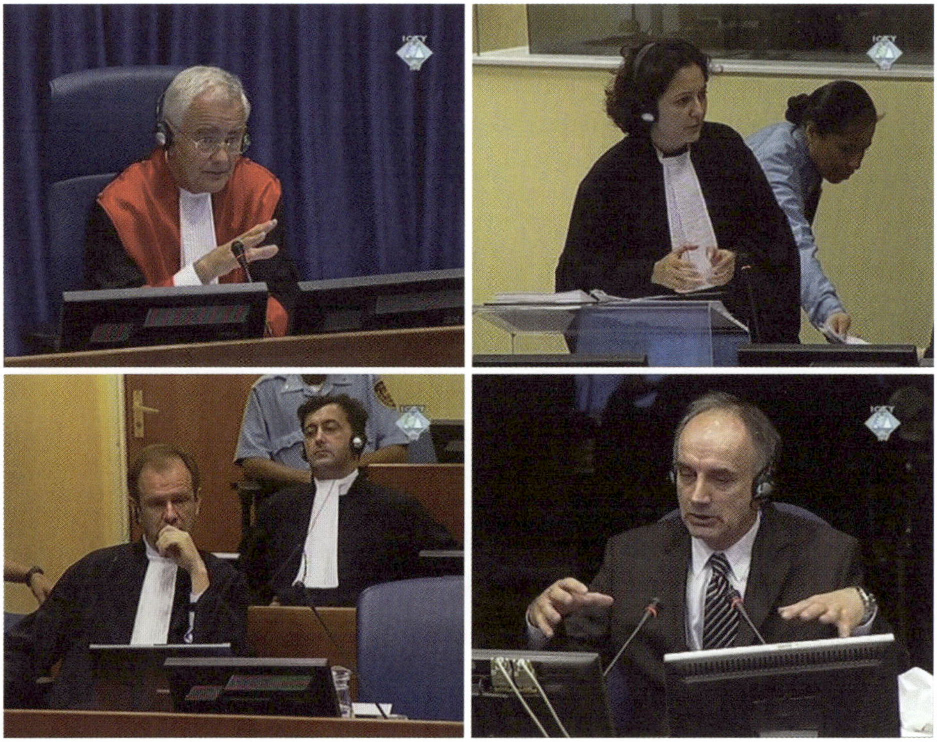

Figure 8.6
The Prosecutor of the Tribunal versus Milan Milutinović et al., October 26, 2006. Source: ICTY Court Records.

I once had a short conversation with filmmaker Philip Scheffner about *Revision* (2013), a documentary project made with Merle Kröger that uses film as a divining rod to tap into the suppressed memories of landscape. We spoke about the challenges of being in locations where extreme acts of human suffering had taken place, yet not necessarily being able to discern palpable evidence of that history regardless of how recently the events in question had occurred. *Revision* explores the discovery of two bodies, later identified as Romanian, in a farmer's field on the German–Polish border in 1992. Composed of witness testimony, archival documents, and research materials, the film uses the landscape as a mnemonic device for reassembling the past and unearthing fragments that might narrate a contingent truth as to what actually transpired and who was responsible for the killings.[12] Scheffner insists that there is always something to see or to sense if we look with sufficient intensity and are fully aware of what it is

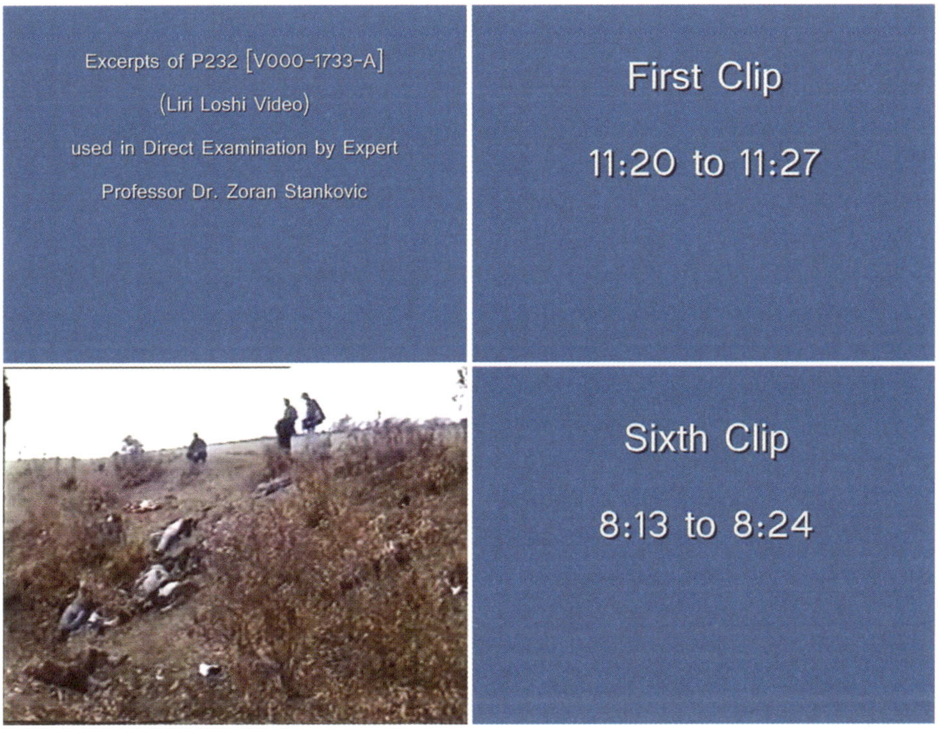

Figure 8.7
Excerpts of P232 [V000-173-A] (Liri Loshi Video) used in Direct Examination by Expert Professor Dr. Zoran Stanković. Source: ICTY Court Records.

that we have actually experienced. Returning to these sites as an artist and researcher, I often wonder whether the burden of historical proof might also be evinced by the sensate materiality of the landscape itself, whose apprehension of the crimes that took place is expressed directly through its enduring presence: something happened, right here, in this very place, that can't simply be ignored no matter how uninflected the scene might appear today. This conviction has also structured the methodology of filming that I bring to such sites: long unwavering shots anchored by a tripod so that the viewer becomes attentive to the landscape in such a way that small details and minute changes are endowed with potential significance.

In Izbica, efforts to hide evidence of the mass killings by Yugoslav and Serb forces were uncovered by aerial surveillance that captured signs of grave tampering at the site where the dead had been buried. As word of the mass killings began to appear in the international media, Serbian forces exhumed the bodies from their impromptu graves and rehid them. "Victims' clothes, blankets, and grave markers were gathered together and stored at a house in the village (Hamdi House) so that they could be burned and destroyed."[13] Some of the victims were disposed of in the local KLA cemetery concealed within the remains of other bodies, while others were hidden hundreds of kilometers away in another mass grave. Thirty bodies from the Izbica massacre were eventually recovered from one of two mass graves found in Petrovo Selo in eastern Serbia. Signs of the massacre and its attempted cover-up (the removal of the dead from their burial site) might well have disappeared, along with any claims that such extreme violence had ever taken place there. Instead it was the ground truth revealed by the surface disturbances of a grassy meadow that produced the legal proof that those massacred at Izbica on March 27 had originally been buried there. Before-and-after aerial photography taken of the burial grounds on May 15, 1999 and June 3, 1999 revealed conclusive evidence of grave tampering. These damning images prompted the ICTY to launch an immediate investigation, which was undertaken by the French Forensic Mission. Between June 28 and June 30, 1999, a team of ten experts, who had experience ranging from medicine, forensic science, criminal research, and ballistics to missing persons, were tasked with finding trace evidence at the three Izbica execution sites, as well as at the clothes and grave marker storage site of Hamdi House. When they arrived in Izbica they found the majority of houses and vehicles burned or fire-damaged. The meadow where the massacre, burials, and subsequent desecrations had taken place still showed partial signs of the earth having been turned over, and a pattern of disturbances indicating where the placement of the graves had been. Tire treads and scored markings from metal tools reminiscent of a mechanized machine, probably that of a tractor's backhoe, were still visible on the surface, indicating that the bodies had been violently disinterred. Broken wood and some items of clothing also still littered the field.[14]

CASE NO. IT-05-87-T

THE PROSECUTOR OF THE TRIBUNAL AGAINST MILAN MILUTINOVIC

Witness for the prosecution Liri Loshi gives evidence before by Prosecutor Ms. Daniela Kravetz, International Tribunal for the former Yugoslavia, Thursday, October 26, 2006

Ms. Kravetz: Q. Now, Mr. Loshi, moving on to another subject. You state in your—in your evidence, in your written evidence, that a month later after filming the—this—these sites you left Izbica and Kosovo and headed to Albania to try to distribute the tape. Did you later return to Kosovo after the war?

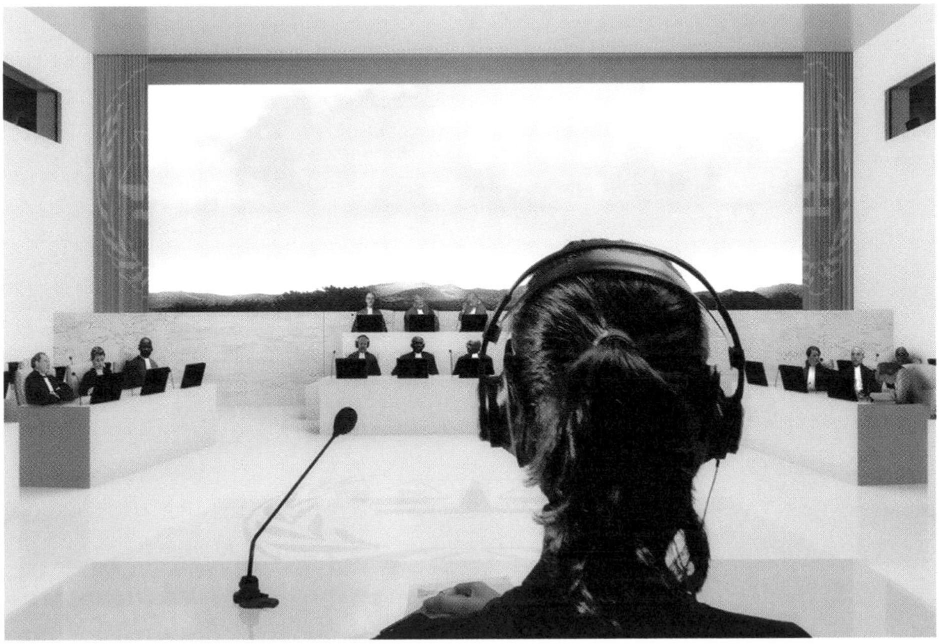

Figure 8.8
Architectural proposal for the new premises of the International Criminal Court (ICC) in The Hague, 2008. The OMA design, which was ultimately not selected, embodies an idealized conception of the law as transcendent and transparent. The wide-screen format of one of the courtroom's windows, evident in this render collage, peers into the skies of Scheveningen, further emphasizing the transformation of the court into a cinematic space. Source: Office for Metropolitan Architecture.

A. Yes, I did. I returned to Kosovo after NATO got in. I was there by 22nd of June and went to Izbica. And now I had my own camera. [. . .] So I used it to tape—to tape that burial site which was—which was with no graves anymore. There were no bodies, no graves. Everything was flattened.

Q. What do you mean there were no graves? [. . .]

A. I just heard rumours. Like they were taken—somebody said they were taken again in two directions. Somebody said they were taken in the direction of Klina, which is on the right side when you go to Turiqevc, and somebody else told me that later on they were found in Mitrovica somewhere. But this information wasn't clear to me, so I don't know much about this.

Q. Okay. Very well. Thank you very much.

Ms. Kravetz: Your Honour, these are all my questions for this witness. I would like to tender this witness—the video that this witness has been referring to which is Exhibit P232. There are also a set of photographs which are still photos from the same video which are referred to in his statement dated 23rd to 25th September 2001, and these are Exhibits P230 and 231.

Judge Bonomy: Well, these will be admitted. The other film that's just been referred to taken after the 22nd of June isn't an exhibit, I don't think?

Ms. Kravetz: I don't think that's an exhibit in this case.

The Witness: Your Honour, I never brought the tape here because I was never asked for that. But if the Prosecution needs that, I would provide them with it, if they need it as an evidence.[15]

Probative Pictures

A significant aspect of my ongoing research has focused on examining the issues that arise when media and other nontextual forms of evidence enter public forums as *material witnesses* entrusted with the task of testifying to history, particularly within the high-stakes war crimes tribunals of The Hague. How does the copying, editing, digitizing, and handling of media artifacts impact upon their evidentiary capacities to produce the truth claims that are required for "the justice of law" to answer to the "injustices of war"?[16] Materials that come out of conflict zones are often shot or recorded under extremely challenging conditions, which might impinge upon their ability to deliver legal truth but can still tell us a great deal about the hazardous conditions under which such material was procured. A particularly useful example that highlights this feature is the investigation "Decoding Witness Testimony" (Drone Strike Investigation #3) that Forensic Architecture conducted for the 2013 UN Inquiry into allegations of extraterritorial lethal counterterrorism operations led by Special Rapporteur on counterterrorism and human rights Ben Emmerson, QC.[17] The case concerned a US drone strike on March 30, 2012 that discharged its Hellfire missiles directly into the dense urban fabric of Miranshah, a city in North Waziristan, Pakistan. The immediate aftermath of this devastating attack was filmed surreptitiously by someone using a hand-held recording device—either a mobile phone or a camcorder—and over a period of several months was smuggled out of Pakistan to the US, where it was eventually aired by Rachel Maddow on MSNBC (June 29, 2012). Although there was no attribution indicating who shot the video, the documentation was obtained under difficult conditions and at considerable risk to the videographer (who was undoubtedly a male). This is evidenced by the nervous camerawork as he moves rapidly from side to side, positioned deep from within the recess of the room, always careful to avoid the open window. The agitation of the image and its sheltered point of view thus combine to offer us valuable clues as to the likely dangers attached to such acts of real-time documentation. Through our research we were already aware of the general prohibition against the use of recording technologies of any kind in the Federally Administered Tribal Areas of Pakistan, a ban corroborated by the cautious camerawork revealed by the video. Yet rather than detract from its evidential qualities, the lack of image stability offers an additional proof, not only of the event depicted but also of the manner of its witnessing. The affective dimensions of the war on terror were in this instance both registered and materialized by the camera's own nervous movements. While the video's anonymous nature, in combination with this agitation, serves to intensify its urgency when it is broadcast on television, within a legal context this may give rise to additional questions. Well-composed and unadulterated materials, whose authorship can be determined, are the ideal technical witnesses for asserting the legal merits of evidence. The poor quality of many videotapes in the custody of the Office of the Prosecutor could certainly raise legal challenges, the probity of which the court would need to prove or disprove through the work of technical experts and corroborating testimony. However, throughout this book, defects, disturbances, and disorder provide a valuable source of additional knowledge about events. Indeed, they are one of the very means by which the conditions and stakes of the political are disclosed.

Today the reporting of human rights abuses has been significantly aided by mobile modes of media capture and social media, yet a great deal of this content is reworked for its online distribution. Under most circumstances this would be an acceptable practice, and would not necessarily hinder the capacity of such materials to produce a public truth. However, such evident processing troubles the court and tests the admissibility standards that might allow such user-generated content to advance a legal truth. Whenever possible, raw unedited files, ideally burned directly to disk without being previewed in a software package, are considered the gold standard by forensic investigators—something I learnt while on my training course in forensic photography for human rights workers. In all the documents I have perused on how to prepare evidence for legal submission, writing to a master CD/DVD or directly to a secure server is still considered best practice, despite the obsolescence of CDs and DVDs in the consumer marketplace. The international nonprofit organization witness.org, founded in the aftermath of the Rodney King beating, has been particularly successful in training activists and citizens in the use of video to expose human rights abuses and to produce legally rigorous evidence. Guidelines governing admissibility standards for social media evidence are also crucial, but it may take quite some time to establish agreed-upon principles, a status not yet achieved for satellite imagery.[18] However, poorly shot, copied, or edited media are often the only materials that prosecutors have in the evidence vault to support or deny a legal claim. Disputes around allegations of genocide and war crimes are thus archived by media whose evidential assertions could be contested in terms of what they show, as well as the ways in which they were produced and handled. Technical inconsistencies, corrupt data, and irregular file management can all raise legal doubts as to the veracity and integrity of materials that will require cross-examination and possibly lead to further forensic examination. When the Tribunal in The Hague began, Bob Reid (Chief of Operations, OTP), who was then an Investigations Team Leader, was dispatched to Bosnia to oversee the seizure, bagging, and logging of evidence, including biohazardous materials such as bloody clothing, ligatures, and blindfolds. I asked him whether any issues had ever arisen pertaining to uncertain audit trails of evidence gathered during the chaos of an ongoing war, and he told me it was rare. In the early days of the Tribunal he personally oversaw trucks being loaded with material evidence from Prijedor, escorted via the British Military to the Bosnian border, from where the evidence was taken to the Zagreb field office. There it was sealed overnight, photographed, put back into the trucks the following day, and transported overland to The Hague. Yet regardless of how materially compromised evidence might be prior to entering the administrative circuits of the court (decomposed objects recovered from a mass grave, clothing soiled by bodily fluids, documents damaged by moisture, videos hurriedly shot and copied), a parallel story unfolds as one makes one's way through the court records and evidential holdings of the Tribunal: namely, the degree to which the ICTY itself is a "processing machine" that also works over the materials that enter its legal infrastructure and in the course of its operations, I claim, also actively transforms them.[19]

Witness for the prosecution Liri Loshi gives evidence before Judge Iain Bonomy, International Tribunal for the former Yugoslavia, Thursday, October 26, 2006

[Videotape played]

Judge Bonomy: Q. Now, I have a question to clear up with your statement of 19 May 1999. The first page of that statement you're describing the videotape that we've seen portions of here today. And you say in that statement under oath: "I recorded this videotape myself on March 31st, 1999, and this original exhibit has been in my constructive possession from the time of filming until now."

Now, we already know, thanks to the testimony that you gave in the statement you made under oath is not true and accurate because Mr. Thaqi is the one who recorded the video.

Now, is it also the case that the second part of this statement, that is to say that you had the original tape in your constructive possession at all times before delivery to the Prosecutor, that statement is not accurate and in fact is false. Isn't that correct?

The Witness [Liri Loshi]: A. No. This is correct, but I believe this is a misunderstanding.

Because what I was—what I said there or what I was trying to explain there, and I did—I believe I did so, was that just after the taping was done by Sefedin Thaqi in—after a few days, I believe this was April 3rd or 4th, I can't remember it now, we transferred the whole filming from his tape to VHS tape, which I had it all the time in my possession.

But that tape I couldn't bring with myself to Albania because I found it very dangerous to take it with myself. Later on I meant I could and I would, but I never did because I found it too dangerous.

And then I was trying to get a hold of Sefedin Thaqi's tape, which I did. And this is how this Sefedin Thaqi's tape got into Tribunal and not my tape that you're referring to, which, of course, like you said, was in my possession all the time. And I believe now it's in a possession of Tribunal of The Hague as well.

Q. Now, with respect to Mr. Thaqi's tape, am I correct that this tape was at one point in time stolen by some thieves?

A. Yes. At the time where I was looking for this tape, his own camera was stolen, I believe not because of the tape but because—the tape was stolen because of camera. The thieves didn't even know what was in. And then with the help of Shaban Dragaj I get a hold of this tape again.[20]

Having now spent a great deal of time reviewing the video footage that Loshi and Thaqi shot at Izbica since my return from Kosovo, and after poring through the hundreds of related pages of ICTY court transcripts again, I have come to the realization that the affective or surplus remainder of the Izbica massacre has not in fact been entirely flattened by the legal protocols to which it was subjected, as I had initially surmised. On the contrary, an "informed material" was produced in the sense advanced by Isabelle Stengers, in which the video's physical handling and institutional management, combined with its discursive legal uptake as disputed evidence, resulted in its progressive informational enrichment.[21] As the video and its copy transited through

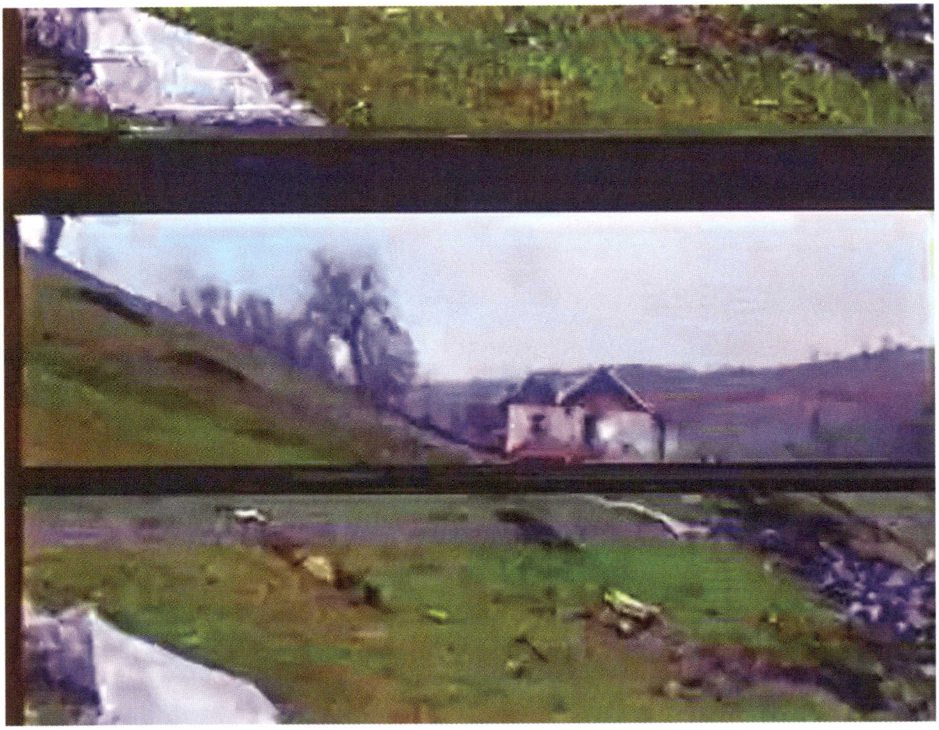

Figure 8.9
IT-05-87: Milutinović et al. [ASF] Video tape of Killings at Izbica taken by Liri LOSHI and Sefedin THAQI. Document Type: Exhibit P00232.2. Date: 03/09/2002. By: Prosecution. Source: ICTY Court Records.

the Tribunal, from its pretrial proceedings and disclosure to its presentation before the Trial Chambers in the cases of Milošević, Milutinović, and Đorđević, they furnished a great deal of insight into its complex legal role. Furthermore, each time the original video was copied, first as an analog VHS recording, later as a digital file in order to facilitate playback on the E-court system and then eventually as an edited-down sequence of five short clips by ICTY Special Prosecutor Dirk Ryneveld, it also accrued information pointing to these administrative proceedings. The more Loshi testified about the events surrounding the massacre and gave evidence regarding the production and custodial care of the video, the more he was also cross-examined, resulting in an ever-increasing number of pages of court transcripts, each of which was translated into the official languages of the ICTY, English, French, Bosnian/Croatian/Serbian, plus Albanian and Macedonian when required. Through these various forms of mediation,

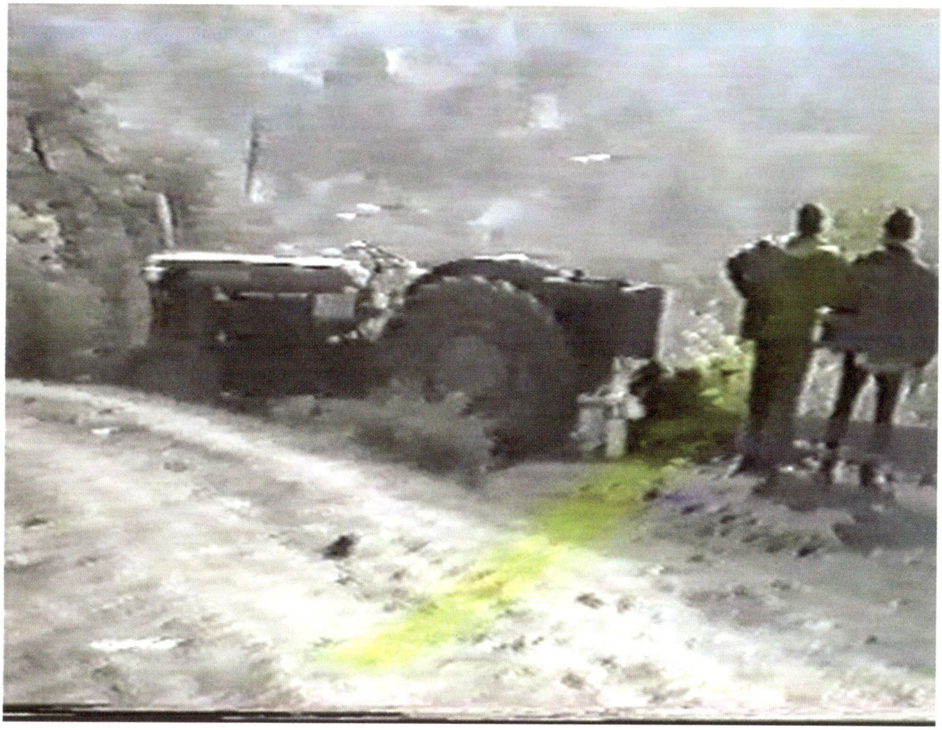

Figure 8.10
IT-02-54: Milosević [WMV] Compilation of excerpts of exhibit 13 videotapes. Document Type: Exhibit P13/1. Date: 20/02/2002. By: Prosecution. Source: ICTY Court Records.

a technopolitics of the legal event begins to emerge that, I argue, is capable of restoring some of the affective dimensions of the original localized event, albeit as a potentially new mode of violence in which the renewal of the emotional force of the video reappears not so much in its singular presence as a discrete media object but in its inexorably distributed appearance across a series of legal events.

Two histories are, in effect, archived by the Izbica video: that of the massacre site, including documentation of the burial of victims, and that of the legal processes through which the video journeyed as a *material witness*. At each juncture in its evolution from a technical object created by Loshi and Thaqi on site in Kosovo, including its concealment and recovery during the war, to its eventual entry into the legal archives of the ICTY as Exhibit No. P232, the video was subject to the entropic vagaries of time. Sometimes these material transformations can be discerned directly as extraneous visual data that encroaches upon the image in the form of scan lines and surface noise (see figure

8.10). These are characteristic of taping over previously recorded material, copying, playback, and possibly even moisture damage due to the camera's subterranean burial. The video also shows signs of image loss, indicating that it may have been reprocessed by incorrect video codecs when transferred using Thaqi's generator. While I have not discovered whether the Hi-8 and VHS tapes they used for filming were new or had been previously recorded on, given the context of a war and the scarcity of such technology it is quite likely that they reused existing tapes. In addition to the visible defects and digital artifacts that one can note in the visual field, the video's informational quotient also results indirectly from the paperwork, transcripts, and court sessions wherein it featured, enabling me to track the tape as it moved through the various stages and cases of the Tribunal: sometimes as an aid to testimony, at other times as direct evidence. The footage that Loshi shot documenting the digging of improvised graves and burial proceedings occurred in real time, thus confirming the video's status as direct evidence of events; whereas the scenes depicting the dead record the aftermath of the massacre, and are therefore corroborating evidence that points to the commission of "serious crimes," allegations that were widely supported by witness testimony. My own observations come at a considerable distance from these events (at the remove of historical time as well as from the perspective of someone who is not a legal practitioner). This enables a different form of critical proximity, whereby the power to witness events is also constituted by a form of reflexivity in which those who have stakes in the events of March 29 might come to examine the complex interactions, discursive frameworks, and histories expressed by law. The original violence captured at the scene of the crime thus returns in a mediated form, both via the damaged materiality of the tape itself and through its protracted legal afterlife, specifically the procedural mechanisms of the court and the legal requirements to which it was repeatedly submitted.

Witness for the prosecution Liri Loshi gives evidence before Senior Prosecutor Mr. Dirk Ryneveld, International Tribunal for the former Yugoslavia, Tuesday, February 10, 2009

Q. My next question—there are only going to be two more questions, and that is going to conclude my cross-examination. So my first question has to do with the authenticity of the footage in relation to the date when it was made. Is there some compelling evidence that would prove the date when this was taken? Was it exactly June 1999? [. . .]

A. With regard to your first question, my sentence uttered on the tape is, "We are in Izbica, 23rd of June, 1999, 1215 is the time, 15 minutes after noon." This is my opening line when the recording starts, and then I explain what I'm doing.[22]

Q. My final question, sir: You've told us, both in the statement and under cross-examination, about the actual videotapes, and you talked about differences in format and then re-recording. The first format of the original tape, I'm holding up a very small videotape. Would you look at it, please. Is that the original format of the tape which was designated as 1733, is that the format of the original tape?

A. From the format that I can see from here, I can't make it out all that clearly, but it could well be the cassette that I brought to this court.

Q. Then I'm holding up a larger, normal size videotape that is usually in use at video stores, et cetera. Is that the size of videotape that you recorded or re-recorded what was on the smaller tape? Is that the two different sizes?

A. Which one, the small one or the big one?

Q. Now looking at a bigger one.

A. Yes. That's the size of the cassette that I used to transfer the material from the small cassette to the large one, because later I used a small cassette of the kind that you're holding in your other hand.[23]

Technical Witness to a War Crime

Appearing initially as an energetic field of interference patterns, eventually these magnetic encodings disappear to expose a pictorial field, a meadow, in which the mute horror of dead bodies begins to reveal itself. The image degradations evidenced in the Izbica massacre tape, or Exhibit P232, immediately alert us to the material violations of the body proper that will soon begin to emerge out of the depths of the image. In this sense the tape registers a strange kind of confluence between the actual violence of the events depicted and the damaged or precarious nature of the material tasked with documenting the crime. The technical witnesses and media artifacts that result from times of war often struggle to meet the court's legal demand for coherent accounts of history. However, rather than diminishing their ability to stand convincingly before the tribunals of history as witnesses to a crime, the degraded quality of such evidential material should, in point of fact, augment their capacity for testimony. The epistemic demand of institutional forums that call for a stable and ordered image field, which can account convincingly for situations of historical violence, is challenged by such defective media. Yet as I have argued, poorly recorded materials serve both to register the radical incomprehensibility of what has taken place and to provide extraneous information about the conditions of documentation itself. An indistinct or compromised image might signal the inherent physical risks of filming in certain situations such that the photographer's nervous movements are folded into the recorded event, or may be a consequence of the scarcity of recording material available in a conflict zone, or even result from the technical vagaries of the media's production and processing.

In classical cinema, frenzied distortion in the visual field has come to signal immanent danger and threat as the stability of a world organized as a coherent picture falls apart and is consumed by violence—a filmic technique that director Michael Haneke has actively resisted, opting instead to extrude sublimated violence from restrained and deliberately passive images. The flat and clinically ordered image stripped of all affect is most terrifying in a Haneke film, and the rupture when it occurs is all the more ferocious. His 2005 film *Caché* is paradigmatic in this regard. On the other hand, artist and theater director Rabih Mroué has suggested that the semiotics of camera movement can be decoded to reveal the ideologies of state power or, conversely, also those of political struggle and resistance. In his well-known performance lecture *Pixelated Revolution* presented at Documenta 13, which explored the role of media during the early days of the Syrian uprising, Mroué claimed that stable images shot with the use of a tripod designate the controlling machinic eye of the state, whereas blurry low-res footage shot in haste belongs to the aesthetic domain of the revolutionary. Although Haneke rejects a reductivist reading of camerawork that would locate political struggle solely within the formal register of chaotic movement, the tyranny of his methodical images has direct recourse to the kinds of coercive power and state violence suggested by Mroué; a motif that is central to *Caché*, with its narrative of repressed and racialized violence rooted in the colonial legacies of the Algerian war. The clean and ordered images so coveted by legal professionals are a sign of the testimonial power given over to the aesthetic condition of transparency as best able to narrate history: unequivocal images devoid of blurred movement and focal flaws; whereas poorly produced and damaged media cannot perform their truth claims entirely within the register of representation, and require further elaboration and forensic analysis. The productive force of impure images recovers violence not in order to do battle with the state and its history-making institutions but in the name of an ethics that demands a different response to acts of witnessing.

The massacre video cannot, of course, be directly compared to the narrative constructions of cinema or the conventions of journalism, as its status is that of legal evidence of a war crime. But the impoverished condition of the videotape, with its at times destabilized image field, is disturbingly resonant with chilling affect, reminding us of the political program that sought to eradicate difference through ethnic

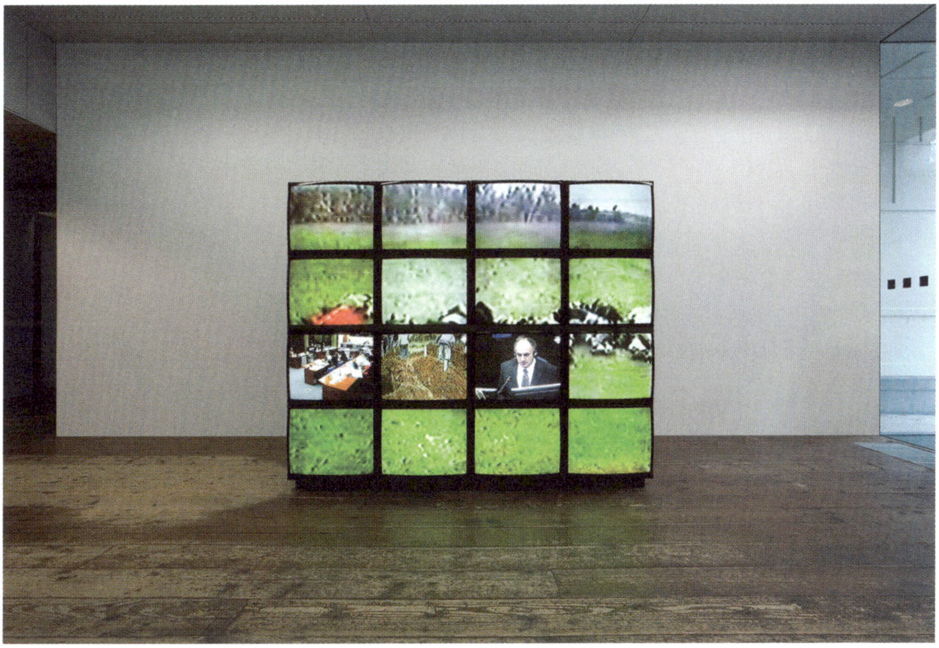

Figure 8.11
Installation view, *Evidence on Trial*, Sequence: Izbica Massacre, Susan Schuppli. *See you in The Hague* exhibition program curated by Brigitte van der Sande, 2014. Photo credit: Stroom Den Haag.

cleansing. In order for an object to bear witness legally, given that it cannot swear to tell the truth, it must move through a sequence of bureaucratic stages that address its relevant features or structurally recompose it. However, literary critic Shoshana Felman has argued that it is the very difficulty of producing an intelligible narrative in the face of historical trauma that characterizes the true act of bearing witness. Drawing upon the filmed documentation of the Eichmann Trial in which a witness, Yehiel Dinoor/K-Zetnik, fainted while attempting to testify, she asks: under what circumstances, and in what ways, can the withdrawal of the legal conventions of speech constitute a form of legal testimony in its own right?[24] The true capacity to bear witness occurs not through (Felman suggests) acts of coherent testimony but through technologies of imperfect inscription: the fainting body, shaky camerawork, incorrect codecs, etc. Rather than reducing its capacity to perform its truth claims before the Tribunal, the inconsistent quality of Loshi's videotape enhances its testimonial credence insofar as the epistemic dimensions of an image regime called to account for historical violence through explicative narration are supplemented by an ontological truth that might require the intervention of a forensic expert endowed with the task of extracting meaning from errant electrons or executed bodies.

Writing about Francis Bacon's paintings, Gilles Deleuze contends that "photographs cannot produce an intensity of sensation, or rather cannot produce differences within sensation" in that, unlike painting, they do not activate the body and provide different ways of seeing. Rather, photographic images are merely a recording and a semblance of what we see.[25] Painting, says Deleuze, requires the cooperation of the artist's hand, which is always in a relationship of imbalance with the eye. What the eye sees can never be registered absolutely by the hand: something different always intervenes to arise from within the depths of paint. I contend that many of the media artifacts presented during the legal proceedings of the ICTY emphatically register this imbalance at the level of the machinic, which is irreducible to the visual field. Sensation can evolve directly out of the technical reorganization of the image event, that is to say, out of its material depths (analog or digital) rather than necessarily out of its mimetic regime. A different stratum of knowledge about these events of crisis—knowledge that arises out of processing—is impelled into presence, activating the sensorial domain of testimony at the moment that the plane of resemblance—the appearance of things—gives way to the furtive emissions of the ontological substratum. At these moments of intensified image compression, a new *material witness* might be said to emerge from within the depths of magnetic particles or pixels.

Witness for the prosecution Liri Loshi cross-examined by Defense Attorney Dan Ivetić, International Tribunal for the former Yugoslavia, Thursday, October 26, 2006

Q. Okay. Now, as far as the filming of the tape is concerned, you had already stated that you did not accompany at all times Mr. Thaqi as he filmed. Now, in particular with the segment that we saw earlier today, the first segment where we saw the set of bodies, as a medical doctor would you have expected there to be more blood at such a dramatic and large-numbered amount of corpses in the same location, particularly more blood on the ground surrounding these bodies?

A. Would I expect it as a medical doctor?

Q. Yes.

A. I don't know. I don't know.

Q. Okay.

A. But I'm telling you that I saw lots of blood there. And if you look carefully at those tapes, you will be able to see some of it too.[26]

Evidence on Trial

When I interviewed Bob Reid, I was extremely fortunate to also tour the evidence vault of the OTP and peer into several of its evidence boxes. It is in this archive that the most sensitive and rare materials are stored, including all the exhumation records and X-rays from Srebrenica as well as the 18 Mladić notebooks, containing 3,500 pages of meticulous handwritten notes documenting every meeting that he (General Ratko Mladić) attended during the war in Bosnia from 1992 to 1995. These constitute, in fact, one of the few OTP seizures whose authenticity was questioned by the defense, requiring their extraction from the vault, and their scientific examination and verification by the Netherlands Forensic Institute. This forensic testing was demanded despite the fact that Mladić said they were his notebooks, Karadzić confirmed it, and they were found hidden behind a wall in Mladić's house.[27] The authenticity and condition of the two copies of the Izbica massacre video did not arouse legal concerns necessitating further forensic video analysis: this despite the fact that under cross-examination Loshi told a rather confused story about the sequence of events surrounding the filming, and even contradicted his own previous testimony. He also admitted that he left the VHS copy of the video in the Istok Mountains of Macedonia for a period of months and that, back home in Izbica, Thaqi's hidden camera containing the original Izbica tape had been discovered and stolen. Fortunately, he was able to enlist KLA help in recovering it. These are all factors that could challenge the tape's chain of custody, and impede its verification. Even Milošević, while cross-examining Loshi, does not doubt the fact that dead bodies are depicted in a meadow. He casts doubt on the capacity of the video to prove what happened and how, given that Loshi arrived on the scene after the events in question: "But what I would like you to tell me is how, by showing a picture of a body in a meadow, you set out to prove that death was caused by execution?"[28] Yet as has been emphasized to me by an ICTY prosecutor, the point is not so much whether the state of a given piece of evidence is dubious but, rather, whether expert opinion, forensic analysis, or witness testimony can duly enhance or diminish its probative value. The task of courtroom procedures is to transform uncertainty into convincing and plausible legal narratives. Loshi's admissions and stumbles under cross-examination corroborate the state of a video shot in the midst of a warzone and the great personal risks that attended both himself and Thaqi in their efforts to bring these images to the world's attention. In the end, equivocations as to its evidential status were minimal. What the remarkable account of the videotape as a *material witness* to a crime can tell us about the historic and horrific events of Izbica corresponds to Loshi's own testimony and the struggles he too experienced at various points to meet the court's demand for coherent accounts of history.

Witness for the prosecution Liri Loshi cross-examined by Senior Prosecutor Mr. Dirk Ryneveld, International Tribunal for the former Yugoslavia, Tuesday, September 3, 2002

Q. Very briefly, Dr. Loshi, you've had an opportunity, as we all did, to see this very brief edited tape. Do you recognize the scenes from this edited video as being part of the videotape that you provided to investigators of the OTP?

A. Yes.

Q. And although obviously very shortened, are these scenes that we have seen true and accurate depictions of what you saw on the days that you took the video?

A. Everything that was filmed was true.[29]

Witness Liri Loshi testifying before Judge Iain Bonomy, International Tribunal for the former Yugoslavia, Thursday, October 26, 2006

[Defence counsel confer]

Judge Bonomy: Do you think this tape has been doctored in any way or does it represent what you saw at the scene?

The Witness: No, I don't think so, that—because I have the other VHS tape which is in Tribunal possession now, and these two can be compared very easily.[30]

9 EXPERT WITNESS

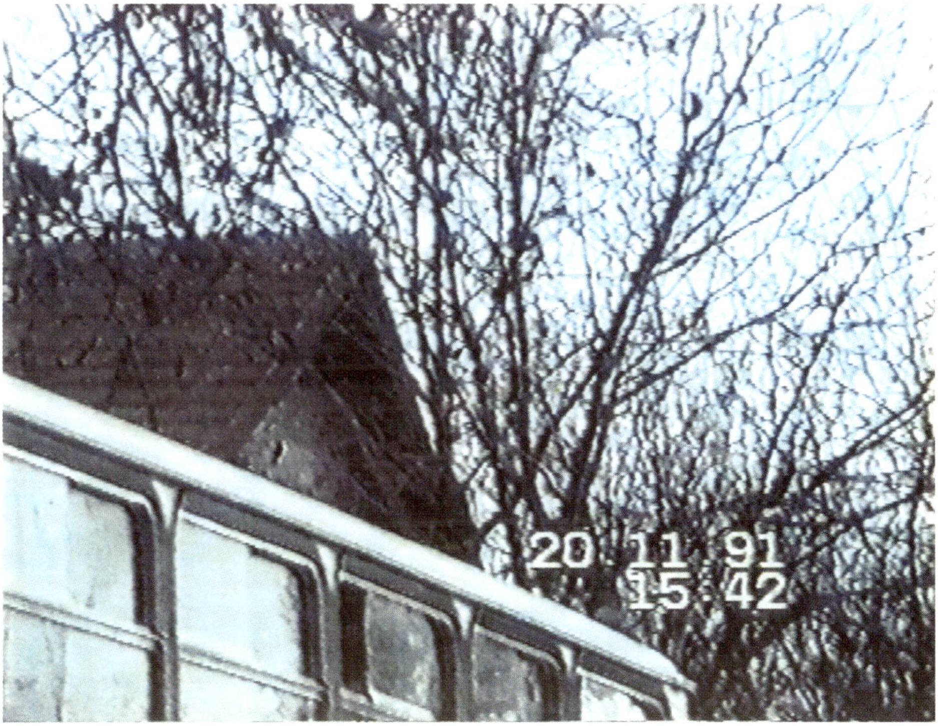

Figure 9.1

IT-95-13a: Dokmanović [JPG] Video still of Exhibit D2 at 15:42. Document Type: Exhibit 217. Date: 17/06/1998. By: Prosecution. Source: ICTY Court Records.

Case No. IT-95-13-A

THE PROSECUTOR OF THE TRIBUNAL AGAINST SLAVKO DOKMANOVIC

Expert Witness Paul Tabbush gives evidence before Prosecutor Mr. Clint Williamson, International Tribunal for the former Yugoslavia, Thursday, June 18, 1998

Q. As you traveled this route, were you also able to recognize any of the trees which you believe might have been depicted in the video segment marked 15.42?

A. Yes.

Q. What kind of tree did you initially recognize there?

A. Well, the original one was a Lombardy poplar I had seen on the video still, segment 15.42, what appeared to be the outline of a Lombardy poplar or a tree of similar appearance.

Q. Is there something distinctive about this Lombardy poplar?

A. Yes. It's a very distinctive tree with upswept branches.

Q. I would like for you at this time to view Prosecutor's Exhibit 222, and if this can be displayed on the ELMO as well, and if you would point out the tree you're talking about?

A. I'm referring to the very upswept branches of this tree here with a very straight central stem and then upswept branches with a very tight angle between those branches and the main stem.

Q. Now, after spotting the Lombardy poplar, did you recognize another tree in that immediate area?

A. Yes, I did.

Q. How did you recognize this tree?

A. This tree bears a certain spatial relationship with the building behind it.

Q. Did you have an opportunity to examine the tree more closely?

A. Yes. In fact, I had a video still with me of the building and of this particular tree, and I examined the branch angles and the arrangement of the main branches of that tree in relation to the image on the video.

Q. What did you look for in trying to determine if this tree that you were examining was the same one depicted in the videotape at 15.42?

A. Firstly, there is the spatial relationship with the Lombardy poplar. It had to be some distance from it because of the way in which it appears in the video. Also, it bears a relationship with a building which has its gable close to and facing the road.

Q. At this time, I would like for you to look at Prosecutor's Exhibit 218. Is this the tree that we're talking about?

A. Yes, indeed. This is the tree I inspected.

Q. What kind of tree is this?

A. It's a walnut tree.

Q. What was your conclusion after examining this tree as to whether it was the same one seen in the video segment at 15.42?

A Yes, I recognized this tree immediately.

Q. Now, after you located these various trees from the videotape, did you document their locations on this map which we have marked as Prosecutor's Exhibit 241?

A. Yes, that's correct. [. . .]

Q. Mr. Tabbush, are there certain characteristics unique and distinctive to a particular tree which would differentiate it from other trees and allow you to positively identify it?

A. Yes. The arrangement of the major branches on a tree are caused by a combination of genetic and environmental factors so that no two trees will be exactly the same.

Q. In this regard, trees are somewhat like people, are they not, except perhaps even more unique, since environment also affects their appearance?

A. That's right. Not only environment, of course, but they are—people are symmetrical about a central access. Trees aren't symmetrical about any access. So if two identical trees were rotated through ten degrees, you would see a different image of branching.

Q. If you have two trees that are genetically identical planted next to each other, would their appearance be the same?

A. It would be extremely unlikely. Even if there were no environmental factors, it would be cxtremely unlikely that they were both planted in the same radial orientation. In other words, one is more likely to be rotated around its vertical access with respect to the other one. It would be very unlikely that they would both be planted in the same orientation.

```
Q. Is there any doubt in your mind that this walnut tree that you
examined and on which you have done these comparisons is the same
one that is depicted in the videotape at 15.42?

A. None at all.[1]
```

Trees Are Somewhat Like People

This exchange between expert witness Professor Paul Tabbush and Prosecutor Mr. Clint Williamson takes place during the war crimes prosecutions of the International Criminal Tribunal for the former Yugoslavia (ICTY), specifically the trial of Slavko Dokmanović. From January 19 to June 25, 1998, the ICTY heard the trial against Dokmanović, who was charged with participating in the mass execution of more than 200 people at the Ovčara farm southeast of Vukovar, Croatia, on November 20, 1991. What makes this exchange particularly noteworthy is that the videotape alibi provided by Dokmanović and his Defense Counsel (Toma Fila and Vladimir Petrović) was proven to be false, based upon a detailed media reconstruction conducted in February 1998 documenting the route that the accused claimed to have traveled and filmed on the day of the massacre. Although this investigation was conducted more than six years later, and at a different time of year, it allowed for a comparative mathematical analysis of various trees that appeared in the videotape alibi as well as in its subsequent reenactment.

Dokmanović maintained that he could not have been at the Ovčara farm during the time of the massacre since he was traveling far south of Vukovar and had shot video footage with a time code and date stamp along the way that matched the exact date and time of the mass killings. His Defense team duly entered this tape into evidence as Defense Exhibit 2.[2] However, the Prosecution was skeptical, not least because two survivors, Berghofer and Čakalić, had provided eyewitness testimony placing Dokmanović at the scene: "Two witnesses confirmed that they personally saw Slavko Dokmanović for a short while two to five minutes in the hangar at the Ovčara farm in the interval between 2 and 4 p.m."[3] The fortuitous existence of the video alibi raised considerable doubts, prompting the Prosecution to enlist the aid of one of the ICTY's investigators—Vladimir Dzuro—in reconstructing Dokmanović's movements on the afternoon in question: "With camera in hand, Dzuro hopped in a vehicle and retraced the route Dokmanović claimed he took on the afternoon of Nov. 20, 1991, recording the drive in the same way the Defence claimed Dokmanović had done."[4] Ultimately, a Lombardy poplar, a mulberry, and a walnut tree would come to stand as crucial *material witnesses* in the prosecution of an alleged war criminal.

According to the indictment issued by the ICTY on April 3, 1996, and amended on December 2, 1997, Slavko Dokmanović "aided and abetted" the Yugoslav People's Army and Serbian paramilitary, under the command of Mile Mrkšić, Miroslav Radić, and Veselin Šljivančanin, in the forced removal and transport of approximately 260 non-Serbs who had taken refuge from the siege of Vukovar in the local hospital. "Among those removed in this way were wounded patients, hospital staff, soldiers who had been defending the city, Croatian political activists, and other civilians. By the time the medical staff meeting with Major Šljivančanin concluded, the soldiers had removed almost all of the men who were at the hospital."[5] From the Vukovar Hospital the captives were taken to a farm in Ovčara, where they were beaten at great length. They were then moved to a location between the farm and Grabovo, where they were shot and killed. Dokmanović was charged with personal criminal responsibility for various events that took place that day, each of which was subject to areas of jurisdiction granted to the ICTY under Resolution 827: grave breaches of the Geneva Conventions, violations of the laws or customs of war, and crimes against humanity.[6]

When OTP Investigator Dzuro reconstructed and recorded the exact route taken by Dokmanović, according to specifications provided by his Defense Counsel as well in statements he gave when interviewed in Scheveningen prison, the well-established trees that appeared at the end of the alibi videotape, which also designated the endpoint of Dokmanović's journey, were nowhere in sight. In their place grew an entirely different grouping of mature trees. Unfortunately, or perhaps deliberately, the original recording was shot out of a car window, and all that is visible at the end of the tape are buses, the roof gable of a house, and the tops of trees. While the architecture of buildings that were still standing years later would have provided easy points of cross-reference had they been filmed, in their absence the intricate lacework of branches growing over a period of six seasons required an unusual form of expertise for a war crimes tribunal: a specialist in the taxonomic classification and identification of wooded plants—a dendrologist. (Dendrology is a specialized field of botany situated within the broader domain of silviculture, which is itself concerned with the growth, establishment, and management of forests.) Since no two trees ever grow in a precisely identical manner, the complex geometry generated by their branch structure functions as a kind of arboreal signature that is considered more distinctive than the whorls of human fingerprints. A frame-by-frame video analysis conducted by British silviculturist and "tree expert" Paul Tabbush, detailing the unique growth pattern of several trees pictured along the route that Dokmanović had purportedly driven, overturned his alibi and confirmed that he had in fact made a U-turn back to the vicinity of the farm. Although the disputed video, with its mute bystanders, could not prove Dokmanović's specific involvement in the perpetration of a war crime, it did offer corroborating evidence in support of testimony given by the two surviving eyewitnesses, who insisted that Dokmanović was indeed present at the time of the mass execution, something he had vehemently denied. The trial thus turned upon a remarkable conjunction between disparate forms of evidence and multiple modes of testimony; from eyewitness accounts, investigative reports, and media documentation to the geometrical expression of natural objects and the analytic observations of an expert who could decode the fingerprints of trees. On June 29, 1998, Dokmanović committed suicide whilst in the ICTY Detention Unit. The Trial Chamber consequently terminated all proceedings against him two weeks later.

Should Videos of Trees Have Standing?

In his well-known text, Christopher D. Stone raised the provocation, by way of his title—*Should Trees Have Standing? Toward Legal Rights for Natural Objects*—as to whether nature should be entitled to a form of legal recognition independent of the humans who might make use of it for commerce or pleasure. He posed this question in order to advance the possibility that natural objects such as a forest be taken seriously as legal actors and thus accorded certain rights, privileges, and obligations under the law.[7] To stand before the law means to be recognized and treated as an equal in the eyes of the judiciary regardless of one's station in life or wealth. Historically, this condition of equal legal recognition effectively designated white men and not women or slaves as the sole holders of rights, but the point was that "to stand before the law" meant to be recognized by the judiciary as a rights-bearing agent. While a nature reserve may be a protected entity whose stewardship is governed and protected by environmental legislation, and even enforced by law, such a natural object does not in and of itself have any recourse to the law except insofar as its destruction or misuse might impact upon the humans who avail themselves of it as a source of respite and space of leisure. The nature reserve, together with forests, rivers, or mountains, are therefore legally "rightless," that is to say, subject to the law but not the bearer of rights themselves.

Environmental policies may protect an old growth forest such as Cathedral Grove on Vancouver Island insofar as it is conserved for our continued enjoyment and use, but these regulatory controls have not been drafted with a view toward granting such ancient trees their own legal rights independent of their specific use value to humans.[8] There are few exceptions to this global legal framework, apart from the recent adoptions of the Pachamama Constitution or Law of Mother Earth in Bolivia and Ecuador.[9] These new legal arrangements have transformed nature into a subject and bearer of rights rather than a mere object upon which the actions of other rights-bearing agents are performed. Many of the entities engaged in the willful destruction of nature are themselves nonhuman actors such as mining companies or oil and gas refineries, whose legal rights have been historically enshrined within the concept of corporate legal personhood.[10] Indeed, Stone reminds us that the legal world has long been "peopled with in-animate rights-holders: trusts, corporations, joint ventures, municipalities, Subchapter R partnerships, and nation-states, to mention just a few."[11] These lifeless rights-bearers do not necessarily have the capacity to speak directly to the court and must rely upon lawyers as mediators, which is also what most people do who find themselves subject to the law.[12] Today the notion that nonhuman entities such as corporations can operate as fully recognized legal persons that can own property, sue for damages, or be found liable for their deeds may not seem as counterintuitive as it once did.

Stone's innovation was to propose a further extension of the concept of legal personhood to a new group of nonhuman agents, namely natural objects. The ontological condition of the human as *the* proper body that could stand before the law was replaced by the legal condition of personhood established in the late nineteenth century in which rights and obligations could accrue to nonhumans. Trees are ontologically given as "standing" in terms of their vertical inclination toward the sun and soil from which they derive their nourishment and strength of purpose, but their capacity to stand legally before the law as rights-bearing and obliging agents does not proceed from any such *a priori* natural "bearing" or physiological comportment. The ironic demand invoked by Stone—that trees should have standing when they are obviously already literally standing—serves to highlight the degree to which the "laws of nature" and the "legal rights of nature" remain largely incommensurate categories of assembly despite their suggestive semantic borrowings. In adapting Stone's title and leading question, I aim to reflect upon the legal status of another group of nonhuman objects, namely media, specifically photographic and videotaped images of trees, but not with a view toward advancing their legal agency as rights-bearing entities; rather, with the intention of asserting their considerable agency to bear witness to "legal rites," specifically those evidentiary practices and protocols that governed the war crimes prosecutions of the ICTY, which recently concluded with the trial of Ratko Mladić in December 2017. In the case of the Dokmanović videotape, which required the wholesale reconstruction of the tendered evidence many years after the alleged time of the crime, its probative value was contingent upon a level of accuracy and clarity sufficient to allow Tabbush to conduct his comparative analysis and render his expert opinion. However, the numerous constraints encountered by Czech Investigator Dzuro in making a precise copy of the Dokmanović journey and his alleged alibi recording led, at times, to the production of a rather poor-quality videotape and substandard photographic images, as is revealed by his testimony in court.

Investigator Vladimir Dzuro gives evidence before Prosecutor Mr. Clint Williamson, International Tribunal for the former Yugoslavia, Thursday, June 18, 1998

[Videotape played]

Vladimir Dzuro: A. Here I turn left towards Ovčara. It's very difficult to film it because the quality of the road is very bad.

Q. Has the condition of this road deteriorated since you have been traveling to Vukovar?

A. Yes. As I said yesterday, for the first time, it was August 1996 when we did the exhumation, and it's clear to see that the quality of the road is—there's no maintenance and the quality of the road is worse than it was in 1996.

Mr. Williamson: Q. In viewing these videotapes, Mr. Dzuro, the times to go between the various locations are not identical to the travel times that you talked about a few moments ago when you went through your measurements to the court. Why is that?

A. Yes, you're right, the time is not the same. But for the purpose of making the video, I really had to drive very slow. You can see even with the slow driving, the quality of the video is not what I want it to be, but you just need more time to travel at a very slow speed; and the measurements I did for my report, there I was driving about 50 kilometers an hour. It was much, much faster than the one I did when I filmed the video.

A. Mr. Fila, we did our best to enhance the quality of this video as much as we could. But unfortunately, the tape itself doesn't give us any more option, yes.[13]

The contingency of image quality does at times seem to assume the character of a moral agent that is able to confer or withhold a determination of truth unless experts intervene to establish the status of images. While the presumed veracity of blurry, real-time footage functions convincingly within popular culture, in legal domains jurists cannot read such semiotics as a sufficient index of fact. Within court, the truth claims of evidence must be produced. Dzuro's painstaking reconstruction, in which he measured distances between roof angles, roads, and trees in order to retrace Dokmanović's steps, combined with the detailed arboreal analysis of Professor Tabbush, were able to establish both the deceit of the original footage and the credibility of the investigative reproduction. The moral order of the image was, in this case, arrived at retroactively through the manufacture of *new* evidence. Dzuro's investigative media work, and especially the insights provided by Tabbush, signal the expanding role that technical knowledge and scientific expertise play in establishing where received knowledge about the truth in images resides. Unlike the Balkan Wars, which ran during the transition from analog to digital media and still generated substantial analog materials, as demonstrated by the ICTY's archival holdings, the preponderance of online media streaming out of conflict zones today requires juridical attention that is progressively directed toward the testimonials encoded in pixels and code—that is to say: the truth claims of metadata, which carries extraneous information about the image event, such as date, time, and GPS coordinates. Together these are capable of substantiating, but also overturning, the self-evident claims of images as representations of events. Troubling the aesthetic fallacies of "naive realism" demands cross-examination not only of people—witnesses and experts—but also of images themselves.[14]

Within legal proceedings such as those of the ICTY, evidential truths are generally corroborated by eyewitness testimony and expert reports, and reinforced by the broader context of the conflict, forgoing the need for scientific testing of evidence. However, the option remains for the judiciary, public prosecutors, and defense counsel to request further scientific analysis of evidence, and the Netherlands Forensic Institute was on standby to provide these services. Outside of the courtroom, within the domains of journalism and popular culture, degraded image quality has become a standard and widely used signifier of real time, to the extent that the graininess of a surveillance image has attained an aesthetic value equivalent to that of indexical truth—not despite its visual deficiencies, but precisely because of them.[15] Media theorist Thomas Y. Levin argues that the aesthetics of real-time image capture has reinvented the photographic index as a predominantly temporal rather than spatial attribute. "By adopting the rhetorics of real-time broadcast so characteristic of television and a certain economy of CCTV—not to mention that of webcam culture—cinema has displaced an impoverished spatial rhetoric of photo-chemical indexicality with a thoroughly contemporary, and equally semiotically 'motivated' rhetoric of *temporal indexicality*."[16] Yet the visual poverty of media evidence presented during the war crimes prosecutions of the ICTY was more often than not a direct consequence of the limited availability of recording technology and the haste with which footage was shot. In the case of Dzuro's reenactment video, its shortcomings are not an index of its having been obtained under conditions of political duress, but rather a consequence of the passage of time in which some of the physical features of the landscape had changed. Transformations in the postwar landscape around Vukovar would ultimately require that videos of trees be

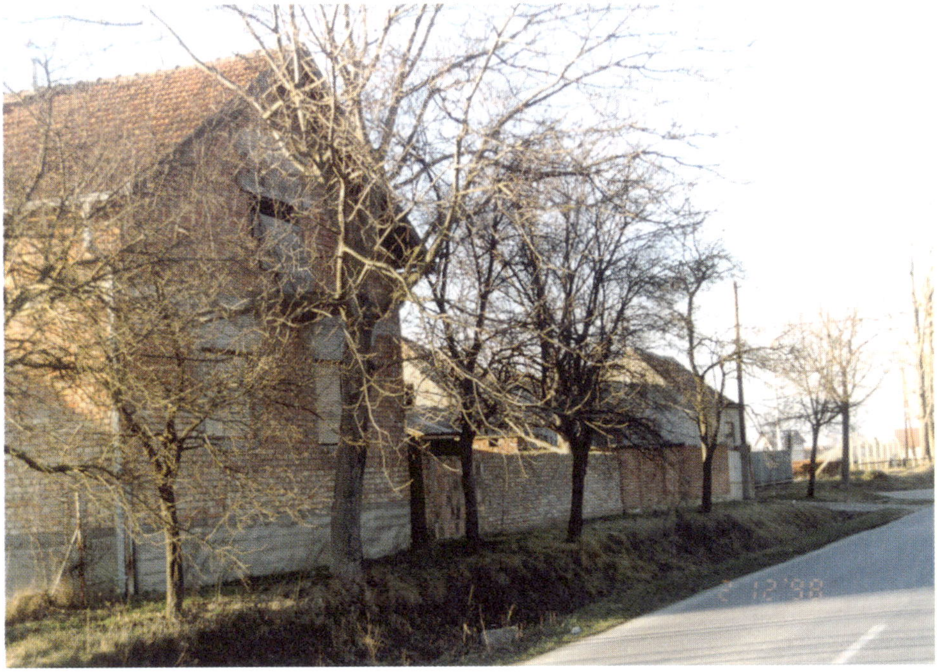

Figure 9.2
Dokmanović [JPG] Photograph taken by witness on February 12, 1998, depicting house at the alleged location recorded on Exhibit D2 at 15:42. Document Type: Exhibit 226. Date: 18/06/1998. By: Prosecution. Source: ICTY Court Records.

called to the witness stand to testify before the judiciary as *material witnesses* to a crime. Throughout his extended testimony in court, Dzuro recounts the many difficulties he faced in his objective to produce an exact temporal and spatial replica of the journey as it was undertaken in 1991, including the position of a traffic sign which had long since disappeared, save its concrete base. Dzuro was attempting to re-create the exact video stills that the FBI laboratories at Quantico in Virginia had extracted from the Dokmanović alibi video. In the exchange that follows we are able to gain some insight into the methods employed by Dzuro in his determination to produce video evidence with the highest possible probative value despite the passage of many years.

`Investigator Vladimir Dzuro gives evidence before Prosecutor Mr. Clint Williamson, International Tribunal for the former Yugoslavia, Thursday, June 18, 1998`

Q. Mr. Dzuro, at the point where we left off yesterday, we were talking about this trip that you had gone on to Vukovar in February of this year to investigate scenes that were depicted in the videotape. When you were on this visit to Vukovar, did you take any photographs of locations that you visited?

A. Yes, I did.

Q. At this time, I would like for you to view the first photograph, which I will mark as Prosecutor's Exhibit 224, and if you can explain to us what is depicted in this photograph? I would ask you, Mr. Dzuro, if you could display this on the ELMO, please? Can you explain what is depicted in this photograph, please?

A. I photographed this area. This is the spot I depicted on the map as well, which I marked as the location at 15.42. This is the house with the gable facing the road, the tree in front of it, the branches. Also, the electric post, the grass area on the right side of the road, the shed, and then in the background here is this tree with the very specific top (indicated). I will talk about that later. [. . .]

This the area right here in front of the shed (indicated). If you look on this photograph and the still I took from the video, it is obvious there is something missing. There is a traffic sign in this area—there is a traffic sign in this area on the still which is not on this photograph, so I did an investigation into this, and I thoroughly walked in that area around, and I discovered the concrete base with the metal bar which is the same one which is used in that area for the traffic signs. So I took a photograph of that and the exact location where I discovered that, and this is the photograph.

Q. Now I am going to show you the next photograph which we will mark as Prosecutor's Exhibit 228, and if you can indicate what is depicted in this photograph, please?

A. So what I did afterwards, I—I wanted to reconstruct the scene. For that reason, first I took the picture of the scene the way it looked, which is the photograph—the first one I presented. [. . .]

Q. Which was marked as Prosecutor's Exhibit 224, correct?

A. That's correct. And then I went to the UNTAES and asked for their assistance because I needed to obtain a traffic sign, this traffic sign which shows to the drivers that you are driving on the main road. The UNTAES, they weren't able to provide me with that, but they were happy to assist, so we went to the local police and asked them to provide a traffic sign, but unfortunately, the conditions in Vukovar the way they are, they also were not able to assist us with the traffic sign. So I asked for the police, traffic police car, the

```
patrol car, and we went together back to the scene. What I didn't
want to do, I didn't want to remove the traffic sign from the other
direction because it could cause some traffic problems, so I asked
the Croatian police for their assistance. [ ... ] I wanted to have
the traffic sign here. There is a particular reason for that. But if
I can explain a little bit later?

Q. Perhaps that would make more sense, yes. Now, as I understand it,
just to make this absolutely clear, this photograph is identical to
the one that has been presented as Prosecutor's Exhibit 224 except
for the fact that you have attempted to reconstruct what was seen in
the videotape by putting the sign back in place; is that correct?

A. Yes, that's correct. I wouldn't call it identical because I'm not
sure I managed to take the same angle because it is very difficult
to find the same angle if you do two photographs. But this is the
photograph of the same location. The only difference is that on this
one, I put the traffic sign back.[17]
```

Branching into Law

In bringing this case to a close, I would like to return to the scene of evidence-making with which I began, namely the examination and cross-examination of Professor Tabbush around the growth pattern of trees featured in the Dokmanović videotape alibi, as well as in the investigative video and photos produced by Dzuro some years later. In this final act of the trial proceeding, nature emerges as a bearer of legal truths, one whose testimony will repudiate even that of the human witness whose lies it "unearths." Through Tabbush's detailed account of the cartographic constancy retained by the branch structure of trees as they mature and grow, the tree is transformed into an irreproachable and unbending *material witness* that can be mapped onto its erstwhile video doppelgänger. Its wooden features secure its singular identity and act as temporal indices that allow us to travel back in time to the day of the crime. "Q. Is there any doubt in your mind that this [mulberry] tree is the same one as depicted in the video segment marked 15.36? A. None at all."[18] But what is fundamentally distinctive about these particular species of video trees is that they are "unnatural" in the extreme. That is to say: they are vegetative matter encoded within the image matter of technical media. To gain access to the informational quotient that such mediated trees can yield requires not only expertise in the natural sciences, but also skills in media analysis and production. Together these competencies combine to create new categories of legal evidence in which unnatural objects—videos of trees—can bear upon questions of legal truth and even determinations of war crimes.

Q. Are you affiliated with any professional organisations?

A. I'm a member of the UK Institute of Chartered Foresters. I am also a member of the International Poplar Commission, which is a United Nations organisation.[19]

At the time of the trial, Tabbush was himself a member of the International Poplar Commission, one of the oldest statutory bodies created by the Food and Agriculture Organization of the United Nations. Founded in the ruinous wake of the war, it designated the cultivation, conservation, and utilization of poplar and willow trees as key factors in efforts to repair the countryside and rebuild the industrial economies of Europe.[20] There was thus already recognition, in 1947, that the environmental devastation wrought by the war would require the establishment of new legislative frameworks for ensuring the productive agency and protection of nature. In response, the fast-growing poplar was strategically enlisted by the UN to participate in the rehabilitation of Europe's degraded lands and diminished rural livelihoods: an entanglement between nature, military violence, and an international body that prophetically gestures toward the very same tree that will make an appearance within the UN's prosecution of Dokmanović some 50 years later. While Stone's 1972 provocation that nature becomes a rights-bearing agent has yet to be fully realized, the crucial role that nonhuman forms of testimony and new forms of evidence, such as videos of trees, have played in resolving questions of legal truth does position them as active agents in the production of jurisprudence.

In the Dokmanović trial much was made by Defense Counsel of the unreliability of eyewitness testimony advanced in support of his alibi. Two statements that placed him at the scene were refuted. This was done by way of reference to two entirely unrelated cases prosecuted by the ICTY, in which prior acts of witnessing were cited as representative of the vagaries of eyewitness testimony.[21] Given criminal law's foundational reliance upon legal precedent, is it not possible that trees will also come to be regarded as much more than mere background features of crime scene imagery, and might serve as valuable "natural" resources for the production of new legal axioms?[22] Since its establishment on May 25, 1993, the operations of the ICTY have generated millions of procedural records and processed a staggering number of exhibits. Out of this vast archive of evidential holdings a videotape of a mulberry, walnut, and poplar tree has emerged to stand as a steadfast *material witness* before the law.

Expert Witness Paul Tabbush gives evidence before Prosecutor Mr. Clint Williamson, Cross-examined by Defense Counsel Mr. Toma Fila, International Tribunal for the former Yugoslavia, Thursday, June 18, 1998

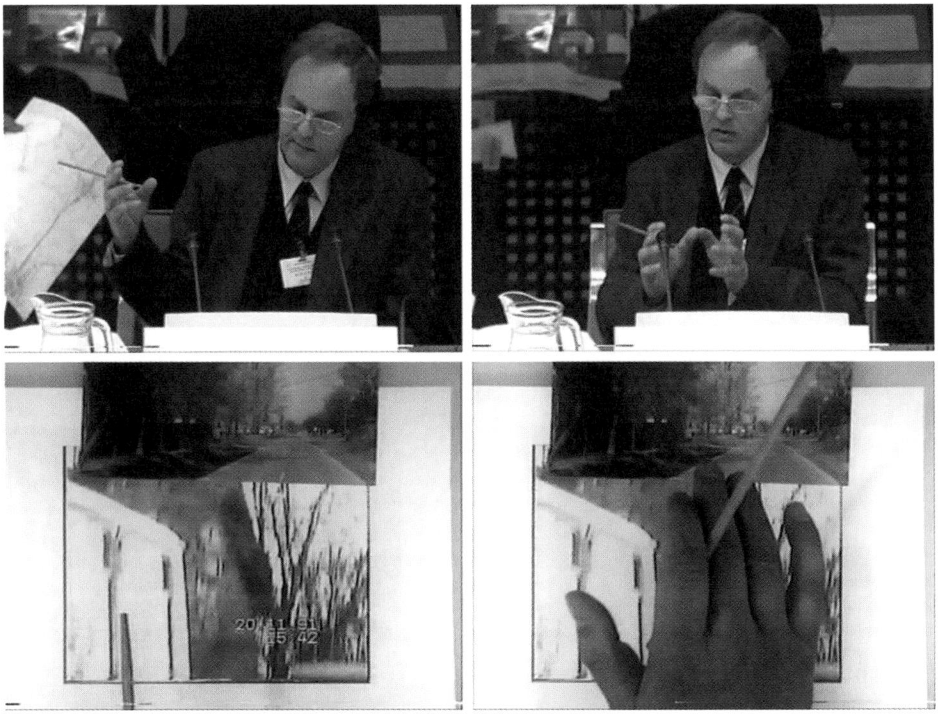

Figure 9.3
IT-95-13a: Dokmanović [MPG] Expert witness Paul Tabbush describing the manner in which trees grow and comparing a photograph from February 12, 1998 and a video still of the same tree from November 20, 1991 on the ELMO. Source: ICTY Court Records.

Mr. Williamson: Q. During the course of the initial consultation with the Prosecution in April, did you have an opportunity to view some photo stills which had been made from a videotape?

A. Yes, I did.

Q. Did you also have an opportunity to view portions of that videotape that had time displays of 15.36 and 15.42?

A. Yes, that's correct.

Q. Based on what you saw, did you feel that there was sufficient material available which would allow you to positively identify the trees which were depicted?

A. Yes. Some of the video stills were of sufficient quality to make out major branch angles and the positions of major branches.

Q. Now, subsequent to that time, in May of this year, did you have occasion to travel to the Vukovar area in order to personally examine the trees that were in question?

A. Yes. [...]

Q. I would like for you at this time to view Prosecutor's Exhibit 215, and also I'll ask him to view 232, [...]

Q. What is different, if anything, between the two photographs?

A. Based on the time line on the video, six growing seasons have passed between these two images, and therefore, the fine branch tracery has extended and become thicker. [...]

Q. Did you use these photographs to create a set of photographic overlays?

A. Yes, I did.

Q. How did you go about doing this?

A. I used imaging software and a flatbed scanner to scan the images and the photographs in such a way that I was able to scale them to the same scale. And then I cropped the image taken from the photograph so that it was small enough to fit over the video still image. This then, because it's at the same scale, allows you to see whether the branches coincide. [...]

Mr. Tabbush [cross-examined by Mr. Fila]: Q. But I want to ask: Professor, if I understood you correctly, you were in Vukovar at the time of full vegetation whereas your compilations and analysis were based on the photographs and the video stills made by Mr. Dzuro; did I understand that correctly?

A. Yes. Yes, that's correct.

Q. Then my second question would be: Does this tree which we see in front, Prosecutor's Exhibit 218, you said that after a certain time, it grows wider, not—it doesn't grow upwards. I mean the walnut.

A. Yes. Can I explain?

Q. Yes. That's what I would like you to explain.

A. Trees extend from their tips, they don't grow, as it were, in the middle of branches, so they leave behind them the major branch angles which represent where buds were set as the tree grew.

Q. Not there, on the other one. Please show that.

A. For instance, this major branch angle here would remain once it was formed by the terminal bud, as it grew upwards, it would remain behind as a major branch position and would not change its height with time (indicated).

Q. Well, in which—so I understand you correctly, in which period of growth does the tree reach its maximum height above which it doesn't grow any longer? How many years does it take?

A. Yes. I'm sorry, I don't think I've made myself clear. The tree grows in height throughout its life, but as it grows, it leaves behind it the significant pattern of branching which doesn't change with time, but, of course, the height of the tree changes continuously throughout its life.

Q. So am I correct in my understanding that, for instance, relative to this roof or the bus, the widening of the angle is not the same, but in the course of growth, this changes?

A. The angles remain as they are. What changes as the tree grows is that the branches get fatter, they increase in girth, but the bud positions remain as they were when they were laid down throughout the life of the tree.

Q. But the height, but the height growths, so this bud is not always in the same position relative to a fixed point?

A. As this—if I may point at this branch here? At the end of a certain year, the tree was at this height. It then produced two buds. One bud produced a side branch and the other one produced a more vertical branch. At the end of the next year, this branch was here and this branch was somewhere around here (indicated). I can't see exactly. So the tip is extending, but the position left behind remains as it was at the time that this node, i.e. this branching position was formed during the development of the tree.

Q. I understand that. I understand that much, yes. But this part of the tree which you've just shown us, this branching position, does it grow relative to the ground? Do I make myself clear?

A. Yes.

Q. Does it grow in height like a person grows? A person, for instance, has a big nose, but he grows in height. Is it the same with trees?

A. No. No, it's not the same. It's not the same with trees. Trees—this point here does not progress up the tree as the tree grows; it's left behind. The bud then extends from here for a year, sets another bud, and then continues to extend, but this angle will always be at the same height above the ground as it was when it was formed (indicated).

Q. I see. Look, for instance, at the edge of the bus and then look at this lower part, the first branching position, above the bus. That's it. And a bit to the right. That's it. Up to which year did this grow and when did it stop growing relative to the roof? I don't know which way to explain it better. Does it always have the same parallel or does it grow, because the house doesn't grow. At least that much we can assume.

A. I can't tell exactly in which year this fork formed, but let us say—

Q. That's exactly what I'm asking.

A. Yes. But when it was formed, which was several years ago, you can tell that from the growth rate of the tree, it formed in this exact position above the ground and then remained there as the tree grew above that point.

Mr. Fila: I apologise, Your Honour. I feel a little stupid, like a parent explaining something to a child and then starting with butterflies, but I'll try to make myself as clear as possible.

Q. In the eight or seven years since the event and the pictures made by Mr. Dzuro, did this ratio change between the tree and the house, just in terms of height, not in terms of angles, not in terms of anything else?

A. The height—this is six—

Q. That's exactly this part which I'm interested in, relative to the house. Please draw a line to the house, to the left. Did that remain the same for the past seven or eight years, or is it lower or higher than it used to be at the time of the event?

A. The same.

Mr. Fila: It remained the same for the past seven years. That's what I wanted to know. Thank you. No more questions.[23]

United Nations
Nations Unies

International Criminal Tribunal for the Former Yugoslavia

Tribunal Pénal International pour l'ex-Yougoslavie

Office of the Prosecutor

Bureau du Procureur

INTERNAL REPORT

Thursday, 11 June, 1998

I am Vladimir DZURO, I am an investigator for the Office of the Prosecutor (OTP) of the ICTY in The Hague.

On 26 and 27 November 1997, Investigator Dennis Milner and I interviewed Slavko Dokmanović in the Scheveningen prison in The Hague. During the course of the interview, Mr. Dokmanović mentioned that he was in possession of video recordings, which he intended to produce to support his alibi. This was the first indication that an alibi video existed.

On 19 January 1998, I was informed by Legal Advisor Clint Williamson that Mr. Fila had supplied the mentioned video tape to the Court and that the OTP would get access to it soon afterwards.

As soon as the OTP obtained a copy of the tape, my colleagues and I had the opportunity to view it. I was tasked by the Prosecutor to identify places shown on the video in Vukovar.

At that time, I began the process of attempting to determine various locations depicted on the videotape, particularly those in relative proximity to Ovćara.

I started my task at the ICTY Video Unit where I printed a number of stills out of the video tape. I also studied the city plan of Vukovar, a map of the Vukovar region, and the statement given to us by Mr. Dokmanović in the Scheveningen prison.

Relying on the above sources, I tentatively established the route that Mr. Dokmanović is alleged to have taken on 20 November 1991.

In February 1998, I travelled on a mission to Vukovar. My primary task at that time was to positively identify locations shown on the videotape and also to determine if the times displayed on the videotape were consistent with actual travel times between the apparent locations.

Based on my on-scene investigations, I was able to establish that at the indicated times the following actions were depicted on the videotape at the locations described below:

15.17 - The group with the cameraman appears to depart from Velepromet

15.26 - The group with the cameraman appears to arrive in the centre of Vukovar

15.30 - The vehicle passes through Sajmište Street travelling in the direction of the southern outskirts of Vukovar towards Negoslavci

15.36 - The vehicle passes the last houses on the southern side of Vukovar as it travels in a southerly direction (on the Vukovar-Negoslavci road).

15.42 - Buses travelling in a southerly direction are filmed at a location approximately 370 meters north of the scene depicted at 15.36 (i.e., approximately 370 meters back toward the centre of Vukovar.

10 BURDEN OF PROOF

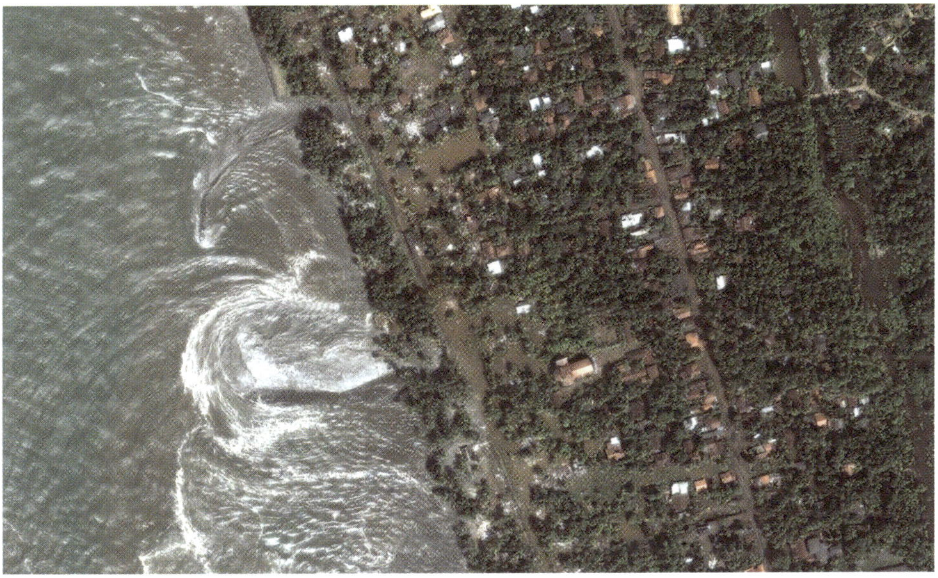

Figure 10.1
Tsunami Strikes Sri Lanka: DigitalGlobe's Quickbird satellite captured an image of the devastation around Kalutara, Sri Lanka, on December 26, 2004, at 10:20 a.m. local time—about an hour after the first in the series of waves hit. Source: NASA/DigitalGlobe.

Fractures and Forces

On December 26, 2004, the tectonics under the Bay of Bengal shifted dramatically when the Indian Plate was forced under the Burma Plate to sink into the earth's mantle. The relatively shallow seismic activity took place less than 30 kilometers below the seabed, fracturing over 1,200 km of the deep-water canyon known as the Sunda Trench. As the powerful faulting grew, its vibrations triggered a series of deadly tsunamis that crashed into the bordering coastal communities, from its epicenter off the coast of Sumatra to as far away as Somalia. It was one of the longest and most devastating earthquakes on record, registering a magnitude at between 9.1–9.3 and lasting upward of 500 seconds. "NASA scientists using data from the Indonesian earthquake calculated it affected Earth's rotation, decreased the length of day, slightly changed the planet's shape, and shifted the North Pole by centimeters. The earthquake that created the huge tsunami also changed the Earth's rotation."[1] The intensity and duration emitted by the energetics of geological matter beneath the Indian Ocean had rocked the entire planet. Almost a quarter of a million people died in its aftermath and 1.74 million have been reported as injured, displaced, or have vanished.

> We'd never seen signals from an earthquake of this size, and the availability of this instrumentation was a real breakthrough in being able to see the complete rupture process of one of these truly monstrous events. ... Two hours after the earthquake has occurred, the wave is spreading out from the Bay of Bengal. Two satellites went over, with the capability of measuring the elevation of the ocean surface. The satellites saw the south-going wave and the north-going part of the wave. It was just good luck that the passage of the satellites caught the tsunami in motion.[2]

In Sri Lanka the civil war between its minority ethnic Tamil population and Sinhalese government forces was still raging in 2004. The destructive forces of the tsunami intensified the politics of aid delivery to its war-torn coastal regions such that the numbers of those killed through political violence were indiscriminately recombined with the death toll produced by the tsunami. Although humanitarian conflicts and crises are consistently reduced to mathematical expressions of misery—statistics that monitor the dead and dying, with relief workers forced to respond in equally calculated measures that can result in disaster management by numbers—the complications of an ecological disaster unfolding amidst a civil war served as a useful alibi for hampering aid and skewing the numbers.[3] As the body count grew, the consequences of 26 years of armed struggle for an independent Tamil State made it difficult to disentangle political deaths from those arising out of natural disaster. The estimated 19,000 Tamils who are said to have perished from the tsunami are still not represented in any of the official tallies. Certainly the ongoing military conflict exacerbated obstacles to delivering aid, as the distribution and allocation of funds was once again fiercely contested between representatives of the Sri Lankan government and the Tamil Tigers. "We've had a long experience in dealing with all sides," said Bernard Barrett of the ICRC.[4] Reports have since established that there was indeed a bias in donor allocations toward Sinhalese-majority areas in the south that were less directly affected by the tsunami than the northeastern rebel-controlled areas. According to a *Joint World Bank-UN Project on the Economics of Disaster Risk Reduction,* expenditures related to relief efforts and rehousing were directed toward Sinhalese-majority areas that historically demonstrated high levels of support and identification with the ruling Sri Lankan Freedom Party (SLFP) of then-President Mahinda Rajapaksa. It remains an open question as to whether the tsunami ultimately aided or abetted efforts toward a ceasefire.

> Taken together, the tsunami and the relief effort constituted at minimum a net $150 million dollar transfer to the southwest of the country relative to the northeast before taking into account the cost in loss of life. The unfavorable distribution of within-district impacts for the Tamil population could only have exacerbated LTTE challenges in resource extraction and manpower recruitment. While these imbalances could not have been decisive in a renewed conflict, they could certainly have altered the GoSL [Government of Sri Lanka] calculus for assessing the potential costs and benefits to pursuing a military solution. The two years immediately following the tsunami saw annual increases in defense spending amounting to 40% per year.[5]

During 2013 I traveled to the former LTTE (Liberation Tigers of Tamil Eelam)-controlled Vanni region of Tamil Eelam for the first time with cinematographer Steffen Kraemer to shoot footage exploring the ways in which the material strata of the landscape might still disclose its complex entangled histories of violence, despite the end of the war in 2009 and tsunami damage slowly receding into the subterfuge of regenerative growth.[6] The northeastern coast of Sri Lanka remains a palimpsest of encrypted histories: a dense living archive of "sensible" traces—part military; part ecological; and now also financial, as a newly minted tourist economy forcefully imprints itself across the land. Although the war has officially ended, ethnic tensions persist in many diverse forms, and today the country's future remains even more uncertain amidst claims of a coup on October 26, 2018, when the current President—Maithripala Sirisena—sacked Prime Minister Ranil Wickremesinghe, replacing him with the former strongman President Rajapaksa. This move to dissolve parliament has since been overturned by the country's Supreme Court, but political unrest has taken hold despite Wickremesinghe's return to office. As we traveled throughout the Vanni region in late 2013, the past was frequently put on display by the victors in the form of improvised

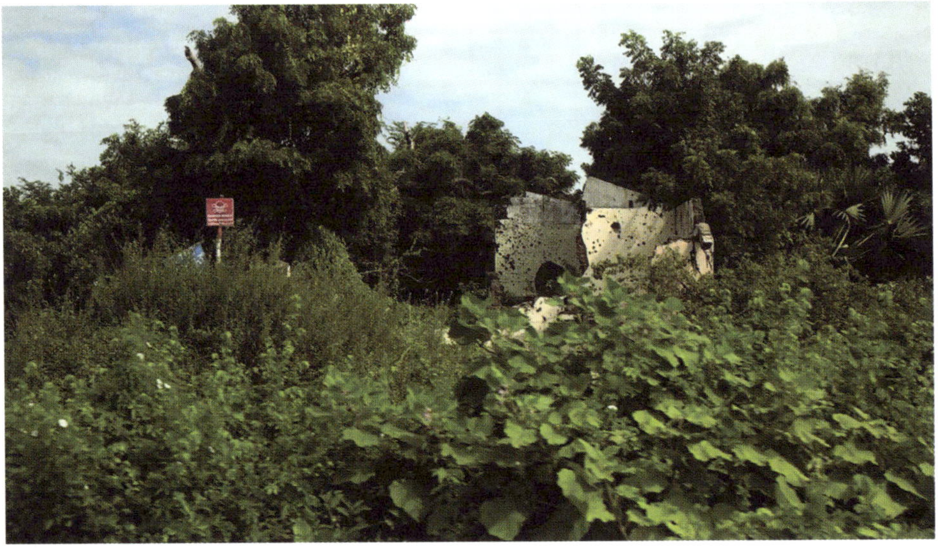

Figure 10.2
Landmines, Tamil Eelam, 2013, *Material Witness*, Susan Schuppli, 2014–2015, HD video, color with sound, 34 minutes.

monuments (destroyed tanks, water towers, a roadside munitions museum, and a Sea Tiger submarine graveyard) that reclaimed sites of political struggle as part of a new global lexicon around the war on terror. The material traces and sites of resistance and armed conflict for an independent Tamil State are systematically being transcoded by the government into universal signifiers of extremism and terror. Everywhere the public language of ethnic division has been strategically recast to reflect a post-9/11 idiom. Against this backdrop, unofficial signs of the recent conflict are disclosed in more subtle and quotidian ways: expressed, for example, by palm trees still devoid of their leafy canopies that preside over the landscape as so many war-torn sentinels, the particular significance of which might go entirely unnoticed. It is out of this slowly evolving geography that a case of extrajudicial killing emerged—executions committed during the final phase of the war that were captured by an anonymous mobile phone recording.

In the aerospace of this new "peace," the commercial arm of the Sri Lankan Air Force has begun operating weekly flights from Triconmalee to Jaffna, capital of the Northern Province and home to its majority Tamil population; a service that sutures the transportation arteries severed during the decades of civil war. As we took off, the dawn light pushed back the lingering cloud cover to reveal the tropical coastline below.

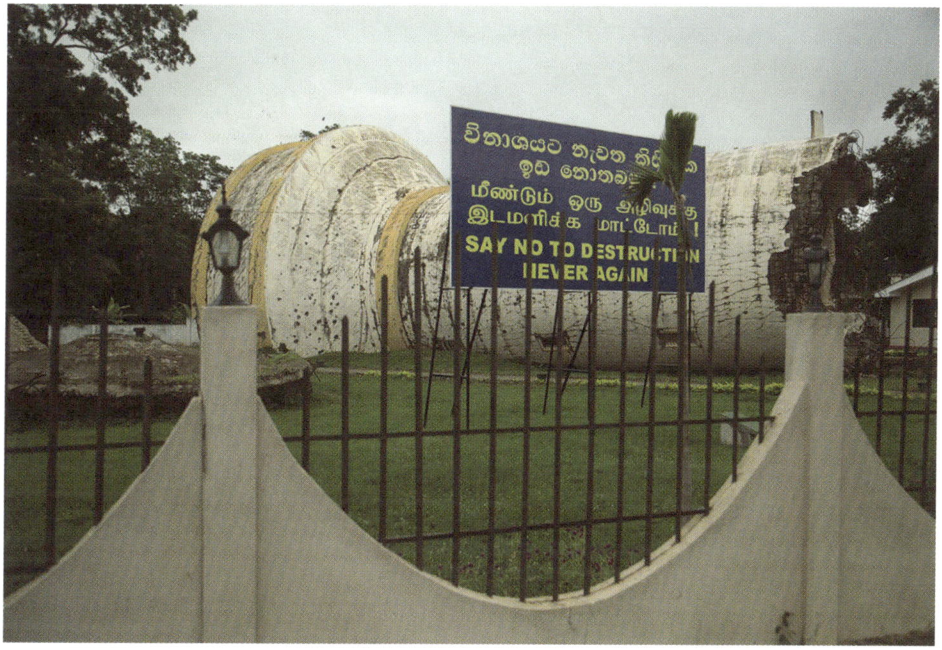

Figure 10.3
Water tower destroyed by the LTTE as government troops advanced onto Kilinochchi in 2009, now a makeshift antiwar monument, *Material Witness*, Susan Schuppli, 2014–2015, HD video, color with sound, 34 minutes.

Gaining altitude unmoored land and sea, dissolving the boundaries between solids and liquids. Our camera's aperture began to struggle with this material fluctuation, as if to remind us of the instability of the events we were attempting to bring into focus. As the ethnic conflict in Sri Lanka came to its deadly close in the winter of 2009, the shelling intensified, forcing thousands into the "no fire zone"; an ever-shrinking strip of land where the aerial bombardment continued unabated despite its legal censure. During the war's final months, more than 40,000 people were killed. Somewhere beneath our flight path, in January 2009, a series of graphic executions were captured by a mobile phone, the anonymous low-resolution video eventually making its way to the United Kingdom, where ITN's Channel 4 News aired it in August of that year, unleashing a furore. The authenticity of the anonymous video, questions around its disturbing content and its mode of production, as well as its potential status as evidence of "serious crimes," ignited widespread public debate and launched two UN inquiries. Experts were commissioned, metadata interrogated, and pixels cross-examined to assess their

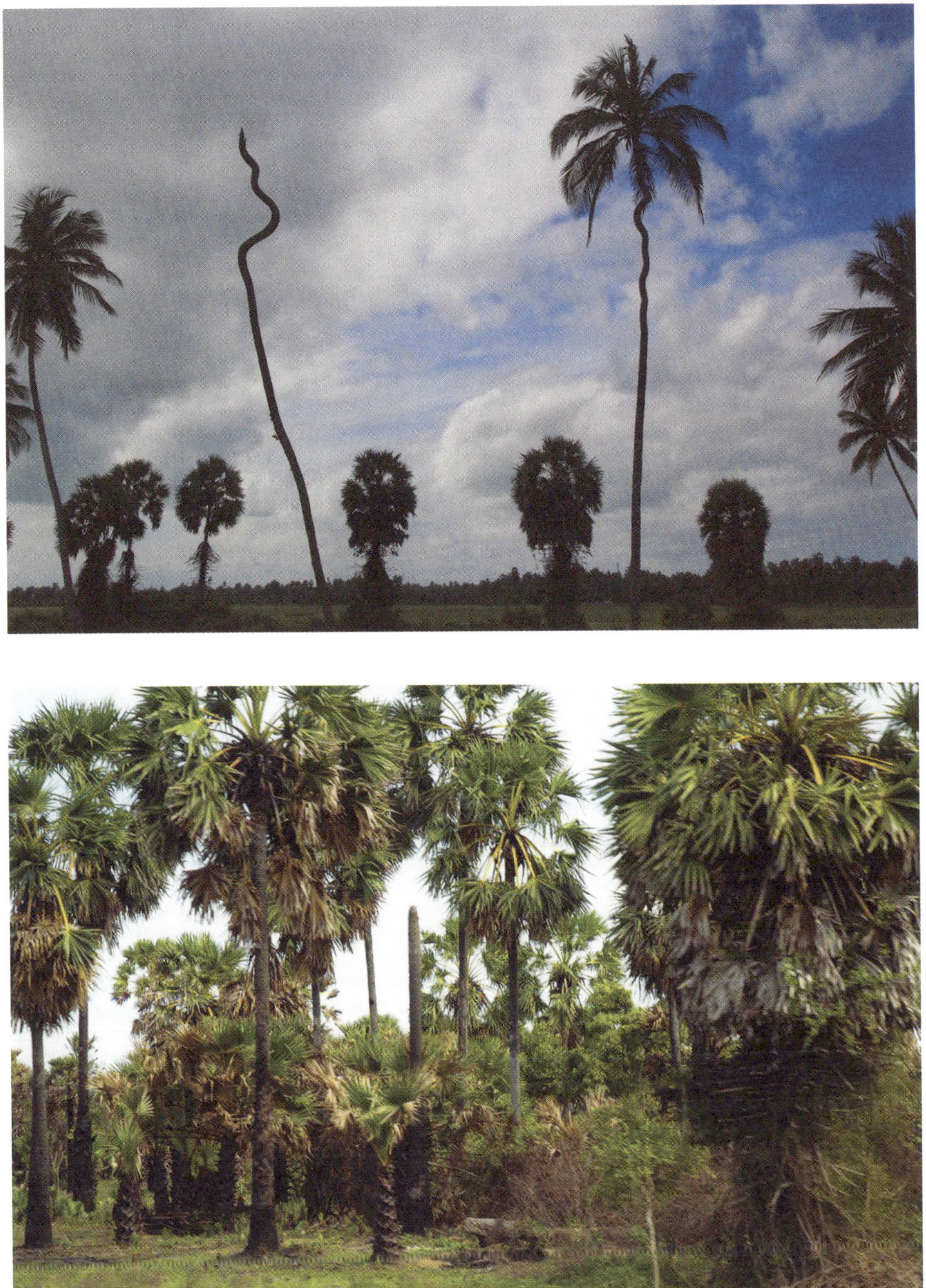

Figure 10.4
Decapitated palm trees, Tamil Eelam, 2013. Photo credit: Kraemer/Schuppli.

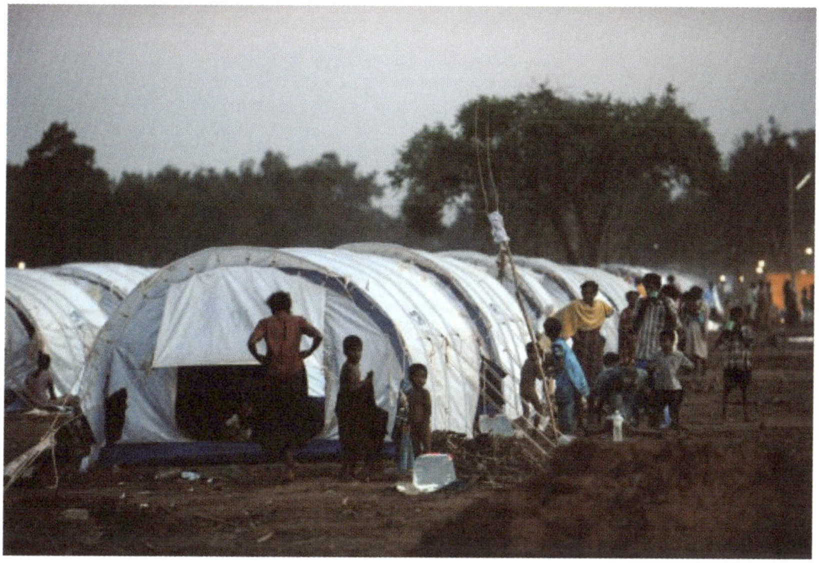

Figure 10.5
Manik Farm refugee camp located on the outskirts of the northern Sri Lankan town of Vavuniya, 2009. Source: unknown.

postprocessing truth claims. The one-minute video stream transformed into a *material witness* that would indict the highest levels of the Sri Lankan State, despite vociferous counterclaims targeting the credibility of Channel 4's journalism and the findings of its forensic experts. No one knows for certain exactly where the footage was shot. But somewhere, in a place where sandy marsh meets the sea, heinous crimes were committed.

Seventeen Frames

This graphic and gruesome piece of media footage depicts what appear to be Sri Lankan personnel engaged in acts of summary execution, sexual violence, and defilement of bodies presumed to be Tamil. "There is no indication of the ethnicity of the dead men, but the group which obtained the pictures claim the victims are Tamils. The killers are speaking Sinhala; they are wearing what appear to be Sri Lankan Army uniforms."[7] The origins of the video, who shot it, and how it was obtained by a group of exiled journalists and then sent on to the UK, have not been made public.[8] The journalists who secured the execution video did so on condition that they maintain the confidentiality

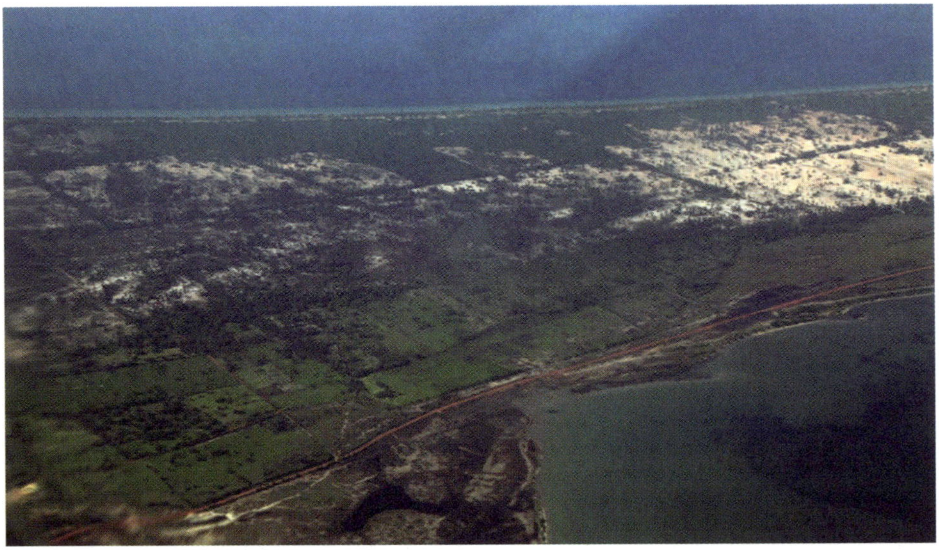

Figure 10.6
Aerial view northeastern coastline, 2013, *Material Witness*, Susan Schuppli, 2014–2015, HD video, color with sound, 34 minutes.

of their sources—no doubt fearing local reprisals—but given the proximity of the camera to the crimes depicted, it is believed to have been shot on a mobile phone by an insider, perhaps in exchange for financial compensation, although Channel 4 News did not pay for the footage, nor would ever do so. As this chapter unfolds, it will become clear that the moral register and political demands provoked by the video would not be met entirely by an analysis of what can be seen in the foreground of the footage—in the field of representation—but needed to consider the ground of the image itself. That is to say: both its mode of manufacture (camerawork and editing) and its computational arrangements (coding and metadata).[9] Even the blurry coastal backdrop, against which the defiled bodies are pictured, came to feature in the forensic analysis that ensued. While compromised-looking images generally have greater difficulty in carrying the burden of legal proof, the aesthetic deficiency of certain images can also work productively to establish counterclaims, a condition that the Sri Lankan State exploited fully in mounting their opposition and declaring the execution video an LTTE-fabricated hoax. When the mobile phone footage eventually surfaced, several extraneous factors came to play a decisive role in its authentication, such as the perceived bias of the UK's media channels as well as the track record of one of the UN's investigative experts—considerations, in short, of many elements external to the image proper that combined

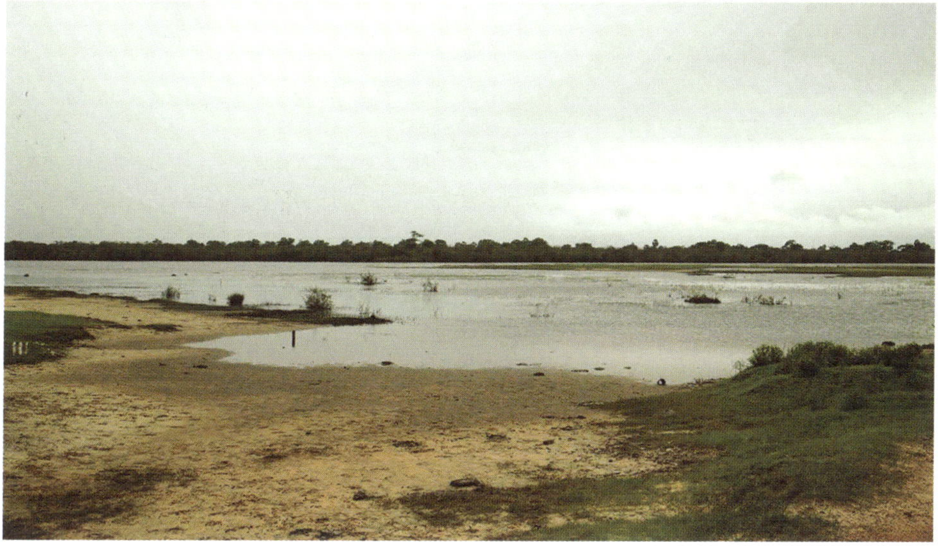

Figure 10.7
Mullaitivu District, 2013, *Material Witness*, Susan Schuppli, 2014–2015, HD video, color with sound, 34 minutes.

to lay the groundwork whereby the mobile phone footage would gain its intelligibility and authorial presence to answer to grave breaches of international law, and possibly even allegations of war crimes.

Before airing the footage publicly on television, Channel 4 News secured the assistance of various professionals, from medical experts to specialists in munitions, to help establish the credibility of the events depicted, as they were well aware of the incriminatory nature of the media and the political stakes that would attend its release. Despite the shadow of international war crimes prosecutions that loomed, and still does to this day, Britain has participated actively and continuously in financial dealings and trading with its Commonwealth compatriot Sri Lanka. As I journeyed into the north, filmmaker and journalist Callum Macrae, who has been an outspoken critic of the regime, had just been banned from traveling in the same areas. Channel 4 News Foreign Affairs Correspondent Jonathan Miller, who first broke the story of the execution video and whom I interviewed in 2012, is on the record as saying: "The existence of such footage had been rumoured for months; these pictures were reportedly filmed in January 2009, but only smuggled out of Sri Lanka two days before Channel 4 News broadcast them. A Sinhalese human rights investigator who watched the material on the day it was broadcast believed it to be genuine."[10] While the provenance of the video has never been

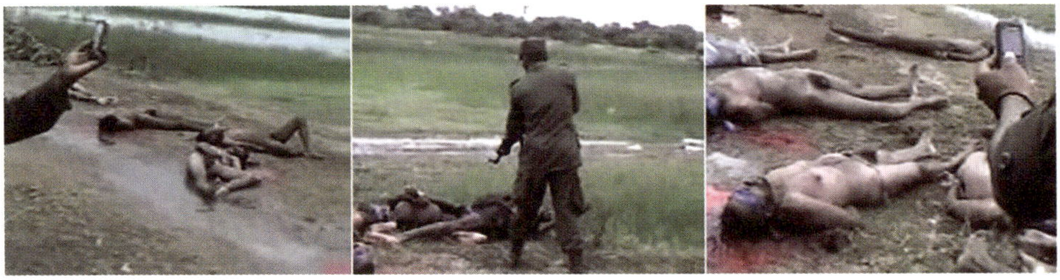

Figure 10.8
Execution video, Sri Lanka, 2009 (frame grabs from mobile phone footage). Source: unknown.

disclosed, the identities of some of the victims were matched to corpses—in particular, the striking resemblance of one brutalized female victim to that of well-known Tamil news presenter Isaipriya, who had disappeared, offering yet further evidence that the video depicted real events. However, immediately prior to its broadcast on August 25, the Sri Lanka High Commission released the following statement:

> The High Commission of Sri Lanka categorically deny that the Sri Lankan armed forces engaged in atrocities against Sri Lankan Tamil community. They were only engaged in a military offensive against the LTTE.
>
> The High Commission has noted that in many instances in the past, various media institutions used doctored videos, photographs and documents to defame the Sri Lankan government and armed forces. Therefore, we request you to verify the authenticity of the video footage before the telecast.

Experts in firearms evidence and forensic pathology were enlisted by Channel 4 News to analyze the video in order to assess whether the killings carried out and injuries depicted were consistent with the kinds of weapons the soldiers are seen firing in the video. Specialists in video forensics also looked for indications of image manipulation and modification of the video's metadata. Ultimately, 17 errant frames at the end of the video were all it would take to ignite the counterclaims of the Sri Lankan State—pixels indicted and accused of perjury. On September 7, 2009, the government issued a "Consolidated Response" reporting that it had conducted four independent and impartial investigations into the authenticity of the video, and "have now scientifically established beyond any doubt that this video is a fake."[11] In particular, the government's investigation concluded that the video had "not" been shot on a mobile phone, as claimed by Channel 4, but had been produced using professional video equipment and then reedited to appear like clandestine low-resolution footage typical of that era's mobile phone technology, in order to heighten its realism and "discredit the Government."[12]

> As Minister Samarasinghe explained to the media and the representatives of the international community on 07 and 08 September respectively, the GoSL condemns and dismisses in its entirety the video and its contents as being false and fabricated. This conclusion is based on the consolidated findings of four separate investigations initiated by the Government.[13]

In light of the State's wholesale dismissal of the video as "false and fabricated," Philip Alston, who was UN Special Rapporteur on Extrajudicial, Summary or Arbitrary Executions at the time, commissioned his own independent evaluations of the Channel 4 video. He had already previously called for an "independent probe" into the veracity of the video when the Government of Sri Lanka released its own findings to the Diplomatic Community and Multilateral Agency Heads on September 8, 2009. Alston's view of their "Consolidated Response," which included the expertise of two members of its own Armed Forces, was that the report was "impressionistic rather than scientific." Perhaps not unexpectedly, given Sri Lanka's continued impunity by the international community for its abysmal human rights records, the United Nations Human Rights Council (UNHRC) in Geneva requested that Alston retract his demands and issue a formal apology to the Government of Sri Lanka. He did neither, embarking instead on his own forensic investigation.

The UNHRC's request that Alston rescind his call for an independent inquiry into the authenticity of the video highlights the complex negotiations around what claims could actually be made in its name, and the political stakes that attend the making of such claims. At these conflictual moments, disputes around fiercely contested materials that depict alleged acts of grave wrongdoing, as was the case with the execution video, are oftentimes less directly concerned with the visual and informatic content encoded by matter than with the rhetorical capacities of such media to mobilize different points of view. Furthermore, what or who counts as a credible witness able to demand public accountability for such events might be challenged by the very institutions entrusted with safeguarding the rights of those who are powerless to make such demands. The utility of the *material witness* as a concept works to highlight the manner in which a media object like the execution video can become an agent of translation between differing versions of events or contestations between stakeholders. For the footage to convey its histories and be made to "speak," it was not a simple question of bringing the right kinds of technical methods and forensic experts to bear upon the video, and thus secure its "testimonials." It was rather, as Michel Foucault has suggested, a consequence of the political conditions that govern the limits of what can be spoken at any given time.[14] Given the partisan response to Alston's call for an inquiry by the very agency that is assigned the "promotion and protection of all human rights around the globe," the documentation of what appear to be war crimes in northern Sri Lanka discloses this limit condition on the part of the UNHRC in no uncertain terms.

In his *Technical Note* as to the authenticity of the Channel 4 video, which Alston went on to present at the United Nations in New York on January 7, 2010, he does in fact highlight key anomalies that are difficult, although not impossible, to account for: "There are a small number of characteristics of the video which the experts were not able to explain. This included the movement of certain victims in the video, seventeen frames at the end of the video, and the date of 17 July 2009 encoded in the video."[15] This despite the lack of an ironclad explanation for these oddities, the mystery of which can be conclusively solved only through direct examination of the actual phone that shot the footage, and upon corroboration by witnesses/perpetrators present at the scene. Nonetheless, the opinions of the three "independent and impartial" experts contracted, forensic pathologist Dr. Spitz, forensic video analyst Jeff Spivack, and firearms expert Peter Diaczuk, were able to provide substantive and plausible explanations for these peculiarities. They all came to the same conclusion: that there was strong and convincing evidence that the video was authentic. With this verdict in hand, Alston called for further examination into the prospect that war crimes had been committed during the civil war: "Given these conclusions, and in light of the persistent flow of other allegations of extrajudicial executions by both sides during the closing phases of the war against the LTTE, I call for the establishment of an independent inquiry to carry out an impartial investigation into war crimes and other grave violations of international humanitarian and human rights law allegedly committed in Sri Lanka."[16] UN Secretary-General Ban Ki-moon likewise notified the Government of Sri Lanka that he too was thinking about establishing a Commission of Experts to look into widespread allegations of grave human rights abuses and systematic breaches of the provisions and principles of international humanitarian law (IHL) that govern the armed conduct of states during hostilities.[17]

Alston's eventual successor to the post of UN Special Rapporteur on Extrajudicial, Summary or Arbitrary Executions, Christoph Heyns, was able to shed further light upon the already noted irregularities in the footage when he conducted a much more elaborate inquiry into the authenticity of the video in 2011. It turns out that Alston's report was based upon an examination of the original video aired by Channel 4, whereas Heyns was able to work with the extended 5-minute 25-second version. "The appearance of an 'A' in the last 17 frames of the first video was also a matter of concern," said Heyns.[18] However, as Jeff Spivack, who was recommissioned to conduct further forensic analysis of the video, writes in his report: "The fact that editing in any form has been applied to the recordings submitted for authentication will quite understandably

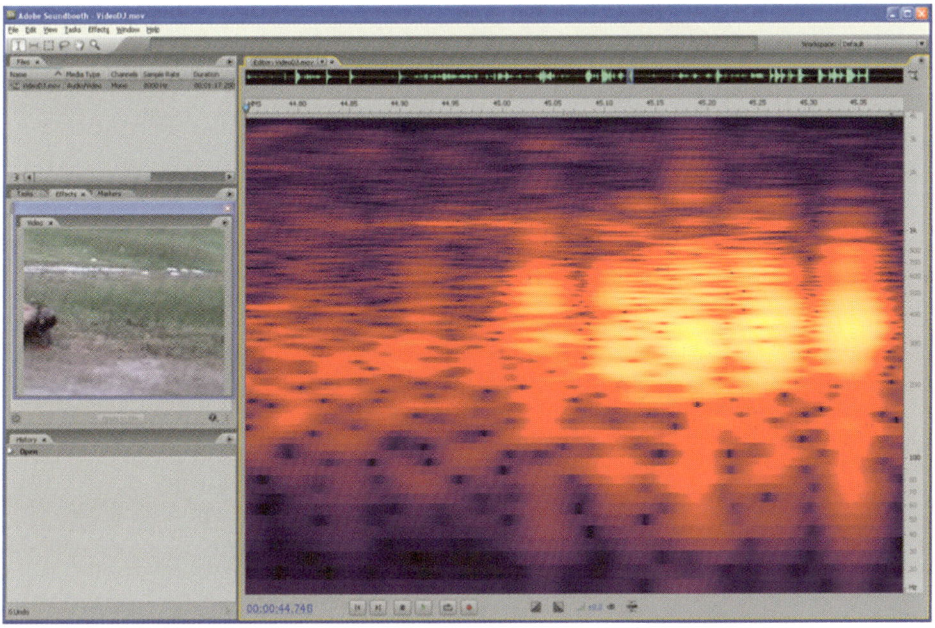

Frame 333 with Corresponding Wind Noise Spectrograph

Figure 10.9
Forensic Video Analysis Report by Jeff S. Spivack, CFC. Re: Authenticity of Digital Video / Audio Recording of Purported Sri Lanka Executions. Source: Technical Note Prepared by the Special Rapporteur on Extrajudicial, Summary or Arbitrary Executions, Philip Alston, in relation to the authenticity of the "Channel 4 videotape."

generate scepticism or even suspicion. However, it is important to understand the distinction between the type of rudimentary editing possible on a mobile phone (that all available evidence indicates was used in this case) and the capabilities of a powerful computer based non-linear editing system with sophisticated filters and effects."[19]

Forensic Findings

Spivack is right to alert us to the potential dangers that something as seemingly benign as a simple edit or camerawork can elicit when the status of truth is perceived to be so radically contingent. During my own "Crime Scene and Evidence Documentation" training course with the International Forensics Program/Physicians for Human Rights, equal emphasis was always placed on what might be missing in our evidential records in addition to what was explicitly present.[20] Image files deleted in a numbered

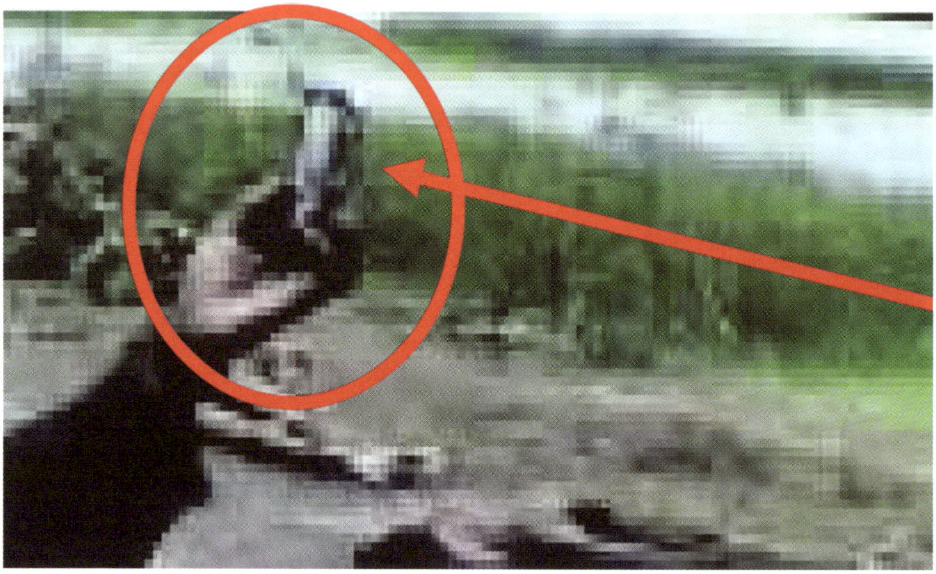

Figure 10.10
Forensic Video Analysis Supplemental Report by Jeff Spivack / Authenticity of Digital Video / Audio Recording of Purported Sri Lanka Executions. Source: United Nations: A/HRC/17/28/Add.1.

progressive sequence can suggest intentional erasure; a direct frontal view of a scene or structure that is taken without corresponding 360° shots to show what or who else was present and out of sight behind the photographer's back can also be indicative of willful deception. The objective is to create documentation that clearly demonstrates where items and bodies are in relation to each other across a crime scene. All incidental events, whether an inadvertent shot of one's foot while walking or an off-color remark recorded during a moment of stress, must be included in the final evidence package to ensure full disclosure. As Stefan Schmitt, Director of the International Forensic Program, put it, the reality that we are able to construct through our documentary practice and the demonstrated proof of its thoroughness will ultimately determine which version of the truth will be accepted in court. Any break in a succession of information, which includes a cut in a video or even abrupt camera movement, raises the possibility that crucial information of some kind was deliberately removed or averted. When footage is shot by nonexperts, as was the case with the execution video, establishing the probity of evidence becomes much more technically and legally difficult. As Figure 10.10 highlights, even the ambient sound of the recorded wind in relation to the specific movement of blowing marsh grasses was used to provide essential clues.

Uncertainties or doubts as to veracity of media can also serve to open up an investigative space in which factors external to the photograph or video will play a significant role in advancing its truth claims. For example, with respect to the execution video, these included reports of similar crimes having been committed, the rhetorical strategies of institutional agents and authority figures to make public pronouncements, the credentials of the experts hired, the prejudicial views and assumed bias on the part of various stakeholders, etc. In her discussion of video forensics and CCTV, surveillance studies theorist Kelly Gates emphasizes the considerable cultural labor required to produce juridically robust evidence: "I want to call attention to the amount of work that goes into establishing the credibility of these [indeterminate] images and others like them—the discourses, procedures, technologies, and forms of labor that work to define the images as authoritative proof."[21] The relationship between the production and management of forensic crime scene evidence and the interpretative possibilities that govern the range of claims that can be made in its name are therefore inversely proportional. The more rigorous the documentation procedure, the less room for narrative conjecture; the more holes or gaps in the evidence dossier, the greater the likelihood of counterclaims being made.

Macrae has produced three documentaries for Channel 4 examining the final months of military escalation and deepening humanitarian crisis. A detailed forensic analysis of the execution video was included in his first documentary, *Sri Lanka's Killing Fields*, released in June 2011, segments of which he also referenced in his two subsequent films.[22] Not surprisingly, the Sri Lankan State was once again quick to denounce the claims put forward in these documentaries, assailing the integrity of Channel 4's investigative journalism and questioning its interpretations and findings. These public aspersions were cast through various means: a Sri Lankan Commission of Inquiry (2011), a television documentary, *Lies Agreed Upon* (2011), produced by State television under the auspices of the Sri Lankan Minister of Defense, and a book, *Corrupted Journalism* (2013).[23] As Miller emphasized when we spoke together about the execution video and its elaborations within the film *Sri Lanka's Killing Fields*, ITN made sure that all the claims and allegations advanced in the documentary could be corroborated through extensive interview material or substantiated by materials that they had gathered through many years of journalism covering the war in Sri Lanka, thus meeting the strong legal requirements that such volatile and potentially incriminatory material commands.[24]

Indeed, one of the primary counterarguments leveled against Channel 4 was that their analysis and that of their experts was based largely upon "an external examination" of the actions depicted in the video, and was therefore open to misinterpretations that could lead to false conclusions. The Sri Lankan State argued, for example, that there is a history of LTTE fighters disguising themselves as government forces by wearing Sri Lankan Army uniforms in order to infiltrate enemy lines, thus implying that the video was stage-managed and produced by the LTTE.[25] "While it's true that Tamil Tiger insurgents were known to masquerade in government uniforms, what makes the video credible is that tell-tale casual dialogue between the killers as they dispatch their helpless captives," explains Miller.[26] The authors of the book accusing Channel 4 of bias also advanceded the absurd suggestion that what looks like the sexual violation of a naked dead woman (identified as Isaipriya) could be a misreading of standard military search practices to look for hidden explosives that a would-be suicide bomber might have secreted in her bra or underwear, a tactic claimed to have been invented by the LTTE.[27] According to this contradictory logic, the soldiers in question would admittedly need to be Sri Lankans caught in the act of carrying out such dubious duties, not Tamil fighters masquerading as troops. The authors of the book also argue that Isaipriya was an active member of the LTTE militia, therefore technically not a civilian, and could thus be legally killed under IHL. This is clearly beside the point, as the sexual assault of captives would also be in breach of the Geneva Convention relative to the Treatment of Prisoners of War. They also make comparisons with the behavior of American soldiers in Afghanistan and Iraq, from prisoner abuse to the posing of US troops beside dead bodies, in order to substantiate the charge that ITN's Sri Lanka coverage was deliberately prejudicial in singling out Sri Lanka's antiterror tactics when such actions are widespread and, as they put it, "a feature of most wars." This point is perhaps the most convincing, as there is certainly truth in the assertion that the West always looks for its criminal perpetrators elsewhere, especially in the so-called Global South, where virtually all of the ICC's arrest warrants have been directed to date.

> Naked and partially-clothed female bodies are not automatic evidence of rape or sexual assault. … This has been a feature of most wars, and certainly most recently in Afghanistan and Iraq. In September 2005, for example, the US Army opened an investigation into video footage of American soldiers standing around what appear to be dead bodies. Other photos include graphic images of severed body parts and what appear to be internal organs spilling from bodies onto the ground. The *New York Times* reported that "The images are said to come from Afghanistan as well as Iraq. Their authenticity has not been determined." Lewd behavior on the part of some of the people searching the bodies for weapons or explosives, or posing with bodies, may have been in bad taste but it does not constitute the sorts of war crimes alleged by Channel 4.[28]

The precedent of abhorrent behavior and wrongdoing on the part of the US is obviously no excuse for such continued practices, especially if the execution video eventually proves itself to be genuine within an international prosecution. While Sri Lankan officials concur that the actions depicted are deplorable, they continue to contest the video's authenticity, arguing that the visual evidence is not conclusive as to who the perpetrators in the execution video actually were, and what motivated their acts of apparent sexual violence. This is a crucial argument which turns, in part, on the distinction between the humanitarian needs that organize the forensic analysis of material evidence and its legal requirements as constituted by a tribunal.[29] While forensic experts such as medical pathologists may be able to help establish probable cause of death, and even aid in the identification of victims seen in the video, in order for prosecutors to proceed with charges of war crimes they need to be able to prove criminal intent, something that would be difficult were the video treated as an isolated occurrence. However, many years of NGO work and investigative journalism, combined with first-person witness accounts, confirm rampant human rights abuses being committed against the civilian Tamil population, as well as toward LTTE rebels, while still recognizing that acts of resistance, violence, and terror were also the stock in trade of the LTTE militia.[30] In light of this overwhelming body of evidence, the explanations offered to justify or account for the gruesome acts documented by the execution video remain highly implausible.

When Heyns assumed the mandate of UN Special Rapporteur from Alston in August 2010, one of the first investigations he turned his attention to was an exhaustive review of the extended version of the execution video. In addition to determining whether the video and events depicted were real, the investigation set out to address the unexplained issues that had arisen during Alston's investigation, which the government of Sri Lanka had vociferously exploited in their own denunciation of the video. Key excerpts from the findings of Heyns's report conclude this chapter. Like Alston before him, Heyns contracted independent forensic experts to answer the challenges that the material anomalies raised. One of these experts was forensic video analyst Grant Fredericks, a name I recognized from a completely unrelated case that he had worked on in Canada: the death of Polish immigrant Robert Dziekański, who was tasered by RCMP (Royal Canadian Mounted Police) officers in the international arrivals area of Vancouver International Airport on October 14, 2007.

> Dazed and confused after more than 15 hours of travel, unable to communicate in English and scared because he couldn't find his mother, Polish immigrant Robert Dziekański was jolted by a taser just 24 seconds after being confronted by police in Vancouver International Airport. … "Unbelievably, these people were probably no more than 150 to 200 feet apart for at least five hours, and she was unable to get any message to him. And no one on the other side [of the glass walls] thought to interview him or come outside or vice versa," Mr. Kosteckyj said.[31]

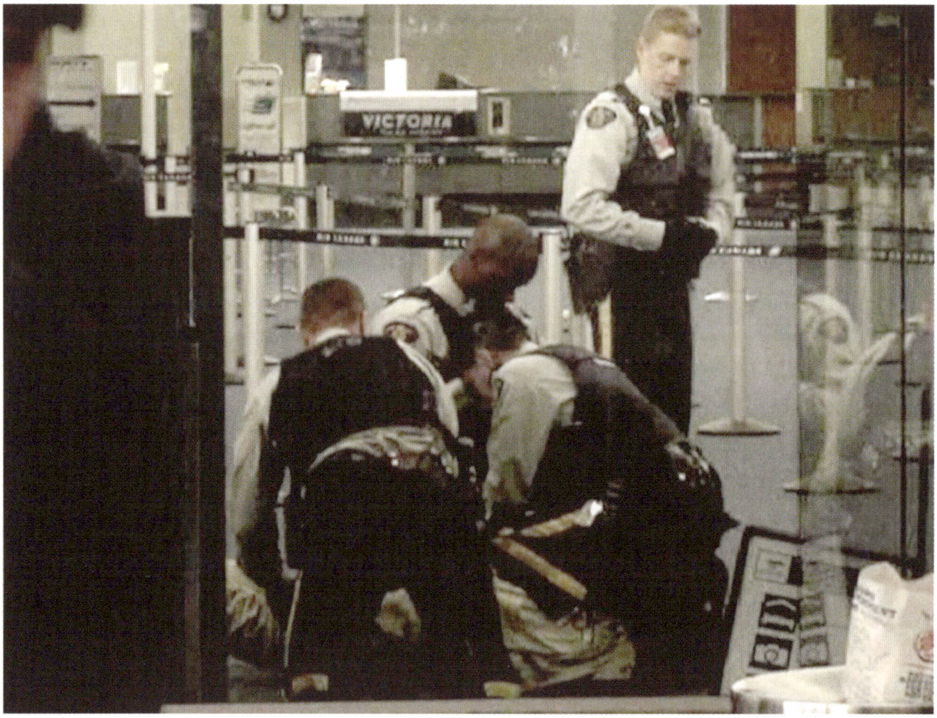

Figure 10.11
Video shot by eyewitness Paul Pritchard at Vancouver Airport of the tasering of Robert Dziekański, October 14, 2007. RCMP Cpl. Monty Robinson is seen at right kneeling on Dziekański. Source: Hand-out Photos.

The death of a frantic lost passenger, who spoke no English and had wandered airport arrivals for ten hours waiting for his mother to arrive, prompted a Commission for Public Complaints Against the Royal Canadian Mounted Police, which released its findings and recommendations on December 8, 2009. It also resulted in the Braidwood Inquiry (report released July 2009) that looked into the use of the taser by law enforcement agencies in the province of British Columbia. Public outrage toward the conduct of the RCMP centered on the use of excessive force by its four officers, specifically their deployment of a conducted energy weapon, or taser, to try and placate Robert Dziekański. Official inquiries also focused their criticisms of the RCMP and its officers on their: use of forced restraints (handcuffs and kneeling upon the victim, which hampered his breathing), disregard for RCMP protocols in managing a low-level disturbance; failure to provide adequate medical care for the victim after he is immobilized;

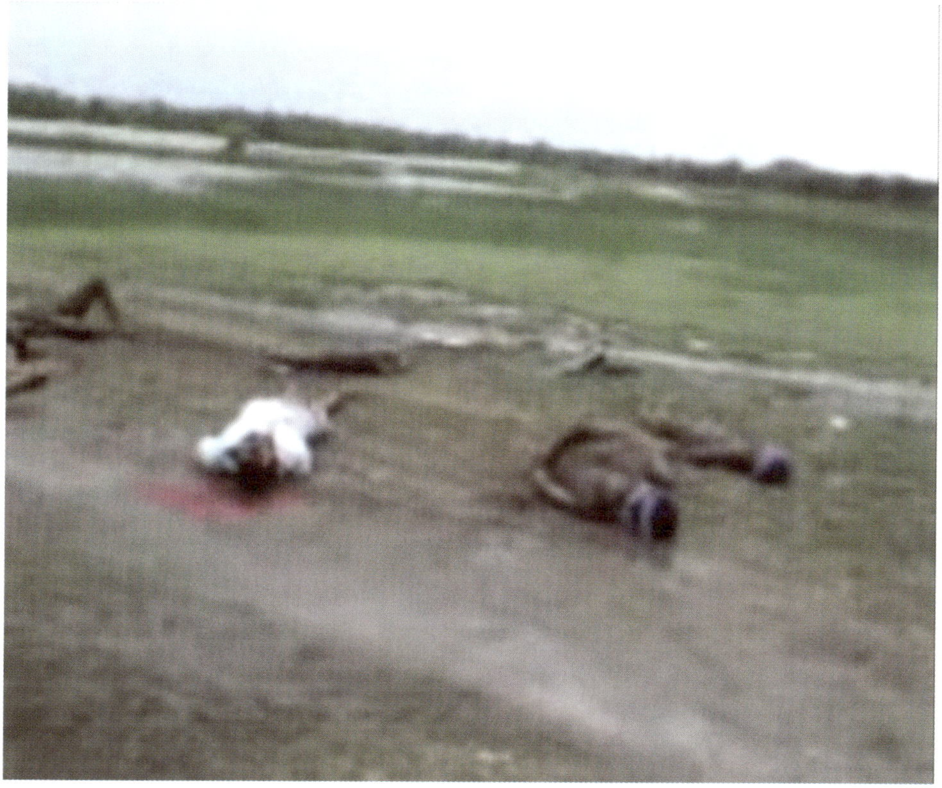

Figure 10.12
Execution video, Sri Lanka, 2009 (frame grab from mobile phone footage). Source: unknown.

unlawful seizure of amateur video footage; internal collusion in manufacturing public statements; and on their in-custody death investigation, which found no fault with any of the officers involved.[32]

Paul Pritchard, another passenger waiting in the arrivals hall, shot a ten-minute video of the events as they unfolded with his digital camera, which was immediately confiscated by the police and returned only after Pritchard hired a lawyer to initiate legal proceedings. Pritchard's firsthand video account clearly refutes the RCMP's version of events, and testifies to their unequivocal involvement in the death of Dziekański. Expert witness Grant Fredericks was hired by the RCMP to forensically deconstruct the Pritchard video and determine whether Dziekański's actions had threatened the police, warranting his submission by taser. Fredericks's analysis corroborated the police account against the combined evidence of eyewitness testimony, CCTV surveillance footage, and the overwhelming proof offered by the video images themselves. In exonerating the RCMP and its officers from any misconduct, he also vindicated TASER® International, the US company which manufactures the highly controversial "nonlethal" stun guns. Under cross-examination, Fredericks admitted "that he has no training in photogrammetry and no more expertise in the science of making measurements by use of photographs than the average layperson"[33]—an admission corroborated by Mark Hird-Rutter, an instructor in geomatics and certified photogrammetrist who subsequently took the stand, stating: "there were numerous flaws in the testimony of the RCMP witness."[34] After repeated denials, Fredericks also conceded that TASER® International was one of his own corporate sponsors, thus muddying his status as an impartial and independent expert, the foundation upon which expert testimony is built. During the escalation of efforts to disprove the authenticity of the Sri Lankan video footage, the name "Grant Fredericks" reappeared. As one of the expert witnesses contracted to the second UN investigation, Fredericks was revealed to have a dubious past. His expertise was demonstrably flawed in the Dziekański case, and his objectivity as an unbiased witness was overturned. Although his track record was used to cast doubt on the merits of his findings, the preponderance of corroborating evidence was such that the authentication of the execution video did not turn exclusively on Fredericks's UN report.

> Detailed report May 27 2011: The overall conclusion reached by the experts is that the video is authentic and the events reflected in the video footage occurred as depicted. The Special Rapporteur has concluded that the video footage indicates the commission of serious crimes, which should together with any other available evidence be examined systematically and professionally by domestic investigators appointed by the Sri Lankan Government, as well as by an independent, international investigational body, with a clear mandate to establish who should be held accountable for the killings.[35] (Christoph Heyns, UN Special Rapporteur on Extrajudicial, Summary or Arbitrary Executions)

However, the situation does highlight the degree to which factors beyond the immediate purview of the case itself, such as the past history of an expert witness, can play a significant role in shoring up or diminishing evidence and, with it, opportunities for potential action. As I have already suggested, these externalities can also include the reluctance of international bodies to call states to account for human rights abuses, regardless of what the evidence purports to reveal. In recent years, several human rights groups have successfully filed lawsuits or used legal tools to try to redress this lack of progress. The work of the European Center for Constitutional and Human Rights in Berlin is one such example. Through its international crimes and accountability program, ECCHR has been pressuring Foreign Ministries in the United Kingdom, Germany, and Switzerland to declare several high-ranking Sri Lanka officers "*personae non gratae*," which would lift their diplomatic immunity. For example, both Jagath Dias, former General of the 57th Division, and Prasanna De Silva, former Major General of the 59th Division, were given diplomatic posts in Europe after the war. ECCHR, along with Track Impunity Always (TRIAL) and the Society for Threatened Peoples (STP), filed a criminal report with the Office of the Attorney General in Switzerland; this action compelled Sri Lanka to recall Dias in early September 2011. Defense attaché De Silva, who was posted to the Sri Lankan High Commission in London, was recalled in 2012 when he was faced with the prospect of similar legal pressure, although the Foreign Office never took any measures to launch a criminal investigation. More recently, in August 2017, the South Africa-based International Truth and Justice Project filed multijurisdictional lawsuits in Brazil and Colombia calling for war crimes prosecutions against Jagath Jayasuriya, Sri Lanka's ambassador to Argentina, Brazil, Chile, Colombia, Peru, and Suriname. General Jayasuriya was a commanding officer during the final months of the war, which saw the intensification of government shelling against tens of thousands of civilians pushed into the no-fire zone. As news of the accusations emerged, Jayasuriya was already on a direct flight out of Brazil to Colombo via Dubai. And while the Sri Lankan government claimed that his ambassadorial assignment had duly concluded, the timing of these two events suggests that these activist legal strategies are succeeding where other reports and investigations, like those of the Human Rights Council, have largely failed in producing the transitional justice that is demanded and required. In early 2018 another incident came to light, indicating that Sri Lanka had sent probable war criminals, including a senior task force officer alleged to have ordered the summary executions of Tamils, to support UN peacekeeping operations in Mali, Lebanon, Darfur, and South Sudan.

Legal Media

The shocking execution video that first came to light in summer 2009 has since been followed by further video evidence of a similarly disturbing nature. In 2014, a video surfaced showing Sinhala-speaking soldiers "laughing and cheering, as they celebrate the deaths of the Tiger fighters and perform acts of grotesque sexual violation on the bodies."[36] This video, too, has undergone extensive scrutiny by forensic pathologist Dr. Richard Sheppard, who concluded that the injuries depicted are real, suggesting that the video was not doctored, and a forensic image analyst whose expertise is frequently enlisted by the British courts, who came to the same conclusion. Considered in sum, these trophy videos corroborate the growing archive of visual evidence that Sri Lankan Army personnel were regularly involved in the execution and sexual violation of prisoners of war and civilian detainees.[37] Once again, the Sri Lanka High Commission responded in kind:

> Your latest attempt to denigrate Sri Lanka is a continuation of your pernicious campaign that has already been exposed in the book *Corrupted Journalism Channel 4 and Sri Lanka*.
>
> Your allegations are such unmitigated and unsubstantiated rubbish that you make even gutter journalism appear to be Pulitzer Prize-winning professionalism.
>
> What makes your journalism doubly dubious and obnoxiously unbalanced is that you expect us to comment on footage which, in fairness, we have not even been given the opportunity of seeing or hearing.
>
> It is a pity that your continuing propagandist vendetta against Sri Lanka only continues to undermine the process of reconciliation and healing that we have undertaken after a near three-decade-long terrorist war.
>
> It is certainly not going to help those in Sri Lanka you pretend you are helping but who only wish to live in peace without external meddling and posturing.
>
> Your crude journalism exposes both Callum and your calumny.
>
> —Sri Lanka High Commission, March 7, 2014

The systematic nature of these heinous acts, should international legal proceedings eventually go forward, would carry the grave charge of individual criminal responsibility—war crimes—under the tenets of international humanitarian law. Sri Lanka's poor human rights record had previously resulted in its losing its seat on the UN Human Rights Council in 2008; however, this censure was overturned only a year later, despite reports of the most grievous abuses being committed during the closing months of the war. "Notwithstanding evidence of widespread abuses in the final stages of the conflict, the UN Human Rights Council, rather than condemning these or even expressing concern, passed a resolution on 27 May 2009 commending the government and ignoring widespread international calls for investigation into abuses."[38] As a concept that aims to disclose evidence of events, but also to offer insight into the event of evidence, the *material witness* offers the possibility for unfolding evidence—the execution video—into a corroborating network where its relation to other actors and events can serve to further establish its politics. The distressing singularity of the video is the very precondition whereby the high stakes of its image will come to matter as more than a singular isolated aberration. In *Sensible Politics*, Meg McLagan and Yates McKee argue that all images perform their truth claims as a consequence of the networked circuits of relations and discursive frameworks that combine to establish their claims as fact. Any analysis must proceed from an understanding that takes this distributed condition into account: "It is not about the image, but the image complex, the channels of circulation along which cultural forms travel, the nature of the campaigns that frame them, and the discursive platforms that display and encode them in specific truth modes. This involves form-sensitive analysis of the specificity of differing platforms that chart the imbrication of aesthetic form, medial practice, and political intent into one assemblage."[39] In reconceptualizing the execution video as a widely distributed media event, we also expand the field of analysis, and possibly even shore up the video's legal credibility by demonstrating patterns of systematic abuse and escalating violence. Staying with the image as a self-sufficient representation of things will get us only so far, politically as well as juridically. Yet it is also this very networked condition in which evidence is dispersed across sovereign jurisdictions that challenges prosecutors' abilities to obtain evidence for international criminal proceedings. As law professor Jacob Katz Cogan writes, in reflecting upon this condition:

> International criminal courts will be judged by their fairness to defendants as well as to victims. In a very practical way, such claims will hinge, inter alia, on the ability of prosecutors and defendants to gain reasonable access to probative evidence. In domestic legal systems prosecutors have at hand the resources and the coercive powers of the state, subject to certain constitutional limitations, as they pursue leads and conduct investigations. In the international system no such procedures exist. When a state requires evidence that is in the possession of another state, it must resort either to already existing mutual legal assistance treaties or to diplomatic negotiations. When international criminal courts seek such cooperation, prosecutors and investigators must depend on states to provide them with evidence or access to evidence. Without such assistance, trials cannot go forward lest the legitimacy of the proceedings and, by extension, the court itself, be called into question.[40]

Although Sri Lanka has not ratified the Rome Statute of 1998, which brought about the creation of the International Criminal Court in 2002, and is therefore not subject to its jurisdiction, it could be compelled to respond to charges if the UN Security Council decided to refer the country to the ICC. The Court was conceived as a legal instrument that would complement national jurisdictions; but when impunity for serious crimes prevails on a domestic state level, international demands for legal accountability can be brought to bear upon nonsignatories. Over the years there have been various attempts to bring certain actions and events before the Court and other international bodies. When an aerial attack on a girls' school in the Mullaitivu District resulted in the slaughter of 61 children and injured upward of 120 later in the same year (August 14, 2006), the Sri Lankan government responded to UNICEF's condemnation by saying that if children were indeed being trained as soldiers, then their status as innocent civilians was surely in doubt. A version of this argument is frequently used in Gaza, whereby Palestinians lose their legal protection as civilians if they are duly warned of an imminent attack by Israel and do not vacate their premises in a timely manner, resulting in their death.[41] The Tamil Tigers, too, face prospects of being charged for grave abuses in using civilians as suicide bombers and human shields. In 2006, a group of Sri Lankan expatriates living in California appealed to UNICEF to urge the ICC to prosecute LTTE leaders for recruiting child soldiers.[42] In 2014, Ban Ki-moon's panel of experts determined that there was sufficient evidence of violations of IHL to warrant an international inquiry, which the UNHRC duly authorized. One year later, the same intergovernmental body (UNHRC) delayed release of its highly anticipated inquiry into such war crimes allegations, succumbing to pressure from newly elected Sri Lankan President Maithripala Sirisena.

> February 2015: The United Nations Human Rights Council on Monday agreed to defer the release of a landmark inquiry [OHCHR Investigation on Sri Lanka/OISL] into possible war crimes in Sri Lanka, after an intense Lobbying campaign by the country's newly elected government and what the United Nations' top rights official described as "signals of broad cooperation" from Sri Lankan officials. The release of the report on suspected rights abuses during a quarter-century of war with the rebel Liberation Tigers of Tamil Eelam has been put off until September. The report's release was originally scheduled for March.[43]

> August 2015: Local mechanisms have completely failed to deliver justice, and the continued reliance on domestic mechanisms will continue to produce the same results. The administration of President Sirisena made promises to the international community following his election in January 8, 2015, but there has been no progress on the ground. The government obtained a deferral of the OISL investigation report in February, over our strong objections, stating that it needed time and space to implement its own credible domestic processes. Eight months later, nothing has happened, and war affected communities are no closer to truth, justice, redress or guarantees of non-recurrence.[44]

This Human Rights Council report was eventually released on September 16, 2015, but its recommendations regarding reconciliation and accountability have yet to be acted upon, and the political instability unfolding in Sri Lanka with the attempted return to power by Rajapaksa in 2018 suggests that there may well be even less motivation to do so now. The International Crisis Group has warned that unless Sri Lanka "steps back" from destabilizing its constitution and its agenda of reform, including its human rights record, supporters of Rajapaksa and his 2016 Sri Lanka Podujana Peramuna Party will be further emboldened: "Tamil activists and journalists, who already face intense police and military surveillance, as well as threats of violence, will be at risk of increased harassment or worse. So, too, will critics of the Rajapaksa family and dissenters throughout the country."[45]

Massacre v. Execution Video

The case of the Sri Lankan execution video is echoed by my earlier discussion of the Izbica massacre tape, which was recorded ten years earlier in Kosovo, also within the context of an ethnic violence, but with many significant differences: most notably the lack of any formal legal process aimed at investigating the alleged war crimes perpetrated by Sri Lankan Army personnel as depicted, and thus no consequential accountability for the extrajudicial killings that took place. Furthermore, whoever shot the footage probably did so with the intention of producing a trophy video to dramatize the spoils of war rather than to document the violations being perpetrated against Tamil civilians. The work of the *material witness* to reveal the norms that adjudicate over the conversion of certain media objects into evidential agents capable of "showing truth to power" must also work equally to reveal the manner in which materials are impeded or entirely prevented from performing such a role. Sadly, we are all aware that there is never a guarantee that the self-evident nature of any documented violation will result in convictions or even, for that matter, prosecutorial action. The preceding discussion has tried to examine the ways in which a series of political truth claims were variously enacted through the mobile phone footage and the digital processes that managed its visual encodings. In doing so I sought to highlight the multiple forms of professional expertise, technical approaches, and rhetorical labor required to transform a conditional truth into one that can make public assertions, and perhaps even advance a legal argument. The challenges put on images to explain events, especially within legal forums where higher standards of proof must prevail than in the courts of public opinion, is an issue of significant urgency and concern. This is where the *material witness* can really do its productive work. For example, during a particularly aggressive cross-examination of witness Liri Loshi by former Yugoslav President Slobodan Milošević during legal proceedings in the ICTY, Milošević asked a provocative question about the evidential status of images, questioning how a picture can actually "prove" anything at all. Loshi, along with Sefedin Thaqi, had shot lengthy video footage documenting the aftermath of a brutal massacre at Izbica, Kosovo, in 1999, in which more than 100 victims, including members of his own family, were found in a farmer's meadow. This case is discussed in detail in chapter 8, "Cross-Examination," but it is cited here again by way of comparison to highlight the lack of consequential response to the execution video.

> Mr. Milosevic: Yes. We're going to look at all that very carefully, don't you worry about that. And experts will take a look at that too, never you mind. But what I would like you to tell me is how, by showing a picture of a body in a meadow, you set out to prove that death was caused by execution. And then you go a step further and say that death occurred through execution and that the execution was carried out by the Serb army and police. How do you prove that by showing the picture of a dead body, of a dead man in a meadow?[46]

The Sri Lankan execution video, by contrast, has had to be mediated without any witnesses who can testify to what they saw at the scene. Moreover, contrary to the many objections raised by the State challenging both Channel 4 and the UN's forensic

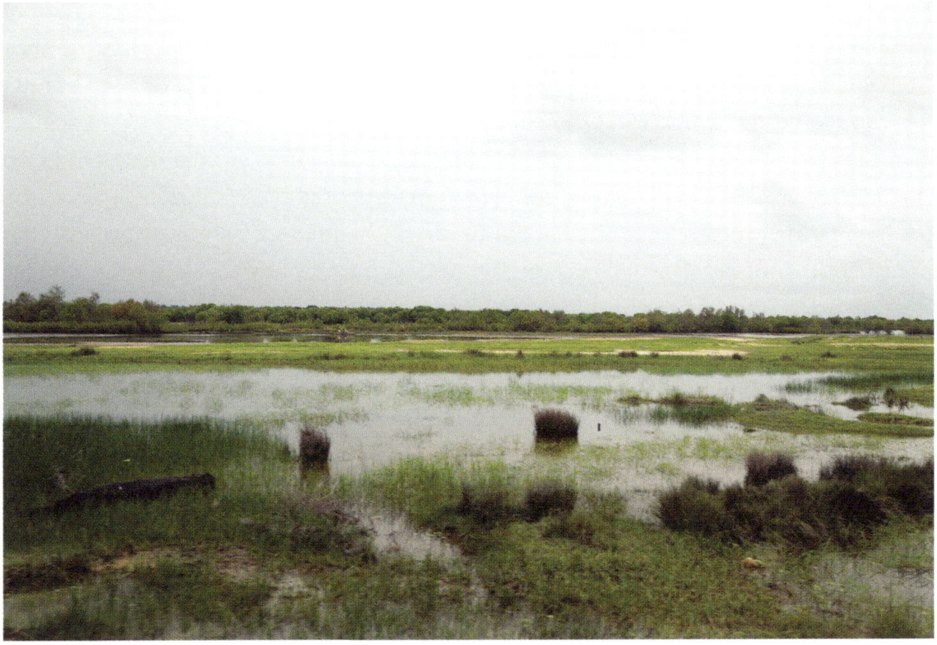

Figure 10.13
Location shot, Mullaitivu District, 2013, *Material Witness*, Susan Schuppli, 2014–2015, HD video, color with sound, 34 minutes.

reports confirming the execution video's authenticity, no allegations of evidence tampering or wrongdoing were raised during the legal determinations concerning Loshi's massacre video, despite the fact that the camcorder containing the original Hi-8 video had at one point been stolen, and was recovered only much later. The period during which the tape was out of Loshi's custodial care could have been cause for concern, prompting its censure as legally admissible evidence, yet the Tribunal was well able to establish its overall credibility. Unlike the claims of fraud leveled at the Sri Lankan execution video, the massacre tape was duly entered into evidence as Exhibit P232. In the former, the Tribunal had already indicted hundreds for the commission of serious violations of international humanitarian law—genocide, war crimes, and crimes against humanity—in the territory of the former Yugoslavia. The videotape would enter a context in which there was little doubt, legal or otherwise, that credible evidence of war crimes existed; thus its veracity was never in question. Nor did Milošević's objections ever doubt the tape's authenticity, he merely offered a counterinterpretation to the events depicted. In giving evidence to the court, Loshi testified to what he saw when he arrived on the scene, as well as corroborating various aspects of the video's production and handling, excluding the time when the original tape was not in his possession.

Even though the executions in Sri Lanka were caught on camera in the very act of killing, and eyewitnesses were clearly present on the scene (as perpetrators and/or videographers), no legal trial has yet taken place. Nor is there any certainty that the person[s] responsible for the filming will ever be located and compelled to testify, or perhaps even made to stand trial and answer criminal charges. Notwithstanding the forensic findings of two investigations launched by successive UN Special Rapporteurs Philip Alston and Christoph Heyns, verifying the authenticity of the video and therefore the criminal nature of the activities depicted, no accountability measures or substantive repercussions have followed, save those I mentioned that were compelled by the actions of the ECCHR, etc. For the moment, a *de facto* victor's court is all that is being seriously considered by Sri Lanka, despite the many formal recommendations that an internal judicial process is not sufficient for ensuring transitional justice in the face of such grave accusations.[47]

When I began this chapter, I made reference to the ecological disaster of 2004 in which the entanglement between natural and political forces produced a condition of obfuscation whereby the responses to crisis were unequally distributed between communities—a strategic recasting of the conflict to the operations of the environment itself. As my analysis of the execution video unfolded, we gained certain insights into how technical ambiguities in both the field of the image and its digital processing enabled radically divergent interpretations to stake their claims in the space opened up by these uncertainties. Ultimately, a definitive or irreducible account of the video and the actions depicted may never be achieved, because it requires access to domains of verification some of which cannot be arrived at through expert analysis and opinion but require direct examination of the recording device, as well as full disclosure and identification of the subjects present on the scene. However, the forms of abuse and violence the video documents were repeated across the conflict zones of the civil war and thus register a pattern of violation, which was multiplied at all scales of the struggle, including enlisting a environmental disaster to skew casualty figures. The execution video's status as juridical evidence lies in wait for a future hearing, when it may be called into court—not only to answer any lingering doubts as to its legitimacy, but to testify as a *material witness* to credible allegations of grave and serious crimes. Until then the video, and the others that have surfaced, will continue to circulate within the *ad hoc* courts of public opinion, and campaigns of human rights work and legal activism. At the time of writing, the perpetrators of the executions captured by mobile phone still remain at large, secure in their anonymity and continued immunity.

Appendix

I. INVESTIGATIONS INTO A VIDEO FOOTAGE WHICH ALLEGEDLY DOCUMENTS MEMBERS OF THE SRI LANKAN ARMY COMMITTING EXTRAJUDICIAL EXECUTIONS.

Commentary by the Special Rapporteur:

On 30 November 2010, the UK television station Channel 4 provided video material of around five minutes in duration to the United Nations Special Rapporteur on extrajudicial, summary or arbitrary executions, Mr. Christof Heyns. The video allegedly depicts Sri Lankan soldiers summarily executing Tamil prisoners during the civil war in Sri Lanka.

The Special Rapporteur, delivered a communication to the Government on 15 December 2010, informing them that he would be investigating the video. On 26 April 2011, the Special Rapporteur informed the Government that he had concluded the technical assessment to establish the authenticity of the video footage and transmitted electronic as well as hard copy versions of the reports of the investigation to the Government (one annexure was inadvertently left out but provided in electronically on 29 April). When the Government submitted its Response on 11 May, it was stated that there were problems with reading parts of the hard copy of the material, but the complete report was made available by 29 April.

The overall conclusion reached by the experts is that the video is authentic and the events reflected in the video footage occurred as depicted. The Special Rapporteur has concluded that the video footage indicates the commission of serious crimes, which should together with any other available evidence be examined systematically and professionally by domestic investigators appointed by the Sri Lankan Government, as well as by an independent, international investigational body, with a clear mandate to establish who should be held accountable for the killings.

The Special Rapporteur has also reproduced below the (a) A technical note in relation to the authenticity of the second extended "Channel 4" video footage regarding Sri Lanka (b) Report of Mr. Daniel Spitz, a forensic pathologist; (c) Report of Mr. Jeff Spivack, a forensic video analyst; (d)

Report of Mr. Peter Diaczuk, a firearms expert; and (e) Report of Mr. Grant Fredericks, a forensic video analyst. The Special Rapporteur has also reproduced communications between the Special Rapporteur and the Government of Sri Lanka.

Reports of the Technical Assessment conducted by the Special Rapporteur on extrajudicial, summary or arbitrary executions.

A. Technical Note by the Special Rapporteur on extrajudicial, summary or arbitrary executions, Mr. Christof Heyns, in relation to the authenticity of the second, extended Channel 4 videotape regarding Sri Lanka

A. Background

1. On 30 November 2010, the UK television station Channel 4 made available video material of around five minutes in duration (in this note called the 'extended video') to the United Nations Special Rapporteur on extrajudicial, summary or arbitrary executions, Mr.

Christof Heyns. It described this video, extracts of which had been aired by Channel 4 around the same time as a longer version of an earlier video of approximately one minute (in this note called the 'first video'), which was aired by Channel 4 on 25 August 2009 and was said to depict Sri Lankan soldiers summarily executing Tamil prisoners during the civil war in that country.

2. The first video has been the subject of extensive communication between the Government of Sri Lanka ('the Government') and the former Special Rapporteur Mr. Philip Alston, in the form of an exchange of letters and press releases, as well as a 'Consolidated Response' to the Channel 4 video by the Government and a subsequent 'Technical Note' by Mr. Alston.

3. In reacting to the screening of this video by means of a letter of allegation to the Government of Sri Lanka, Mr. Alston's contention was that the video necessitated an impartial investigation into the question whether war crimes had been committed. The Secretary-General of the United Nations as well as other diplomats also expressed their concern about the contents of the video. The Government, however, denied the authenticity of the video.

4. In order to support this contention, the Government presented a 'Consolidated Response' to the media and the diplomatic community. It cited four reports of investigations into the authenticity of the video which the Minister of Disaster Management and Human Rights said it had obtained from its experts. While those cited seem to be regarded by the Government as experts in the field of video and audio technology, the Government also relied on their opinions on matters of forensic pathology and ballistics. According to the Minister these reports proved that the video was 'false and fabricated'. The claim was made that the Government's investigations proved that the recording was not made on a cell phone, as stated by Channel 4, but on a high quality digital camcorder or similar equipment, and then edited to reflect the atrocities and to make it appear to have been made on a cell phone, in order to discredit the Government.

5. Mr. Alston commented that he had not seen the original version of three of the four reports and asked to see them. Mr. Alston also questioned the impartiality of those who conducted the investigation, pointing out that two of the four were members of the armed forces (one was a Major, the other a Brigadier), the body which actions have been called into question, and the other two were apparently also citizens of Sri Lanka who had previously acted as advisers to the Government.

6. Mr. Alston then commissioned a study of his own by three independent experts with no links to the country or government under consideration. In addition to a video and audio expert, he engaged the services of a forensic pathologist as well as a ballistics expert, who worked independently of one another. They contested the scientific nature of the comments attributed by the Government to its own investigators. On the basis of these reports Mr. Alston concluded that 'while there are some unexplained elements in the video, there are strong indications of its authenticity.' He made the full reports available to the Government.

7. In its subsequent reactions, the Government has relied on these 'unexplained elements', clearly acknowledged by the Rapporteur, to contest his claims that the video was authentic and to justify rejection of his continued calls for an independent investigation.

8. In particular, the following issues were identified as unexplained: The date inscribed on the video was after the hostilities had ceased; there is an 'A' in the last 17 frames of the video, which suggests that some editing had been done; one victim's leg remains upright after he has apparently died; and another's dead body moves without an apparent reason.

9. It appears from the record of communication between the Government and the Special Rapporteur that the Government's contention regarding the first video is confined to the question whether the video is authentic or 'doctored' or 'a fake'. Issues such as whether the members of the military depicted in the video wear Sri Lankan uniforms (except for one soldier who wears a white T-shirt) and whether they speak Sinhala (this is in fact recognized in the excerpts of the report provided by Maj Bandara) or for that matter whether the setting of the video is in Sri Lanka, are apparently not contested. It is also not contested that the actions depicted in the video, if they reflect real events, constitute serious international crimes and violations of international human rights law. While the independence of those whom the Government say have written reports for it has been questioned by the Special Rapporteur, the independence and expertise of the experts engaged by the Special Rapporteur has not been placed in doubt.

10. The single point of contention that has emerged from the intensive communication over several months between the Special Rapporteur and the Government is therefore the authenticity of the first video, in the sense that the Government contends that it had been 'doctored'.

B. The new, extended video

11. On the extended video additional executions are shown, as well as bodies that lie on a track of ground. The faces of some of the soldiers are visible. Also clearly visible is that others are filming the scene with cell phones. One of the voices on the extended video says: 'Do not use the phone, we will be reprimanded.'

12. The extended video offers the opportunity to see the first video (which forms one segment of the extended video) in a broader context, and in particular to test the results of the earlier investigations, to see whether anything stated by the independent experts has been disproved by this new video, and whether answers to the unexplained issues may be provided by the new material.

13. I as Special Rapporteur, who took over the mandate from Mr. Alston in August 2010, informed the Government on 15 December 2010 that I would be investigating the extended video. Upon request from the Government I informed of the names of the experts who have been commissioned to conduct the investigation, and the Government was supplied with a copy of the video as received from Channel 4, to enable it to do its own investigation.

14. In view of the fact that the expertise and independence of the experts who investigated the first video was not questioned by the Government, and the fact that they were already familiar with part of the material, the services of the same experts were again obtained, to comment within their fields of expertise on the authenticity or falsity of the video. As in the past they agreed to do this free of charge, as a form of public service.

15. In addition, some further evidence was obtained and considered by the current me that would be useful in better understanding the context of the video. This included a translation of what is being said in the video, from the original Sinhala. A large number of additional pictures and other material were received from NGOs who have concerns surrounding these events. However, as will be explained below, the latter were not investigated in any detail by me.

16. Enquiries were also made by me about the origins of the video from Channel 4. However, given that the video was more than likely filmed by an insider, and then made available to the media (whether this was done for compensation or not is not known), it is not a surprise that the journalists in question maintain that they have obtained the videos on

the conditions of confidentiality from their sources. While such information would no doubt be very useful in any subsequent criminal trials, not least because it would provide one with an eye-witness of the events who could identify those involved (also those not seen on the video) it is not regarded as indispensable for current purposes, which is simply to ascertain the authenticity of the video itself.

17. The authenticity of a video such as the one under consideration can be established through a comprehensive forensic investigation, covering the different aspects of the video, which should include at least the audio and video quality. Forensic pathologists and ballistics experts can also contribute in important respects to such an investigation. In order to be credible such investigations have to be conducted by independent people of recognized expertise. Independence in this context, according to well-established jurisprudence means there should not even be a perception of bias. Close connections to the Government or State under consideration – such as nationality and/or employment – are bound to create a perception of bias and a perceived conflict of interest.

18. The new reports of the three experts on the extended video provided to me are attached. The picture that emerges is that the events that are reflected in the video in fact occurred as depicted. These videos – both the first and the extended version - show real people who are being summarily executed.

19. The first report on the extended video, contained in Annexure 'A', is by audio and video expert Mr. Jeff Spivack. His qualifications and experience are detailed in his report, as was the case with his previous report.

20. According to his report the extended video in fact consists of five segments, not in chronological sequence. This appears to be the result of the rudimentary editing that is possible on a cell phone. In this case the meta-data indicates the use of Philips software, which can be used on a variety of cell phones. However, cell phone editing capacity could not have been used to produce the images of executions captured on the video. 'At most, integrated mobile phone editing software could delete evidence that occurred before or after the remaining video, or reorder video sequences.' Cell-phone editing '... could not possibly create even a crude simulation of the subject matter present in these recordings, much less a realistic simulation.' (p 13)

21. He concludes that '... the results of testing procedures and content analysis are persuasive that the events depicted on the available video/audio recordings are authentic.' (p 13)

22. The second report, contained in Annexure 'B', is by Mr. Daniel Spitz. His biography and expertise are also described in his report. His conclusion upon having studied the extended video is as follows: 'Subsequent to my review of these materials, it is my opinion that the execution shootings shown in the videos represent real executions of multiple individuals secondary to close range gunshot wounds using high powered assault rifles.' (p 1)

23. The third report, contained in Annexure 'C', is by Mr. Peter Diaczuk, a firearms evidence expert, who comments on the three clips in the extended video where firearms are being discharged. His experience and training is indicated in his report. His conclusion is as follows. 'The three video sequences reviewed accurately depict firearms being discharged, and the recoil observed is consistent with the firing of live ammunition.'(p 4)

24. Of special importance is the fact that the extended video material has now enabled the experts to address the issues identified as 'unanswered' during the first round, and relied upon by the Government as proof that the video was not authentic.

25. The date of 15 (alternatively 18) July 2009 is encoded in the video, while hostilities had ceased in May 2009. One explanation is that the date provided on such a video is determined by the device's date setting, which can be changed by the person using the device. However, according to Mr. Spivack, if the rudimentary editing that is possible on a cell phone is done, and if five segments are put together as we now know was the case here, the date reflected for the video as a whole will be the date of such editing. (p 7)

26. The appearance of an 'A' in the last 17 frames of the first video was also a matter of concern. According to Mr. Spivack the rudimentary editing possible on a cell phone can produce such an effect. (p 13)

27. It was previously unclear why one of the apparent victims on the ground next to a victim being shot shows movement of his left lower extremity. However, Mr. Spitz reports that from the extended video it is clear that the bullet passed through the one person to hit the body of the other (p2).

28. The way in which the leg of one of the victims was maintained in an upright position was likewise not readily explicable when only the first video was available. Dr Spitz now explains that a review of the current video 'better shows the position of the leg and why it maintained an upright position'. The reason is that '... the ankle is supported by resting against the outer aspect of his right leg.' (p3)

29. The integrity of the process followed by these experts in respect of the first video finds confirmation in the fact that they marked certain aspects of that video as unresolved, when they did not have sufficient evidence to express themselves on those points. This uncertainty has now been resolved on the basis of the newly available evidence, which could not have been foreseen at the time when the first reports were being written. The above sequence of events show that they were describing the facts as they presented themselves, and were not out to prove any point.

30. The above serves as a coherent and credible foundation for the conclusion that the extended video is authentic, and thus warrants calling for the accountability of those responsible for these atrocities. It should be stressed however that the claim is not being made here that any specific individuals are guilty or that State responsibility has been established – the point is rather that there is a well-founded case for the government to answer.

31. Reference was made in the Technical Note of Mr. Alston to an article in *The Times* newspaper where an expert, whom it had commissioned, Grant Fredericks, also regarded the first video as authentic.

32. The Government told the Office of the High Commissioner for Human Rights in Geneva, when it was provided with the names of the experts who were going to investigate the extended video, that it would be more persuasive if a report by someone who was not part of the team of Mr. Alston during his investigation were made available. Because the independence of these experts was not challenged by the Government when their first reports were considered, it is hard to see the foundation for this point. However, to err on the side of caution, the current writer has asked Mr. Fredericks as well to do an independent investigation into the extended video. His report is attached as Annexure 'D'.

33. Mr. Fredericks – whose credentials are set out in his report – is of the opinion that Phillips software was used, probably on a Nokia cell phone to make the extended video. (p28) He concludes as follows: 'Giving consideration to my research and to the observations listed in this report, I have found no evidence to suggest that [the extended video] contains fabricated images or audio elements. The execution scenes contain no 'virtualization' (computer generated effects). I have therefore formed the opinion that [the extended video] is authentic in that it accurately portrays what it purports to show.' (p 29).

34. As was noted at the outset, the current Special Rapporteur was provided with numerous pictures and other material said to depict the last phases of the civil war in Sri Lanka. Sources at Channel 4 have also indicated that a much longer version of the extended video exists and could become available. The material that has already been provided includes pictures and videos of a Tamil journalist named Isaipiriya who bears a striking resemblance to one of the persons whose dead body is captured in the extended video. The material also includes pictures of the dead body of Charles Anthony (son of the late LTTE leader Prabhakaran) who was killed during the final phases of the war, in a group of pictures containing one that corresponds with images captured in the last section of the extended video. Channel 4 has also provided the Special Rapporteur with a video that captures the removal of the naked bodies of women by soldiers, said to be government troops. On this video – as is the case with the extended video – the faces of those in uniform can clearly be seen, and soldiers using cell phones as cameras are also visible.

35. These and other links with the extended video have so far not been investigated in any detail by the Special Rapporteur, in view of the limited nature of his capacity for fact-finding and forensic investigations. In view of the serious nature of the material covered by the growing body of potential evidence, it should be investigated by a body with the necessary capacity to do a comprehensive, thorough study. The material mentioned above will be made available to the Government upon request, and to such an international body, in order to assist any credible enquiry.

36. There is no indication at present that either the Attorney-General, or internal structures within Sri Lanka, such as the Lessons Learned and Reconciliation Commission, have given serious consideration to this video, or its implications, in their work.

C. Conclusion

37. The present note confines itself to the question of the authenticity of the extended video, based on the results of the independent, multi-disciplinary forensic studies that have been commissioned. The conclusion that emerges from these reports is that the video is authentic.

38. The outstanding issues identified during the investigation of the first video have now been resolved. This includes the apparent inconsistent date on the first video. However, even if that had not been done, the question could be asked how material that issue was in the first place. If someone had manufactured a false video of the events during the final stages of the war, with the malicious intent of portraying the Government's conduct during the war in a negative light, the last thing one would expect such a person to do is to provide the video with a date that falls months after the completion of the war. Likewise, it appears highly unlikely that a person who wants to create the impression that a cell phone was used would be so careless as to leave an 'A' on the frames if that can only be done on a high quality video camera. However, irrespective of how much weight could legitimately have been accorded to these issues, it is submitted that they have now been resolved.

39. On the basis of the available evidence the process of determining accountability for the crimes that have been committed should proceed with sufficient speed to avoid a situation where witnesses, accused or evidence disappear.

40. The extended video should be considered in the context of the growing body of evidentiary material which appears to relate to the events during the civil war in a comprehensive manner, covering possible atrocities by all concerned, by an institution with

the necessary capacity and level of technical skill to cover such an extensive enterprise in a professional and comprehensive manner, on the basis of a clear mandate to perform this function.

41. What is reflected in the extended video are crimes of the highest order – definitive war crimes. Judging by the use of cell phones by soldiers in the video, there may well be other records of the same events available. There appear to be links that can be made to other evidentiary material, which is already available or may still be brought to light, giving a clearer picture of what happened during the last phase of the war. Investigating the identity of those whose faces are captured so clearly on these videos cannot be difficult for the Government, which may contact the commanders of the troops who participated in the last phases of the war. Similarly, an international investigation with appropriate powers of inquiry and witness protection mechanisms will also be well placed to address these issues.

42. As has been pointed out in correspondence with the Government, it is the primary duty of the State to investigate this compelling evidence of horrendous crimes – crimes which the international community cannot allow to go unpunished. This is stated in clear terms in paragraphs 9 and 10 of the United Nations Principles on the Effective Prevention and Investigation of Extra-legal, Arbitrary and Summary Executions, adopted on 24 May 1989, with provides under the heading 'Investigations' as follows:

9. There shall be thorough, prompt and impartial investigation of all suspected cases of extra-legal, arbitrary and summary executions, including cases where complaints by relatives or other reliable reports suggest unnatural death in the above circumstances. Governments shall maintain investigative offices and procedures to undertake such inquiries. The purpose of the investigation shall be to determine the cause, manner and time of death, the person responsible, and any pattern or practice which may have brought about that death. It shall include an adequate autopsy, collection and analysis of all physical and documentary evidence and statements from witnesses. The investigation shall distinguish between natural death, accidental death, suicide and homicide.

10. The investigative authority shall have the power to obtain all the information necessary to the inquiry. Those persons conducting the investigation shall have at their disposal all the necessary budgetary and technical resources for effective investigation. They shall also have the authority to oblige officials allegedly involved in any such executions to appear and testify. The same shall apply to any witness. To this end, they shall be entitled to issue summonses to witnesses, including the officials allegedly involved and to demand the production of evidence.

43. This obligation on the State to investigate cannot be discharged by simply denying that anything untoward has happened. It can also not be discharged by assembling a group of people tied in one way or another to the government under question who are asked to comment on the videos, and expecting the international community to accept their expertise in all matters ranging from forensic analysis of videos to pathology to ballistics, without even seeing the full text of their reports or establishing their expertise in these fields. Denials based on such evidence are not credible.

44. The mandate of the domestic mechanism that the Government of Sri Lanka has created does not require a fact-finding investigation into violations of international law and international humanitarian law, and its *modus operandi* so far does not indicate that it is doing this. In addition to whatever steps can be taken to rectify the domestic process, an international investigation by an independent team with full investigative powers and capabilities should be initiated. It should make recommendations on any possible prosecutions or other measures to be taken.

45. In conclusion, what has been said above should be re-emphasized, to avoid any misunderstandings: This note does not purport to find the Government or any of its agents

guilty of any offence. This can only be done by a court of law. Instead, the claim is made here that the extended video provides credible evidence that serious crimes have been committed within the context of the Sri Lankan civil war, which should together with any other available evidence be examined systematically and professionally by domestic investigators, as well as by an independent, international investigational body, with a clear mandate in this regard, in order to establish who should be held accountable for these cold-blooded killings.

11 FAILURE TO APPEAR

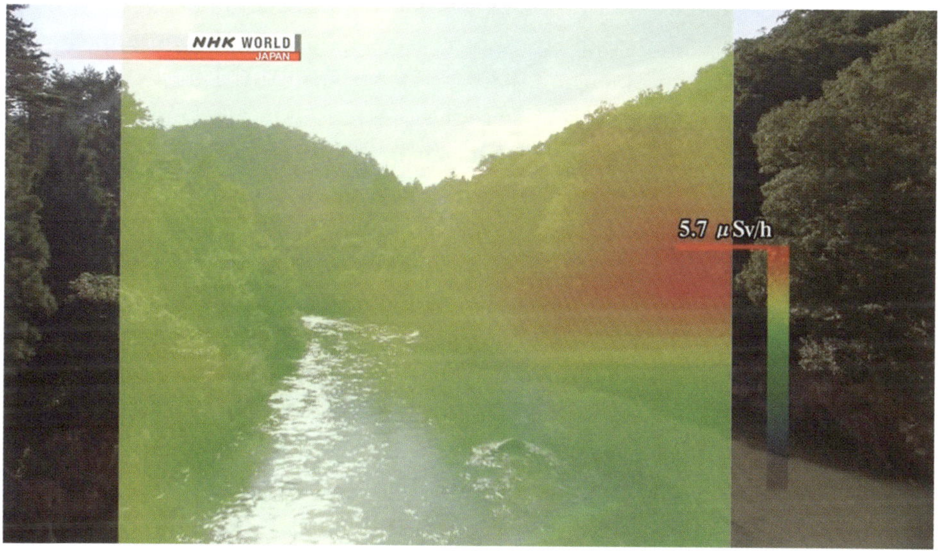

Figure 11.1
Radioactive hotspot in a ditch in the Iitate valley. Film still from *Radioactive Forest*, NHK, 2016, documentary film, 78 minutes. Source: NHK World.

Japan's Fatal Forests

Under dense vegetative cover, in the shadow of Mount Fuji, there is a verdant killing field: a suicidal forest whose magnetic soil is so rich in alluvial deposits of iron oxide that it can lure lost souls to their death. In the aftermath of the publication of Seichō Matsumoto's 1960 crime novel *Kuroi Jukai* (translated as "Black Sea of Trees") in which doomed lovers willfully perish in a rugged woodland whose thick foliage conceals their whereabouts and hampers recovery of their remains, the Aokigahara Forest of Japan has become the second most suicidal geography in the world after the Golden Gate Bridge in San Francisco. Upward of 50 persons take their final walk in this fatal forest each year, many believed to lose their bearings due to the heavily mineralized volcanic loam that renders compass readings askance. Japan's enduring animistic traditions, found throughout its Shinto religion, have also led to the belief that the Aokigahara Forest is possessed by an otherworldly spirit that exercises its deadly but invisible powers on all those who enter, only to lose their way in its vast arboreal lair.

Further north on Honshu Island, in the Iitate valley of the Sōma District, another forest exerts its lethal force, afflicting all biota, ground water, and soil with its powerful presence. Rather than succumbing to the darkness of despair in the forest's gloam, or dying from prolonged exposure to the elements as besets the spellbound wanderers of the Aokigahara, entities that move through the forests of Iitate are exposed to elemental arrangements of a radically different kind: namely high levels of radioactivity, in particular caesium-137, whose half-life of 30 years poses the greatest harm. Located just 39 kilometers from the blown-out reactors of the Fukushima Daiichi Nuclear Power Plant, which went supercritical on March 11, 2011, after an earthquake and tsunami combined to unleash their destructive energies on the coast, the forest ecosystem—which in fact comprises the largest area of concentrated radioactive contamination from the accident—absorbed airborne fallout for months, while disaster relief efforts were directed toward the more populated regions. As the days and weeks went by, an unseen enemy had moved like a stealth agent through the forest, weaponizing trees and transforming topsoil into a covert nuclear threat.

Most radionuclides are highly soluble in water, and thus extremely mobile in natural environments, whether discharged into ponds and oceans or absorbed by the moisture in soil. Airborne contaminants that settle on the forest canopy can migrate quite easily when it rains, or when vegetable matter in the form of falling leaves and branches decomposes. Many mosses and lichens extract their nutrients directly from the atmosphere because they have no developed root system, and thus act like radioactive sponges drawing in pollutants and storing isotopes that will eventually make

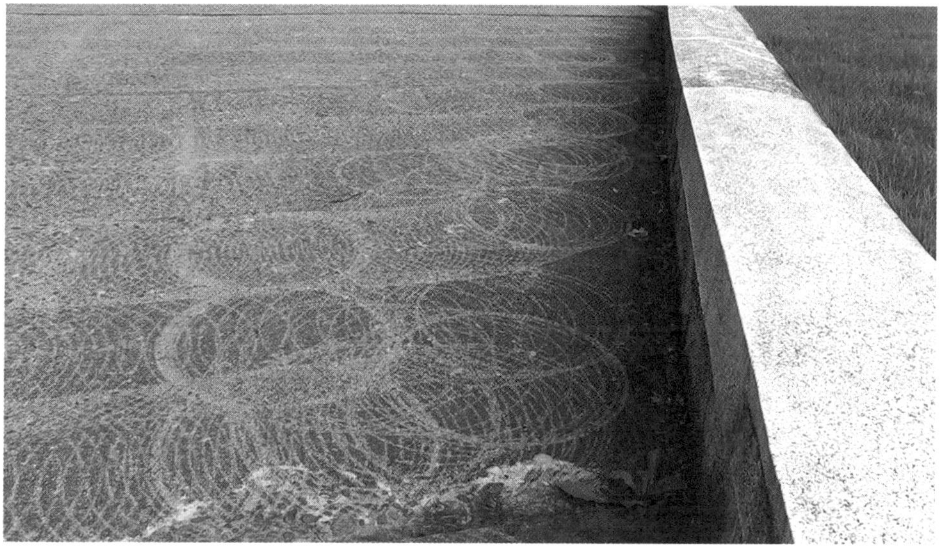

Figure 11.2
Scouring contaminated surfaces in Fukushima Prefecture, Japan, July 2014. Photo credit: Susan Schuppli.

their way into biological systems. This is why 80 percent of Sweden's reindeer meat was controversially destroyed in 1986, when fallout from the accident at Chernobyl threatened the food supply of the Sámi people via heavily contaminated lichen, the primary staple of reindeer in winter.[1] In a report detailing the dispersion of radioactive material throughout the natural environment around Fukushima, its authors remind us that "Forest ecosystems consist of tree biomass (above-ground: boles, branches, and leaves; below-ground: roots), small dead organic matter on the soil surface (termed litter), dead trees on the soil surface (termed coarse woody litter), and soil."[2] Because of the recursive dynamics of such forest ecologies, decontamination strategies that were utilized in the built environment of the Fukushima Prefecture, such as the washing and scouring of surfaces, do not work. Instead, areas of vegetative contamination require the wholesale removal of soil, litter, and leaves: a staggering effort that must be repeated, given that contaminants will reemerge when radioisotopes move through the life cycles of plants and fungi, eventually entering into animal and human food chains or returning as a dangerous latency to despoil the forest floor.

> Trees, grasses, other plants, and fungi trap radionuclides through their basic life cycle: When leaves and needles transpire (release water), the plant draws more water up from the roots. Water-soluble salts of caesium and strontium are chemical analogues of potassium and

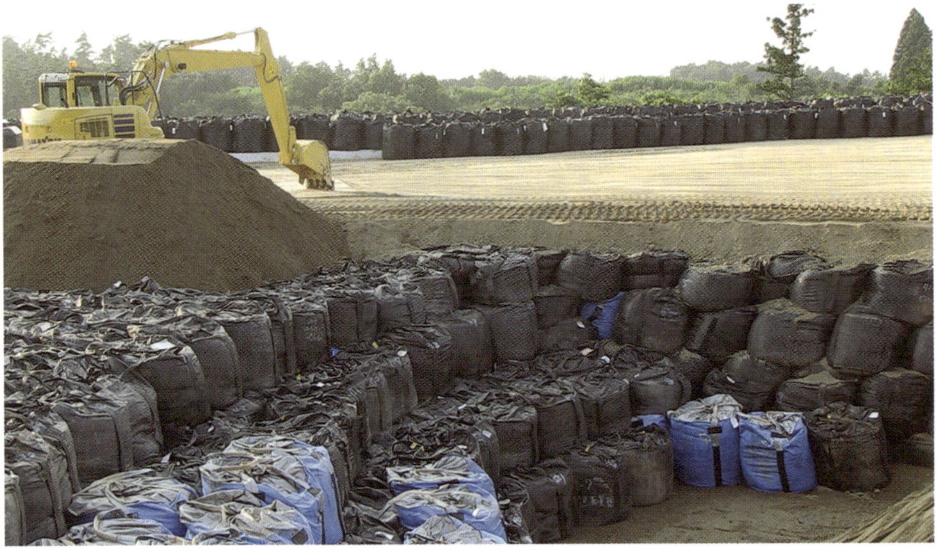

Figure 11.3
Removal, bagging, and burial of contaminated topsoil from Fukushima Prefecture, Japan, July 2014. Photo credit: Susan Schuppli.

> calcium, respectively, and are taken up in place of these crucial nutrients. In evergreens, the radionuclides gradually accumulate in needles as each season progresses. The needles then fall to the ground, becoming part of the "litter"—the discarded vegetation that covers the forest floor—and returning the radioactive salts to the top layer of the soil in a natural cycle that takes 10 to 12 years to complete. Without the trees or other permanent groundcover, contaminants would migrate out, blown in dust or carried by water.[3]

The health risks associated with exposure to ionizing radiation are further complicated if we consider that the hazard is not simply one of direct contact with the source of contamination, as is commonly assumed when nuclear accidents occur, nor even a consequence of the extremely protracted decay rates of certain isotopes that can take millennia to degrade, but also results from the redistribution and accumulation of contaminants as they move through different environments and bodies over time. While the nervous clicks of the Geiger counter have long signaled the paradigmatic warning indicating one's proximity to irradiated matter, the challenge of locating hotspots in a faulty power plant, let alone in expansive outdoor environments with varying moisture patterns, is thwarted by such technologies, as radiation contamination is also extremely localized and can return readings that vary dramatically only meters apart. This is why a Geiger counter might spike near a water-filled depression, whereas the banks of the same creek would return far less elevated levels of contamination.

Gamma Rays

Figure 11.4, provided by the Japanese Power and Electric Company or TEPCO, the company that owns and operated the Fukushima Daiichi plant, reveals a highly uneven distribution pattern of contaminants inside one of its failed reactor units, with the concentration of red-orange pixels near the upper reaches of the structure indicating an area of maximum caution. This unusual image, which is in fact a video still, was produced by the Toshiba Gamma Camera, the world's first portable gamma ray camera. It was designed expressively for detecting radiation levels inside the Fukushima Daiichi Nuclear Power Plant as well as in its environs. The camera has even been used outside in local playgrounds and parks, and in 2016 it was taken by a group of scientists from the University of Tokyo into the open-air laboratory of the Iitate valley, where it was used to investigate radioactivity within the forests. As a technology for sensing gamma radiation it permits far greater insight into the spatial distribution of contaminants, as well as the scalar cartography of their concentrations. Using an adapted video camera outfitted with 128 semiconductor sensors that can detect and translate gamma ray emissions into a visual field of color-coded pixels, the Toshiba Gamma Camera permits real-time large-area observation of the changing conditions of nuclear contamination.

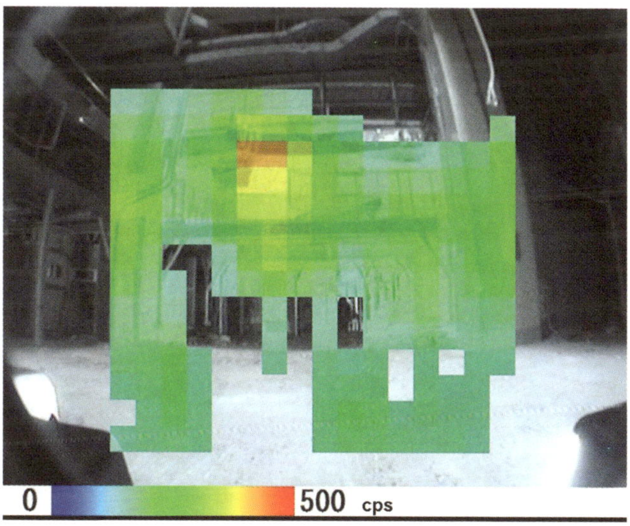

Figure 11.4
Radioactive hotspot inside the Fukushima Daiichi Nuclear Power Plant. Gamma Camera view from the large equipment service entrance to the south side airlock, May 22, 2011. Source: TEPCO.

Within the history of radiation detection, locating the distribution of contaminants within a complex spatial environment such as a building has been particularly demanding. When there is a leak in a power plant the dosimeters worn by workers may set off alarms, but finding the actual source can be extremely difficult. While variations of gamma cameras, also known as scintillation cameras, have existed since the late 1950s for applications in nuclear medicine, they are large, cumbersome machines that are fixed in place. The innovation of the Toshiba Gamma Camera lies in its compact size (it weighs only 8.9 kilos) and portability (three-hour battery life), as well as in its capacity to visualize the spatial distribution of gamma rays in real time. The camera's specialized sensors are able to detect the direction as well as intensity of high-frequency wavelengths emitted by radioactive materials in as little as three seconds, depending upon the volumetric scale of the space in which it is filming. This data is then downloaded to an attached computer whose software calibrations translate these geolocated readings (taken in sieverts per second or hour) into a field of color-coded pixels. The multicolored grid, indicating the distribution pattern of contaminants, is superimposed onto standard resolution (640 x 480) video footage that is shot simultaneously by the Gamma Camera, resulting in a composite image sourced from two different sensors. Unlike the high-frequency emanations that create the pixelated gamma grid, the background video is produced by medium wavelengths of visible light reflected by the objects or entities located in the space, which are in turn registered by a light-sensitive microchip, or CCD (charge-coupled device). In combining information from across the electromagnetic spectrum, the Gamma Camera transposes the emissions of the invisible into the realm of the sensible.[4]

My invocation here of the controversial 1976 Franco-Japanese film *L'Empire des Sens*, directed by Nagisa Oshima, which translates as *In the Realm of the Senses*, is deliberate. The film's title was adapted from French philosopher Roland Barthes's fictive book about Japan, *The Empire of Signs* (*L'Empire des Signes*), written in 1970, on the aesthetics of the surface. Barthes argued that in Japan there is no metonymic displacement, as events are always immanent to the situation in which they literally take place. Sex, he suggests, is not distributed throughout society in the form of innuendo or insinuation, as so often happens in the West, but exists solely within the act itself. There is no recourse to the transcendent regime of the figurative or symbolic, only immanence. Due to the sexually explicit subject matter of Oshima's film, it had to be optically censored by blurring key segments before its public release in Europe; an entanglement between the filmic operations of the "censor" that also bears upon an understanding of the gamma sensor. Inasmuch as the Gamma Camera can make visible the alarming presence of radiation, it also acts as a kind of graphic veil that prevents us from seeing

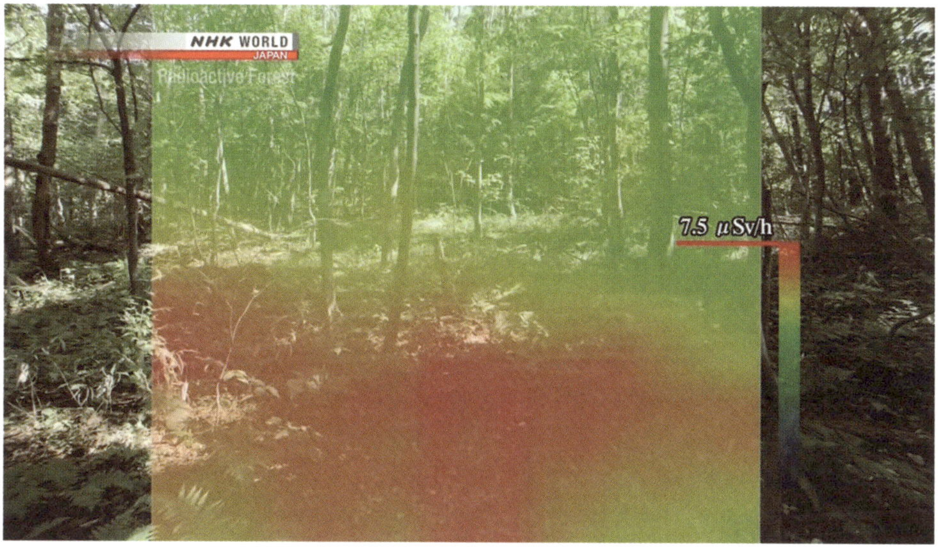

Figure 11.5
Radioactive hotspot in the forests of the Iitate valley. Film still from *Radioactive Forest*, NHK, 2016, documentary film, 78 minutes. Source: NHK World.

into the most explicitly dangerous parts of the image. The pixelated field that floats on top of the surface of the image alerts us to the ontological threats that lurk within its gridded space, the transgressive nature of which can never be fully known, since the latency of radiation is so extremely variable.

As I have argued elsewhere in this book, the nuclear aesthetics of the *material witness* are always radically indexical to themselves. In the case of the Iitate valley, this would be akin to saying that radiological contamination has rendered the forest ecosystem a living trace of the disaster. Moreover, in capturing traces of the real, the woodland also became image matter in waiting: an arboreal archive whose photogenic capacity would come to be actualized only with the invention of the portable Gamma Camera, which forced the ontological condition of the forest as contaminated into presence. The camera *makes* the forest radioactive. The same could be said for the sonics of the Geiger counter, or even the mutating actions of cancerous cells that make known the illness of the body. This is an inductive process rather than a deductive one of assembling clues. In my formulation the trace assumes an asignifying function that induces the real into presence, whereas classically the trace was used to deduce a prior history. In *Camera Lucida*, Barthes himself seems to intuit operations suggestive of the Gamma Camera when discussing the photograph as a material instantiation of a radiating force that emanates from a source to touch a perceiver:

> The photograph is literally an emanation of the referent. From a real body, which was there, proceed radiations which ultimately touch me, who am here; the duration of the transmission is insignificant; the photograph of the missing being, as Sontag says, will touch me like the delayed rays of a star.[5]

Inasmuch as the photograph posited here is a documentary recording of circumstances that precede it, the alchemical event of "contact" between light-emitting photons and a glass plate or negative is already suggestive of a material index that is evidential to itself, which is to say, internal to the organization of technical matter; whether that between photonic emanations and light-sensitive film, or between radioactive emissions and semiconductor sensors. These an-indexical events of chemistry or circuitry exist prior to their externalization in the form of a representation, and are thus all the more ontologically real. Likewise, the radioactive forests of the Sōma District were fully camera-ready prior to subsequent investigations by scientists. This insight further extends Paul Virilio's arguments around the primal accident in stressing not only that the possibility of a nuclear accident had been latent at the Fukushima Daiichi Power Plant since the technical realization of a self-sustaining nuclear chain reaction in 1942, but that oftentimes the accident as a potential latency is inaugurated only when a new type of procedure or sensor is invented that can retroactively reveal the lurking presence of the event. Through the intercession of the Gamma Camera the forest was reinvented as an abiotic "media" ecology attuned to its radioactive becoming.

Reconceptualizing the gamma sensor as part of a radiating process that brings forth the image censor by way of a pixelated shroud produces a situation in which superimposition does not so much act to signal subversive content but, rather, works to express the deeply political nature of the electromagnetic spectrum in which the realm of human vision still constitutes the privileged domain of action. In essence, the Gamma Camera reveals the paradox of visibility that has lain at the heart of contemporary politics. As the American environmentalist Aldo Leopold once remarked: "We can be ethical only in relation to something we can see, feel, understand, love, or otherwise have faith in."[6] But even then, Leopold adds, the images of nature that we hold on to are often mere figures of speech rather than images that disclose genuine understandings of how complex ecosystems actually work. In suggesting that ethical action requires an identification whose affective primacy is conditioned by sight, he admits that mere knowledge of an environmental catastrophe is not wholly self-sufficient for bringing about change. Despite our enduring conviction in the power of images, says media theorist Thomas Keenan, the visual representation and disclosure of devastation and suffering is by no means contracted to the public sphere as a call to action or prompt for humanitarian intervention.[7] Today we are witnesses to an even greater surge of images—still and moving, uploaded and streaming—that clearly depict self-evident violations of human rights or catastrophic accidents, but whose rhetorical capacity to overturn such wrong-doings, let alone convict legally, has failed miserably. Despite the demand for justice that such documentary images may perform publicly, when they enter into institutional infrastructures and forums, especially legal ones, they cannot guarantee that the regime of representation will be adequate to the task of providing accountability or, indeed, result in a criminal conviction. Nonetheless, the realm of the visible rather than the "sensible" is still venerated in Western contexts as the requisite condition for producing a transformative politics; an aesthetic challenge that has become considerably more urgent with the advent of algorithmic processes or the degradation of life worlds within our toxic commons.[8] When it comes to the fallout of nuclear matter, the slow and invisible violence of ionizing radiation cannot compete with the spectacular detonations of mushroom clouds.[9]

Powerful Particles

However, before the atmospheric particle became the delivery system *par excellence* whereby lethal toxins would be carried into the terrifying narratives of modernity, as suggested by Peter Sloterdijk in his thesis of "atmoterrorism," the nuclear capacities of the twentieth century were preceded by two key developments in photo-imaging technology:[10] the discovery of the X-ray in 1895 by Wilhelm Röntgen, followed by Henri Becquerel's chance encounter with spontaneous radioactivity a year later. Both of these pioneering physicists identified processes that were capable of transforming solid matter into a spectral image trace without the arbitration of an external light source, which had until that point been a necessary precondition of all early photographic practices. The transgressive spectral agency of the nuclear is perhaps its defining aesthetic property, which is also why the terrifying potency of the evil spirits that are said to lurk in the Aokigahara Forest of Japan offers an uncanny parallel to the contaminated forests of Fukushima; the mineralized soils of each are rich in powerful particles that can interfere with the natural order of things.

In late February 1896 Becquerel was experimenting with uranium salts and phosphorescence to produce contact prints, but when a series of cloud-covered days disrupted his research he put his prepared materials away in a drawer, where they lay hidden for several days, "sheltered from the excitation of incident rays."[11] Inside the darkness of

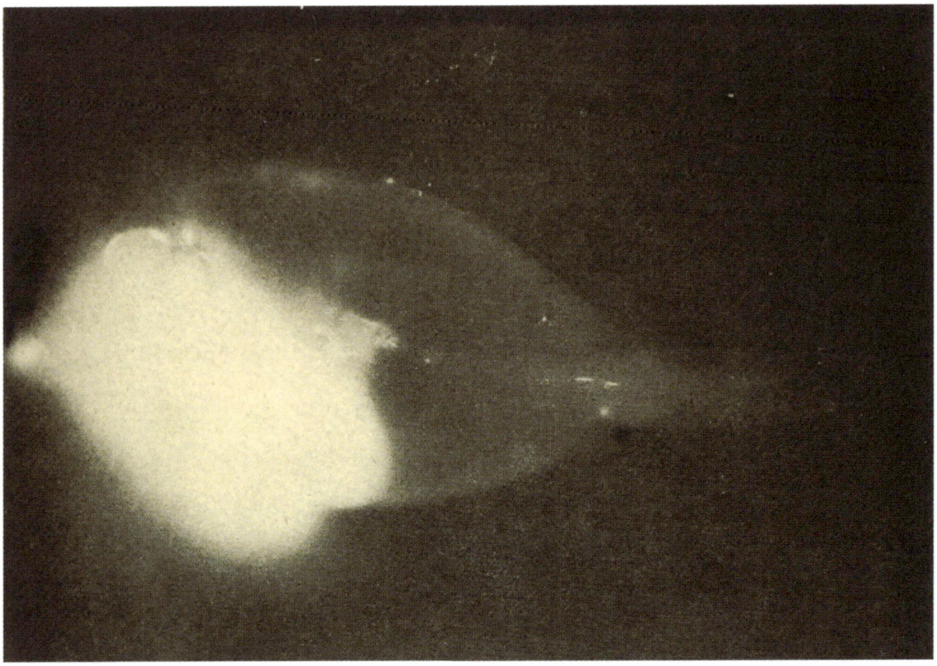

Figure 11.6
Radio-autograph of a tropical pufferfish. Source: Operation Crossroads: The Official Pictorial Record, 1946.

this enclosure was a copper cross that Becquerel had placed between a photographic plate wrapped in paper and a uranium-salted glass slide. Upon resumption of his work, and for some inexplicable reason, Becquerel decided to develop this sequestered but unexposed plate. To his surprise, an incredibly bright and detailed image of a Maltese cross appeared. Uranium salts, it turned out, emitted radiation (specifically beta particles and gamma rays, as alpha particles would have been blocked by the paper wrapping), which the copper object had absorbed, producing an entirely new kind of image: a radio-autograph. This technique of direct contact printing by means of decaying radioactive emissions would come to provide technologists with a crucial diagnostic tool for detecting the presence of contaminants in natural systems. However, as photohistorian Kelly E. Wilder stresses, Becquerel's ultimate objective was to create evidential images in which the isolated qualities of alpha, beta, and gamma radiation could be specifically studied. "Henri Becquerel's method was singular because he used photography in an entirely different way. Instead of picturing objects by illuminating them with radiation, he made the illumination the object of his images, as a spectroscopist would do."[12]

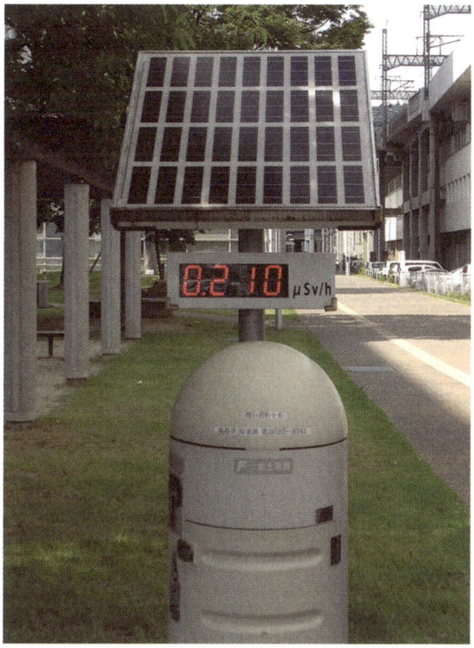

Figure 11.7
Public solar-powered Geiger counters are installed throughout the Fukushima Prefecture. July 2017. Photo credit: Susan Schuppli.

Chief amongst early proponents of radio-autography (also known as autoradiography) was US Army medical doctor David Bradley, who worked as a radiological monitor or "Geiger man" during Operation Crossroads, the first postwar atomic weapons test. Bradley pioneered the use of biological organisms as a proto-gamma ray sensor that could record direct evidence of exposure to radioactivity.[13] Working with the method of contact printing, Bradley was able to translate the relative degree of contamination found within marine biota into a visual information system that could be further analyzed and compared with other species and locales. For example, using tropical pufferfish caught in the aftermath of the atomic testing in the Bikini Atoll in 1946, Bradley would carefully slice open one of these small fish along the length of its body, arranging flesh so that its splayed tissue pressed against a photographic plate. After several hours the fish was removed and the film was developed. This whole process was carried out in complete darkness without the aid of an enlarger to generate the negative imprint of the organism, as would be the case when producing a standard photographic contact print. Instead, the ghostly apparition that emerged out of

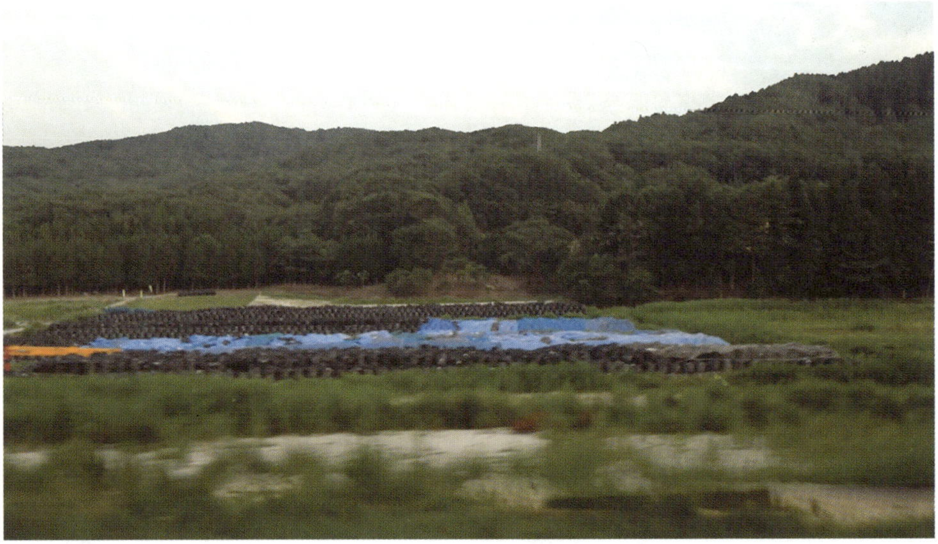

Figure 11.8
Removal and bagging of 5 cm. of contaminated topsoil from forests in the Iitate valley, Japan, July 2014. Photo credit: Susan Schuppli.

the developing solution was a 1:1 analog detailing the gradient levels of radioactivity present within the soft tissue of the biological creature.

The contaminated flesh of the pufferfish, as evidenced in Figure 11.6, especially its gills, liver, intestines, and reproductive organs, are all areas where toxicity has settled in greater concentrations. There is also an indication that a significant deposit of radioactive algae has yet to be digested by the fish. During the postwar period the nuclear signature of such tropical fish was enlisted as a kind of biocalculus for measuring the degree to which radiation exposure could accumulate within living tissue, especially that of humans.[14] Scientists sought out these aquatic specimens because their planar morphology and relatively consistent tissue depth made them ideal living analogs to the photographic plate. Not only did their irradiated tissue render the nuclear visible in the form of a negative image, but it was also the source of its visualization, as radioactive decay and the emission of energetic particles effectively lit the organism from within. The radiological wound revealed within the defective tissue of this small fish is no less momentous than that of the mushroom cloud, and is equally disturbing, as the compromised interiority of living matter highlights the extensive dispersion and global circulation of contaminants within an ecological system as vast as the Pacific Ocean: a nuclear legacy that today is carried by Pacific Bluefin tuna, which spawn in the heavy waters off Japan's Honshu Island to eventually make their way to the California coast. Anthropologist Joseph Masco has discussed Bradley's work and the emergence of the radio-autograph as signaling a "new modernity" defined by an ecology of contaminated nature; an observation he made in 2006 that had yet to confront the fallout of Fukushima Daiichi but to which his insight remains equally relevant.

> If the pre-Cold War radio-autographs of irradiated fish from Operation Crossroads offer us an image of a nuclear ecology of damaged organs, a corrupted food chain, and death, another image of radioactive nature in the post-Cold War period privileges survival. The Chernobyl site, which is, for many people, now the primary reference for radiation exposure, provides perhaps the clearest illustration of this new formation.[15]

Image Safe Areas

Efforts to visualize the unseen forces of radiation have organized our scientific as well as nuclear imaginaries for more than 100 years. But it is Becquerel's breakthrough photographic plate fogged by its direct exposure to uranium salts that has become a source of conceptual intrigue for contemporary art practices in particular. The furtive emissions of radioactive decay, with their capacities for self-illumination, have led many an artist to work with irradiated materials as a form of "cameraless" photography: a process of analog image-making that does not require the intercession of a negative or external light source to produce an exposure. But I do worry about the overly poetic sensibility that guides some of these projects, whose outcomes seem wholly captivated by the spectral dimension of the radiological without any critical commitment to investigating the nuclear infrastructures, whether those of uranium mining, weapons testing, or energy production, that underwrite such ghostly propensities. Film theorist Akira Mizuta Lippit once referred to this incorporeal seduction as a kind of "sadistic metaphysics" that revels in the transmutation of bodily matter by way of the cosmic potency of atomic light.[16] I too am not immune to the nuclear's imaginative hold in beginning this chapter with an analogy to the supernatural powers of the Aokigahara Forest. However, the gamma ray visualizations produced by advances in medical physics, which I reference here with respect to the Gamma Camera and its historic predecessor in the radio-autograph, are decidedly informatic in rendering perceptible the distribution and concentration of radioactive contaminants. Understanding the technicity of such ghostly forces must always balance our affective enchantments, otherwise the agency and politics of nuclear materials are all too quickly transformed into signs that can be read, and are expressive of cultural value, but eschew their evidential capacity to testify to events.

Unlike conventional devices and dosimeters, Toshiba's portable Gamma Camera allows scientists to pinpoint the whereabouts of hotspots quickly, without having to grid out a space and take measurements across intervals, as would be the case with standard Geiger counter readings. As a spatial tool for detecting potentially harmful but invisible events, the Gamma Camera is usefully positioned for identifying areas of potential concern, thus aiding in environmental remediation, but this is not to suggest that it is now safe for the 80,000 evacuated residents of the Iitate valley to return home. With the 2020 summer Olympics looming on the horizon, and nine nuclear power plants back in full operation, State assurances as to the limited dangers of return have been met with fierce criticism and outright rebuttal. According to a 2015 report, most displaced communities, especially those of Iitate, do not wish to go home, despite a government pledge to move two-thirds of all evacuees back within less than a decade of the accident.[17] Many have controversially argued that the Japanese state and TEPCO's elusiveness as regards the risks governing cleanup efforts at Fukushima Daiichi, as well as more widespread public health concerns, has been even more deliberately evasive than the Soviet Union's response to Chernobyl; both events registered as Level 7 nuclear incidents. Although such comparisons may be skewed, given that the release of radioactive carcinogens by the accident in the Ukraine was tenfold that of Japan, issues of foot-dragging, conflicting information, and public transparency remain.[18] Even the presence of public solar-powered Geiger counters installed throughout the Fukushima Prefecture might be argued as functioning in a somewhat obfuscating manner. While they aid in monitoring, and can alert inhabitants to the ongoing potential for elevated levels of radioactivity to flare up within the urban fabric, as stand-alone devices their public syntax of risk is largely recast as a symbolic form of powerlessness. People are totally unable to ascertain the source, direction, and scope of any spike in readings, let alone mitigate any potential harm. Indeed, many have taken to conducting their own radiological readings, but this is not an appropriate measure either, given the need for systematic calibration and accurate analysis.

In this regard, the technical image produced by the Gamma Camera in the forest ecologies of the Iitate valley is much more "operational" than that provided by more conventional detection methods in furnishing detailed sensor data across geographic scales that can be used to locate key areas of danger and thus, one could hope, direct decontamination as well as remediation efforts. Although I must say that the Herculean task of removing contaminated topsoil and vegetative matter from the forest floor, which I witnessed personally, seems like an impossible feat. Everywhere activity is underway to deal with the disaster: from rebuilding and fortification of the destroyed seawall, the scrubbing of surfaces and roadways, to the removal of soil. At last count,

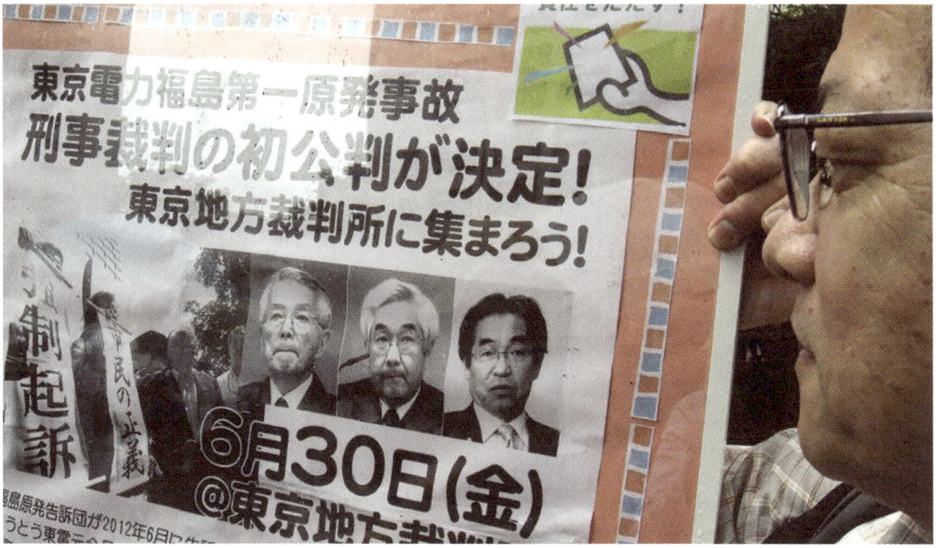

Figure 11.9
A poster showing the three executives now on trial for alleged negligence over the Fukushima nuclear disaster of 2011. The trial began in Tokyo district court on June 30, 2017. Photo credit: Koji Sasahara. Source: AP.

10 billion dollars has been spent in cleanup efforts and 2.9 million bags of topsoil have been removed and buried in toxic waste sites throughout the prefecture.[19] I spent a day filming the reconstruction of the seawall and the repairing of other tsunami damage in the reclassified sector of the Exclusion Zone, which is now called the "Restricted Residents' Zone," but I did wonder who exactly is supposed to benefit from these efforts? Such activities are perhaps more aptly understood as a form of state-sanctioned penance—a parliamentary apology that comes too late, but makes overtures toward crisis response in face of the systematic inaction documented by the Fukushima Commission (2012). This is why the invisibility of radiation contamination has to be countered by a suite of practices—technical, social, activist, and otherwise—that render the problem legible, and thus potentially knowable, as the very abstract nature of an imperceptible threat reinforces the already secretive tendencies of the Japanese State and TEPCO. And while sensor technologies are not exclusively organized by optical or visual regimes *per se*, they do allow us to register differences across domains, and to convert this information into datasets that can be aggregated and acted upon. From readings of moisture content, barometric pressure, air quality, temperature levels, spectral emissions to electromagnetic feedback, sensing brings something into presence as a difference in degree.

Moreover, I would suggest that the semiconductor sensor array of the Gamma Camera also produces different kinds of information about the radiological event, as seemingly invisible rays are transformed into a public truth with a rhetorical force that can address the real scope of the nuclear disaster and, by implication, the lack of accountability across the political spectrum. Today, full public disclosure about the extent and levels of fallout from the accident at the Fukushima Daiichi Power Plant are still subject to ongoing censure and controversy. "In a telling move in a country where litigation is relatively rare, more than 10,000 have joined some 20 class action lawsuits to demand more compensation so they can afford to choose for themselves whether to return, or to build new lives elsewhere."[20]

Tokyo Trial

On June 30, 2017, three former TEPCO executives, Tsunehisa Katsumata, Sakae Muto, and Ichiro Takekuro, pleaded "not guilty" to charges of professional negligence resulting in death and injury in a hearing held at the Tokyo district court. "The charges are linked to the deaths of about 40 patients at Futaba Hospital in the town of Futaba who were forced to flee the Fukushima area and later died. The trial was set when a previous judgment by prosecutors not to pursue charges was overturned by an Inquest of Prosecution—a rare procedure that can be used to appeal such a decision before a panel of ordinary citizens."[21] It is the only legal proceeding aimed directly at TEPCO's senior management to have advanced in the six-year period since the accident at the Fukushima Daiichi Nuclear Power Plant, although many more lawsuits have been brought forward by Fukushima evacuees against the State on the grounds of emotional distress or for compensatory damages related to loss of personal property. In March 2017 the Maebashi district court ruled that negligence on the part of the State also contributed to the "man-made" disaster at Fukushima Daiichi. It is the first such ruling to have found the government liable, and it awarded damages of ¥38.55m (£270,000) to 137 evacuee plaintiffs.

In the criminal action pursued against TEPCO's executives, it is alleged that its management was fully aware of the potential risks to the plant that breaches to the seawall posed in the face of an offshore earthquake and tsunami. According to a 641-page report published by a parliamentary panel (Fukushima Nuclear Accident Independent Investigation Commission) in 2012, TEPCO had already run simulations as early as 2008 modeling the impact of seismic activity on the power plant, knowing that it was located in a region of the world prone to such events. Any earthquake with a magnitude of 8.3 or higher was demonstrated to be fully capable of creating a coastal wave of 15.7 meters, which would prove devastating to the plant's security perimeter. "The 2008 data were relayed to Takekuro and Muto, who were in charge of TEPCO's nuclear business at that time, and were also 'very likely' to have been reported to Katsumata by June 2009 at the latest, according to an independent committee of citizens that reviewed the prosecutors' decision not to press charges" prior to the current trial.[22] In a 2002 report drafted by the government's Headquarters for Earthquake Research Promotion, experts established that there was a one in five chance of a combined magnitude-8 earthquake and tsunami occurring off the northeast coast of Honshu Island within the next 30 years. Apparently both of these official reports, with their dire predictive warnings, went unheeded. Moreover, the parliamentary commission of 2012, led by Kiyoshi Kurokawa, Professor Emeritus at Tokyo University, determined that the combined natural forces unleashed by the earthquake and tsunami were not the sole causal agents that contributed to the triple reactor core meltdown at Fukushima Daiichi, but that the disaster was also human-made, and part of a culture of collusion and blind bureaucratic adherence to systems of decision-making.

> The Fukushima nuclear power plant accident was the result of collusion between the government, the regulators and TEPCO, and the lack of governance by said parties.
>
> They effectively betrayed the nation's right to be safe from nuclear accidents. Therefore, we conclude that the accident was clearly "man-made."
>
> We believe that the root causes were the organizational and regulatory systems that supported faulty rationales for decisions and actions, rather than issues relating to the competency of any specific individual.
>
> Across the board, the commission found ignorance and arrogance unforgivable for anyone or any organization that deals with nuclear power. We found a disregard for global trends and a disregard for public safety.
>
> —Fukushima Nuclear Accident Independent Investigation Commission (NAIIC)

It is doubtful that the *material witness*, narrowly conceived as a juridical concept, can do the considerable work that is required to address matters of environmental justice and accountability for the radiological afterlives emerging out of Fukushima. The spatial migration of contaminants and temporal latency of their metabolic effects, which may take years or even decades to reveal themselves, complicate this immeasurably. "I apologize for causing the serious accident," said TEPCO's former Chairman Tsunehisa Katsumata in court, before adding the proviso "it was impossible to predict." One of his two co-defendants, Sakae Muto, a former Vice-President at TEPCO, made a similar declaration to absolve himself of any criminal wrongdoing: "When I recall that time, I still think it was impossible to anticipate an accident like that. I believe I have no criminal responsibility over the accident." However, when it is adapted to situations that include but are not limited to the legal sphere, the *material witness* offers an initial attempt at inventing a new conceptual framework for critical analysis; one that in taking the "accident seriously" also takes seriously the evidential capacities of materials to express their own condition, and labors to unfold such disastrous events into much larger networks of affiliation.

In the aftermath of the meltdown at Fukushima Daiichi, the regulatory body tasked with overseeing nuclear operations in Japan came under heavy criticism for its close and "collusive" ties with the nuclear industry. A new nuclear watchdog has been appointed, but the moratorium imposed upon the restart of Japan's nuclear reactors in 2011 has already been overturned as two power plants at Sendai were brought back online in 2015, followed by seven others since then. Japan's Prime Minister, Shinzo Abe, is a staunch proponent of nuclear energy, and plans are in place to continue to move a fifth of Japan's energy needs back to the nuclear sector by 2030. When I visited Toshiba's Nuclear Energy Systems and Services Division to demo their portable Gamma Camera in 2014, the scientists working there were similarly convinced that Japan's nuclear power plants would systematically be brought back online in due course. In the lobby, a model of a reactor design that Toshiba had just sold to the United Kingdom was proudly displayed, although plans to build three new reactors at Moorside in Cumbria have been thrown into doubt with the bankruptcy filing of Toshiba's nuclear subsidiary Westinghouse in March 2017. Meanwhile, back at the trial in Tokyo, Katsumata apologized again "for the tremendous trouble to the residents in the area and around the country because of the serious accident that caused the release of radioactive materials."

12 CLOSING ARGUMENTS

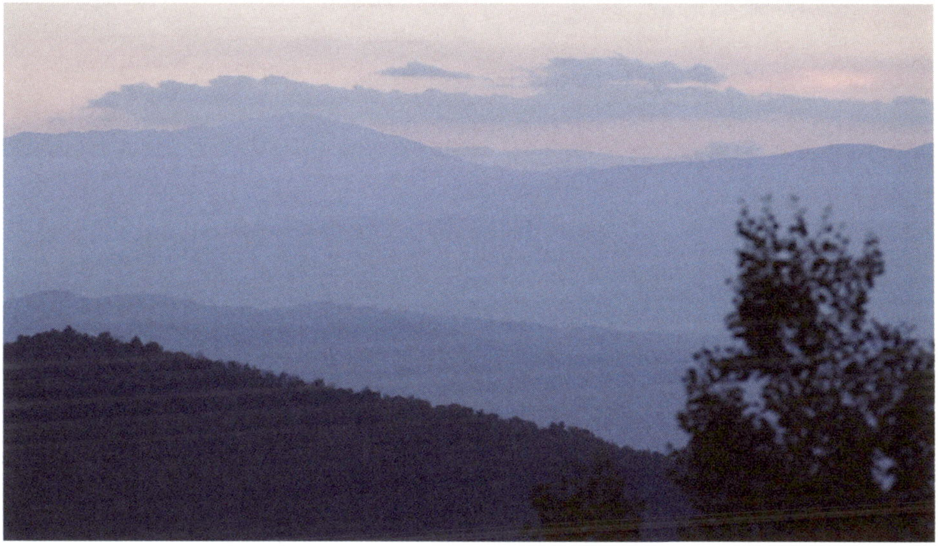

Figure 12.1
Mountains of Kozara and Grmeč, *Memorial in Exile*, Susan Schuppli and Steffen Kraemer, 2012, HD video, color with sound, 25 minutes.

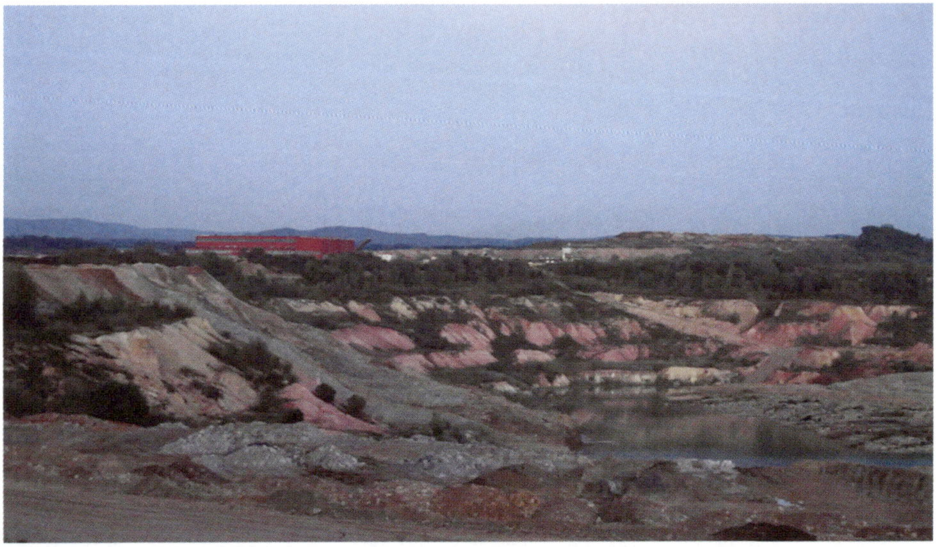

Figure 12.2
Omarska Mine, *Memorial in Exile*, Susan Schuppli and Steffen Kraemer, 2012, HD video, color with sound, 25 minutes.

Earth Evidence

In 1912, a German geophysicist and meteorologist, Alfred Lothar Wegener, made the daring proposition that the continents once formed a supercontinent called Pangaea, which had fractured and whose landmasses were still slowly drifting apart. His proposition was roundly rejected at the time, and relegated to the realm of fiction until the 1960s when, as Isabelle Stengers puts it, "the movement, not of the continents but of the plates on which they rested, confessed to their mobility."[1] The evidence that testified to Wegener's proposition was quite literally a *material witness*—the earth's crust itself—whose plate tectonics provided the crucial proof to support a theory of continental drift. However, the acceptance of the theory by geologists took decades, emphasizing the degree to which the capacity for evidence to testify convincingly requires not only the development of new technical probes for the detection, measurement, and analysis of the dynamics of matter, but that it also be tested in the appropriate public forums in which such witnessing can properly take place. Today these tend to be juridical and scientific forums, whereas in the premodern era theological courts held sway over the miraculous appearance of evidence.[2] However, as we have seen throughout the preceding chapters, such enunciative frameworks still

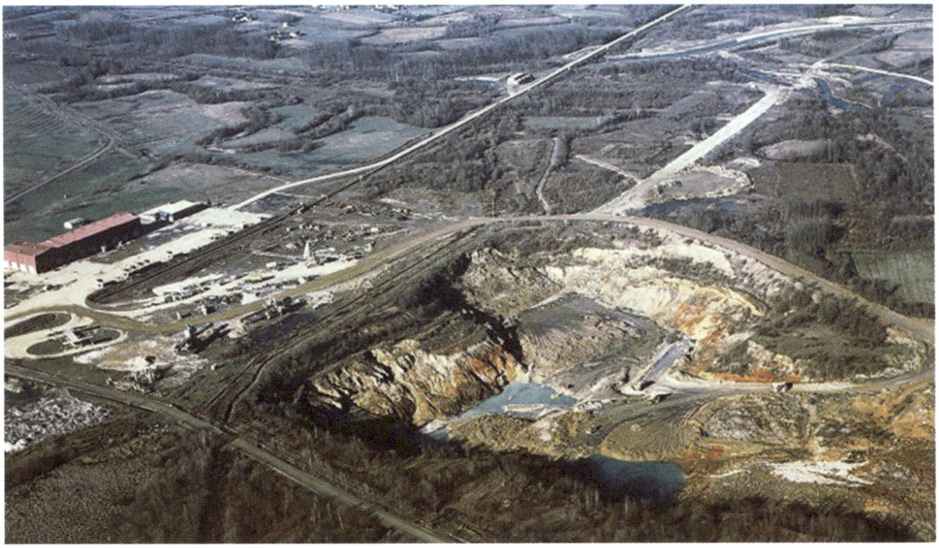

Figure 12.3
Aerial view of the Omarska mine, Ljubija mining complex. *Memorial in Exile*, Susan Schuppli and Steffen Kraemer, 2012, HD video, color with sound, 25 minutes.

remain highly partisan in nature, strictly governed by agreed-upon practices and rules of procedure.

In the mineralized landscape of northern Bosnia and Herzegovina there is an open pit mine called Omarska that was used as a Serbian death camp in 1992. According to recent geological assessments there are still some 347 metric tonnes of limonite and carbon ore reserves in the river valleys of the Sana, Una, and Gomjenica, which lie between the mountains of Kozara and Grmeč, a region that was heavily impacted by the Balkan Wars of the 1990s. In 1992, 12 years after the war crimes committed there, the world's largest steel producer—ArcelorMittal—assumed 51 percent ownership of the Ljubija mining complex, an acquisition that included Omarska. The ICTY's findings proved that crimes against humanity had been carried out at the mine site and its earth-moving equipment had been used to dispose of bodies, yet no space of public commemoration exists despite the company's repeated public commitments to financing and building a memorial on its grounds. Instead, an infrastructure once directed toward lethal extermination has been reenlisted in the lucrative operations of a global mining concern overseen by one of Britain's richest residents, Lakshmi Mittal.

As Senior Research Fellow on Forensic Architecture, I worked alongside survivors, archaeologists, and the Belgrade-Prijedor-Graz-based collective Working Group Four

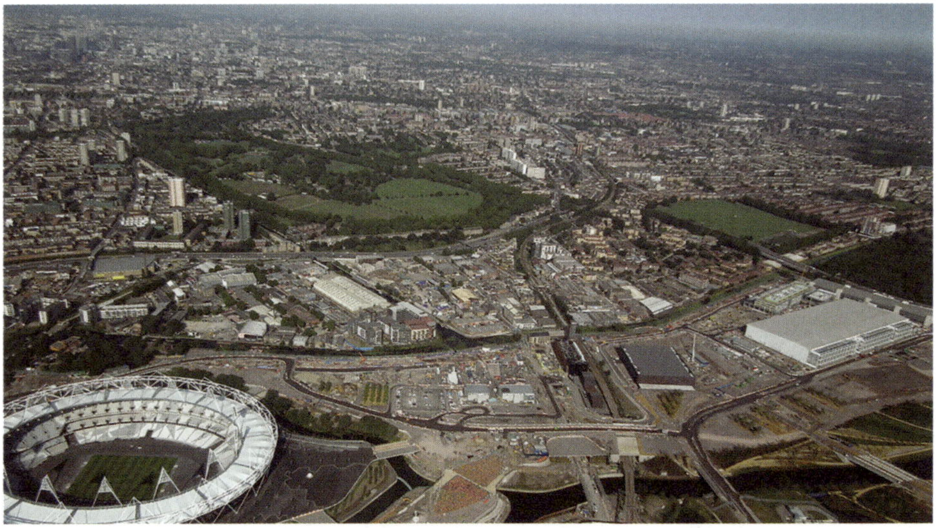

Figure 12.4
Aerial view of London Olympic Park under construction, June 11, 2011. Source: EG Focus/CC BY.

Faces of Omarska on the "Living Death Camps" investigation (2011–2012) into two historic concentration camps in the region: Staro Sajmište, a location in the heart of Belgrade repurposed by the Germans during World War II, and Omarska.[3] When word of ArcelorMittal's purchase first came to light, journalist Ed Vulliamy immediately raised the specter of buried bodies, and even potentially mass graves, being found at the Prijedor mines: "Work has just concluded at one mass grave only two miles from the Omarska site, from which the remains of 420 men murdered in the camp were retrieved. In October 2001, another mass grave containing 353 bodies was found within another mine in the complex."[4] He also interviewed Amor Mašović, president of the Bosnian government's Commission for Tracing Missing Persons, which conducted the exhumations; he vehemently maintains: "There is no doubt whatsoever that there are bodies as yet unfound within the mine of Omarska and its vicinity."[5]

Prijedor is in the region of Bosnia and Herzegovina that is referred to, after the Dayton Peace Agreement, as Republika Srpska, an area whose demographics were dramatically affected by the war, and where ethnic cleansing was at its most intensified and ultimately successful. In addition to the more than 70,000 Bosniaks killed (a figure that includes both civilian and military deaths), more than 25 percent of the overall population now live in exile. Bosnian Muslims, who have returned to Prijedor under the Agreement, spoke to us of daily harassment and continued discrimination, including

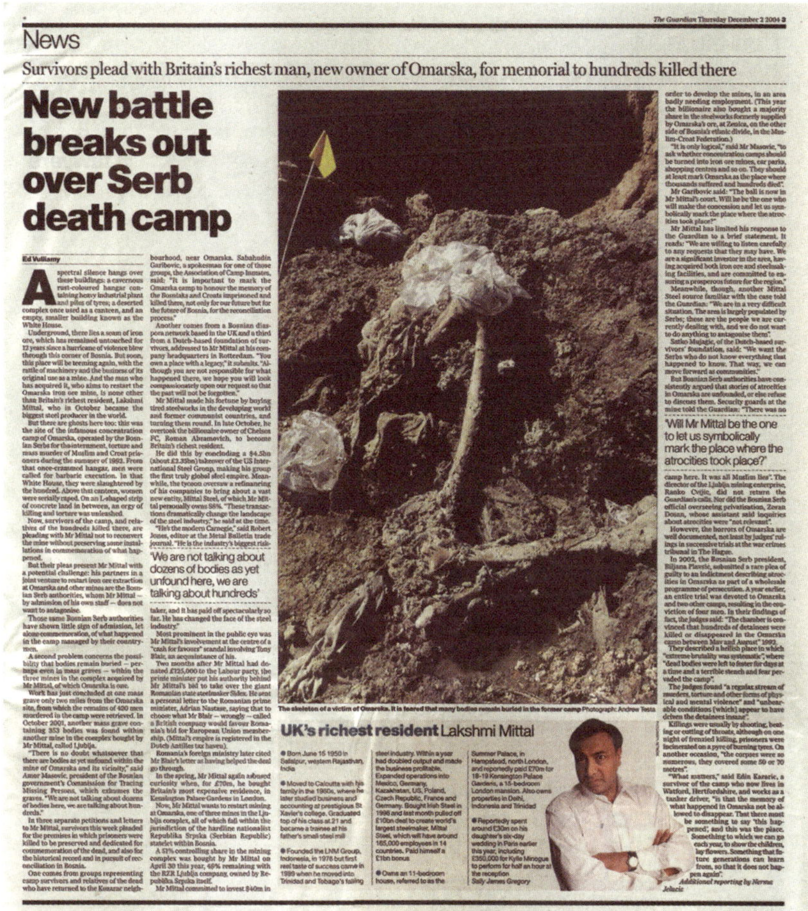

The Guardian Thursday December 2 2004 3

News

Survivors plead with Britain's richest man, new owner of Omarska, for memorial to hundreds killed there

New battle breaks out over Serb death camp

Ed Vulliamy

A spectral silence hangs over these buildings: a cavernous rust-coloured hangar containing heavy industrial plant and piles of tyres; a deserted complex once used as a canteen, and an empty, smaller building known as the White House.

Underground, there lies a seam of iron ore, which has remained untouched for 12 years since a hurricane of violence blew through this corner of Bosnia. But soon, this place will be teeming again, with the rattle of machinery and the business of its original use as a mine. And the man who has acquired it, who aims to restart the Omarska iron ore mine, is none other than Britain's richest resident, Lakshmi Mittal, who in October became the biggest steel producer in the world.

But there are ghosts here too: this was the site of the infamous concentration camp of Omarska, operated by the Bosnian Serbs for the internment, torture and mass murder of Muslim and Croat prisoners during the summer of 1992. From that once-crammed hangar, men were called for barbaric execution. In that White House, they were slaughtered by the hundred. Above that canteen, women were serially raped. On an L-shaped strip of concrete land in between, an orgy of killing and torture was unleashed.

Now, survivors of the camp, and relatives of the hundreds killed there, are pleading with Mr Mittal not to reconvert the mine without preserving some installations in commemoration of what happened.

But their pleas present Mr Mittal with a potential challenge: his partners in a joint venture to restart iron ore extraction at Omarska and other mines are the Bosnian Serb authorities, whom Mr Mittal – by admission of his own staff – does not want to antagonise.

Those same Bosnian Serb authorities have shown little sign of admission, let alone commemoration, of what happened in the camp managed by their countrymen.

A second problem concerns the possibility that bodies remain buried – perhaps even in mass graves – within the three mines in the complex acquired by Mr Mittal, of which Omarska is one.

Work has just concluded at one mass grave only two miles from the Omarska site, from which the remains of 400 men murdered in the camp were retrieved. In October 2001, another mass grave containing 353 bodies was found within another mine in the complex bought by Mr Mittal, called Ljubija.

"There is no doubt whatsoever that there are bodies as yet unfound within the mine of Omarska and its vicinity," said Amor Masovic, president of the Bosnian government's Commission for Tracing Missing Persons, which exhumes the graves. "We are not talking about dozens of bodies here, we are talking about hundreds."

In three separate petitions and letters to Mr Mittal, survivors this week pleaded for the premises in which prisoners were killed to be preserved and dedicated for commemoration of the dead, and also for the historical record and in pursuit of reconciliation in Bosnia.

One comes from groups representing camp survivors and relatives of the dead who have returned to the Kozarac neighbourhood, near Omarska. Sabahudin Garibovic, a spokesman for one of those groups, the Association of Camp Inmates, said: "It is important to mark the Omarska camp to honour the memory of the Bosniaks and Croats imprisoned and killed there, not only for our future but for the future of Bosnia, for the reconciliation process."

Another comes from a Bosnian diaspora network based in the UK and a third from a Dutch-based foundation of survivors, addressed to Mr Mittal at his company headquarters in Rotterdam. "You own a place with a legacy," it submits. "Although you are not responsible for what happened there, we hope you will look compassionately upon our request so that the past will not be forgotten."

Mr Mittal made his fortune by buying tired steelworks in the developing world and former communist countries, and turning them round. In late October, he overtook the billionaire owner of Chelsea FC, Roman Abramovich, to become Britain's richest resident.

He did this by concluding a \$4.5bn (about £2.35bn) takeover of the US International Steel Group, making his group the first truly global steel empire. Meanwhile, the tycoon oversaw a refinancing of his companies to bring about a vast new entity, Mittal Steel, of which Mr Mittal personally owns 88%. "These transactions dramatically change the landscape of the steel industry," he said at the time.

"He's the modern Carnegie," said Robert Jones, editor at the Metal Bulletin trade journal. "He is the industry's biggest risk-taker, and it has paid off spectacularly so far. He has changed the face of the steel industry."

'We are not talking about dozens of bodies as yet unfound here, we are talking about hundreds'

Most prominent in the public eye was Mr Mittal's involvement at the centre of a "cash for favours" scandal involving Tony Blair, an acquaintance of his.

Two months after Mr Mittal had donated £125,000 to the Labour party, the prime minister put his authority behind Mr Mittal's bid to take over the giant Romanian state steelmaker Sidex. He sent a personal letter to the Romanian prime minister, Adrian Nastase, saying that to choose what Mr Blair – wrongly – called a British company would favour Romania's bid for European Union membership. (Mittal's empire is registered in the Dutch Antilles tax haven).

Romania's foreign ministry later cited Mr Blair's letter as having helped the deal go through.

In the spring, Mr Mittal again aroused curiosity when, for £70m, he bought Britain's most expensive residence, in Kensington Palace Gardens in London.

Now, Mr Mittal wants to restart mining at Omarska, one of three mines in the Ljubija complex, all of which fall within the jurisdiction of the hardline nationalist Republika Srpska (Serbian Republic) statelet within Bosnia.

A 51% controlling share in the mining complex was bought by Mr Mittal on April 30 this year, 49% remaining with the RZR Ljubija company, owned by Republika Srpska itself.

Mr Mittal committed to invest \$40m in order to develop the mines, in an area badly needing employment. (This year the billionaire also bought a majority share in the steelworks formerly supplied by Omarska's ore, at Zenica, on the other side of Bosnia's ethnic divide, in the Muslim-Croat Federation.)

"It is only logical," said Mr Masovic, "to ask whether concentration camps should be turned into iron ore mines, car parks, shopping centres and so on. They should at least mark Omarska as the place where thousands suffered and hundreds died".

Mr Garibovic said: "The ball is now in Mr Mittal's court. Will he be the one who will make the concession and let us symbolically mark the place where the atrocities took place?"

Mr Mittal has limited his response to the Guardian to a brief statement. It reads: "We are willing to listen carefully to any requests that they may have. We are a significant investor in the area, having acquired both iron ore and steelmaking facilities, and are committed to ensuring a prosperous future for the region."

Meanwhile, though, another Mittal Steel source familiar with the case told the Guardian: "We are in a very difficult situation. The area is largely populated by Serbs; these are the people we are currently dealing with, and we do not want to do anything to antagonise them".

Satko Mujagic, of the Dutch-based survivors' foundation, said: "We want the Serbs who do not know everything that happened to know. That way, we can move forward as communities."

But Bosnian Serb authorities have consistently argued that stories of atrocities in Omarska are unfounded, or else refuse to discuss them. Security guards at the mine told the Guardian: "There was no camp here. It was all Muslim lies". The director of the Ljubija mining enterprise, Ranko Cvijic, did not return the Guardian's calls. Nor did the Bosnian Serb official overseeing privatisation, Zoran Dosan, whose assistant said inquiries about atrocities were "not relevant".

'Will Mr Mittal be the one to let us symbolically mark the place where the atrocities took place?'

However, the horrors of Omarska are well documented, not least by judges' rulings in successive trials at the war crimes tribunal in The Hague.

In 2002, the Bosnian Serb president, Biljana Plavsic, submitted a rare plea of guilty to an indictment describing atrocities in Omarska as part of a wholesale programme of persecution. A year earlier, an entire trial was devoted to Omarska and two other camps, resulting in the conviction of four men. In their findings of fact, the judges said: "The chamber is convinced that hundreds of detainees were killed or disappeared in the Omarska camp between May and August" 1992.

They described a hellish place in which "extreme brutality was systematic", where "dead bodies were left to fester for days at a time and a terrible stench and fear pervaded the camp".

The judges found "a regular stream of murders, torture and other forms of physical and mental violence" and "unbearable conditions [which] appear to have driven the detainees insane".

Killings were usually by shooting, beating or cutting of throats, although on one night of frenzied killing, prisoners were incinerated on a pyre of burning tyres. On another occasion, "the corpses were so numerous, they covered some 50 or 70 metres".

"What matters," said Edin Kararic, a survivor of the camp who now lives in Watford, Hertfordshire, and works as a tanker driver, "is that the memory of what happened in Omarska not be allowed to disappear. That there must be something to say 'this happened', and this was the place. Something to which we can go each year, to show the children, lay flowers. Something that future generations can learn from, so that it does not happen again".

Additional reporting by Nerma Jelacic

The skeleton of a victim of Omarska. It is feared that many bodies remain buried in the former camp Photograph: Andrew Testa

UK's richest resident Lakshmi Mittal

- Born June 15 1950 in Sadulpur, western Rajasthan, India
- Moved to Calcutta with his family in the 1960s, where he later studied business and accounting at prestigious St Xavier's college. Graduated top of his class at 21 and became a trainee at his father's small steel mill
- Founded the LNM Group, Indonesia, in 1976 but first real taste of success came in 1989 when he moved into Trinidad and Tobago's failing steel industry. Within a year had doubled output and made the business profitable. Expanded operations into Mexico, Germany, Kazakhstan, US, Poland, Czech Republic, France and Germany. Bought Irish Steel in 1996 and last month pulled off £10bn deal to create world's largest steelmaker, Mittal Steel, which will have around 165,000 employees in 14 countries. Paid himself a £1bn bonus
- Owns an 11-bedroom house, referred to as the Summer Palace, in Hampstead, north London, and reportedly paid £70m for 18-19 Kensington Palace Gardens, a 15-bedroom London mansion. Also owns properties in Delhi, Indonesia and Trinidad
- Reportedly spent around £30m on his daughter's six-day wedding in Paris earlier this year, including £350,000 for Kylie Minogue to perform for half an hour at the reception

Sally James Gregory

Figure 12.5

"New battle breaks out over Serb death camp," Ed Vulliamy. Source: *The Guardian*, December 2, 2004.

hiring practices at the mine. In 2012, the local municipality had a hardline Serbian Mayor in Marko Pavić, who personified the culture of denial that still persists in the region, an attitude reinforced by ArcelorMittal's reluctance to build a memorial on the site. Pavić has insisted that Omarska was used only as a transit and interrogation center, and even prohibited the use of the term genocide in any public commemorations, although the ICTY indicted both Karadžić and Mladić for the crime of genocide in Prijedor.[6] The material continuities between a site of historical violence and its mineralized remains persist in the present, highlighting the limitations of prosecutorial processes that are by necessity focused on past events organized by specific testimonial proofs, and therefore cannot adjudicate over the ways in which such violence might reorganize itself in the future.

> **PRESS RELEASE 29 JUNE 2011:** ArcelorMittal confirms that the 2,200 tonnes of steel being used in the ArcelorMittal Orbit—London's Olympic tower—will contain symbolic quantities from every continent in the world where the Company has operations, reflecting the spirit of the Olympic Games, which draws together athletes from across the globe.

In a chance meeting on April 14, 2012, in the parking lot of Kozara mountain, Mladen Jelača, Director of ArcelorMittal Prijedor, confirmed to Eyal Weizman, Director of Forensic Architecture, and artist Milica Tomić, of the Working Group Four Faces of Omarska, that the "ArcelorMittal Orbit" commissioned for the London 2012 Olympics, designed by artist Anish Kapoor and engineer Cecil Balmond, was indeed fabricated with iron ore that came in part from the Omarska mine. According to Weizman and Tomic, "Mladen Jelača said that parts of the Mittal Orbit would be made from Omarska resources. He was very proud. He also said that metal (iron) is being taken out from three different mines in Europe. One of these is Omarska." However, in their Press Release of June 29, 2011, promoting this Olympic project, ArcelorMittal neglects to mention that it even has European mining operations in Bosnia and Herzegovina—a curious omission in and of itself, which reads [at least to me] as a deliberate attempt to distance themselves from this troubling connection.[7]

Rising to the soaring height of 114.5 meters and outstripping even the Statue of Liberty by two meters, the ArcelorMittal Orbit boasts an impressive compendium of statistics: 1,500 metric tonnes of steel, 35,000 bolts, 19,000 liters of paint, 770 visitors per hour/5,000 per day, vistas of 20 miles into the distance, and a overall price tag of £22.7million, £19.6million of which was funded by ArcelorMittal. Another series of facts: 3,400 Bosniaks and Croats from Prijedor went missing or were killed during 1992, the summer of the massacre, at least 3,334 were imprisoned in the camp at Omarska, 700–800 were exterminated, 37 female detainees were repeatedly raped and tortured, upward of 150 men were singled out daily for execution. Still missing: 1,200 men,

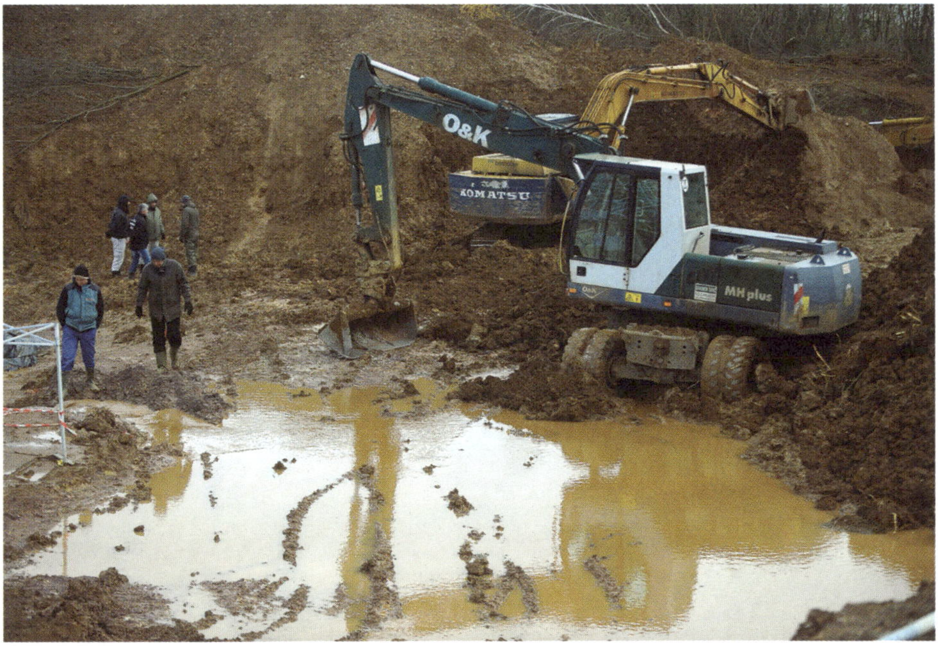

Figure 12.6
Forensic experts, members of the International Commission on Missing Persons (ICMP), and Bosnian workers inspect a rain-drenched mass grave site in the village of Tomašica, near the western Bosnian town of Prijedor, on November 25, 2013. Forensic experts have excavated the body remains of 430 victims so far, but believe there are many more yet undiscovered as they excavate a 7-meter-deep trench to find human remains believed to have belonged to Muslims and Croats killed by Serb forces during their campaign to eliminate all non-Serbs from parts of the country they controlled during the 1992–1995 Bosnian war. Authorities are still searching for 1,200 Muslims and Croats missing from the area of Prijedor. Photo credit: Elvis Barukcic. Source: AFP/Getty Images.

women, and children from the Prijedor region. The facts and figures of the ArcelorMittal Orbit, the towering showpiece of London's 2012 Olympics, are materially intertwined with the history of war crimes that took place on the very grounds from which ArcelorMittal subsequently began to extract not only its soaring global profits but iron ore that the Director of ArcelorMittal Prijedor boasts was used in the construction of the Orbit.

A "hellish orgy of persecution" is how Judge Almiro Rodrigues described the extreme violence that took place at the mine site during the war crimes tribunal in 2001:[8] a disturbing history that cannot simply be reconciled with the economic instruments of

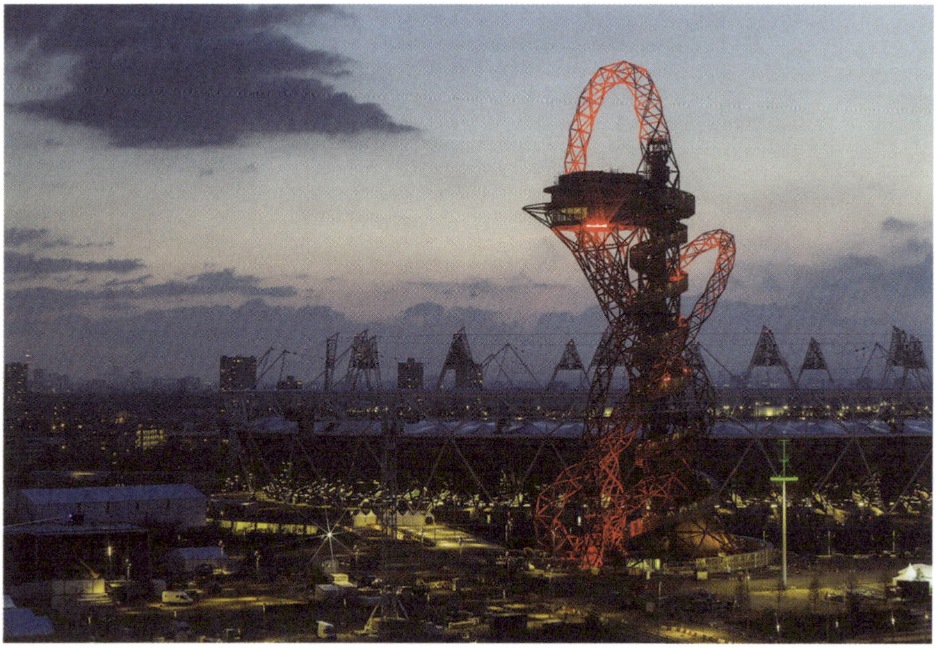

Figure 12.7
ArcelorMittal Orbit, London Olympic Park, 2012. Source: unknown.

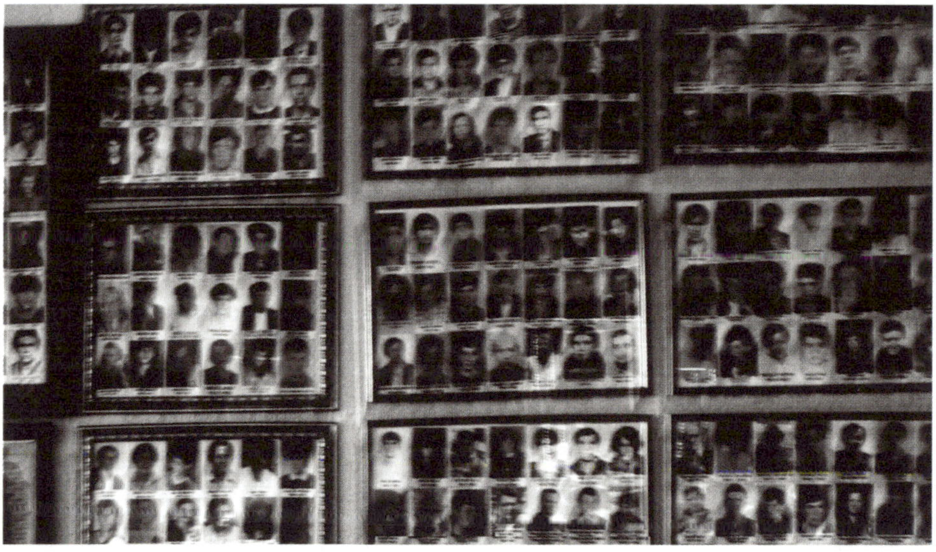

Figure 12.8
Photos of the missing, Prijedor, *Memorial in Exile*, Susan Schuppli and Steffen Kraemer, 2012, HD video, color with sound, 25 minutes.

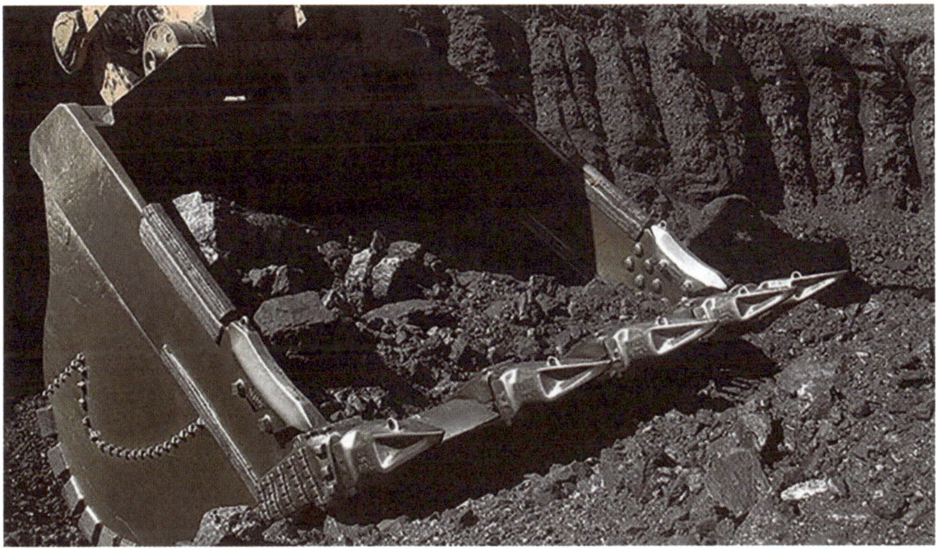

Figure 12.9
Memorial in Exile, Susan Schuppli and Steffen Kraemer, 2012, HD video, color with sound, 25 minutes.

postwar normalization, especially when communities are still in pain and responsibilities are neither faced nor acted upon. Surely the ArcelorMittal Orbit, as the material consequence of wealth generated by the world's most lucrative mining operations, to which Prijedor contributes 1.5 million metric tonnes of iron ore concentrate annually, needs to be able to stand up to the tyrannies of history, and not merely swagger over London as a fanciful, albeit now failing, tourist attraction. When public pressure mounted in the immediate runup to the opening of the Games, the company finally acknowledged that the events in Bosnia and Herzegovina were indeed tragic, but was still careful to note that their ownership was subsequent to the horrific events in question.

> **PRESS RELEASE 5 MAY 2012:** ArcelorMittal's mining operation at Omarska, near Prijedor in Republika Srpska, Bosnia and Herzegovina, includes some areas where well-documented war crimes took place in 1992. It continues to be controversial, as demands for access to the site and a permanent memorial intensify during this 20th anniversary year. ArcelorMittal acknowledges the suffering of the victims of the conflict of the 1990s, and fully respects the feelings of survivors and relatives of those affected.

As Stengers's invocation of Wegener suggests, materials offer themselves up for propositional thinking, and are thus powerfully operative in forging relations between seemingly disparate events and geographies. Materials are thus also propositions for making new claims, and whilst they may not be admissible within the institutional contexts of juridical or scientific forums, they can make demands that require the creation of other forms of public debate whereby acts of *material witnessing* and *evidence-making* can assume a more activist stance. When the trauma and ethnic divisions of the past endure in innumerable different ways, the affective propensities produced by the confrontational presence of steel are evidence enough for reclaiming Omarska as the ArcelorMittal Orbit's defining condition. Irrespective of whether the metal oxides from which it is fabricated actually still carry the mineralized traces of the dead, as many survivors claim, if steel is the "fabric of life," as proclaimed by ArcelorMittal in describing the Orbit, then what of the dead of Omarska? On July 2, 2012, in an activist forum and protest at the Olympic Park to mark the lack of meaningful progress, we undertook a collective action to reconnect the metallurgical traces of violence that link London's Olympic landmark with the death camp at Omarska by radicalizing the ArcelorMittal Orbit and declaring it *The Omarska Memorial in Exile*.[9]

Solar Dispute

One hundred years before Wegener's audacious thesis, physicist and optical lens-maker Joseph von Fraunhofer embarked upon a series of experiments to explore the optical spectrum of the sun. His work would eventually come to be used by scientists to determine the chemical composition of a remote object—our sun, some 149.6 million kilometers away—not through direct testing but by treating it as an image, one whose chromatic variance could be translated into the complex language of chemistry. Fraunhofer's absorption and emission lines enabled scientists to conduct spectral analyses of different gases suffused by sunlight as they passed through the Earth's atmosphere over the course of a day's rotation, thus changing the ways in which sunlight would come to be studied and known today. His assertion that the essence of objects could be determined by virtue of the aesthetic judgment of chemistry would prevail, setting the course for the primacy of the visual in deliberating truth claims.

In a roundabout way, the narrative arc of this book is indebted to yet another solar provocation: that posed by a US judge in 1886, when he asked the rhetorical question "Can the sun lie?" during deliberations over the probative value of photographs as testimonial agents.[10] In pondering the sun's aesthetic capacity and animistic potential for deception, the judge implied that nonhuman entities and technical processes would come to play a crucial role in the production of evidence. Indeed, he gestured toward key attributes of the *material witness* in suggesting that the mode of appearance of the media object, the photograph put before a jury, was equal in consideration to the

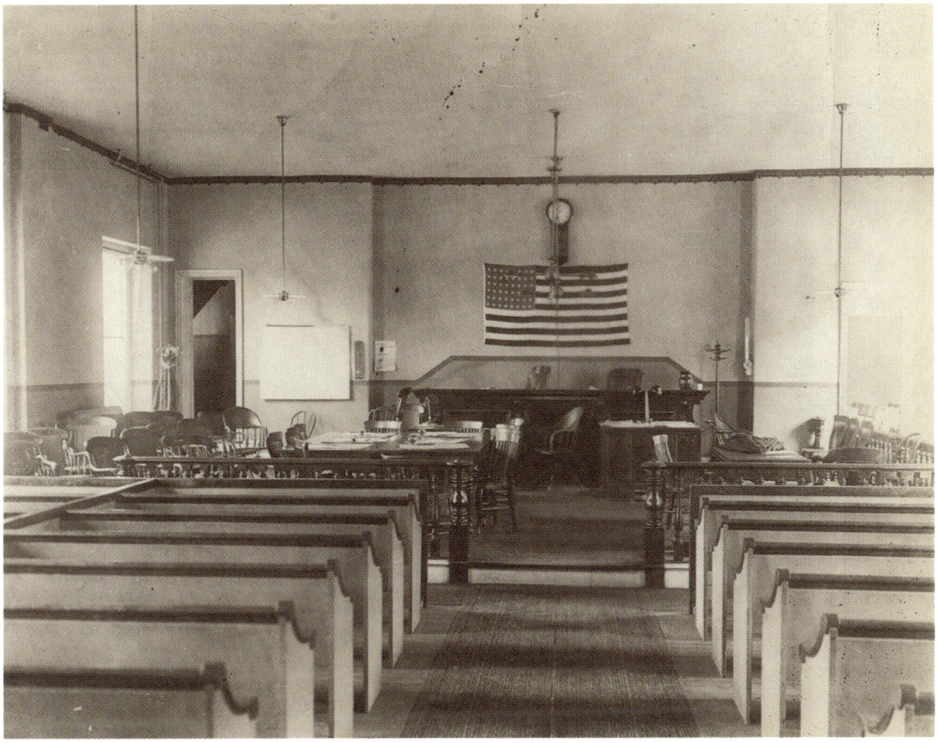

Figure 12.10
US courtroom interior, nineteenth century. Collection of the author.

epistemic claims that could be made on behalf of its representational stance. But when he was faced with the improbable prospect of cross-examining the sun directly—after all, the sun obeys only the laws of nature, not those of anthropos, as once believed by the geocentrics of the ancient world—he also opened the proceedings of the court to the influence of scientific norms and, with it, new forms of expert knowledge that would progressively be called upon to ventriloquize the object world. The judge continued: "Perhaps we may say that though the sun does not lie, the liar may use the sun as a tool. Let us, then, beware of the liar who lies in the name of the sun."[11]

The legally sanctified gaze of the human had a rival in this new technical witness, which deeply troubled the courts. Photographs taken in the aftermath of a crime or for the purposes of legal explication were not only presented as aids to memory to assist with testimony but also positioned as demonstrative evidence in their own right. If evidence could be deliberately manufactured after the fact, then the self-evident facts

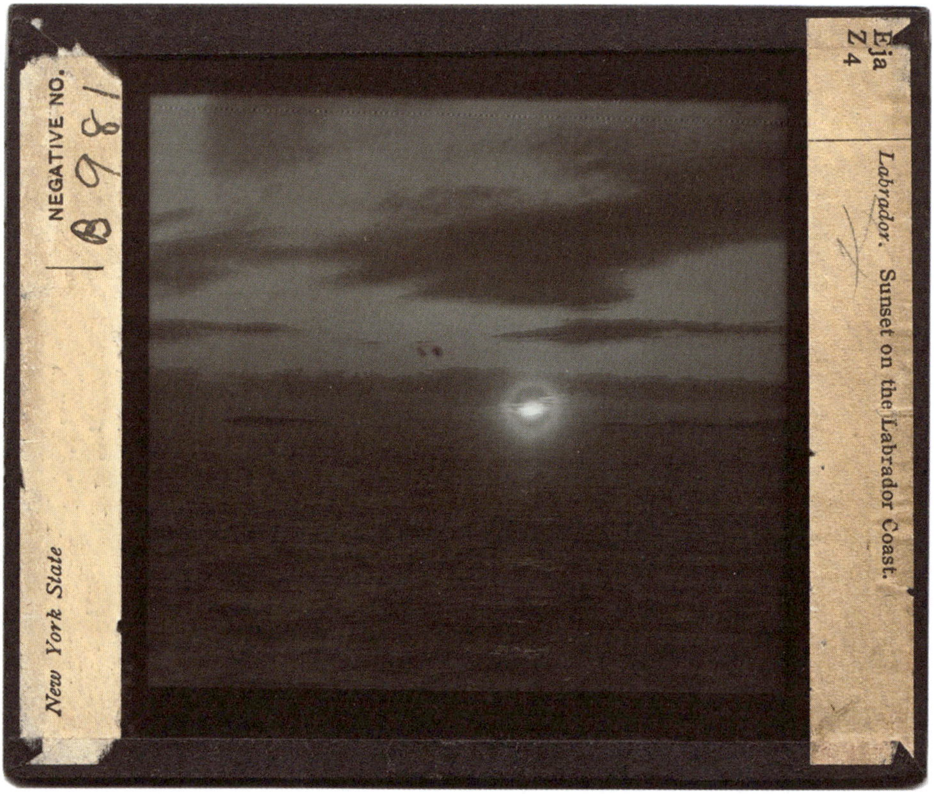

Figure 12.11
Sunset on the Labrador Coast. Glass negative. Collection of the author.

of the case could themselves be thrown into doubt. The introduction of these photographic materials into legal trials came to inaugurate a significant transformation in evidence law as the sovereignty of the human eyewitness was called into question by new modes of machinic witnessing, contributing to what has been referred to as an episteme of mechanical objectivity.[12] While objects in the form of models and diagrams had already entered into legal proceedings in cases of patent law, or to assist with clarifying property disputes, the arrival of photographic materials must be understood as singularly unique, because of sunlight's persuasive power of analogization.[13] Chemically provoked by the radiological emissions of the sun, the resulting photograph produced such a convincing picture of the "real" that the subjective processes of human recollection and memory could, it seemed, be set aside in favor of a new regime of scientifically produced truth. Indeed, proponents of the legal aid provided by sunlight were swift to dismiss any doubts as to its fidelity, and countered such reservations with statements such as the following:

> We cannot conceive of a more impartial and truthful witness than the sun, as its light stamps and seals the similitude of the wound on the photograph put before the jury; it would be more accurate than the memory of witnesses, and as the object of all is to show truth, why should not this dumb witness show it?[14]

This historical controversy around the objectivity of manufactured proofs, the testimony of nonhuman agents, and the opposition between lay and scientific knowledge has only been exacerbated with the advent of an ever-increasing range of technologies for measuring, monitoring, and recording data. Indeed, the very lack of agreed-upon protocols governing the use of many new technologies—satellite imagery is a case in point—and absence of consensus as to the interpretation of their datasets have, if anything, reanimated such debates. This is particularly evident within the context of climate change disputes, and especially so with regard to interaction between the different regimes of witnessing: notably those represented by scientific expertise and indigenous knowledge traditions such as storytelling. Historically considered a denigrated mode of knowledge transfer, indigenous observations and their oral transmissions are forcefully reshaping the epistemic frameworks that are required for understanding long-term environmental transformations. This constitutes a reordering of expertise and its claims to truth that turn on the evidence proffered by nature itself: the changing expressions of matter that are at the heart of indigenous life worlds.

The vicissitudes of *material witnessing* are perhaps best exemplified by the range of stakeholders, knowledge claims, moral values, and risk strategies that gather around issues of global warming. For example, in Zacharias Kunuk and Ian Mauro's film *Inuit Knowledge and Climate Change* (2010), several Inuit elders make the repeated observation that the setting sun has slowly been moving further west, and that the location of the stars has also altered. Has the earth shifted on its axis, they ask, causing the position of the sun and stars to change?[15] When their documentary was prescreened at the Copenhagen Climate Change Conference (COP15) in December 2009, the filmmakers were admonished by the scientific community for presenting such a spurious hypothesis on the part of the Inuit, despite the fact that they had clearly looked to Western physics in attempting to explain this extraordinary transgression on the part of the sun. "We had a litany of scientists come back to us, responding after seeing this news, saying, this was great to be speaking to indigenous people about their views, but if you continue to perpetuate this fallacy that the Earth had tilted on its axis, [the Inuit] … would lose all credibility."[16] The Inuits' deep ancestral knowledge of the environment in which they lived and the events that they had witnessed was insufficient

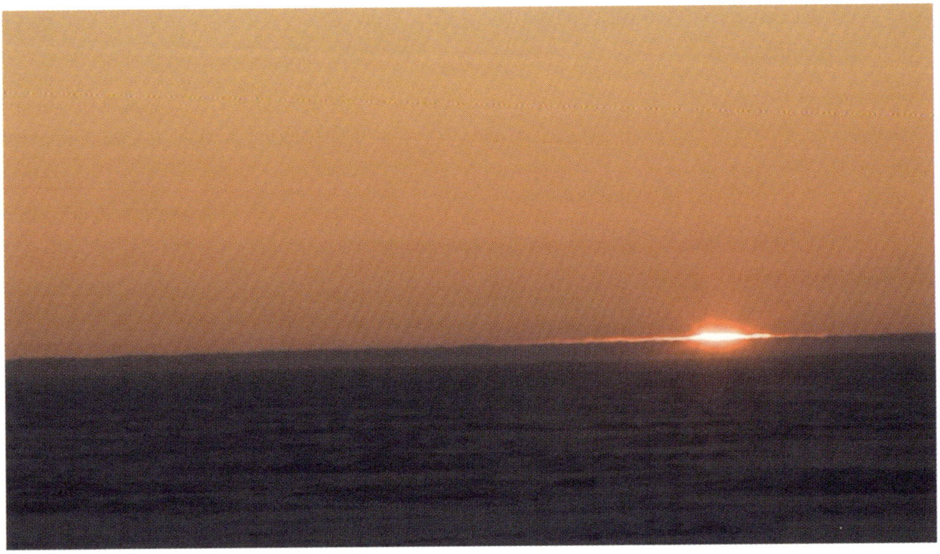

Figure 12.12
Inuit Knowledge and Climate Change, Zacharias Kunuk and Ian Mauro, 2010, film still. Courtesy: Isuma TV.

for conferring a contingent legitimacy on their speech acts if their testimonials ran counter to widely accepted scientific truths and their hypothesis seemed spurious. Yet how else should they have explained the dramatic migration of the setting sun? The epistemic virtue of objectivity turned, not upon a distinction between Western rationality and native cosmology, as might have be expected by their critics at COP15, but on who has the authority, and thus the expertise, to speak on behalf of science itself?[17] Linguist Paul Goodwin diagnoses this condition as the "professional vision" of trained judgment: "Different professions—medicine, law, the police, specific sciences such as archaeology—have the power to legitimately see, constitute and articulate alternative kinds of events. Professional vision is perspectival, lodged within specific social entities, and unevenly allocated."[18] Although the Inuit may have come to the wrong scientific conclusion in speculating that a physical realignment of the earth's axis had caused the locational drift of the sun, rather than the cumulative effects of industrialization resulting in the production of greenhouse gases, their observations were not in and of themselves flawed—their eyes had not deceived them.

Indeed, the rapid and extreme environmental changes that have overturned established perceptions of the natural world throughout the North suggest that only an equally radical proposition might begin to explain the hallucinogenic dynamics of matter—now evident—in these transformative geographies. Not only is Arctic sunlight bending and deceiving the eyes that have tracked the position of the sun for generations, but as black carbon deposits accrue throughout the region, and rising temperatures diminish sea ice, melt glaciers, liquefy snow packs, and thaw permafrost, the natural indexicality of such Northern topographies has also become increasingly suspect.[19] Ecological registration systems that formerly directed Inuit hunters home with cartographic certainty are distorting as the contours of snow-encrusted landscapes are resurfaced by climatic aberrations. No longer can the wind-carved tongues of snowdrifts alone offer up the icy signs that permit confident action. Matter is dramatically out of place in these mutating Arctic environments, and nature has itself become a hostile witness, antagonistic to the deep historical testimonies inscribed into its once frozen landscapes.

In Camera

Indeed, the nineteenth-century suspicion once directed toward the sun's capacity to mislead, to turn stable realities into distorted versions of the real, is refracted in this twenty-first-century corollary as climate change transforms the surfaces of the earth into a vast array of proto-photographic plates, each of which is recording the atmospheric chemistry of terrestrial change differently. For the Inuit, the world that they once knew finds no analogy, no mirror image, in the world that they now see. In the Circumpolar North, this process has accelerated at between two and four times the global average, and intensified as tropospheric warming and temperature inversions trap ever-greater concentrations of atmospheric pollutants within particles of ice and snow, whereas previously they would have been diffused at higher altitudes. Snow and ice produce different spectral variations. The visible spectrum of light is better refracted by snow, whereas the optical properties of ice have superior absorption capacities toward the spectrum of the near infrared.[20] This is why, in part, indigenous observations of the changing pathway of the sun are made in regions covered by continuous snow. The material registration of light by silver halide particles that came to define the photographic process is warped in a landscape where matter is out of place and sunlight lies. Not only do granular snow particles absorb and capture light, converting billions and billions of grains into a vibrating plate of solar-charged particles, they also act as vast networks of finely ground crystal lenses focusing and refracting light across the Polar region. As chemical impurities increasingly saturate the snow, and temperature increases reshape the density of the snow pack and liquefy its crystalline structure, the snow also becomes a developing solution, overexposing and distorting rays of sunlight

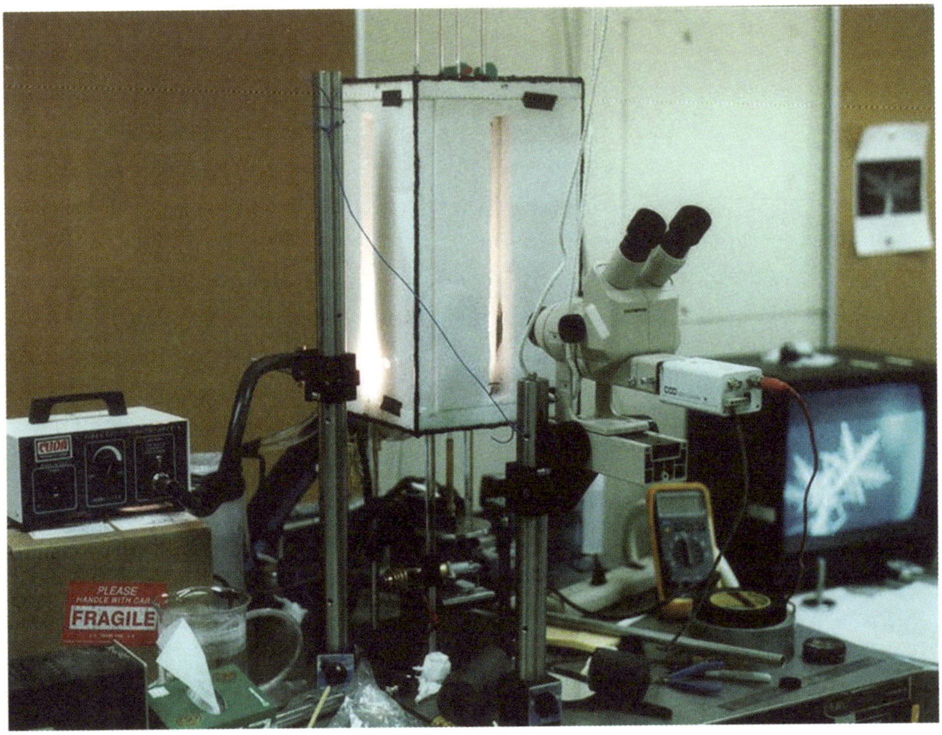

Figure 12.13
Can the Sun Lie?, Susan Schuppli, 2014, HD video, color with sound, 13 minutes.

as they are redirected back up into the atmosphere. Snow is, in effect, camera lens and photographic substrate, refractive technology and radiant media.

Planetary Processing

Paleoclimatologist Andrew Bush has likened Arctic ice cores to the inscriptive mechanisms of a tape recorder. "*Ice cores are like a tape recorder of climatic history, and that history is disappearing worldwide.*" Although Bush is making an analogy here, glacial ice sheets have been registering and thus *recording* the slow accretion of carbon, allowing scientists to *playback* the histories of climate change. Polluted environments do function as vast sensor networks that are transmitting information about industrialization and its aggregating effects. The planet is a "vast machine" for processing climatic data.[21] Analogies are important if they help us in grasping a new concept or emergent condition, but I really wish to push beyond the analogy and challenge what counts as

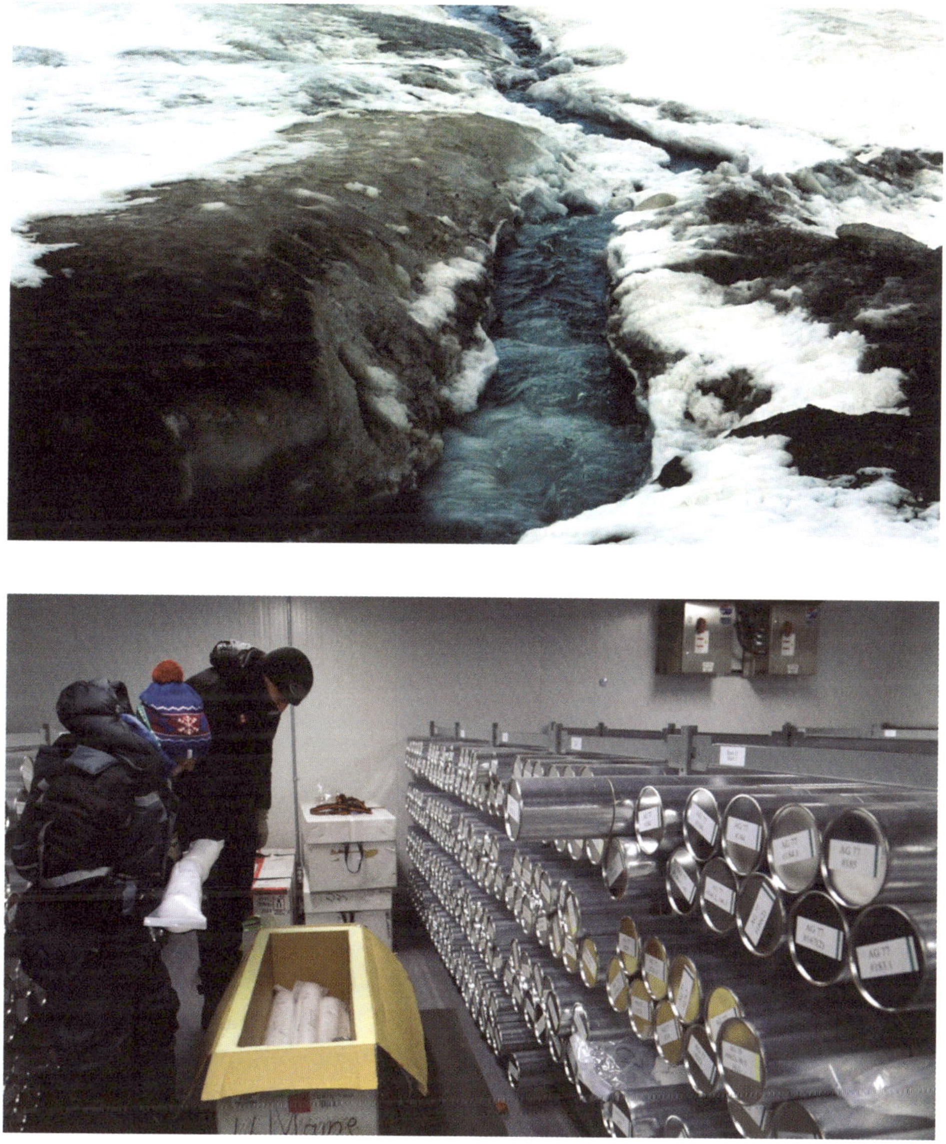

Figure 12.14

Learning from Ice, Susan Schuppli, 2019, HD video, color with sound, production stills detailing the Athabasca Glacier and the Canadian Ice Core Archive, University of Alberta. Commissioned by the Toronto Biennial of Art 2019–2021, curated by Candice Hopkins.

a technical image or media system and thus, ultimately, a *material witness* to events: in short, to insist upon the agency of the aesthetic inasmuch as legal agency has already been extended to various nonhuman actors: for example, the Pachamama constitution of Ecuador that allowed Nature, in the form of the sea, to represent itself in a lawsuit against British Petroleum for the 2010 oil spill in the Gulf of Mexico under the principle of universal jurisdiction.

The epistemic convictions that have organized the material world in order to render it sensible and thus knowable, especially within legal and scientific discourses, must be supplemented by a detailed consideration of the ontological arrangements that matter itself evinces as a sensate mediator and *material witness* to historical events without immediate recourse to the linguistic forms of expression deemed constitutive for the production of human subjectivity, or to positivist notions of the physical world as directly given through empirical observation and technical measurement. While many new scientific probes and modified methods for deducing environmental transformations have been developed, indigenous people are often positioned as having recourse to such "aesthetic" events only through the sense-making operations of myths and stories, so that their knowing is disavowed and their sensing denigrated as a feeling for nature rather than a form of radical empiricism.[22] *Material Witness* does admittedly give a great deal of prominence to the technical operations of machines and the technicity of matter as a means for generating many of its insights, but it also aims to highlight the limits to which all evidence-making practices are subject. Additionally, through my creative practice as an artist-researcher I have opened up parallel lines of inquiry into many of these case studies that both explore and situate the incommensurate relations that emerge between ways of seeing, knowing, and sensing that, in turn, govern the advent of different forms of evidence. These aesthetic projects function as investigative proxies, forging new categories of assembly across disparate events and domains of practice that also serve to generate many of the insights that I bring to this writing.

In spring 2018, I produced a new body of work for the SculptureCenter in New York, "Nature Represents Itself." This was an experiment in which I set out to realize a conceptual argument around the self-imaging capacities of environmental systems catalyzed by chemical pollutants and contaminants. Technically speaking, many environments convey changes in ways that are fundamentally comparable to how analog media—photography and film—disclose perturbances as visible aesthetic effects. The chlorophyll found in algae and plants offers a paradigmatic account of a photochemical process found in nature whereby the direct capture of light brings about a series of visible transformations. As environmental scholar Adrian J. Ivakhiv notes, "All life on this

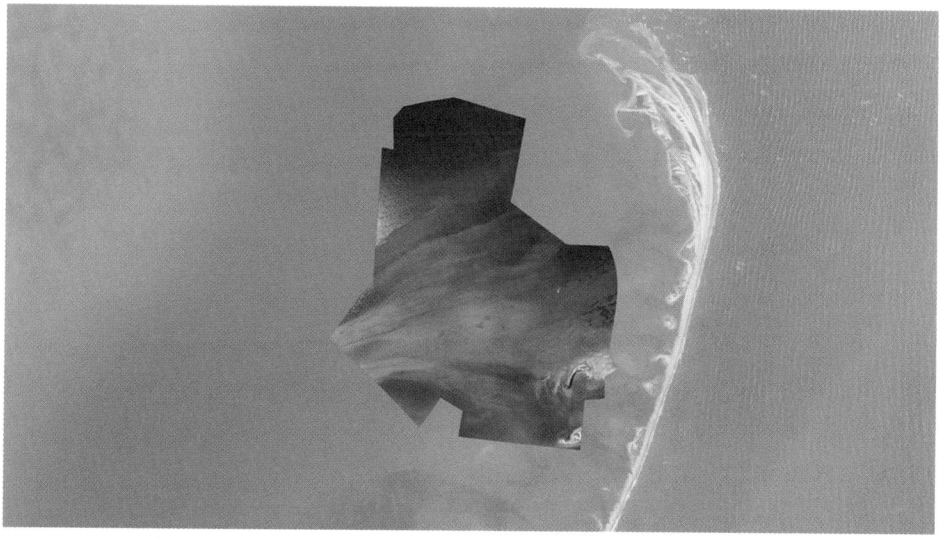

Figure 12.15

Public Lab, Chandeleur Islands, Louisiana, May 9, 2010. Mapped by Shannon Dosemagen, Stewart Long, Mariko Toyoji / Cartographer: Stewart Long. 29.802910103410355 N, –88.86611555841014 E Ground resolution: 8.31 cm/px. Capture date: 2010-05-09 T00:00:00 Publication date: 2010-05-16 T00:00:00 License: Public Domain.

planet is the product of one or another permutation of the interaction between energy (heat and light) originating from the sun and the surface of the Earth that it strikes."[23] Surfaces, it has been suggested, constitute a "separate state of matter, distinct from solids, liquids, and gases," and are the sites where the "properties of matter change most rapidly."[24] Scientists call these kinds of natural sensors "in-situ imagers." Because of the nagging problem of direct measurement, as well as the problems that invasive technologies pose for fragile ecologies, visible-light imagers have become very useful for monitoring changes taking place across large-scale and often inaccessible ecosystems like a forest. For example, there is a clear correlation between the spectral properties of leaves and their photosynthetic outputs, which plants and trees express as visual information. Changes in their pigmentation caused by external factors such as pollution, soil degradation, or drought result in precise changes in the reflectance properties of visible wavelengths. Scientists can mobilize these vegetative features as "powerful biological sensors" to monitor the CO_2 uptake and health of a vast forest ecology. Such transformations in the state of affairs of matter are dramatized by the operations of technical processes that help to make even minor changes perceptible.

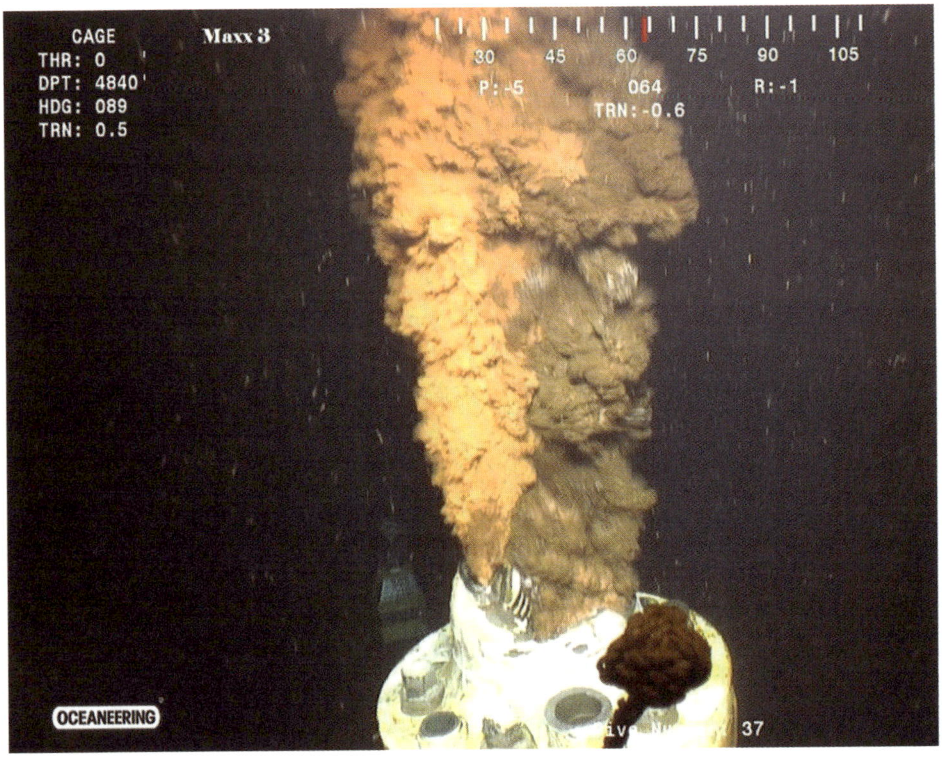

Figure 12.16
Underwater video feed of attempts to cap the Deepwater Horizon Well. Dive 37, June 3, 2010. Source: Oceaneering Deepwater Technical Solutions.

> Given an image-based model of CO_2 uptake, we can begin to predict photosynthesis on a much larger scale than is possible to measure traditionally. For example, estimating the CO_2 uptake of an entire forest would now be feasible. This information can then be used to more accurately track the global release of CO_2 into the atmosphere, a nearly intractable problem currently.[25]

Yet as some scientists ponder whether we have entered a new geological epoch—the Anthropocene—to reflect the West's considerable impact upon Earth, aesthetics is still not a salient feature of this debate, notwithstanding the fact that the term designates a condition in which cultural production writ large—terraforming and human industrial activity—is its constitutive force. By contrast, the concept's considerable uptake within the arts and humanities has spurred wide-ranging theoretical work and cultural imaginaries. Anthropogenic matter is relentlessly aesthetic in throwing disturbing material rearrangements back at us: dirty pictures of dramatically contaminated landscapes and polluted atmospheres that both intoxicate and repel.[26] Any discussion that lays claim to the possibility that we have entered a new geologic era should by extension also consider the Earth as thoroughly geo-media-logical. Not only is our planet permeated and encrusted with media and its infrastructures—what Peter Haff and others have referred to as a "technofossil assemblage"—ecological matter has long been performing a series of technical operations akin to the functions of various media systems.[27] As Douglas Kahn notes in *Earth Sound Earth Signal*, "media's proximity to nature" is not as "counter-intuitive" as one might think, given the electromagnetic energies and currents that have always swathed the Earth. "In fact, nature was broadcasting globally before there was a globe."[28]

When I was working on my 35mm vertical cinema project *Atmospheric Feedback Loops* (2017) with climate scientists in the Netherlands, the unprocessed data coming from the clouds was considered "noise," and their digital tools were directed at extracting "signals" out of this vaporous clamor. This conceptual and practical shift in their understanding of atmospheric phenomena demarcates a mediatic condition rather than a metaphoric attribution in which nature is subsumed into formulations drawn from computer science. My own understanding of damaged environments as comprised of capacities that can actively sense evidence of external events, and even disclose these under certain conditions, is to posit the aesthetic realm as ontologically continuous with the reformulations of matter. Fraunhofer's now historic insight was, in in this respect, a radical intervention into the field of representation.

Etymologically, "aesthetics" is a twofold concept that refers both to the senses' capacity to perceive external events and to the ways in which the mind itself is attuned to such appearances. It is both the apprehension of things by the senses and the cognitive awareness of things. For example, the photochemical smog that engulfs many contemporary cities modifies the visible spectrum of light, because pollutants interfere with the chemistry of the atmosphere as it interacts with the sun. What is significant is not that we can actually "see" these smog-shrouded cities from afar, but rather that photochemical smog alters the optical properties of the atmosphere such that the "way" we actually see is modified along with the thing itself. Might the emergence of such extreme forms of environmental image-making, considered in light of the original Greek conception of aesthetics as both sensing and knowing, work to denaturalize vision and construct new modes of perception?

The poorly produced and low-resolution images with which I began my analysis have, in these final pages, given way to the much dirtier pictures of anthropogenic climatic change and global warming. As the investigative entities of *Material Witness* expand to include compromised landscapes such as the crude oil film that spread across

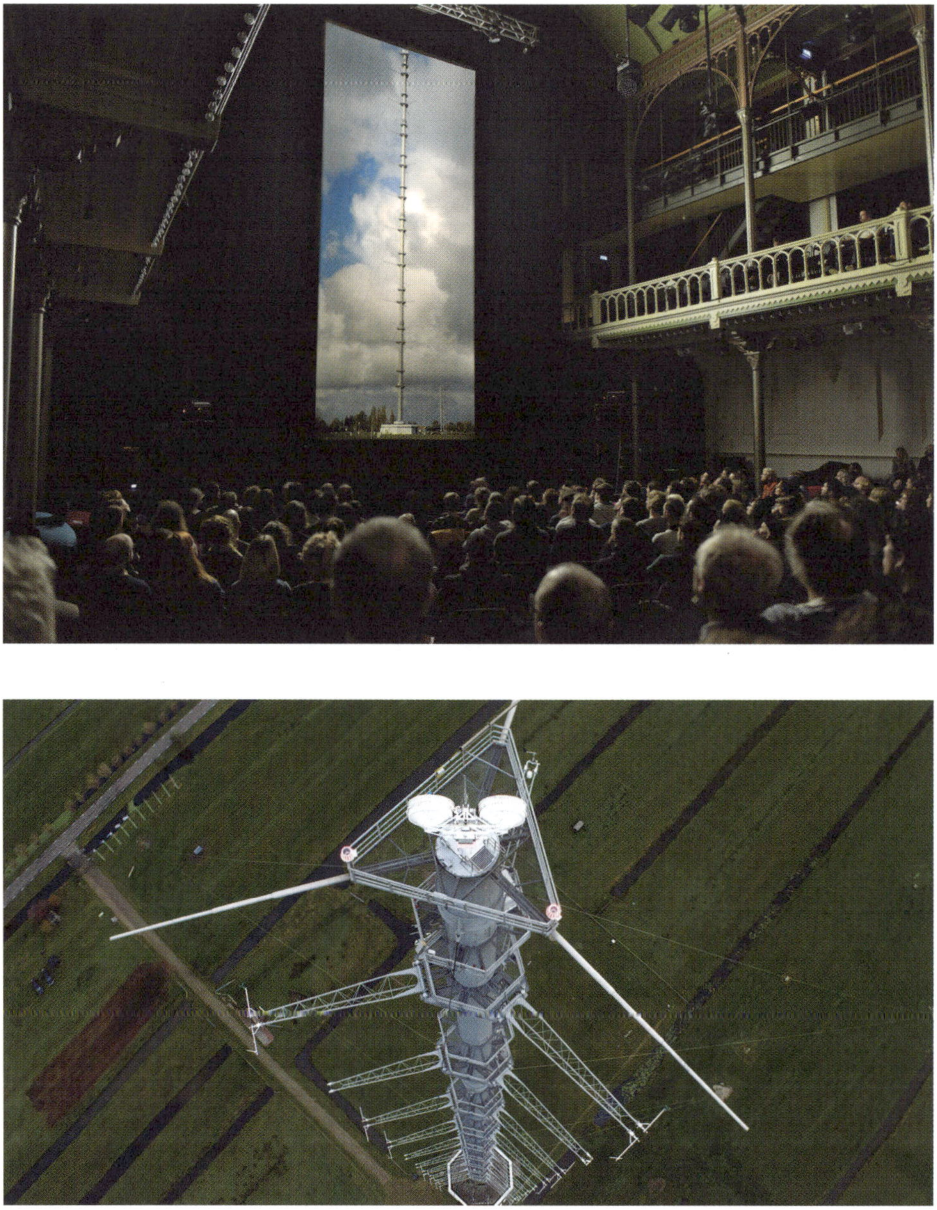

Figure 12.17

Atmospheric Feedback Loops, Susan Schuppli, 2017, 35mm vertical color film with stereo sound, 18 minutes. Source: Sonic Acts, Amsterdam.

the Gulf of Mexico in the wake of the Deepwater Horizon disaster, the case with which I will shortly conclude, our (colonial capitalism's) complicity in bringing about these entanglements is not to be overlooked. Reconceptualizing environmental systems as fully realized aesthetic agents that are expressive of their own damaged condition does not negate the myriad ways in which certain human activities are the source of their impurity. Nor can these hazardous environments be "contained" according to the conventions of the pictorial or the exclusion zone, because they are always multiscalar and multitemporal, stretching back in time as well as throwing their contaminants forward into the far distant future. In sum, this might entail giving up the image of the holistic blue marble exemplified by Stewart Brand's 1966 provocation: "Why haven't we seen a photograph of the whole Earth yet?" Rather than picturing the Earth as a discrete object floating in space, which continues to spur fantasies of managerial control, would it not be more relevant to consider all of the ways in which its Earthly image matter exceeds such singular capture?[29] Surely the complex and nonlinear modes of causation that give rise to the Earth's dynamic forms of material expression—its evidential and damaged surplus which is also a consequence of specific forms of excess—produce a surfeit of image matter that adamantly refuses coherency and objectification. Only when the world is transformed into a scalar dataset and simulated do we seem to get a glimpse of these planetary processes interacting as one unified whole, whereas our actual lived experience of these events remains partial and local to the end.

Moreover, alternate modes of perception that come out of entirely different cultural contexts suggest that ways of knowing and ways of seeing need not be bound exclusively to ocular-centric traditions or technological systems. Indigenous people, for example, may have intergenerational knowledge of the land that is guided by an acute sensitivity to the many changes taking place in their immediate environment. But even when technological sensors are deployed, this acquired data must be integrated into a broader network that includes the observations and lived experiences of humans as well as information gleaned from more-than-human entities that are also engaged in the direct sensing of their environments, such as plants and animals. Researcher and theorist Jennifer Gabrys has referred to certain forms of sensor technology such as the Moss Cam, a webcam for monitoring growth patterns of Starr Moss in the James Reserve in California, as producing a "data layer" rather than a representation.[30] By this she means that the image information provided by the webcam contributes a dataset derived from the technical observation of a living organism that is itself already "expressing sensory responses to human-altered worlds." This image data is then combined with an array of other distributed sensor technologies to produce a more complex understanding of the many changes taking place within a given environment.[31] The data layer of the

Moss Cam image enables a shift in scale from an expression of situated local conditions to its aggregation within planetary processes, allowing it to be further modeled, computed, and mediated. This insight is helpful for conceptualizing images as part of a larger sensorial assemblage, thus breaking with pictorial conventions that would place the viewing subject outside and at a distance from that which is perceived, stressing instead our critical proximity to and mutually imbrication with one another. "A new image [wrote the poet Jacques Bousquet] costs humanity as much labour as a new characteristic costs a plant."[32]

Nature Represents Itself

QUITO, ECUADOR 26 NOVEMBER 2010

THE HONOURABLE SECRETARY GENERAL CONSTITUTIONAL COURT OF ECUADOR

In reference to: Lawsuit on behalf of the rights of nature under the principle of universal jurisdiction

Under the principle of universal jurisdiction, we, **Vandana Shiva**, an Indian national, holder of passport number Z2009264, member of the Research Foundation for Science, Technology and Ecology (RFSTE); **Ana Luz Valadez**, a Mexican national, holder of passport number G01913571, member of Desarrollo Alternativo; **Diana Murcia**, a Colombian national, holder of passport number 52198871, member of the Instituto de Estudios Ecologistas del Tercer Mundo; **Blanca Chancoso**, a Kichwa Ecuadorian national, holder of national identity document number 170410079-9, member of ECUARUNARI; **Cecilia Cherréz**, holder of national identity document number 1701597930, member and president of Acción Ecológica; **Nnimmo Bassey**, a Nigerian national, holder of passport number A01707016, member of the OILWATCH network; **Delfín Tenesaca**, a Kichwa Ecuadorian national, holder of national identity document number 060192169-5, member and president of ECUARUNARI; **Alberto Acosta**, an Ecuadorian national, holder of national identity document number 1702088822; and **Líder Góngora**, an Ecuadorian national, holder of national identity document number 080092916, member and president of C-CONDEM, hereby submit, in defence of the rights of the sea—understood as an integral part of nature which the Ecuadorian Constitution of 2008 recognizes as a subject of rights and which we recognize as a giver of life of which we form part—the present lawsuit filed under the principle of **universal jurisdiction** against the transnational corporation British Petroleum PLC, headquartered in the United Kingdom, as the responsible party for the environmental disaster that struck the Gulf of Mexico on 20 April 2010.

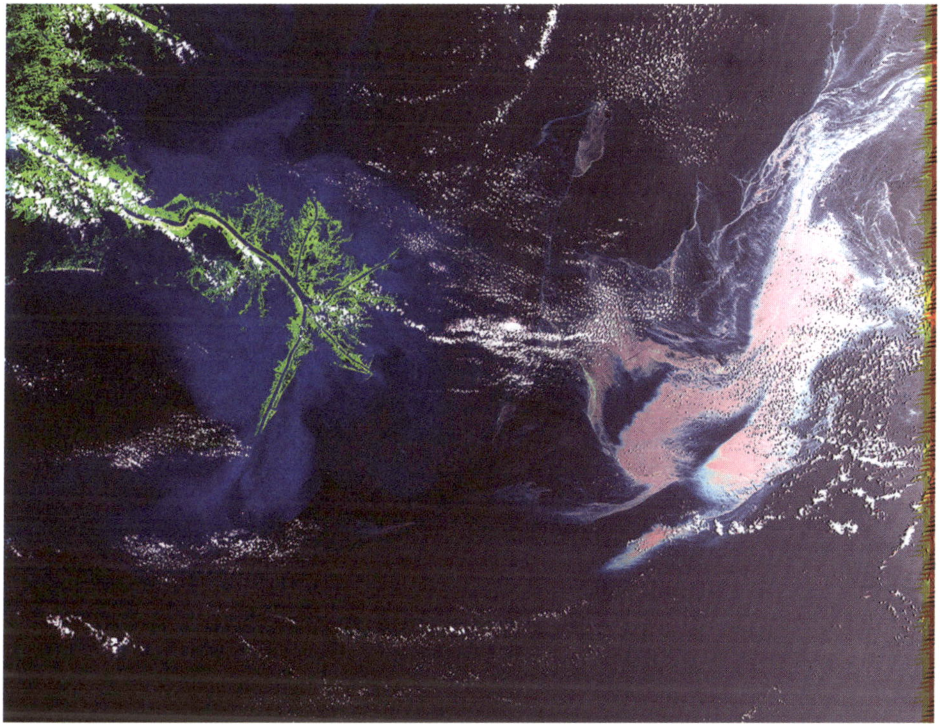

Figure 12.18
False-color composite image of the Deepwater Horizon Oil Spill captured by NASA's Landsat 7 earth observation satellite using ETM+ bands 7,4, and 2. The image falls on Landsat WRS-2 Path 21 Row 40. Acquired May 1, 2010.

ADMISSIBILITY

We, the plaintiffs, are filing this lawsuit because it is an ethical imperative in these times when even the most optimistic voices warn that humankind is losing its future, because the model of growth, overexploitation and plunder based on fossil fuel is robbing us of that future; because the oil decline is pushing the industry beyond the limits of reason and operations are moving into extraordinarily fragile areas, where there is no turning back

Because we recognize ourselves as men and women who depend on the air to breathe; on the water to revitalize us, refresh us, and give us life; on the species that surround us to maintain the balance of life and the planet, to astonish us with their beauty and amaze us with the immense capacity for collaboration and solidarity among the species found in nature; on the sea, which holds the secrets of existence in its vastness, and is the birthplace of life as we know it.

Because it is the only way that we can honour our original ancestors, who safeguarded and protected nature in order to offer us the legacy of a place where we could make our dreams a reality; and because, in turn, it is the only way we can pass down to the men and women that our children will become a place where they can make their dreams a reality.

Because the international system of rights does not recognize the rights of nature, and as a result, the precautionary principle and compensation for impacts on nature are limited to uses and abuses as they relate to people, and do not extend to nature or *Pachamama* in her own right, nor to the different species with whom we coexist.

We are filing this lawsuit because the international system of rights is clearly biased towards protecting the interests of transnational corporations that make excessive, irresponsible and predatory use of their rights to property and free enterprise, based on a development philosophy that is antagonistic to nature.

We are filing this lawsuit to break with the longstanding colonial logic of positive rights, which closes the doors to us for demanding fulfilment of the rights of *Pachamama* in formal spaces and limits us to alternative spaces such as Courts of Opinion, where, although we honourably exercise our right to have and to demand our rights, decisions are not binding on the transnational corporations or on the governments who back them, and thus they do not serve as an effective means to guarantee that the crimes denounced will not be repeated.

We submit as grounds for the admissibility of this suit both factual and legal grounds. With regard to the former, as we will presently demonstrate, the oil spill has global impacts: it impacts the ecosystems of every one of the countries of which the plaintiffs are nationals. With regard to the latter, we base our claim on the Ecuadorian Constitution of 2008, which obliges all public officials, including constitutional court judges, to protect subjects of rights, establishing as duties of the Ecuadorian state, among others:

- To guarantee the rights of nature (Art. 277).
- To protect nature from the negative effects of anthropogenic disasters (Art. 389).
- To establish effective mechanisms for the prevention and control of environmental pollution, for the recovery of degraded natural areas, and for the sustainable management of natural resources (Art. 397-2).

We the plaintiffs invoke the principle of universal jurisdiction to request that this collegiate body authorize Magistrate Nina Pacari to carry out this act of recognition of one of the subjects most overlooked in history and whose rights have been most violated: nature or *Pachamama*.

We consider it a landmark challenge to the colonial model of legal positivism to submit this case to the justice system in Ecuador, the only country in the world that recognizes the rights of nature, and for it to be overseen by Magistrate Pacari, an indigenous woman who has inherited the wisdom of the original peoples who, despite the genocide and violence that has been and continues to be perpetrated against them, have protected nature and risen up as the most committed collective environmental conscience of our planet.

We believe that Magistrate Pacari's examination of this matter could fulfil the spirit of the Ecuadorian Constitution of 2008 with regard to the protection of *Pachamama*, through an interpretation that would most effectively promote the enforcement of rights, as stipulated by Article 11-5 of the Constitution.

In the past, Dr. Pacari has exercised her duties as Magistrate in accordance with the Constitution by recognizing that "*in the traditional imagination the state has been conceived and rights have been recognized exclusively from a Western perspective, in which the only legally protected rights tended to be so-called individual rights, and particularly those of a White-Mestizo majority, as citizens of organizations constituted under the protection of the freedom of association as a notion constructed by the hegemonic culture, invisibilizing Indigenous, Afro-Ecuadorian, Montubio and other peoples and nationalities. [. . .]*" As such, she has generated jurisprudence in which she recognizes the interpretive value of cultural and intercultural diversity and therefore, the rights of nature.

Having demonstrated the admissibility of this suit under the principle of universal jurisdiction for the defence and protection of the rights of the sea, the vital blue segment of nature, we submit as grounds for this suit the following:

In the late evening of April 20, 2010, an explosion ripped through the British Petroleum (BP)-leased Deepwater Horizon oil rig, killing 11 people and discharging a compressed stream of hydrocarbon atoms into the coastal waters of the Gulf of Mexico. As these chains of carbon and hydrogen were released from their subterranean containment some four kilometers beneath the sea floor, their natural photonic properties began to interact with the unstable and energetic surface molecules of the water, recombining to produce an iridescent image of dread: a horror film in fact. Transfixed by the televisual

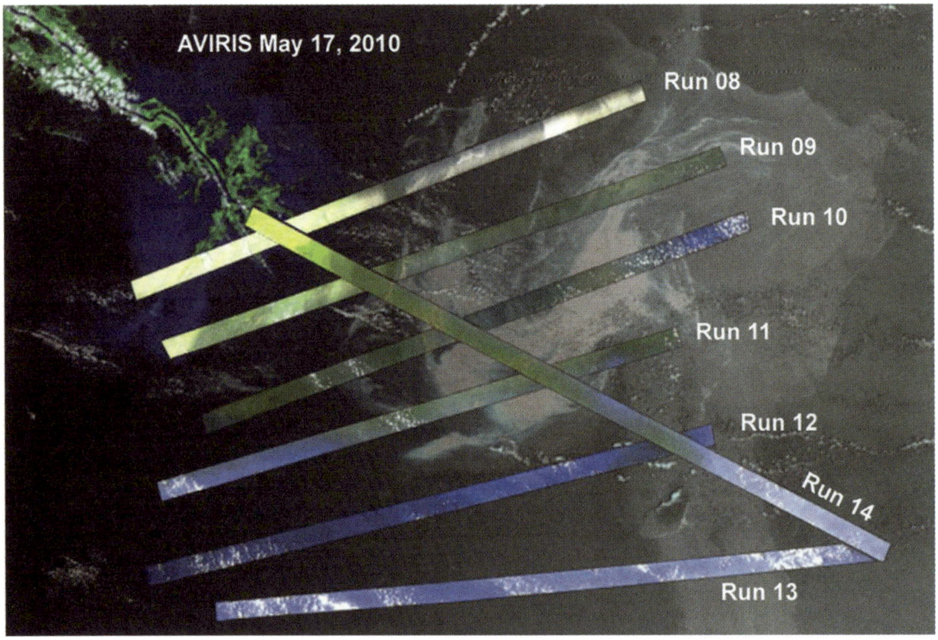

Figure 12.19
AVIRIS flight lines over the Deepwater Horizon oil spill. The background image is from MODIS Terra. Both acquired May 17, 2010.

coverage of an crude oil chimera whose tentacular reach grew daily as it moved ever closer to the shores of the Mississippi River Delta, we watched as biological systems were ensnared and devoured by this creeping hydrocarbon hazard. Out of this refractive and monstrous shimmer a new breed of hybrids emerged as oil transformed living organisms into an abject surface of technogenic sludge. Birds and wildlife became coextensive with the "black lagoon" that had spawned them and would soon reclaim its brood. By June 2010 the oil slick had reached the barrier islands of Alabama and the western Panhandle of Florida.

During the initial days of the disaster—before the drilling rig sank into the sea—its image regime was localized at the site of the blowout (although not necessarily the scene of the crime, which was distributed across corporate actors around the globe, as the various investigative commissions would eventually expose) and dominated by spectacular shots of the burning rig engulfed by flames and bilious toxic smoke: the kind of dramatic images that demand our immediate attention, and which literary theorist Rob Nixon's thesis of "slow violence" indicts as standing in the way of ecological justice.[33] When the disastrous object disappeared from view into the murky depths below, its image-making capacities and modes of image capture began to multiply across various forms of technical media and distribution platforms. Soon our public gaze was suspended between two new media geographies: the real-time underwater cameras that streamed blurry images of gushing crude as it defied all efforts to cap the leak, and the Earth observation satellites that transmitted aerial datasets tracking the spill's expansion across the surface waters of the Gulf, from the Landsat 7 that charted its migrating pathway to the NASA near-infrared AVIRIS instrument that was repeatedly flown across the spill, mapping the location and distribution of thick oil floating on water. Yet in contrast to these highly technical satellite images, which appeared primarily in scientific contexts and government reports, the underwater cameras returned the accident to the domesticated sphere of online spectatorship, allowing us to peer into its proximate and abject space with the click of a mouse. The magnitude of the leak registers its full visceral force, not in the satellite imagery documenting a creeping mass that threatens to dwarf all terrestrial features, but in the low-resolution underwater footage. Here the oil spill is encountered as a torrential surplus: matter out of place. I confess that I was mesmerized by the underwater battle being waged to plug the leak in the blowout preventer. As the days, weeks, and months passed we collectively learnt a new lexicon: "top kill," "junk shot," "cut-and-cap," "static kill," and "relief well"—a petroleum patois that marked each stage and strategy in efforts to arrest the flow. Subsequent reports from oceanographers indicate that the plume of oil was in fact far greater in volume below the surface than that which could be monitored from above.[34]

Yet this impoverished real-time video feed was somehow deemed insufficient by BP, which decided at a certain point to doctor a scene of their employees monitoring the remote-controlled underwater cameras in their Houston Command Center. In the original photograph three of the video feeds were turned off, but in the later version of the press image, all video streams are shown in full operation, suggesting comprehensive round-the-clock coverage. This altered image featured prominently on BP's website with the caption "HIVE at Houston Command Center, July 16, 2010," and was promoted as evidence of their continued and comprehensive oversight of the accident. Blogger John Aravosis, who was following the crisis in the Gulf, noticed this crude photoshopping and remarked: "I guess if you're doing fake crisis response, you might as well fake a photo of the crisis response center."[35] By the time the wellhead was finally capped, on July 15, 2010, it had spewed an estimated 4.1 million barrels of crude into the Gulf, permanently damaging its marine biology, destroying coastal wildlife, polluting habitats, and shutting down the fishing communities reliant upon the ecological bounty of the Gulf.[36] According to the US Department of the Interior

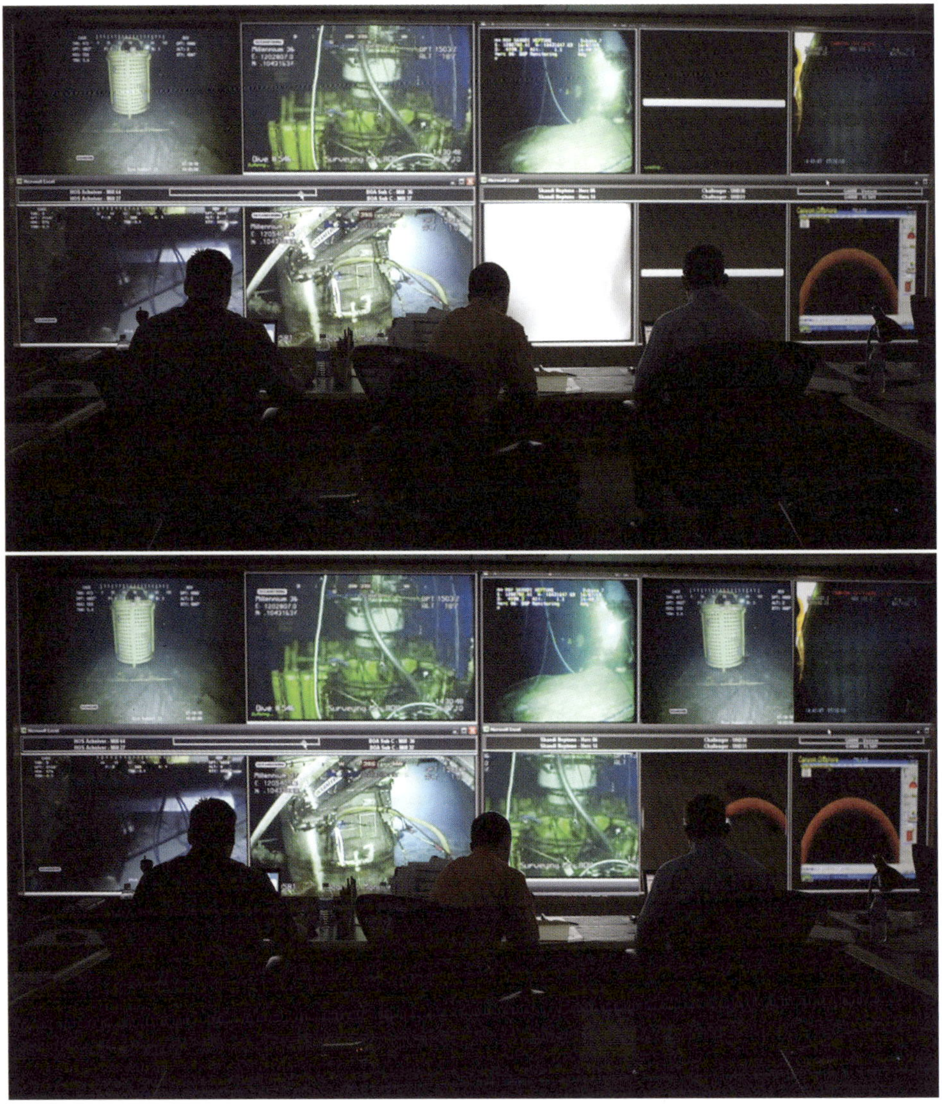

Figure 12.20

Top: HIVE at Houston Command Center, July 16, 2010. Original image. Source: BP. Bottom: Altered image. Source: BP.

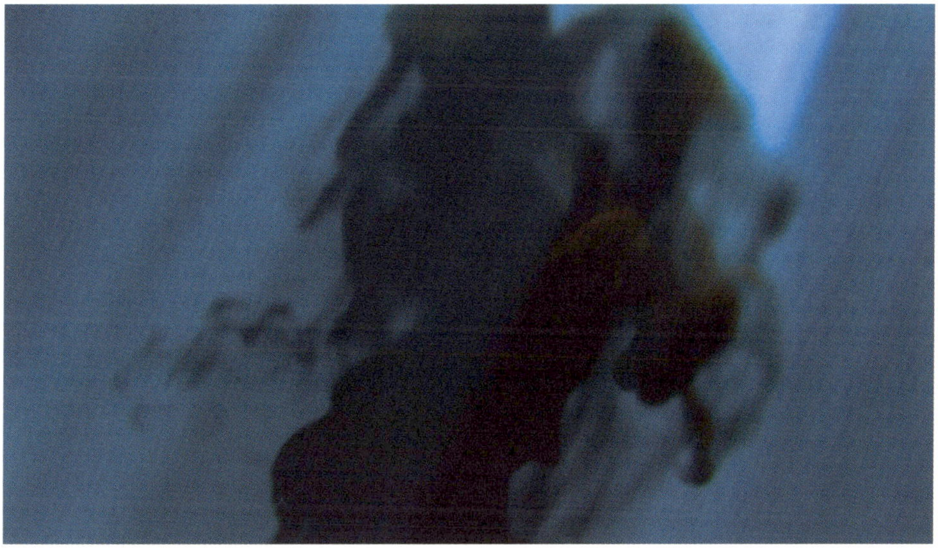

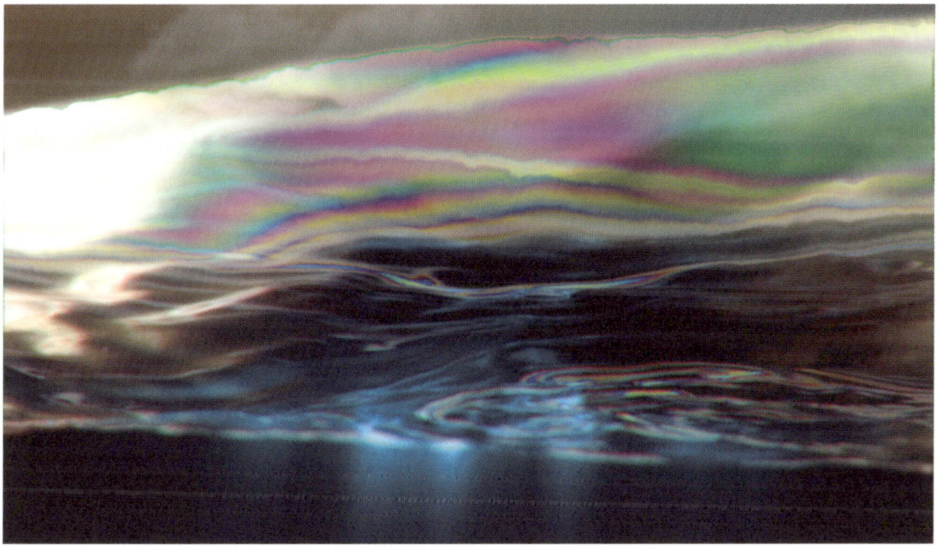

Figure 12.21

Nature Represents Itself, Susan Schuppli, 2018, CGI video produced in collaboration with Harry Sanderson, color with sound, 6:27 minutes, oil film simulation of surface slick as well as deep subsurface plumes resulting from the Deepwater Horizon oil spill. Commissioned by Sculpture-Center for the exhibition *74 million, million, million tons*, curated by Ruba Katrib and Lawrence Abu Hamdan.

Minerals Management Service (Gulf of Mexico Region), as of October 1, 2014, there were some 3,060 offshore rigs in the Gulf drilling at depths ranging from 200 meters to over 800 meters.[37]

> Documents and testimony from Congressional hearings revealed a series of potential failures and warning signs at the well site in the hours leading up to the rig explosion, as well as questions that had been raised years earlier about the reliability of deepwater technology and the ability of the industry to deal with "worse-case scenarios" of accidents. The Minerals Management Service, the government agency with lead oversight of offshore oil and gas activity, came under heavy criticism for lax environmental planning and for sacrificing sound stewardship of a public natural resource for the narrow economic gain to private industry.[38]

Until the night of the disaster, future dividends from the Macondo Prospect oil field, which included the Deepwater Horizon, were already being pumped into the combined coffers of BP, Haliburton, and Transocean Ltd., the three major corporations involved in developing the exploratory well. My interest in the case of the Deepwater Horizon lies not in telling another tale of technogenic failure, environmental catastrophe, and corporate malfeasance, but in examining the proto-cinematic properties of oil slicks, or "oil films," as they are properly called. However, rather than merely revel in the hallucinogenic appearance of the slick, I shift my analytical focus to forward an argument around the aesthetic agency of such damaged ecologies as fully capable of self-representation both before the law and as environmental media systems. Oil films are thin emulsive layers of molecules that ride the surface tension of water, refracting light to create a form of natural photonics.[39] In fact it was Fraunhofer's experiments in optics that first led him to discover the refractive properties of thin-film coatings in 1817, using the transparent incident medium of glass rather than that of water, as is the case with an oil spill.

In animals, especially birds, fish, and insects, the metallic-like reflections we associate with a peacock's plumage, the iridescence of fish scales or a beetle's glittering carapace, are produced by photonic crystals. These are *structural* colors generated by the architectural arrangement of molecules as light waves move across an organism's crystalline surface, not variations achieved by virtue of genetic pigmentation. Such photogenic creatures are, in effect, prismatic agents whose spontaneous coloration is activated by the structural play of light.[40] By comparison, the natural chromatic properties of an oil spill are activated by changes in the molecular density of the film as it spreads and thins, thus modulating the degree to which light wavelengths interact and interfere with one another to produce their polychromatic effects. Contrary to what we seem to see, only one color is ever reflected by a particular thickness of the oil film at any given time.[41] The cinematic capacity of the oil film is not simply a consequence of its representational program as a mirrored watery surface that is capable of projecting an aesthetic event back at us—abstracted and lurid patterns of refracted light—but a feature of its very ontology: its molecular structure and behavior. Understood as such, oil films, following Kahn, might be said to collapse the distance between the surface of the filmstrip and that of the projection screen, a spatial mediation that celluloid cinema resolved by means of the temporal operations of light energy, but which the oil spill uses to generate its refractive effects.[42] Oil films are literally slick images, just as celluloid film is literally a product of oil. In his reflections on *Ecologies of the Moving Image*, Ivakhiv reminds us of the fundamental entanglement between filmic processes and the metabolic, meta-origins of oil.

> It [cinema] has always depended on a powerful combination of at least two forms of solar energy: the capture of reflected solar light itself, and the indirect products of that energy that have been stored and compounded over millennia in the form of fossil fuels and their photochemical derivatives. Cinema is a form of captured, organized, and released light-heat-energy-movement. … Cinema arose alongside the industrialization of material production—that is, alongside the unleashing of productive capacities that had been stored on or beneath the surface of this planet for millennia.[43]

While satellite transmissions, the underwater video feed, and even Public Lab's kite mapping project all combined to document the aftermath of the Deepwater Horizon oil spill, the slick was already operationalizing an independent mode of filmmaking. When the smooth viscosity of oil comes into contact with the rough surface tension of the sea—the point at which water molecules are exposed to air—rapid transformations in the thickness of the oil film occur, resulting in extraordinary and rapid shifts of color. Molecules achieve maximum stability when they are in close proximity with other like molecules, which is why the surface agitation of water molecules is calmed when a film of oil molecules begins to amass itself: a smoothing over that also improves its overall reflective potential. The interference patterns that are visible on the surface of an oil slick are an aesthetic expression of the optical conceits that the oil film shares with other technical forms of moving image production. However, the oil spill is perhaps better understood as engaged in the production of a new form of cinema organized by the found footage of nature itself: one whose indexical operations are pushed to the extreme insofar as the external event to which it gestures—in the case of the Deepwater Horizon, the release of an estimated 4.1 million barrels of crude oil into the Gulf—is transformed into its very mode of image production. The conditions that brought about the disaster are thus reexpressed as an ontological rearrangement of molecular matter: a shift from the representation of the damaged drilling rig and its gushing crude to the actualization of a ruinous image. This event returns us directly to the beginnings of this book, and my discussion of film stock contaminated by Chernobyl's airborne radiation. Although Shevchenko's documentary, shot two days after the reactor explosion, was initially deemed to be ruined by virtue of its contact with radioactive decay as it moved through the body of his camera, his eventual realization that he had captured a trace of "real" was singularly transformative in shaping my thinking around the *material witness*. This conception is pushed further still if we consider contaminated environments like the Gulf of Mexico as engaged in self-imaging without the interpretative intercession of a filmmaker or, indeed, the arbitration of a filmic substrate. In making this case I am returning to representation, but with a difference. There is no oil-based substance that mediates the relationship between representation and the real, no celluloid film stock that carries the traces of incoming toxicity. Representation has become the real.

Despite BP's considerable efforts to control the news cycle by effectively banning media from the Gulf, as the lawsuit filed on behalf of the rights of nature makes clear, damage control was not entirely in their hands. Earth-observing satellites and Public Lab's "community satellites" did manage to capture and produce images that confirmed the extraordinary scale of the spill.[44] Limiting the field of legal liability by limiting the visual field was part of BP's implicit goal but, as my argument contends, in addition to the activist mapping strategies of Public Lab and automated forms of remote sensing, the Gulf was already documenting its own damaged condition, irrespective of the *de facto* media ban imposed. In fact, these photodynamic activities expanded exponentially with the industrial scale of the accident in combination with the various responses to control and contain the spill.

> **Facts I.12.** BP has hindered the possibility of independent observations. It has rented all of the hotel rooms in the area, chartered all of the boats and hired practically all of the fishers left unemployed, in its attempt to keep the press at bay, while paying lucrative sums to scientists for conducting studies with confidentiality clauses. Different forms of censorship have been enforced by BP's private security team. This obstruction of access to information about what is really happening with this environmental disaster directly impacts on the ability of the citizens to know about its impacts on nature and thus to undertake action in its defence.[45]

As the injured party, the Gulf of Mexico, "understood as an integral part of nature," disclosed evidential proof of wrongdoing to which the oil film as a *material witness* testified. Beyond the fact that the slick carried direct evidence of the injurious nature of its contaminants in its molecular makeup, it also provided indirect visual evidence of a range of strategies to hide the crime, thus also disclosing the event of evidence making or, in BP's case, revealing willful attempts at "unmaking" evidence, from unscrupulous media tactics to doctored crisis-management images of the largest ever application of chemical dispersants in US history. With its microimaging particles dispersed, perhaps the accident of April 20, 2010 too would recede into the murky depths of past news cycles—or so BP hoped. To that end, 1.8 million gallons of Corexit 9500 and Corexit 9527 were dumped into the Gulf (applied to the surface and wellhead) to break up oil molecules at an order of magnitude whose consequences remain completely unknown. "As part of the National Contingency Plan required for offshore drilling, one of 18 EPA-approved dispersants must be on hand to handle spilled oil. Each of those dispersants has been preapproved for use."[46] The use of such oil emulsifiers is, however, identified as proven to affect aquatic biota, especially toward the upper reaches of the water column. Environmental scientist Carys Mitchelmore notes: "Dispersed oils are going to be toxic, particularly in the top 10 meters that contains all the sensitive life stages. Anything that has sensitive membranes can be affected by dispersants and dispersed oil."[47] Oceanographers who have sampled the deep waters of the Gulf claim that the application of these emulsifiers, which break up oil density, resulting in particles sinking below the visible surface, means that the submerged plumes are also being carried far from their point of origin, once again pulling apart the causal links that can connect a perpetrator directly to their crime.[48]

In their article on oil spill imaging, Peter Galison and Caroline A. Jones advance a related set of observations: "No longer visible, the treated oil floats in those submerged transparent plumes, unimaged and hence largely unimagined. It may be that in the final analysis, the real role of the dispersant was to remove the spill from the camera—and with it, BP from the glare of popular and political scrutiny."[49] Applied even in very small doses of one drop per 2.5 liters of seawater, Corexit 9500 has been shown to prevent photosynthesis in phytoplankton species specific to the Gulf.[50] Dispersants can also bring about another dangerous photo-based process, known as photo-induced or photo-enhanced toxicity, whereby sunlight interacts with polycyclic aromatic hydrocarbons (PAH) and chemical compounds, transforming an already comprised ecology into an even more harmful event.[51] "Compounds in the oil act as a catalyst to transfer some of the sun's energy into oxygen, converting the latter to a more reactive state that can literally burn up cells. And as fish and other sea life ingest the dispersed oil, it can be broken down into more toxic by-products."[52] As strategies to break up the spill headed into uncharted waters, the Gulf was turned into a "massive uncontrolled experiment" with no clear understanding as to what such chemistry would yield for coastal communities and habitats already struggling with the first wave of the disaster. And whilst BP was generally following the protocols set out by the National Contingency Plan, it becomes clear in reading through the documentation and reports as they relate to the Deepwater Horizon that scientific, environmental, and industry testing differed considerably in determining the datasets upon which levels of acceptable risk were being established: an ambiguity that played into BP's hands.

Just as with Chernobyl, the accident had pushed well beyond the scalar dimensions that any disaster management plan, even one that might have followed the provisions set out by the directives of the EPA and NCP more rigorously than BP had done, could have anticipated. Explanations that turn on the theory of "unforeseen circumstances" are deeply flawed in that the accident is always invented alongside the invention of any technology.[53] Ultimately the facts, legal arguments, and especially the "actions requested" put forward by the lawsuit filed in Quito, were much more proactive in their conceptualization than was reflected in the final consent decree arrived at by United States District Court for the Eastern District of Louisiana, whose response was reactive and organized by financial settlements and the payout of compensation claims.

> BP has been ordered to pay $5.5 billion to settle civil damages claims made by the U.S. as a result of the Deepwater Horizon oil spill. The amount will be paid over the course of 16 years. Despite protests from both Congress and a broad coalition of environmental groups, the final settlement will allow BP to deduct a majority of the costs as an ordinary business expense. ... U.S. District Judge Carl J. Barbier ruled in favor of BP, citing the Oil Pollution Act (OPA) passed in the wake of the 1989 Exxon Valdez spill.[54]

And while the lawsuit filed "in defence of the rights of the sea" was ultimately unsuccessful, it emphasized the degree to which our current mechanisms—regulatory agencies, jurisdictional courts, and national academies—for assessing risk, attributing responsibility, determining remediation, and establishing preventive measures for averting future disasters, are challenged by parametric thinking (the sliding scales of cost–benefit analysis, of pay now or pay later, of worst-case scenarios) that all too often inform decision-making. As Paulo Tavares notes in his essay "Nonhuman Rights" in *Forensis*, the lawsuit reframed public debate around the spill as a political, cultural, and social conflict rather than a problem of drilling technology and corporate malfeasance around which compensation would duly be settled.

> Legal advocacy is of course not a novel strategy in responding to ecological catastrophes. Most notably after the publication in 1962 of *Silent Spring*, Rachel Carson's seminal indictment of chemical pollutants, the alliance between the natural and legal sciences was firmly consolidated as lawyers and ecologists increasingly joined efforts to take action on behalf of the environment. The lawsuit filed against BP in Ecuador draws from this historical tradition, but at the same time projects it anew, appropriating the classic tools of environmental advocacy to expose its own limitations, searching for means to expand the political force of what has been called "environmental justice." More than an action with law as its instrument, the lawsuit was an intervention within the very frames of law itself, which sought to make visible how the existing legal order inevitably legitimizes the ecological violence it should help to restrain.[55]

In bringing *Material Witness* to a close with the case of the Deepwater Horizon, I wish to reiterate the degree to which a conceptual argument about the aesthetic agency of ecological matter as forwarding visual evidence of its own compromised condition is both "sensible" and "grounded," if one considers that corporations like BP itself were accorded the legal status of personhood (rights guaranteed to individuals) as early as the nineteenth century, allowing them to enter into contracts, buy and sell property, and, perhaps most importantly, shift legal liability from individuals to that of an abstract entity. In 2010, US corporations were even given the constitutional right of political speech, allowing for their direct financial involvement in election campaigns, a move that reinforces the notion of the speech acts of things.[56] The emergence of an array of new legal personalities, including nature, surely is precedent enough for me to attribute other forms of agency to matter, of which the aesthetic in the technical form of an oil film are arguably more real than those entities forged out of judicial amendments.

13 CONVICTIONS

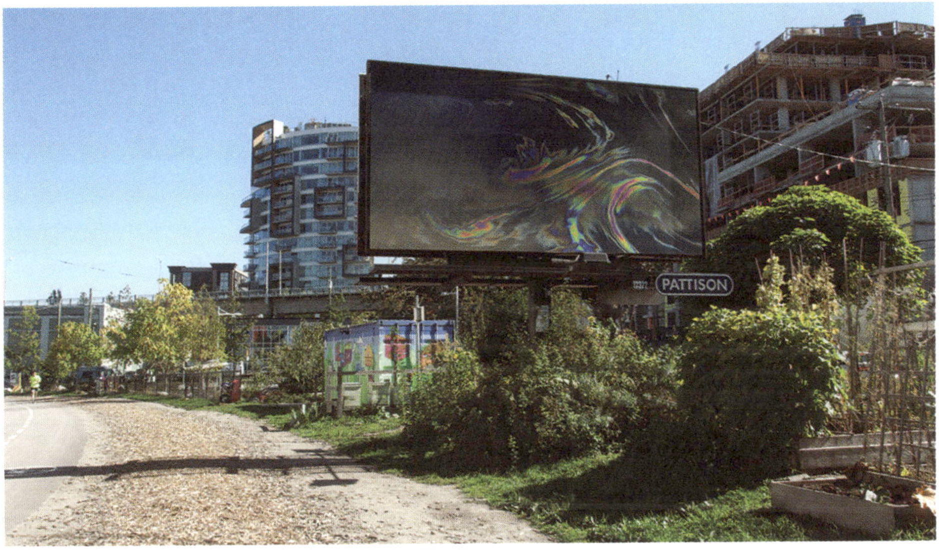

Figure 13.1
Disaster Film, Susan Schuppli, a public billboard series installed throughout Vancouver for the exhibition *Signals from the Sea*, curated by Jayne Wilkinson. Source: Capture Photography Festival, 2019.

Materials, whether naturally occurring, industrially manufactured, or computationally derived, register their complex interactions with the world, producing ontological transformations and informatic dispositions that can be forensically decoded and reassembled back into a history. I have called these nonhuman entities and machinic ecologies *material witnesses*. Throughout the cases presented, I have tried to account for the innumerable ways in which the responsiveness of matter to external forces demands an acute and renewed sense of material and technical specificity in order to grasp the full cultural and political implications that such ongoing changes or interactions might yield. The dare posed by these materials—to invoke Isabelle Stengers one last time—is that they emphasize what is needed from us if we are to think matter differently.[1] Apprehending materials as dynamic and expressive witnesses rather than inert and mute bystanders is achieved not only by means of the specific probes or techniques that can be brought to bear upon them in order to exhort their testimonials and, by extension, the discursive frameworks that have been sanctioned to translate their material encodings into actionable events. It also results from being compelled to reflect upon the limits of our own experience and knowledge. How do subjective modes of perception and our choice of interpretative frameworks play a decisive role in determining what kinds of materials can become evidential? As Stengers reminds us, what is collectively accepted as "mattering" affects our practices, in that it establishes our theoretical frameworks, determines our research pathways, produces our political horizons, and organizes our critical response. In validating certain practices and rejecting others, potential tools for thinking are lost; thus alternate vantage points are ceded. The dual nature of the *material witness*, as both condition and concept, permits its disciplinary interchange and confirms its broader investigative applicability and cultural repurposing. It is in referring both to that which can be factually demonstrated as well as that which can be creatively imagined that the *material witness* becomes fully operative.

I opened with a description of a blurry image seared into the crystalline surface of a video monitor reclaimed from Prison Maze/Long Kesh in Northern Ireland in 2000. The monitor had been turned off almost 20 years earlier, yet still carried an evidential trace of its carceral history in the form of a screen burn. I am closing *Material Witness* with another image medium: a disaster film created when hydrocarbon atoms were accidentally released from their pressurized containment to combine with salt water and sunlight. Both are technical systems whose structural composition responded to the intensification of external forces in uniquely mediatic ways. The registration of political and sectarian violence that was compressed into the phosphorous limit space of the screen is unfolded throughout this book until the media object becomes an extensive and multidimensional eco-aesthetic event, whose violent abstractions are organized by the flows of finance capital and the molecular chaos of crude matter. This constitutes a progression from a discrete artifact to a networked assembly of relations: a transformation that also challenges notions of media that would locate their perceptual coherency and aesthetic repertoire entirely within the unified operations of specific human-centered events. As evidence for events migrates, and assumes ever more materially dispersed and datafied arrangements, our critical investigative practices must take into account alternate modes of witnessing that operate across scales and entities—including the technical and more-than-human—if, that is, we are to challenge the powerful contexts and institutional formats that determine the particular relevance of events or, indeed, to invent new ones.

As caesium-137 becomes trace evidence, as documentary film becomes radioactive fossil, as microfiche becomes search engine, as machinic silence becomes political indictment, as photo reenactment becomes perjury, as 150 kHz becomes humanitarian crisis, as metadata becomes kill list, as atmospheric noise becomes accidental napalm, as Agent Orange becomes class action, as disturbed ground becomes war crime, as video alibi becomes arboreal witness, as anonymous footage becomes forensic proof, as contaminated forest becomes electromagnetic spectrum, as iron oxide becomes exiled memorial, as the sun becomes a liar, as extractive zone becomes toxic common, as grain becomes pixel, as electronic defect becomes testimony, as dust becomes impure matter, as poor image becomes dirty picture, as screen burn becomes oil spill—the *material* becomes a *witness*.

Notes

1: Opening Statements

1 The project Transforming Maze/Long Kesh is part of TRACES, a Horizon 2020 project exploring contentious cultural heritage in different European contexts. In their examination of the material culture of the former Irish prison, artists Martin Krenn and Aisling O'Beirn have photographed objects from Maze/Long Kesh in a dialogical fashion by talking to their owners and custodians in order to devise a title and accompanying text. The resulting title becomes part of the foreground of each object photographed, to form part of a touring exhibition and book. Their broader research is guided by an interest in the ways in which architecture and the built environment can act as witnesses to history.

2 See Laura U. Marks's discussion of the recollection object (Marks 2000).

3 Johnston (1999).

4 Deleuze (1990), 151.

5 See the discussion in chapter 12, "Closing Arguments," that details the lingering trauma and localized racism consequent to the reactivation of the Omarska concentration camp in Prijedor, Bosnia and Herzegovina, as an iron ore mine.

6 Barry (2010), 90.

7 Bensaude-Vincent and Stengers (1996), 206.

8 Galloway (2012), 88–89.

9 The work of Luciana Parisi is exemplary in this regard. See Parisi (2013).

10 See Eyal Weizman's introduction in Forensic Architecture (2014), 9–10.

11 Latour (2004).

12 Donna Haraway, "Primatology is Politics by Other Means," in *Feminist Approaches to Science*, ed. Ruth Bleir (New York: Pergamon Press, 1986), 85.

13 See Kirschenbaum (2008).

14 "I argue that one of the decisive features of the 'era of the witness' has been the reframing of witnessing and testimony as gestures that, given the proper guidance and support, are bound to instigate a subjective transformation and not just produce empirical or metaphysical truths." See Givoni (2014), 126.

15 Agamben (2000), 16–17.

16 Bernard Stiegler summing up one of Jacques Derrida's points in "Phonographies: Meaning—From Heritage to Horizon," in Derrida and Stiegler (2005), 100.
17 Derrida and Stiegler (2005), 93–94.
18 Halewood (2016), 796–797. These insights by Halewood first came to my attention during the one-day conference "Thinking with Stengers" held at UCL in 2015.
19 Barad (2007), 132.
20 See Doyle (1997).
21 Stengers (1997), 140.
22 Massumi (2002b), 20.
23 Jackson quoted in Felman (2001), 242. Original source Harris, Jackson, and Storey (1954), xxix, xxxv–xxxvi.
24 Felman (2001), 244; Arendt (1963).
25 Keenan and Weizman (2012), 10. See also Felman (2002); Wieviorka (2006).
26 Felman (2001), 244; Arendt (1963).
27 Levi (1997), 220.
28 Keenan and Weizman (2012).
29 On 11 February 1994, the United Nations adopted the "Rules of Procedure and Evidence pursuant to Article 15 of the Statute of the International Tribunal for the Prosecution of Persons Responsible for Serious Violations of International Humanitarian Law Committed in the Territory of the Former Yugoslavia since 1991." The Rules of Procedure and Evidence for the ICTY lays down the 125 rules that provide the fundamental legal architecture of the entire Tribunal, from its organizational structure, prosecutorial operations, witness management and evidentiary processes, to its technical and media requirements. International Criminal Tribunal for the former Yugoslavia, Rules of Procedure and Evidence, U.N. Doc. IT/32/Rev.49 (22 May 2013), entered into force 14 March 1994, http://www.icty.org/sid/136.
30 "Obtaining by sense-enhancing technology any information regarding the interior of the home that could not otherwise have been obtained without physical intrusion into a constitutionally protected area constitutes a search for purposes of the Federal Constitution's Fourth Amendment—at least where the technology in question is not in general public use—and is presumptively unreasonable without a warrant. (Stevens, J., Rehnquist, Ch. J., and O'Connor and Kennedy, JJ., dissented from this holding.)" (United States Court of Appeals 2001, 4.)
31 Although the ICTY Court Records represent its unrestricted public offerings, they are but a small fraction of the actual materials gathered and records produced by the Tribunal since its inception in 1993. Full disclosure of all its legal materials with provisions for protected witnesses remains one of the Tribunal's core ambitions, though there has been much dispute as to where and how such a permanent facility should be located and administered. The issue of future appeals and the late arrest of its final fugitive, Goran Hadžić, on 20 July 2011, have also meant that its "Completion Strategy" will need to transfer cases to local judiciaries for prosecution. As a United Nations court, conventionally all materials from its Tribunals return to UN Headquarters in New York, where they are sequestered away at some considerable distance from their primary stakeholders. However, the decision has now been made to keep the archives in The Hague as a legacy project, where access can be made more readily available to those directly affected by the Balkan Wars, or where they can be used as a tool for reconciliation

and legal pedagogy. For a discussion of the memorial function of the ICTY archive, see Kirsten (2013).
32 See 16-channel video installation *Evidence on Trial* in "See you in The Hague," Stroom Den Haag, 2014. Curated by Brigitte van der Sande. See also *Scenographies of Power: From the State of Exception to the Spaces of Exception*, La Casa Encendida, 2017. Curated by Maite Borjabad López-Pastor.
33 See Barad (2003), 802–804.
34 Stengers (1997), 126.
35 Ibid.
36 See Kirschenbaum (2008), xii.
37 Two authors who address related aspects of degraded images are Steyerl (2009); Takahashi (2006).
38 See Pottage (2011); Mnookin (1998).
39 http://gazaplatform.amnesty.org, https://blackfriday.amnesty.org
40 https://www.forensic-architecture.org/case/saydnaya
41 "During the final months of its existence the Committee was asked in a Polish case (Commission No. 7150) to determine whether ten Germans, all of whom had been heads of various Departments in the Forestry Administration in Poland during the German occupation (1939–1944), could be listed as war criminals on a charge of pillaging Polish public property. It was alleged that the accused in their official capacities caused the wholesale cutting of Polish timber to an extent far in excess of what was necessary to preserve the timber resources of the country, with a loss to the Polish nation of the sum of 6,525,000,000 zloty. It was pointed out that the Germans, who had been among the first as a nation to foster scientific forestry, had entered Poland and wilfully felled the Polish forests without the least regard to the basis principles of forestry. The Polish representative presented a copy of a circular signed by Goering under date of 25th January, 1940, in which were laid down principles for a policy of ruthless exploitation of Polish forestry. It was decided by the Committee that prima facie existence of a war crime had been shown and nine of the officials charged were listed as accused war criminals." *History of the U.N. War Crimes Commission and the Development of the Laws of War* (London, 1948), 496, cited in Falk (1976), 14.
42 "For example, in the Second World War, the German General Lothar Rendulic adopted a scorched earth policy in Norway in order to evade advancing Russian troops. General Rendulic ordered the evacuation of all inhabitants in the province of Finmark, and destroyed all villages and surrounding facilities. The Nuremberg Military Tribunal charged General Rendulic with wanton destruction of property, but later acquitted him on the basis that military necessity justified his actions in light of the military situation as he perceived it at the time" (Yuzon 1996, 815). See also Drumbl (1998).
43 Guardian (2016).
44 Ibid.
45 In November 2010 a case was filed by nine plaintiffs from five countries in the Constitutional Court of Ecuador against British Petroleum (BP). On 26 July 2012 the suit was admitted as No.0523-2012 under the Juzgado Segundo de Pichincha (Second Labor Court of Pichincha). The case has been decided.

46 Caroline Hunter, a chemist working for the Polaroid Corporation in 1970, found evidence that her employer was providing the camera system to the South African State to produce photographs for their passbooks. Along with her partner Ken Williams, she formed the Polaroid Workers Revolutionary Movement to campaign for a boycott (Goodman and Gonzalez 2013).
47 See Amaro (2015).
48 "The singularity of an event is based not simply on the coming together of prehensions, but on their becoming together in a particular way. The question as to whether an entity—a scientific artefact or work of art for example—is 'real' or whether it is a 'representation' is thus displaced in favour of the question as to what it can do" (Fraser 2006, 131).
49 "I call the distribution of the sensible the system of self-evident facts of sense perception that simultaneously discloses the existence of something in common and the delimitations that define the respective parts and positions within it. A distribution of the sensible therefore establishes at one and the same time something common that is shared and exclusive parts" (Rancière 2004, 12).
50 Bensaude-Vincent and Stengers (1996), 206.
51 Computer forensics is able to discern "data remanence" or trace evidence of previous data inscriptions that sit alongside more recent encodings. Although erased digital data is "flagged" by the system as space that is now available for overwriting, data may remain in a residual or partial state of inscription until required, which in turn may allow it to be recovered. See "Every Contact Leaves a Trace," in Kirschenbaum (2008). However, I still maintain that the phenomena of data remanence do not produce "thick" or topologically sedimented artifacts but merely extend data in space horizontally.
52 See Clough et al. (2007), 61. See also Caffentzis (1997).
53 See IPCC (2013).
54 The film is based upon the book by Gourevitch and Morris (2008).
55 Brent Pack, Army Special Agent in the Criminal Investigation Division, speaking on camera in Morris (2008).
56 Forensic Architecture's investigation "Black Friday / Carnage in Rafah during 2014 Israel/Gaza Conflict" solved this date/time problem in a unique way by using the smoke plumes of munitions as analog clocks to sync time across thousands of images and videos. https://blackfriday.amnesty.org
57 Brent Pack, Army Special Agent in the Criminal Investigation Division, speaking on camera in Morris (2008).
58 Morris (2008).
59 "What is missing from this image [writes Laura Kurgan, referring to the IKONOS image] is what is missing now from the city or the world, and it is always missing at the limits of one-meter resolution, for all its detail. What is missing are the missing, over 5,000 people now presumed dead. Beneath or beyond the limits of visibility, of data, are the dead. And yet they remain in the image, in the ruin of the image, and ask something of us" (Kurgan 2002, 655).
60 Intact bodies were nowhere to be found, frustrating rescue efforts, which ultimately managed to recover 19,906 human fragments. Of these remains, only 293 were fully intact bodies and only 12 could be identified by sight.
61 See Petraco, Kubic, and Faber (2007), 3.

62 "You have 10-story buildings that leave more debris than these two 100-story towers. Where the fuck is everything? A serious weeklong search and we've found 200 in a pile of 5,000? What's going on? Where is everyone? Why aren't we finding more bodies? Cause it's all vaporized—turned to dust. We're breathing people in that dust." A fireman speaking in a Brooklyn bar who had done a 24-hour shift at Ground Zero (Ketcham 2011).
63 Connor (2009), 71.
64 Locard (1930), 278. See also Burney (2013).
65 Locard (1930), 276.
66 See ICTY (2010).

2: Discovery

1 Ascarelli (2011).
2 Ibid.
3 Ibid.
4 See Forsmark, Monday, 28 April 1986, a chronology of events translated and reprinted in Zetterberg (1996).
5 Ascarelli (2011).
6 Northern Sweden absorbed 5 percent of the radioactive caesium-137 that Chernobyl released into the air.
7 Okumura (2003).
8 Zetterberg (1996), 3–4.
9 The KH-11 spy satellite, part of the Keyhole series of spy satellites, had the capacity to capture data with a resolution of 10–15 cm and was the first to "return film-quality images from orbit electronically, without bucket-dropping because of the invention of the charge-coupled device (CCD) in 1970" (Gilman 2004, 48).
10 Firemen tasked with containing the blaze so that it didn't migrate to the three other working reactors and workers involved in immediate cleanup operations had already died during this time lag. See Lyudmila Ignatenko's harrowing account of her husband Vasily's 14-day death in a clandestine ward in a Moscow hospital. Vasily was one of the first firemen called to quell the flames of Chernobyl during the night of 26 April 1986 (Aleksievich, Gunin, and Tait 2016).
11 Media announcements were given to the *Pravda* newspaper, State television, the Novosti press agency (APN), and the TASS Agency and their correspondent in the Ukraine. Reporter Igor Kostin, who worked for TASS, took the first photographic image of the destroyed reactor at Chernobyl. Like Vladimir Shevchenko's, his film was riven by radioactive contaminants, most of the roll incinerated and unreadable. See Kostin (2006), 10.
12 70 percent of atmospheric fallout fell onto Belarus rather than the Ukraine, a situation that has not been central to the story of Chernobyl save in Svetlana Aleksievich's extraodinary accounts from witnesses. See Aleksievich, Gunin, and Tait (2016).
13 Becquerels per cubic meter denotes the number of decay events per second per quantity, and sieverts per second refers to the unit of ionizing radiation that is an index of its ill-health effects on the human body.

14 Document 3: Henry W. Newson to N. E. Bradbury, director, Los Alamos Laboratory, "Possible Difficulties in Naval Tests," 17 December 1945, Secret. Source: Nuclear Testing Archive/National Security Technologies, Department of Energy contractor, document number NV0120851.
15 Buesseler (2016).
16 Guardian (2015).
17 Ibid.
18 Jönsson and Watson (2016).
19 Bruno (2003), 238.
20 Lutts (1985), 212.
21 Smith et al. (2015), 1314.
22 Greenpeace (2006).
23 Interview with Dr. John Rowat, International Atomic Energy Agency, Department of Nuclear Safety and Security, Waste and Environmental Safety Section, Decommissioning and Remediation Unit conducted by Susan Schuppli, London, UK, 10 February 2018.

3: Hostile Witness

1 Shevchenko (1986).
2 I am indebted to Peter C. van Wyck, whose mention of this filmic incident/accident prompted my search for the film footage and subsequent writing (Van Wyck 2004, 97).
3 Transcription of film voiceover from Shevchenko (1986).
4 Gayatri Chakravorty Spivak, who coined the term, uses it to invoke a planet that is "other" to the human, whereas the globe is an entity entirely circumscribed by anthropocentric logics of jurisdiction and control. She writes: "The planet is in the species of alterity, belonging to another system; and yet we habit it, on loan" (Spivak 2003, 72). Also DeLoughrey (2014), 1.
5 Barry (2010), 95.
6 Artists Jane and Louise Wilson interviewed surviving members of Shevchenko's crew in 2011. Their film production "Toxic Camera" was inspired directly by an earlier partial draft of this chapter, which appeared as Schuppli (2013).
7 See Petryna (2002).
8 Bazin (1960), 4–5.
9 Ibid.
10 Deleuze (1989). See also See Christopher Vitale's useful "Guide to Reading Deleuze's Cinema II: The Time-Image, Part I: Towards a Direct Imaging of Time to Crystal-Images," which is part of his Networkologies project. https://networkologies.wordpress.com/2011/04/29/tips-for-reading-deleuzes-cinema-ii-the-time-image-towards-a-direct-imaging-of-time/
11 Deleuze (1989), 113.
12 Lippit (2005), 44.
13 From Robert Oppenheimer's infamous assertion upon witnessing the Trinity test in New Mexico on 14 July 1945: "I am become Death, the destroyer of worlds," borrowed from Hindu scripture, to the entombment of Chernobyl's remains in a "Sarcophagus" to ward off threats (Crowley and Pavitt 2008, 103).
14 Deleuze (1989), 166.

15 See Bill Morrison's *Decasia* (2002), a cinematic exploration of the decomposition of found silent-film footage. See also Christoph Keller's "Hypnosis" (2007), in which he retrieved a 1936 German science film on hypnosis that had lain deteriorating on the bottom of a lake-bed in Berlin since 1945. See also Filipa César's project "Spell Reel" on revolutionary cinema in Guinea-Bissau (1963–1974).

16 The direct reference to ancient Egypt is not incidental but is, in fact, fundamental to the ways in which strategies around nuclear waste management and storage are being developed today. Built around 2560–2540 BCE, the pyramid complex at Giza offers a paradigmatic case study for assessing the challenges of long-term nuclear containment, for what is effectively eternity. Although they clearly constitute one of the oldest standing repositories for safeguarding precious materials—namely, the pharaonic bodies of kings and queens—these ancient pyramids were frequently broken into and their contents looted. Nor was the physical landscape into which they were built immune from transformations brought about by changing climatic conditions and human activities. While the original site of the pyramid complex was geographically removed from dense patterns of settlement, today it is located in the direct vicinity of upward of seven million people as the urban sprawl of Cairo encroaches. Such human immediacy, with its attendant environmental impacts and industrial stresses, naturally impact upon the material integrity and resilience of the pyramids, despite their once robust engineering. Moreover, the hermetic and unadorned character of these monumental structures devoted to preserving their pharaohs in a state of eternal repose has not held vandals, fortune hunters, archaeologists, vendors, and tourists at bay but, on the contrary, has drawn them all ever closer. As an ancient architecture of enclosure designed to stave off external threats, the variable history of the pyramids at Giza offers a cautionary tale for considering the challenges faced by contemporary efforts at locating, designing, and managing geological repositories for the storage of intermediate-level nuclear waste, let alone those that might be required after an accident.

17 Krauss (1981), 26.

18 See Benjamin (1972)

19 In the scene depicting the Donbass miners digging a tunnel underneath the destroyed reactor, Shevchenko uses the audio from *Stalker*'s tracking shot of the railway work car when the characters cross into the Zone, complete with the electronic effects that Tarkovsky wove into the score. Thanks to Jonathan Littell for bringing this audio reference to my attention.

20 Tyrkin (2001), 2.

21 See Virilio (2000), 212.

22 Virilio (2007), 5.

23 "The Nuclear Power Industry in the Ukraine," *Soviet Life*, 8 February 1986. Statement by Vitali Sklyarov, Minister of Power and Electrification for the Soviet Ukraine, concerning the safety of the Chernobyl nuclear power plant. A shift superintendent at Chernobyl added that "working at the plant is safer than driving a car" (Hartke 1987, 319).

24 The deteriorating state of the Sarcophagus has been the subject of several architectural competitions to design a more permanent and secure burial structure, all of which have come to naught due to the lack of financial resources in the Ukraine for what would become the world's most ambitious work of engineering to date.

25 "At present, the power plant is decommissioned. Some fifteen thousand people conduct maintenance work or service the Zone of Exclusion" (Petryna 2004, 252).
26 Van Wyck (2004), 19.
27 "Our report involved 52 respected scientists and includes information never before published in English. It challenges the UN International Atomic Energy Agency Chernobyl Forum report, which predicted 4,000 additional deaths attributable to the accident as a gross simplification of the real breadth of human suffering. The new data, based on Belarus national cancer statistics, predicts approximately 270,000 cancers and 93,000 fatal cancer cases caused by Chernobyl. The report also concludes that on the basis of demographic data, during the last 15 years, 60,000 people have additionally died in Russia because of the Chernobyl accident, and estimates of the total death toll for the Ukraine and Belarus could reach another 140,000" (Greenpeace 2006).
28 "Defendants Bruchanov V. P., the director of Chernobyl NPP, 52 years old, Fomin N. M., the chief engineer of Chernobyl NPP, 50 years old, Diatlov A. S., the deputy chief engineer of Chernobyl NPP, 56 years old, Kovalenko A. P., the chief reactor hall-2, 45 years old, Laushkin U. A., the inspector of Gosatomenergonadzor in Chernobyl NPP, Rogozkin B. V., the station shift supervisor, 53 years old, are accused of the crime described in the clause 220, part 2, of the Criminal Code of Ukrainian SSR, which implies responsibility for breaking the accident prevention rules in highly explosive plants that led to serious consequences and human sacrifices. Furthermore, accusations were brought on the basis of clauses 165 and 167 of the Criminal Code of Ukrainian SSR, for abuse of power, prevarication and irresponsibility during course of duty."
29 Chicago Tribune (1987).
30 Karpan (2001), 61.
31 "A state injured by radiation will first have to prove that the Soviet Union was responsible for the accident. According to the doctrine of state responsibility, there is a concomitant duty of reparation. An injured state must then prove the Soviet Union liable under international law for the damage sustained. Proving liability may be difficult, depending upon which of the many theories a victim state chooses to assert. The arsenal of theories includes negligence, enterprise liability, strict liability, trespass, and nuisance. A theory must be chosen in light of the type of remedy it affords. Traditional remedies include compensation and injunction. The above-outlined procedure is complex and difficult to administer. One impediment to the implementation of this procedure is that injured nations rarely agree to submit their claims to an international tribunal for adjudication" (Hartke 1987, 321).
32 Flanders (2013).
33 International Atomic Energy Agency (1956). The IAEA was created in response to the deep fears and great expectations resulting from the discovery of nuclear energy, fears and expectations that have changed profoundly since 1945 and continue to fluctuate. As a result, what the IAEA is asked to do about nuclear energy—and indeed, what it can do and does—are much affected by the vicissitudes of national moods, international politics, and technological change. The IAEA's history illustrates these points. Its genesis was President Eisenhower's address to the General Assembly of the United Nations on December 8 1953, though many of the ideas he presented had earlier roots. Diplomats and lawyers, advised by scientists, and drawing on the precedents set by other organizations, developed these ideas into the charter of an international agency, the IAEA Statute, which 81 nations unanimously approved in October 1956 (Fischer 1997, 1).

4: Hearsay

1 See McNichol (2002), 3.
2 NARA (2002b), 2–3.
3 See the National Archives website for more detailed information. http://www.archives.gov/
4 Gerald R. Ford Library and Museum (2006).
5 Paraphrased from Gerald R. Ford Library and Museum (2006).
6 "Although the missing 18 and a half minutes reinforced allegations of a cover up, Nixon was nailed by a different tape—known as the 'smoking gun'—of a conversation three days after his discussion with Haldeman. The president is heard plotting to get the CIA to block the FBI investigation into the Watergate break-in on the pretext of national security. Watergate prosecutors concluded that amounted to criminal conspiracy. Nixon resigned on 9 August 1974, three days after the tape was made public. His successor, Gerald Ford, pardoned Nixon of crimes connected to Watergate" (McGreal 2011).
7 Richard Nixon, in a press interview, 1957 (Time 1973, 15).
8 Lewis (2005).
9 Time (1973), 15.
10 Excerpt from the technical report detailing the operational requirements to erase and re-record sections of Tape 342 (Bolt et al. 1974, 81).
11 Hiss was still convicted on related charges in 1948, in what is seen today as woeful mistreatment by the justice system. See the analysis of this incident in Miller (1999), 265–266.
12 McNichol (2002).
13 See Attali (1985), 33.
14 Vanhanen (2001), 1.
15 Lardner (1973), A01.
16 McNichol (2002), 4.
17 Ibid., 5.
18 Paraphrased from ibid.
19 Ibid.
20 Grosz (1999), 18.
21 NARA archivist John Carlin in NARA (2003).
22 Ibid.
23 "[T]he question of the archive is not, we repeat, a question of the past. ... It is a question of the future, the question of the future itself, the question of a response, of a promise and of a responsibility for tomorrow. The archive: if we want to know what that will have meant, we will only know in times to come, later on or perhaps never. A spectral messianicity is at work in the concept of the archive and ties it, like religion, like history, like science itself, to a very singular experience of the promise" (Derrida 1995, 36).
24 Foucault (2002), 146.
25 Bennett (2010).
26 Kahn (1999), 158.
27 Ibid., 159.
28 Cage (1979), 179.

29 Kahn (1999), 164.
30 Ibid.
31 Attali (1985), 26–27.
32 Barthes (1981), 82.
33 "Phonographies" in Derrida and Stiegler (2005), 107.
34 See Altman (1992), 24–26.
35 Ibid., 24.
36 Morelle (2012).
37 Ibid.
38 Analyzing a series of museum exhibitions in the summer of 2013, musician and critic Seth Kim-Cohen has argued that their turn toward ambience, exemplified by an interest in passive, experiential projects, positions contemporary art as a depoliticizing form that washes over us rather than alerts us to the fierce politics of our time. Yet as the case of the "mains frequency" highlights, ambience is being measured and quantified, and is therefore an acoustic condition that can be instrumentalized, and thus also repoliticized (Kim-Cohen 2016).
39 Socrates speaking to Phaedrus, cited by Derrida (2004), 137.
40 The Uher 5000 tape recorder used by Rose Mary Woods in transcribing Nixon's audio recordings does have an additional "Diction" button, but the Sony TC-800B used by Nixon to record his conversations had the usual five buttons.
41 "The evening broadcast of *ABC World News Tonight* on November 15 demonstrated that Woods would have had to have been in a contorted stretching position for several minutes with her finger on the erase button while talking on the telephone in order for the tapes to have been erased accidentally" (Liebovich 2003, 100).
42 Bolt et al. (1974), 6.
43 Deleuze (1991), 17.
44 NARA archivist John W. Carlin in NARA (2003).
45 Paul Ginsberg quoted by McNichol (2002), 3.
46 Ibid.
47 Camras (1988), 37–38.
48 "When high-frequency bias is used, the record is first demagnetized with an erasing head, which subjects it to an alternating field that diminishes to zero over many cycles. The record then passes through a recording head energized by a mixture of the signal to be recorded and a steady high-frequency, high-intensity current. For audio recorders, the high-frequency component may be 30 to 400 kHz, and its intensity is usually about five to ten times as high as the average recording current. The resultant is not amplitude modulated signal but merely a mixture of high- and low-frequency fields. When the record medium is passed through the composite field, it acquires a residual magnetization according to the output versus input curve, which is linear and symmetrical. The bias is not recorded since its high frequency is beyond the capability of the system" (ibid., 45).
49 Dolar (2006).
50 The origin of the term "tape cut-up" comes from William Burroughs and Brion Gysin's experiments with splicing audiotape to create acoustic montages, or tape recorder cut-ups, as they referred to them. Lecture by Burroughs (1976).

51 Birchall (2014), 25–26.
52 Ibid., 26.
53 Campens, Cooke, and Lam (2008), 13.
54 See Keenan (2004).

5: Motion to Strike

1 Reprieve (2012).

2 See photographic exhibition *Edmund Clark: War of Terror,* Imperial War Museums, 28 July 2016—28 August 2017, London.

3 President Obama signed three executive orders on 22 January 2009, directing the CIA to shut what remains of its network of secret prisons, and ordered the closing of the Guantánamo detention camp within a year.

4 "You know, due process to most of us is a court of law, it's a trial by a jury. And right now, their process is him [Obama] looking at some flash cards and a power point presentation on 'terror Tuesdays' in the White House. For a lot of us, that's not really due process." Senator Rand Paul on Obama's 23 May 2013 foreign policy address at the National Defense University, Washington, DC, in which he addressed the legal use of drones.

5 Foreign Affairs Symposium "The Price of Privacy: Re-Evaluating the NSA," debate between General Michael Hayden and Dr. David Cole. Johns Hopkins University, 1 April 2014.

6 Given the near-complete absence of communications technologies in FATA, survivors of drone strikes may testify only long after the fact when interviewed by lawyers or journalists outside of the region. Reporting of female deaths, for example, also often goes unnoted due to tribal customs that shy away from publicly naming deceased wives and sisters.

7 http://www.thebureauinvestigates.com/2011/08/10/obama-2011-strikes/

8 Interview with Mohammad Kausar (anonymized name), in Islamabad, Pakistan, 26 February 2012 (International Human Rights and Conflict Resolution Clinic 2012, 84).

9 Lavallee (2013).

10 See McChrystal (2013), 226.

11 Chris Woods, then Project Leader of "Covert Drone Wars" at the Bureau of Investigative Journalism, provided me with this estimate. As Chris notes, if we make a comparison of armed drone sorties in Afghanistan to Pakistan, data provided to the Bureau last year for Afghanistan showed that for every 30 armed drone sorties, only one would result in an actual strike. If we used that formula for FATA, under the Obama years, we might expect:

2009: 53 strikes = c. 1500 sorties
2010: 128 strikes = c. 3800 sorties
2011: 75 strikes = c. 2250 sorties
2012: 48 strikes = c. 1500 sorties
2013: Jan-June 14 strikes = c. 420 sorties

http://www.thebureauinvestigates.com/2012/12/04/revealed-us-and-britain-launched-1200-drone-strikes-in-recent-wars/

12 Survivor of a drone strike in Mir Ali, FATA Pakistan. Anon. "4.10.2010 Mir Ali Drone Strike." Ed. Schüller, Andreas. Witness Declaration ed. Berlin: ECCHR, 2013., 1.
13 It is by no means a conceptual vagary that the drone continues to assume a filial link with the insecta class of nature. A new generation of Micro Air Vehicles, or MAVs, based upon the morphologies of insects, are being developed; their sensors will enable them to find, track, and target adversaries, while operating in even less perceptible/detectable ways than the current generation of armed drones. See Russia Today (2013).
14 Data is gathered by its various sensors (including electro-optical and infrared cameras as well as synthetic aperture radar) and relayed back to an operator in Nevada through a system of secure data links with only a 1.2 second delay in transmission relay. 5,000 to 25,000 feet is the altitude ceiling of a typical US Predator drone.
15 Reprieve (2012), 1.
16 See Georgia Tech Research Institute (2009).
17 For a discussion of the technical failures of drone technology, see Benjamin (2013), 23–24.
18 See Sadasivan and Sekar (2001). See also Marmaroli, Falourd, and Lissek (n.d.); Wilshire and Chesnut (1993).
19 International Human Rights and Conflict Resolution Clinic (2012).
20 Ibid., 81.
21 Lavallee (2013).
22 Hill (2010).
23 For example: "The Ministry of Defence has confirmed that a device that can be used as a 'sonic weapon' will be deployed in London during the Olympics. The American-built long-range acoustic device (LRAD), which has been used by the US army to control crowds in Iraq, can emit an ear-piercing beam of sound. An MoD spokesman said the device, which can also be used as a loudspeaker, was among a 'broad range of assets' being used by the armed forces to provide security during the Games" (Guardian 2012).
24 B'Tselem (2010).
25 Ibid.
26 Thank you to Eitan Diamond, Legal Adviser ICRC, for bringing this legal petition to my attention.
27 "(1) The use of sound passes [sonic booms] by the IDF has an intended military purpose that is operationally significant, which is disrupting the capabilities of terrorists, deterrence and reducing the opportunities to continue to harm the State of Israel and its citizens, among others, by launching rockets, creating sense of confusion, Disinformation, danger and surveillance. Making supersonic passes is designed to achieve a purpose that is legal and permitted (principle of military necessity);

(2) The use of sonic passes is not directed towards targeting civilians but against legitimate targets—those who engage in terrorism against Israel and its citizens. Consciousness and psychological effects, expressed feelings of anxiety and fear among the civilian population, as those caused during the execution of sonic passes (and this has not been proven), are considered minor and incidental results for which the passes are made, and legitimate under the law of war. This is typical of the effects of the many means and realities of combat (the principle of distinction);

(3) Even if the damage caused to the civilian population and property (and even this has not been proven), this is incidental, very minor, which are entirely disproportionate to the military advantage outperforms these passes (principle of proportionality); (4) supersonic passes do not cause 'unnecessary suffering' of enemy fighters (the principle of humanity)." Israeli High Court of Justice (2006.)

28 Suisman (2015), 170.

29 See Goodman (2010); also Daughtry (2015).

30 Serle and Woods (2013). See also Strawser (2010).

31 Witness to a drone strike in Datta Khel, FATA Pakistan, 17 March 2011.

32 McVeigh (2013).

33 Barlow, Chorpita, and Turovsky (1996), cited in Chua et al. (1999), 563.

34 BBC (2009).

6: Damages

1 Incidents of military mistakes, friendly fire, and the killing of unarmed civilians were frequent during the Vietnam War, including the shocking massacre that took place at the My Lai hamlet in South Vietnam on 16 March 1968: more than 500 innocent women, children, and elderly men were killed by marauding American troops. Only one man, Lieutenant William L. Calley, Jr., was ever found guilty of this mass violence, but in 1974 his conviction was overturned, releasing him from further imprisonment.

2 Pyle (2000).

3 Keenan (2002).

4 Ibid., 10.

5 Latour and Weibel (2005).

6 Fass and Fulton (1998).

7 O'Brian (1996), 3–22.

8 "What is the photographer's ethical responsibility to the vulnerable subject? Is a living corpse, such as the image of the Sudanese child suggests, capable of being a proper subject? Can photography itself breathe life into this lifeless body in order to win it recognition as to be counted among the living? In short, can Carter's picture confer on this nameless child the status of personhood? These questions are raised here not only in relation to the image but in recognition of a broader debate directed at reaching an equilibrium between pictorial concern and violence in representation." Kevin Carter's image appeared in the *New York Times* on 26 March 1993. See Enwezor (2006), 18.

9 Shaw (2016).

10 In 1992, during an airline stopover in Newfoundland en route to Cuba, where she was studying at the University of Havana, Phúc defected to Canada, where she still lives (Chong 2000).

11 Ibid., 5–6.

12 Lumb (2010).

13 An excerpt detailing Ut's search for his lost negatives follows:

> When Nick Ut returned to the Saigon bureau of Associated Press in the afternoon of June 8, 1972 he brought back eight rolls of black and white Kodak film (400 ASA) from the events around Trang Bang on that day, more than 240 exposures. Most of the original film has disappeared.

> Some was discarded already in Saigon or returned to Nick Ut. In line with AP's policy at the time all possibly useful negatives were forwarded to New York headquarters: This included material selected in the first and second editing process in Saigon and most of the negatives not used. In New York the photo desk passed the material to the Photo Library—to be eventually discarded there, most likely in a big clean-out after the end of the Vietnam war. Negatives of pictures that were used for the wires were archived.
>
> Today 12 negatives of the "Kim Phúc incident" remain with AP. They are locked in a safe and rarely touched. The Pulitzer winning negative (1973 award) shows a major scratch across the sky in the upper part of the negative. The original image has been digitally reconstructed and full-size and cropped print versions of the picture are now produced from this digital information. The pictures used and transmitted from the original film in June 1972 are preserved in the AP's digital archive.
>
> After the war Huynh Cong "Nick" Ut began a search for the remaining material. Working temporarily in the Tokyo AP office from 1975 to 1977, he found a small selection of prints and nineteen original negatives—material that somehow ended up in Tokyo. He now has both in his private collection. The negatives and prints show some of the military operations on the same day, before the "Kim Phúc incident" and add important information to the basic material in the AP Photo Library. (Pyle 2000, 2.)

14 Fehrenbach and Rodogno (2015).

15 Levin, Wong, and Harding (2016).

16 Roberts (2012).

17 Fass and Fulton (1998).

18 DeLanda (2003), 192.

19 Johnston (1999), 27–29.

20 "What can't be coded can be decoded if an ear aye seize what no eye ere grieved for" (Joyce 1976, 482). See also Johnston (1999).

21 See Azoulay (2008).

22 Colonel Jack Broughton cited in Virilio (1989), 84.

23 Lenoir (2002), 375.

24 Wiener (2007).

25 Hayles (1999), 32–33.

26 See ibid., 103.

27 Benjamin (1999), 72.

28 See photo theorist Ariella Azoulay's project *Different Ways Not to Say Deportation*, a collection of drawings and captions for "unshowable" photographs taken in Palestine in 1947–1950, gathered from the International Committee of the Red Cross archives in Geneva (Azoulay 2013).

29 Hunt (2008), 230.

30 Hariman and Lucaites (2007).

31 The US National Archives and Records Administration made public another 500 hours from the 3,700 hours of "Nixon White House Tapes" recorded illegally between 1971 and 1973. This tape release documents conversations recorded primarily during 1972 between then-President Richard Nixon and his staff in which they discuss methods for escalating the conflict in Vietnam, as well as for responding to the mounting domestic opposition to the war (NARA 2002a).

32"Digital technologies in fact have a remarkably weak connection to the virtual, by virtue of the enormous power of their systematization of the possible" (Massumi 2002a, 137).

33 "The Uses of Afro-Pessimism," in Enwezor (2006), 11.

34 Ibid., 18.

35 Solomon-Godeau (1991), 180.

36 https://www.tate.org.uk/whats-on/tate-britain/exhibition/turner-prize-2018
37 Hariman and Lucaites (2007), 182.

7: Toxic Tort

1 See Zierler (2011), 2.
2 Cited in Blaser (1992), 343.
3 Quoted in Noam Chomsky's 1971 foreword to Russell (1967).
4 League of Nations (1925).
5 Zierler (2011), 2.
6 "About 60 percent of the herbicides used in Vietnam was Agent Orange. More than 45 million litres of it were used from 1962–1970. An additional 28 million litres of Agents White, Blue, Purple, Pink and Green were also sprayed" (Stellman et al. 2003).
7 Weinstein (2005).
8 Cited in Rabin (1989), 815.
9 United States District Court (1984).
10 Schuck (1987), 4–5.
11 Ibid., 9. See also Martini (2012).
12 Jasanoff (1995). See also Schuppli (2014).
13 "The field is not a distinct, stand-alone object, nor the neutral background on or against which human action takes place, but a dense fabric of lateral relations, associations, and chains of activity that mediates between the scales and material tendencies of large environments, individuals, and collective action. It overflows any map that seeks to frame it because there are always more connections and relations to be made in excess of its frame. Field causalities challenge contemporary epistemologies because they demand a shift in explanatory models and structures of causation." https://www.forensic-architecture.org/lexicon/field-causality/
14 Schuck (1987), 9.
15 Weinstein quoted in ibid., 114.
16 Weinstein quoted in ibid., 115.
17 Peter Schuck quoting Judge Weinstein in Schuck (1987), 114.
18 Jasanoff (1987), 447.
19 "At the time, the settlement for $180 million was the largest in history. It was to be paid out by the companies in proportion to the amount of herbicides they produced and the degree of the dioxin contamination in the respective 2,4,5-T; as a result, Dow got off rather lightly, having the 'cleanest' herbicides. The settlement was invested, growing into a fund of approximately $330 million by the time the distribution and legal technicalities were worked out. The fund mailed out its first checks to veterans in March of 1989. Those who were rated 100% disabled were eligible to receive a settlement of up to $12,800 paid out over 10 years. For those who had already died of Agent Orange-related illnesses, their survivors were eligible to receive a settlement of $3400. The Fund closed in 1997 after it distributed $197 million in payment to about 52,000 American veterans and their families. The average payment was $3800. The fund also distributed $74 million to social service programs that helped 239,000 veterans. Australian veterans received approximately $7 million of the settlement and New Zealand veterans about $1 million. Legal

fees for the lawyers involved in the case made up almost $50 million of the total fund." http://www.agentorangerecord.com/information/the_quest_for_additional_relief/

20 "Judge Jack Weinstein, like any judge presiding over complex litigation, had tremendous power to frame the legal issues and control the timing of the case, and he used his power to push the parties toward settlement. He warned the defendants that they might not fare so well before a Brooklyn jury. And he all but told the plaintiffs that they would lose a trial on the issue of whether Agent Orange actually caused their health problems. He set a rushed trial schedule that made it even less likely that the plaintiffs could develop a solid case" (Stone 1987, 372–373).

21 "In his analysis of media coverage of the first Gulf War, French film critic Serge Daney proposed a conceptual distinction between the 'image,' which he qualified as cinematic, and the 'visual,' which he attributed to the media (television, advertising, techno-military images)" (Blümlinger 2003, 112; quote by Daney reprinted in Daney 1991).

22 Hecht (2018), 111.

23 Ibid., 112. Thanks to my colleague Kodwo Eshun for making this useful observation.

24 Ibid., 115.

8: Cross-Examination

1 Behar (2014), 81.

2 Ibid.

3 Ibid., 83.

4 ICTY (2002), 9424–9425.

5 Ibid., 9441.

6 Ibid., 9457–9458.

7 Loshi testified as to the videotaping of the massacres at Izbica and Padalishte in the trials of both Slobodan Milošević (September 2002) and Vlastimir Đorđević in relationship to the proceedings against Milan Milutinović (October 2006).

8 Behar (2014), 76.

9 "The Cultural Politics of Preservation in Globalization" Kosovo fieldtrip and seminar was organized by Andrew Herscher and Gayatri Chakravorty Spivak, 16–19 May 2011.

10 An expression coined by journalist Ed Vulliamy in describing the Balkans.

11 "To educate the image-making medium within us, raising it to a stereoscopic and dimensional seeing into the depths of historical shadows." These words are from Rudolf Borchardt's *Epilegomena zu Dante*, vol. 1 (Berlin, 1923), cited in Benjamin (1999), 458.

12 http://revision-film.eu/en/2/synopsis

13 ICTY (1999), 3.

14 Description translated from the French report (TPIY 1999, 3).

15 ICTY (2006), 5369–5371.

16 Kirsten (2013), 247.

17 http://unsrct-drones.com (Emmerson 2014). See the "Secrets" section of Forensic Architecture (2014), 361–480.

18 Purdy and Macrory (2003).

19 It is also interesting to note that the ICTY's Outreach Programme produces its own documentary films—seven of which are available online—taking this practice of "re-processing of legal material" to another level and into quite another domain. http://www.icty.org/en/in-focus/documentaries

20 ICTY (2006), 5390–5391.

21 See Bensaude-Vincent and Stengers (1996), 206. See also Barry (2010), 90.

22 ICTY (2009a), 793.

23 ICTY (2002), 9484–9485.

24 Felman (2002), 131–151.

25 Deleuze (2004), 49.

26 Mr. Dan Ivetić was one of the attorneys assigned to represent Sreten Lukić relative to the Milan Milutinović proceedings (ICTY 2006, 5391).

27 Bob Reid (ICTY Chief of Operations) in discussion with the author, August 2013.

28 ICTY (2002), 9443.

29 Ibid., 9427.

30 ICTY (2006), 5391.

9: Expert Witness

1 ICTY (1998c), 3880–3897.

2 ICTY (1998b), 3768.

3 ICTY (1998a), 1878.

4 Matheson (2015).

5 Goldstone (1995).

6 Slavko Dokmanović was charged on the basis of his individual criminal responsibility (Article 7(1)) and, or alternatively, superior criminal responsibility (Article 7(3) of the Statute)) with: Willfully causing great suffering; willful killing (Grave breaches of the Geneva Conventions, Article 2(c)); Murder; cruel treatment (violations of the laws or customs of war, Article 3); Murder; inhumane acts (crimes against humanity, Article 5 (a) and (i)). He pleaded "not guilty" to all charges on 4 July 1997.

7 Stone (1972).

8 Ibid., 463.

9 Tavares (2014), 553. See also "Ecology and the Law," in Gómez-Barris (2017), 27–29.

10 Dewey (1926).

11 Stone (1972), 452.

12 In my research, I stumbled upon only one case where a nonhuman entity testified entirely of their own accord. In a hearing before the French Court on 10 September 2008, a dog named Scooby was enlisted as a material witness in a suicide case in which there was suspicion of wrongdoing. Judge Thomas Cassuto called Scooby, who was believed to have been at his owner's side when she died, to the stand to see how he would react when confronted with a potential suspect. The dog was said to have "barked furiously," convincing the Judge to go forward with a murder

inquiry. "A spokesman for the Palais de Justice in Paris said the incident marked the first time an animal had been called to testify in France. He said he was 'almost certain' the testimony was unprecedented on the global scale as well." The dog's agitated response to the suspect was accepted as a convincing form of legally admissible speech without the need for interpretation or mediation on the part of an expert witness such as a veterinarian or animal behaviorist. Rather, the general or popular understanding of canine comportment as highly sensitive and fiercely loyal to its owner was sufficient for the Judge to assess the dog's reaction with apparent confidence and assign a particular and incriminatory significance to its barking. The dog had, in effect, spoken (United Press International 2008).
13 ICTY (1998c), 3806–3849.
14 See Kahan (2009). See also Sherwin (2007).
15 See Gates (2013); Scheeres (2002).
16 Levin (2002), 592.
17 ICTY (2009b), 3791–3797.
18 ICTY (1998c), 3880.
19 Ibid., 3874–3875.
20 "Available online": "Poplars and willows are multi-purpose species and form an important component of forestry and agricultural production systems worldwide, often owned by small-scale farmers. They provide a long list of wood and fibre products (sawn lumber, veneer, plywood, pulp and paper, packing crates, pallets, poles, furniture and small handicraft), non-wood products (animal fodder), environmental services (rehabilitation of degraded lands, forest landscape restoration, climate change mitigation) and are grown increasingly in bio-energy plantations for the production of biofuels. These attributes make poplars and willows ideally suited for supporting rural livelihoods, enhancing food security, alleviating poverty and contributing to sustainable land-use and rural development." http://www.fao.org/forestry/ipc/en/. Accessed 16.01.16.
21 In the Grabez case, the court found that the testimony was probably arrived at through coercion, and therefore perjurious, which served to confirm the Defendant's alibi, and in the other, the capacity for recall on the part of the eyewitness was deemed to be diminished as a consequence of their harrowing experience, thus also producing a ruling in favour of the Defendant (ICTY 1998a, 1879–2880).
22 See Capra and Mattei (2015).
23 ICTY (1998c), 3879–3901.

10: Burden of Proof

1 Cook-Anderson and Beasley (2005).
2 Professor Thorne Lay, Seismology Laboratory, Earth and Marine Sciences, University of California, Santa Cruz (Walton 2005).
3 See Weizman (2011).
4 Majumder (2005).
5 Kuhn (2009), 3.
6 *Material Witness*, Dir. Schuppli, Cinematography Steffen Kraemer, 2014–2015, 33.30 mins.

7 Miller (2009).
8 The group consisting of exiled writers, journalists, and human right defenders formed in Berlin on 18 July 2009 as Journalists for Democracy in Sri Lanka.
9 Nancy (2005).
10 Miller (2009).
11 "Since the video's release, the Government of Sri Lanka has claimed that the video is a fake. Over the past four months, I [Philip Alston] have been engaged in a series of communications with the Government about this video, in which I requested it to conduct an independent investigation. While the Government initially refused to do so, on 7 September 2009, it issued a response stating that it had commissioned four separate investigations, and that they 'have now scientifically established beyond any doubt that this video is a fake'" (Alston 2010b, 1).
12 Heyns (2011), 424.
13 Government of Sri Lanka (2009), 3.
14 Foucault (2002), 146.
15 Alston (2010b), 1.
16 Alston (2010a).
17 UN News Center (2010).
18 "Second, the white uppercase 'A' against a red background present for the final 17 frames of VideoDJ.3GP: according to published information from NXP Software, VideoStudio provides the ability to add titles and graphics. It is quite plausible that the producer of VideoDJ.3GP added this text/logo at the end of the video segment, though only those responsible can explain its significance." Report of Mr. Jeff Spivack, a forensic video analyst, reproduced in Heyns (2011), 427.
19 Ibid. 443.
20 http://physiciansforhumanrights.org/justice-forensic-science/ifp/
21 Gates (2013), 243.
22 Channel 4 has produced three documentaries covering the final months of Sri Lanka's civil war: Macrae (2011, 2012, 2013). Sri Lanka responded with its own documentary.
23 Ratnayake (2011); Engage Sri Lanka (2013); Weeratunga (2011).
24 Telephone interview conducted with Jonathan Miller (London, 30 May 2012).
25 Engage Sri Lanka (2013), 160.
26 Miller (2009).
27 Engage Sri Lanka (2013), 164.
28 See, for example, "US condemns troops who allegedly posed with dead suicide bombers in Afghanistan," *World News on msnbc.com*, 18 April 2012; and "Army Investigates Photos of Iraqi War Dead on Web," *New York Times*, 27 September 2005. Engage Sri Lanka (2013), 164.
29 Stover and Weinstein (2004), 85.
30 See International Crisis Group http://www.crisisgroup.org/en/regions/asia/south-asia/sri-lanka.aspx
31 Hume and Dhillon (2007).
32 "I found that the conduct of the responding members fell short of that expected of members of the RCMP. The members demonstrated no meaningful attempt to deescalate the situation, nor did they approach the situation with a measured, coordinated and appropriate response. The failure of the senior member to take control of the scene, communicate with and direct the

more junior and inexperienced members negatively manifested itself throughout the interaction with Mr. Dziekanski. I do not accept the version of events as presented by the four responding RCMP members. The statements provided by the members are sparse in terms of detail of the events and the thought processes of the members as events unfolded. When tracked against the witness video, the recollections of the members fall short of a credible statement of the events as they actually unfolded. The fact that the members met together prior to providing statements causes me to further question their versions of events." KEY CONCLUSIONS FROM THE COMMISSION'S PUBLIC INTEREST INVESTIGATION AND INTERIM REPORT (Kennedy 2009, 1).
33 CBS News (2009).
34 Ibid.
35 Heyns (2011).
36 The British Tamil Forum supplied this video to Channel 4 (Macrae 2014, accessed 24 August 2015).
37 Ibid.
38 Kim and Jeffery (2014), 79.
39 McLagan and McKee (2012), 12.
40 Cogan (2000), 405.
41 See the Forensic Architecture investigation into the Israeli attack on the Salha family home in Beit Lahiya, Gaza, on 9 January 2009, http://www.forensic-architecture.org/case/drone-strikes/
42 Rajasingham (2006).
43 Sengupta (2015), A4.
44 Tamil Guardian (2015).
45 International Crisis Group (2018), 5.
46 ICTY (2002), 9443.
47 High Commissioner for Human Rights (2015).

11: Failure to Appear

1 "Soviet atomic bomb testing in Novaya Zemlya in the 1950s and 1960s produced contamination in reindeer that went unregulated. Herders affected by Chernobyl were shocked to learn that in the 1960s, Swedish reindeer carried contamination levels of 3,000 Bq/kg, a level 10 times the marketability maximum set by the state in 1986." (Blackwell 2003, 2). Sweden would go on to amend its risk calculus the following year and reset its acceptable dosage rates from 300 Bq/kilo to 1,500 Bq/kilo to accommodate a much greater intake of tainted water and food. Norway also followed suited and recalibrated their own maximum exposure levels in response to Chernobyl but none of these risk thresholds ever corresponded between one another.
2 Hashimoto et al. (2012), 1.
3 "A study of soil contamination in the Red Forest found 90% of the strontium documented in 2001 was located in the top 10 cm of the soil. Blame—or credit—the forest, says Sergiy Zibtsev, an associate professor of forestry at the National University of Life and Environmental Sciences of Ukraine in Kiev. Trees, grasses, other plants, and fungi trap radionuclides through their basic life cycle: When leaves and needles transpire (release water), the plant draws more water up from

the roots. Water-soluble salts of caesium and strontium are chemical analogs of potassium and calcium, respectively, and are taken up in place of these crucial nutrients. In evergreens, Zibtsev explains, the radionuclides gradually accumulate in needles as each season progresses. The needles then fall to the ground, becoming part of the 'litter'—the discarded vegetation that covers the forest floor—and returning the radioactive salts to the top layer of the soil in a natural cycle he says takes 10 to 12 years to complete. Without the trees or other permanent groundcover, Zibtsev adds, contaminants would migrate out, blown in dust or carried by water." (Braxton and Bird 2013, A80)

4 The implicit reference to the Franco-Japanese film *In the Realm of the Senses* (directed Nagisa Oshima, 1976) is useful here, in that its highly controversial sexual subject matter required that the film be optically censored using reframing and blurring.

5 Barthes (1981), 80.

6 Leopold (2001), 179.

7 Keenan (2004).

8 With the advent of machine learning, many contemporary forms of violence, from financial transactions to military conflicts, are no longer organized by the thresholds of human perception. See Schuppli (2014); also Schuppli (2017).

9 Nixon (2011), 13.

10 See Peter Sloterdijk's discussion of the advent of gas warfare, as well as his discussion of Zyklon B (Sloterdijk 2009, 9–46).

11 Becquerel (1896), 420–421.

12 Wilder (2009), 165.

13 Bradley (1948).

14 Joint Task Force One (1946), 216. See also Bradley (1948), 125.

15 Masco (2006), 306.

16 Film theorist Akira Mizuta Lippit advances the concept of avisuality when he reflects upon a comment made by the late abstract expressionist painter Willem de Kooning with respect to the "radical visuality" produced by the atomic bomb. "The advent of atomic light signaled, for de Kooning, the absolute transformation of visual representation," inaugurating a new kind of seeing freed by the nuclear foreclosure of figuration's traditional symbolic economy. In the apocalyptic forces unleashed by the bomb, de Kooning located a "transcendent" sublime, as everyone was momentarily reduced to colorless transparency and dispersed into the radioactive dust of angels. Lippit argues that de Kooning's "sadistic metaphysics" confuses the radical avisuality of atomic light with a kind of religious fervor that maps a "redemptive" narrative onto the conversion of the physical body into ghostly spirit matter by the sheer visceral and spectral force of atomic energy (Lippit 2005, 81).

17 Fackler (2015).

18 McNeill (2011).

19 Fackler (2015).

20 Ibid.

21 Kikuchi (2017).

22 Ibid.

12: Closing Arguments

1 Stengers has suggested that we call such an innovative hypothesis a "propositional fiction" in that it may not be verifiable today, or even tomorrow, but that as a proposition it holds out the possibility of becoming fact at a later date. A point she illustrates by referring to the example of Wegener's theory of continental drift, which was retroactively proven to be true by evidence furnished by the Earth's tectonic plates. "To speak of fiction concerning an innovative scientific proposition does not mean saying its only fiction." Stengers (1997), 136–137.

2 See Vidal (2007).

3 http://www.forensic-architecture.org/case/living-death-camps/

4 Vulliamy (2004).

5 Ibid.

6 "Despite the scale of the atrocities, after a careful analysis of the facts and the state of mind of the actors, the Trial Chamber was unable to infer the necessary *dolus specialis* for genocide, this *dolus specialis*—or specific intent to destroy, in whole or in part, a group as such—being the core element of the crime" (ICTY 2003).

7 "To reflect the shared focus on sustainability of both the London Organising Committee of the Olympic Games (LOCOG) and ArcelorMittal, the bulk of the steel comes from Western Europe to ensure 60 percent comes from recycled scrap metal. However, ArcelorMittal has used its global reach to secure small quantities of steel from Africa, Asia, and North and South America to be part of the ArcelorMittal Orbit as well. ArcelorMittal has a presence in the following countries on these continents: Europe—Belgium, Czech Republic, France, Germany, Kazakhstan, Luxembourg, Romania, Spain, Ukraine, Poland, Africa—South Africa, Asia—China, India, N. America—Canada, United States, S. America—Brazil, Argentina, Mexico." 29 June 2011. Press release: http://www.arcelormittalorbit.com/media-centre/words/arcelormittal-orbit-embraces-olympic-spirit-with-steel-from-every-continent

8 "Five Bosnian Serbs were found guilty yesterday of committing crimes against humanity during a 'hellish orgy of persecution' against Muslims and Croats at the most notorious concentration camp [Omarska] of the 1992–1995 Bosnian war. Judge Almiro Rodrigues of Portugal passed sentences of up to 25 years and told the men that they had all known about or participated in rape, murder and persecution aimed at extinguishing the non-Serb population of northern Bosnia. Dragoljub Prca, Milojica Kos, Miroslav Kvočka and Mlado Radi were all camp commanders, and a local taxi driver, Zoran Žwere, was a regular visitor to Omarska and other camps, where he beat prisoners, often to death. … 'You enjoyed using force, you enjoyed inflicting pain. … You also enjoyed humiliating detainees by forcing them to lap up water like dogs or to drink their own blood,' the judge told Žigić." (Andrew Osborn in Brussels The Guardian, Saturday 3 November 2001, 11.58 GMT)

9 http://www.forensic-architecture.org/wp-content/uploads/2014/05/A-memorial-in-exile-in-London's-Olympics-orbits-of-responsibility-openDemocracy.pdf

10 "Can the sun lie? asked the Virginia Law Journal in 1886. Perhaps we may say that though the sun does not lie, the liar may use the sun as a tool. Let us, then, beware of the liar who lies in the name of the sun." (Thurston 1996–2009, accessed 29 March 2013).

11 Ibid.

12 See Daston and Galison (2007).
13 See Pottage (2011).
14 *Franklin v. The State of Georgia*, 69 Ga. 36 (1882).
15 Kunuk and Mauro (2010).
16 Dixon (2010).
17 "There once was a time, a time that includes the present, when scientific observation was equated with objectivity, when perception was thought to be a transparent and neutral act, and when the identification of mind and reason as incorporeal and transcendent over nature was pre-requisite to the determination of truth. Although a plethora of research in the sciences actually contests such ill-informed assertions, this cartoon representation of science fundamentals is widely held. Many science practitioners continue to explain their goals and achievements in such terms, and perhaps ironically, even cultural and social analysts who reject them may require this caricature as their interventionary departure point" (Kirby 2017).
18 Gates (2013), 626.
19 During the 1950s the Soviet Union actually experimented with accelerating glacial melt (climate forcing) by deliberately blackening snow surfaces with coal dust to boost their capacity to absorb solar radiation and thus aid in irrigation and supplement water supplies to areas affected by drought. Today vast swaths of the Arctic are wholly saturated by airborne contaminants including black-carbon deposits from industrialization that combine to "fast-track" the global melting of ice as the surface albedo of snow is reduced. "While climate forcing resulting from black-carbon contamination of snow is considered minor when averaged across the entire globe, regional forcing over the snow-covered regions of the Arctic and the Himalayas is devastating, comparable to the degree of carbon dioxide accumulation in the atmosphere since pre-industrial times." Climate models have demonstrated that the reduction of surface albedo in dark snow is itself a contributing factor to global warming and a source of the decline of ice sheets and glacial melt. Arctic snow has become an unwitting accomplice in bringing about the very changes that were directly responsible for generating its own damaged and dirty condition (Hadley and Kirchstetter 2012, 437).
20 Warren (1982); see also Grenfell and Maykut (1977); Leslie (2016).
21 See Edwards (2010).
22 James (1996).
23 Ivakhiv (2013), 338.
24 Frankel and Whitesides (2007), 8, 14.
25 Hyman, Graham, and Hansen (2007), 1.
26 Schuppli (2016).
27 Zalasiewicz et al. (2014).
28 Kahn (2013), 2–3.
29 A question already answered in part by the next-generation Blue Marbles (2002, 2005, 2010) composited out of multiple satellite image slices. See Kurgan (2013), 10–12.
30 See Gabrys (2016), 57–80.
31 Similarly, the Moss Cam generates images and daily records that contribute to a picture of seasonal patterns and "event effects." These effects might include lack of moisture in the summer, which contributes to mosses "burning through" their CO_2 reserves—in other words, higher

temperatures can correlate to an increased release of CO_2 by mosses, as they consume stored energy and move toward states of dehydration and dormancy. Here, what counts as "sensing" is not a simple matter of observing mosses through a web camera over time, but instead involves observing how the moss is a sensor, or a biomonitor that is itself detecting and responding to changes in the environment (Gabrys 2016, 44).

32 Jacques Bousquet quoted in Bachelard (1983), 3.

33 Rob Nixon contends that "there is a representational bias against slow violence" in favor of spectacular eruptions. "The representational challenges are acute, requiring creative ways of drawing public attention to catastrophic acts that are low in instant spectacle but high in long-term effects" (Nixon 2011, 13).

34 Woods Hole Oceanographic Institute (2014).

35 Mufson (2010).

36 A Center for Biological Diversity Report estimates that over 82,000 birds; about 6,000 sea turtles; and nearly 26,000 marine mammals were killed from either the initial explosion or the oil spill (Center for Biological Diversity 2011). "The U.S. Fish and Wildlife Service reported that up to 32 National Wildlife Refuges were potentially affected by the spill. Concerns were raised about the environmental impacts of chemicals known as dispersants that have been used to dissipate the oil slick. By June 2, 2010, the National Oceanic and Atmospheric Administration (NOAA) had banned fishing in about 36% of federal waters, or 229,270 sq. km of the Gulf" (Cleveland 2010, 4).

37 www.data.bsee.gov/homepg/data_center/platform/platform.asp

38 Cleveland (2010), 5.

39 Horstein (1972).

40 See Kinoshita (2008).

41 "The film of oil creates two imperfect mirrors—surfaces that are flat, approximately parallel, but only partially reflecting. A light wave first encounters the surface between the air and the oil; some of it reflects, some continues on into the oil and encounters the surface between the water and the oil. Here again, some reflects and some continues. When we look at an oil slick, we see the combination of reflected light waves. Because the two mirrors are close—the distance between them is similar to the wavelength of light—light reflecting from them interferes with itself: that is, waves of light reflecting from one mirror augment or annihilate waves reflecting from the second" (Frankel and Whitesides 2007, 14)

42 See Kahn (2013), 21.

43 Ivakhiv (2013), 338.

44 "Public Lab was founded in the wake of the 2010 BP oil disaster. During the spill, there was an information blackout for residents of the coastal region, as well as the rest of the world. No one was accurately tracking what was happening on the ground. In response a group of concerned residents, environmental advocates, designers, and social scientists lofted 'community satellites,' made from balloons, kites and digital cameras, over the spill to collect real time data about its impact. Local citizens collected the images, and through a newly created open source platform, contributors stitch over 100,000 aerial images into maps of the coastline before, during, and after the oil spread. These high-resolution maps were featured by BBC and New York Times, among others, allowing residents to speak their truth about what was going on in the Gulf Coast."

https://publiclab.org/about The success of the grassroots mapping effort galvanized the group to found Public Lab as a new research and social space for the development of low-cost tools for community-based environmental monitoring and assessment.

45 Shiva et al. (2010), 5. See also Angélica M. Bernal's discussion of the 1993 class action lawsuit *Aguinda v. Texaco, Inc.*, filed in US federal courts on behalf of indigenous communities impacted by damage to Ecuador's Amazonian rainforest, and the challenges that eco-political strategies organized by litigation confront. "Environmental disasters, particularly oil spills, increasingly involve a complex intermingling of the national, international and often the transnational. Traditional responses to seeking remediation have pursued the legal path of class action suits against multinational corporations." Bernal (2011), 143.

46 Biello (2010).

47 Toxicologist Carys Mitchelmore in ibid.

48 See the related discussion concerning Fukushima's contaminants and the challenge of proving direct causality—the condition of criminal liability—with regard to environmental crimes in chapter 2, "Discovery."

49 Galison and Jones (2010), 51.

50 Toxicologist Sergio Alex Villalobos in Biello (2010). See also National Research Council (2005), 214, 218.

51 See Alloy et al. (2015).

52 Biello (2010).

53 Virilio (2000), 212.

54 Laursen (2016); see also Barbier (2016).

55 Paulo Tavares, "Nonhuman Rights," in Forensic Architecture (2014), 557.

56 United States Supreme Court (2010).

13: Convictions

1 Stengers (2007b); see also Stengers (2007a).

References

Agamben, Giorgio. 2000. "The Witness." In *Remnants of Auschwitz: The Witness and the Archive*, 15–39. New York: Zone Books.

Aleksievich, Svetlana, Anna Gunin, and A. L. Tait. 2016. *Chernobyl Prayer: A Chronicle of the Future*. London: Penguin.

Alloy, Matthew M., Idrissa Boube, Robert J. Griffitt, James T. Oris, and Aaron P. Roberts. 2015. "Photo-induced Toxicity of Deepwater Horizon Slick Oil to Blue Crab (Callinectes sapidus) Larvae." *Environmental Toxicology and Chemistry* 34 (9): 2061–2066. doi: 10.1002/etc.3026.

Alston, Philip. 2010a. Press Conference by United Nations Human Rights Expert Concerning Authenticity of Channel 4 Videotape Depicting Extrajudicial Executions in Sri Lanka. United Nations Meetings Coverage and Press Releases. New York: United Nations.

Alston, Philip. 2010b. Technical Note prepared by the Special Rapporteur on extrajudicial, summary or arbitrary executions, Mr. Philip Alston, in relation to the authenticity of the "Channel 4 videotape." New York: United Nations.

Altman, Rick. 1992. "The Material Heterogeneity of Recorded Sound." In *Sound Theory Sound Practice*, 15–31. London: Routledge.

Amaro, Ramon. 2015. "Machine Learning and Racial Profiling in Data-driven Decision Making." Neoliberalism Conference: The Self in the Era of New Media, Goldsmiths, University of London, 10 June.

Arendt, Hannah. 1958. *The Origins of Totalitarianism*. New York: Meridian Books.

Arendt, Hannah. 1963. *Eichmann in Jerusalem: A Report on the Banality of Evil*. London: Faber and Faber.

Arendt, Hannah. 1971. "Lying in Politics: Reflections on the Pentagon Papers." *New York Review of Books* (November 18): 28.

Ascarelli, Brett. 2011. *Twenty-five Years after Chernobyl: How Sweden Found Out*. Stockholm: Radio Sweden | Sveriges Radio.

Attali, Jacques. 1985. *Noise: The Political Economy of Music*. Manchester: Manchester University Press.

Azoulay, Ariella. 2008. *The Civil Contract of Photography*. New York: Zone Books.

Azoulay, Ariella. 2013. *Different Ways Not to Say Deportation*. Vancouver: Jeff Khonsary.

Bachelard, Gaston. 1983. *Water and Dreams: An Essay on the Imagination of Matter*. Trans. Edith R. Farrell. Dallas: Pegasus Foundation.

Barad, Karen. 2003. "Posthumanist Performativity: Towards an Understanding of How Matter Comes to Matter." *Signs: Journal of Women in Culture and Society* 28 (3): 801–831.

Barad, Karen. 2007. *Meeting the Universe Halfway: Quantum Physics and the Entanglement of Matter and Meaning*. Durham: Duke University Press.

Barbier, Honorable Carl J. 2016. Consent Decree among Defendant BP Exploration and Production Inc. 2: 10-cv-04536, United States District Court for the Eastern District of Louisiana, New Orleans.

Barlow, D. H, B. F. Chorpita, and J. Turovsky. 1996. "Fear, Panic, Anxiety, and Disorders of Emotion." *Nebraska Symposium on Motivation* 43: 251–328.

Barry, Andrew. 2010. "Materialist Politics: Metallurgy." In *Political Matter: Technoscience, Democracy, and Public Life*, ed. Bruce Braun and Sarah J. Whatmore, 89–117. Minneapolis: University of Minnesota Press.

Barthes, Roland. 1981. *Camera Lucida: Reflections on Photography*. New York: Noonday Press.

Bazin, André. 1960. "The Ontology of the Photographic Image." *Film Quarterly* 13 (4): 4–9.

BBC. 2009. "Barack Obama Swats Fly Mid-interview." *News, World, America*, 17 June, http: // news.bbc.co.uk/1/hi/8104495.stm.

Becquerel, Henri. 1896. "Sur les radiations émises par phosphorescence." In *Comptes Rendus Hebdomadaires des Séances de l'Académie des Sciences*, 420–421. Paris: Gauthier-Villars.

Behar, Eliott. 2014. *Tell It to the World: International Justice and the Secret Campaign to Hide Mass Murder in Kosovo*. Toronto: Dundurn.

Benjamin, Medea. 2013. *Drone Warfare: Killing by Remote Control*. Updated edition. London: Verso.

Benjamin, Walter. 1972. "A Short History of Photography." *Screen* 13 (1): 5–26. doi: 10.1093/screen/13.1.5.

Benjamin, Walter. 1999. "The Task of the Translator." In *Illuminations*, ed. Hannah Arendt. London: Pimlico.

Bennett, Jane. 2010. *Vibrant Matter: A Political Ecology of Things*. Durham: Duke University Press.

Bensaude-Vincent, Bernadette, and Isabelle Stengers. 1996. *A History of Chemistry*. Cambridge, MA: Harvard University Press.

Bernal, Angélica M. 2011. "Power, Powerlessness and Petroleum: Indigenous Environment Claims and the Limits of Transnational Law." *New Political Science* 33 (2): 143–167.

Biello, David. 2010. "Is Using Dispersants on the BP Gulf Oil Spill Fighting Pollution with Pollution?" *Scientific American* (June).

Birchall, Clare. 2014. "Aesthetics of the Secret." *New Formations* 83 (3): 25–46.

Bishop, Ryan. 2011. "Project 'Transparent Earth' and the Autoscopy of Aerial Targeting: The Visual Geopolitics of the Underground." *Theory Culture Society* 28 (7–8): 270–286.

Blackwell, Melanie. 2003. "Effects of the Chernobyl Disaster on Sámi Life." Accessed 25 February 2015. http: //www.laits.utexas.edu/sami/dieda/socio/chernobyl.htm.

Blaser, Arthur W. 1992. "How to Advance Human Rights without Really Trying: An Analysis of Nongovernmental Tribunals." *Human Rights Quarterly* 14 (3): 339–370. doi: 10.2307/762370.

Blümlinger, Christa. 2003. "Harun Farocki: Stratégies Critiques." *Parachute* 3: 112–125.

Bolt, Richard H., Franklin So Cooper, James L. Flanagan, John G. McKnight, Thomas G. Stockham Jr, and Mark R. Weiss. 1974. "The EOB Tape of 20 June 1972: Report on a Technical Investigation Conducted for the U.S. District Court for the District of Columbia by the Advisory Panel on White House Tapes." United States District Court for the District of Columbia, Washington.

Bradley, David. 1948. *No Place to Hide*. Boston: Little, Brown.

Braxton, Jane, and Winifred A. Bird. 2013. "A Tale of Two Forests." *Environmental Health Perspectives* 121 (3): A78–A85.

Bruno, Laura A. 2003. "The Bequest of the Nuclear Battlefield: Science, Nature, and the Atom during the First Decade of the Cold War." *Historical Studies in the Physical and Biological Sciences* 33 (2): 237–260.

B'Tselem. 2010. "The Sonic Booms in the Sky over Gaza." B'Tselem, 6 May 2010, accessed 24 June. http: //www.btselem.org/gaza_strip/supersonic_booms.

Buesseler, Ken. 2016. "Fukushima Site Still Leaking after Five Years, Research Shows." Woods Hole Oceanographic Institution, last modified 7 March 2016, accessed 24 July. http: //www.whoi.edu/page.do?pid=127297.

Burney, Ian. 2013. "Our Environment in Miniature: Dust and the Early Twentieth-Century Forensic Imagination." *Representations* 121 (1). 31–59. doi: 10.1525/rep.2013.121.1.31.

Burroughs, William. 1976. "Origin and Theory of the Tape Cut-Ups." Conference, Jack Kerouac School of Disembodied Poetics. Naropa Institute.

Caffentzis, George. 1997. "Why Machines Cannot Create Value; or, Marx's Theory of Machines." In *Cutting Edge: Technology, Information, Capitalism, and Social Revolution*, ed. J. Davis, T. Hirschl, and M. Stacks. London: Verso.

Cage, John. 1979. "The Future of Music." In *Empty Words*. Middletown: Wesleyan University Press.

Campens, Angelique, Erica Cooke, and Steven Lam, eds. 2008. *For Reasons of State*. New Haven: Yale University Press.

Camras, Marvin. 1988. *Magnetic Recording Handbook*. New York: Van Nostrand Reinhold.

Capra, Fritjof, and Ugo Mattei. 2015. *The Ecology of Law: Toward a Legal System in Tune with Nature and Community*. Oakland: Berrett-Koehler.

CBS News. 2009. "Video Analyst Tells Inquiry Dziekanski was Aggressive toward Mounties." The Canadian Press, last modified 25 May 2009, accessed 4 September 2015. http: //www.cbc.ca/news/canada/video-analyst-tells-inquiry-dziekanski-was-aggressive-toward-mounties-1.812048.

Center for Biological Diversity. 2011. "A Deadly Toll: The Gulf Oil Spill and the Unfolding Wildlife Disaster." In Center for Biological Diversity, *April Report*.

Chicago Tribune. 1987. "Six Chernobyl Officials Sentenced to Prison Terms of Up to 10 Years." *Chicago Tribune*, 30 July, 1.

Chong, Denise. 2000. *The Girl in the Picture: The Remarkable Story of Vietnam's Most Famous Casualty*. New York: Simon and Schuster.

Chua, Phyllis, Michael Krams, Ivan Toni, Richard Passingham, and Raymond Dolan. 1999. "A Functional Anatomy of Anticipatory Anxiety." *NeuroImage* 9: 563–571.

Cleveland, Cutler J. 2010. "Deepwater Horizon Oil Spill." *Encyclopedia of Earth*: 37.

Clough, Patricia Ticineto, Greg Goldberg, Rachel Schiff, Aaron Weeks, and Craig Willse. 2007. "Notes Towards a Theory of Affect-Itself." *Ephemera: Theory and Politics in Organization* 7-1 (Immaterial and Affective Labour: Explored): 15.

Cogan, Jacob Katz. 2000. "The Problem of Obtaining Evidence for International Criminal Courts." *Human Rights Quarterly* (22): 404–427.

Connor, Steven. 2009. "Pulverulence." *Cabinet* 35 (Fall): 71–76.

Cook-Anderson, Gretchen, and Dolores Beasley. 2005. Release 05-0011, "NASA Details Earthquake Effects on the Earth." NASA, Washington, DC.

Crowley, David, and Jane Pavitt. 2008. *Cold War Modern: Design 1945–1970*. London: V&A.

Daney, Serge. 1991. "Montage obligé. La guerre, le Golfe et le petit écran." In *Devant la recrudescence des vols de sacs à main: Cinéma, télévision, information*. Lyon: Aléas.

Daston, Lorraine, and Peter Galison. 2007. *Objectivity*. New York: Zone Books.

Daughtry, J. Martin. 2015. *Listening to War: Sound, Music, Trauma and Survival in Wartime Iraq*. Oxford: Oxford University Press.

DeLanda, Manuel. 2003. *War in the Age of Intelligent Machines*. New York: Zone Books.

Deleuze, Gilles. 1989. *Cinema 2: The Time-Image*. Trans. Hugh Tomlinson and Barbara Habberjam. London: Continuum.

Deleuze, Gilles. 1990. *The Logic of Sense*. Trans. Mark Lester, ed. Constantin V. Boundas. New York: Columbia University Press.

Deleuze, Gilles. 1991. *Bergsonism*. Trans. Hugh Tomlinson and Barbara Habberjam. New York: Zone Books.

Deleuze, Gilles. 2004. *Francis Bacon and the Logic of Sensation*. Trans. Daniel W. Smith. London: Continuum.

Deleuze, Gilles, and Félix Guattari. 1987. *A Thousand Plateaus: Capitalism and Schizophrenia*. Trans. Brian Massumi. London: Continuum.

DeLoughrey, Elizabeth. 2014. "Satellite Planetarity and the Ends of the Earth." *Public Culture* 26 (2): 257–280.

Demos, T. J. 2013. *The Migrant Image: The Art and Politics of Documentary during Global Crisis*. Durham: Duke University Press.

Derrida, Jacques. 1988. *Ear of the Other: Otobiography, Transference, Translation*. Lincoln: University of Nebraska Press.

Derrida, Jacques. 1995. *Archive Fever: A Freudian Impression*. Trans. Eric Prenowitz. Chicago: University of Chicago Press.

Derrida, Jacques. 2004. *Dissemination*. Trans. Barbara Johnson. London: Continuum.

Derrida, Jacques, and Bernard Stiegler. 2005. *Echographies of Television: Filmed Interviews*. Trans. Jennifer Bajorek. Cambridge: Polity Press.

Dewey, John. 1926. "The Historic Background of Corporate Legal Personality." *Yale Law Journal* 35 (6): 655–673.

Didi-Huberman, Georges. 2008. *Images in Spite of All: Four Photographs from Auschwitz*. Chicago: University of Chicago Press

Dixon, Guy. 2010. "New Documentary Recounts Bizarre Climate Changes Seen by Inuit Elders." *Globe and Mail*, 19 October.

Dolar, Mladen. 2006. *A Voice and Nothing More*. Cambridge, MA: MIT Press.

Doyle, Richard. 1997. *On beyond Living: Rhetorical Transformations of the Life Sciences*. Stanford: Stanford University Press.

Drumbl, Mark A. 1998. "Waging War against the World: The Need to Move from War Crimes to Environmental Crimes." *Fordham International Law Journal* 22 (1): 122–153.

Edwards, Paul N. 2010. *A Vast Machine: Computer Models, Climate Data, and the Politics of Global Warming*. Cambridge, MA: MIT Press.

Emmerson, Ben, QC. 2014. "Report of the Special Rapporteur on the Promotion and Protection of Human Rights and Fundamental Freedoms while Countering Terrorism." United Nations Human Rights Council, Geneva.

Engage Sri Lanka. 2013. *Corrupted Journalism: Channel 4 and Sri Lanka*. Great Britain: Engage Sri Lanka.

Enwezor, Okwui. 2006. *Snap Judgments: New Positions in Contemporary African Photography*. New York: Steidl Publishing.

Eshun, Kodwo, and Ros Gray. 2011. "The Militant Image: A Ciné-Geography." *Third Text* 25 (1): 1–12. doi: 10.1080/09528822.2011.545606.

Fackler, Martin. 2015. "4 Years after Fukushima Nuclear Calamity, Japanese Divided on Whether to Return." *New York Times*, 8 August 2015, Asia Pacific.

Falk, Richard A. 1976. "Environmental Warfare and Ecocide." In *The Vietnam War and International Law*, vol. 4: *The Concluding Phase*, 287–303. Princeton: Princeton University Press.

Fass, Horst, and Marianne Fulton. 1998. "How the Picture Reached the World." Accessed 13 July. http: //www.digitaljournalist.org/issue0008/ng4.htm.

Fehrenbach, Heide, and Davide Rodogno. 2015. "A Horrific Photo of a Drowned Syrian Child: Humanitarian Photography and NGO Media Strategies in Historical Perspective." *International Review of the Red Cross* 97 (900): 1121–1155.

Feldman, Allen. 2015. *Archives of the Insensible: Of War, Photopolitics, and Dead Memory*. Chicago: University of Chicago Press.

Felman, Shoshana. 2001. "A Ghost in the House of Justice: Death and the Language of the Law." *Yale Journal of Law and the Humanities* 13 (1): 241–282.

Felman, Shoshana. 2002. *The Juridical Unconscious: Trials and Traumas in the Twentieth Century*. Cambridge, MA: Harvard University Press.

Fischer, David. 1997. *History of the International Atomic Energy Agency: The First Forty Years*. Vienna: Division of Publications International Atomic Energy Agency.

Flanders, Laura. 2013. "'Chernobyl Was Transparent Compared to Fukushima': Harvey Wasserman on Ongoing Crisis." *GRITtv Interview*.

Forensic Architecture. 2014. *Forensis: The Architecture of Public Truth*. Berlin: Sternberg.

Foucault, Michel. 2002. *The Archaeology of Knowledge*. Trans. A. M. Sheridan Smith. London: Routledge.

Frankel, Felice, and George M. Whitesides. 2007. *On the Surface of Things: Images of the Extraordinary in Science*. Cambridge, MA: Harvard University Press.

Fraser, Mariam. 2006. "Event." *Theory, Culture and Society* 23(2–3): 4.

Fromm, Karen, Sophia Greiff, and Anna Stemmler, eds. 2018. *Images in Conflict—Bilder im Konflikt*. Weimar: Jonas Verlag

Gabrys, Jennifer. 2016. *Program Earth: Environmental Sensing Technology and the Making of a Computational Planet*. Minneapolis: University of Minnesota Press.

Galison, Peter, and Caroline A. Jones. 2010. "Unknown Quantities: On Oil Spill Imaging." *Artforum* November: 49–51.

Galloway, Alexander. 2012. "Are Some Things Unrepresentable?" *Theory, Culture and Society* 28 (7): 85–102.

Gates, Kelly. 2013. "The Cultural Labor of Surveillance: Video Forensics, Computational Objectivity, and the Production of Visual Evidence." *Social Semiotics* 23 (2): 242–260. doi: 10.1080/10350330.2013.777593.

Georgia Tech Research Institute. 2009. "The Silent Treatment: Aeroacoustics Research on UAVs Could Lead to Stealthier Surveillance." Georgia Tech Research Institute.

Gerald R. Ford Library and Museum. 2006. "The Battle for the Tapes." *The Watergate Files*, 23 January.

Gilman, Larry. 2004. "Satellites, Spy." In *Encyclopedia of Espionage, Intelligence, and Security*, ed. K. Lee Lerner and Brenda Wilmouth Lerber, 455. Farmington Hills, MI: Gale Group.

Ginzburg, Carlo. 1979. "Clues: Roots of a Scientific Paradigm." *Theory and Society* 7 (3): 273–288.

Givoni, Michal. 2014. "The Ethics of Witnessing and the Politics of the Governed." *Theory Culture Society* 31 (1): 123–142.

Goldstone, Richard J. 1995. Indictment: The Prosecutor of the Tribunal against Mile Mrkšić, Miroslav Radić and Veselin Šljivančanin. Case No. IT-95-13a, International Criminal Tribunal for the former Yugoslavia, The Hague.

Gómez-Barris, Macarena. 2017. *The Extractive Zone: Social Ecologies and Decolonial Perspectives*. Durham: Duke University Press.

Goodman, Amy, and Juan Gonzalez. 2013. "Polaroid and Apartheid: Inside the Beginnings of the Boycott, Divestment Movement against South Africa." *Democracy Now!* (13 December), 17: 49.

Goodman, Steve. 2010. *Sonic Warfare: Sound, Affect, and the Ecology of Fear, Technologies of lived abstraction*. Cambridge, MA: MIT Press.

Gourevitch, Philip, and Errol Morris. 2008. *Standard Operating Procedure*. New York: Penguin Press.

Government of Sri Lanka. 2009. "Consolidated Response of the Government of Sri Lanka to the Telecast by Channel 4 News of the United Kingdom on 25 August 2009 of a Video of Supposed Extra-Judicial Executions in Sri Lanka." Ministry of Disaster Management and Human Rights, Government of Sri Lanka.

Greenpeace. 2006. "The Chernobyl Catastrophe: Consequences on Human Health." Greenpeace International, Amsterdam.

Grenfell, Thomas C., and Garry A. Maykut. 1977. "The Optical Properties of Ice and Snow in the Arctic Basin." *Journal of Glaciology* 18 (80): 445–463.

Grosz, Elizabeth. 1999. "Thinking the New: Of Futures Yet Unthought." In *Becomings: Explorations in Time, Memory, and Futures*, ed. Elizabeth Grosz, 15–28. Ithaca: Cornell University Press.

Grusin, Richard. 2013. *Premediation: Affect and Mediality after 9/11*. London: Palgrave Macmillan.

Guardian. 2012. "London 2012: Army to Use 'Sonic Weapon' on Thames during Olympics." *The Guardian*, page removed, accessed 12 May. http://www.guardian.co.uk/sport/2012/may/12/british-military-sonic-weapon-olympics.

Guardian. 2015. "Fukushima Disaster Radiation Detected off Canada's Coast." *The Guardian*, 7 April.

Guardian. 2016. "Marshall Islands Begins Legal Action Aimed at Global Nuclear Disarmament." *The Guardian*, 10 March. https: //www.theguardian.com/world/2016/mar/10/marshall-islands-begins-legal-action-aimed-at-global-nuclear-disarmament.

Hadley, Odelle L., and Thomas W. Kirchstetter. 2012. "Black-carbon Reduction of Snow Albedo." *Nature Climate Change* 2 (6): 437–440. doi: http: //www.nature.com/nclimate/journal/v2/n6/abs/nclimate1433.html-supplementary-information.

Halewood, Michael. 2016. "Do Those Diagnosed with Alzheimer's Disease Lose Their Souls? Whitehead and Stengers on Persons, Propositions and the Soul." *Sociological Review* 64 (4): 786–804.

Hansen, Mark B. N. 2013. "Ubiquitous Sensation: Toward an Atmospheric, Collective, and Microtemporal Model of Media." In *Throughout: Art and Culture Emerging with Ubiquitous Computing*, ed. Ulrik Ekman, 626. Cambridge, MA: MIT Press.

Haraway, Donna. 1986. "Primatology Is Politics by Other Means." In *Feminist Approaches to Science*, ed. Ruth Bleir, 77–118. New York: Pergamon Press.

Hariman, Robert, and John Louis Lucaites. 2007. *No Caption Needed: Iconic Photographs, Public Culture, and Liberal Democracy*. Chicago: University of Chicago Press.

Harris, Whitney R., Robert H. Jackson, and Robert G. Storey. 1954. *Tyranny on Trial: The Evidence at Nuremberg*. Dallas: Southern Methodist University Press.

Hartke, Victoria Riess. 1987. "The International Fallout from Chernobyl." *Dickinson Journal of International Law* 5 (2): 319–343.

Hashimoto, Shoji, Shin Ugawa, Kazuki Nanko, and Koji Shichi. 2012. "The Total Amounts of Radioactively Contaminated Materials in Forests in Fukushima, Japan." *Scientific Reports* 2: 416. doi: 10.1038/srep00416.

Hayles, N. Katherine. 1999. *How We Became Posthuman: Virtual Bodies in Cybernetics, Literature, and Informatics*. Chicago: University of Chicago Press.

Hecht, Gabrielle. 2018. "Interscalar Vehicles for the African Anthropocene: On Waste, Temporality, and Violence." *Cultural Anthropology* 33 (1): 109–141.

Helmreich, Stefan. 2009. *Alien Ocean: Anthropological Voyages in Microbial Seas*. Berkeley: University of California Press.

Helmreich, Stefan. 2016. *Sounding the Limits of Life: Essays in the Anthropology of Biology and Beyond*. Princeton: Princeton University Press.

Heyns, Christof. 2011. "Investigations into a Video Footage which Allegedly Documents Members of the Sri Lankan Army Committing Extrajudicial Executions." In *Report of the Special Rapporteur on Extrajudicial Summary or Arbitrary Executions / A/HRC/17/28/Add.1*. Human Rights Council, Geneva: United Nations.

High Commissioner for Human Rights. 2015. Report of the OHCHR Investigation on Sri Lanka (OISL). In *Annual Report of the United Nations High Commissioner for Human Rights and Reports of the Office of the High Commissioner and the Secretary-General*. United Nations Human Rights Council, Geneva.

Hill, Amelia. 2010. "Mosquito Youth Dispersal Alarms Face Ban." *The Guardian*, 24 June.

Horstein, Bernard. 1972. "The Appearance and Visibility of Thin Oil Films on Water." US Environmental Protection Agency.

Hoskins, Andrew, and Ben O'Loughlin. 2010. *War and Media: The Emergence of Diffused War*. Cambridge: Polity Press.

Huhtamo, Erkki, and Jussi Parikka, eds. 2011. *Media Archaeology: Approaches, Applications, and Implications*. Berkeley: University of California Press.

Hume, Mark, and Sunny Dhillon. 2007. "Questions Hang over Taser Death." *Globe and Mail*, 26 October, 3.

Hunt, Nancy Rose. 2008. "An Acoustic Register, Tenacious Images, and Congolese Scenes of Rape and Repetition." *Cultural Anthropology* 23 (2): 220–253.

Hyman, Josh, Eric Graham, and Mark Hansen. 2007. "Imagers as Sensors: Correlating Plant CO_2 Uptake with Digital Visible-light Imagery." *Proceedings of the 4th International Workshop on Data Management for Sensor Networks* ACM 978-1-59593-649: 1–6.

ICTY. 1998a. Court Transcript 980421. United Nations, International Criminal Tribunal for the former Yugoslavia, The Hague.

ICTY. 1998b. Court Transcript 980617IT. United Nations, International Criminal Tribunal for the former Yugoslavia, The Hague.

ICTY. 1998c. Court Transcript 980618ED. United Nations, International Criminal Tribunal for the former Yugoslavia, The Hague.

ICTY. 1999. French Forensic Mission Kosovo Summer 1999. In *OTP Reference*. United Nations, International Criminal Tribunal for the former Yugoslavia, The Hague.

ICTY. 2002. Court Transcript 020903IT. United Nations, International Criminal Tribunal for the former Yugoslavia, The Hague.

ICTY. 2003. "Judgement in the Case the Prosecutor v. Dr. Milomir Stakic." ICTY press release (WS / P.I.S. / 774e). United Nations, International Criminal Tribunal for the former Yugoslavia, The Hague.

ICTY. 2006. Court Transcript 061026IT. United Nations, International Criminal Tribunal for the former Yugoslavia, The Hague.

ICTY. 2009a. Court Transcript 090210IT. United Nations, International Criminal Tribunal for the former Yugoslavia, The Hague.

ICTY. 2009b. Court Transcript 090324ED. United Nations, International Criminal Tribunal for the former Yugoslavia, The Hague.

ICTY. 2010. Prosecutor's observations regarding expert report on the authenticity of videotapes IC00820 and IC00821. United Nations, International Criminal Tribunal for the former Yugoslavia, The Hague.

International Atomic Energy Agency. 1956. The Statute of the IAEA. Conference on the Statute of the International Atomic Energy Agency, 29 July.

International Crisis Group. 2018. "Sri Lanka: Stepping Back from a Constitutional Crisis." Crisis Group Asia. Brussels: International Crisis Group.

International Human Rights and Conflict Resolution Clinic. 2012. "Living under Drones: Death, Injury, and Trauma to Civilians from US Drone Practices in Pakistan." Stanford Law School and New York University School of Law.

IPCC. 2013. "Appendix I: Glossary." In *Working Group I: The Scientific Basis*, ed. A. P. M. Baede. Intergovernmental Panel on Climate Change / UNEP and WMO.

Israeli High Court of Justice. 2006. Sonic Booms in the Gaza Strip. HCJ 10265/05. Supreme Court Sitting as the High Court of Justice, Jerusalem.

Ivakhiv, Adrian J. 2013. *Ecologies of the Moving Image: Cinema, Affect, Nature*. Kitchener, ON: Wilfrid Laurier University Press.

James, William. 1996. *Essays in Radical Empiricism*. Lincoln: University of Nebraska Press.

Jasanoff, Sheila. 1987. "Reviewed Work: Agent Orange on Trial by Peter H. Schuck." *Jurimetrics* 27 (4): 446–450.

Jasanoff, Sheila. 1995. *Science at the Bar: Law, Science, and Technology in America*. Cambridge, MA: Harvard University Press.

Johnston, John. 1999. "Machinic Vision." *Critical Inquiry* 26 (1): 27–48.

Joint Task Force One. 1946. *Operation Crossroads: The Official Pictorial Record*. United States. Joint Task Force One. Office of the Historian. New York: W. H. Wise.

Jönsson, Bror F., and James R. Watson. 2016. "The Timescales of Global Surface-Ocean Connectivity." *Nature Communications* 7: 6.

Joyce, James. 1976. *Finnegans Wake*. Harmondsworth, UK: Penguin.

Kahan, Dan M. 2009. "Whose Eyes Are You Going to Believe? Scott v. Harris and the Perils of Cognitive Illiberalism." *Yale Law School Faculty Scholarship Series*, Paper 97.

Kahn, Douglas. 1999. *Noise Water Meat: A History of Sound in the Arts*. Cambridge, MA: MIT Press.

Kahn, Douglas. 2013. *Earth Sound Earth Signal: Energies and Earth Magnitude in the Arts*. Berkeley: University of California Press.

Karpan, N. V. 2001. "Trial at Chernobyl Disaster: Outline after Records of Trial of the Chernobyl NPP Personnel." Kiev.

Keenan, Thomas. 2002. "Publicity and Indifference: Media, Surveillance, Humanitarian Intervention." *PMLA* 117 (1): 104–116.

Keenan, Thomas. 2004. "Mobilizing Shame." *South Atlantic Quarterly* 103 (2–3): 15.

Keenan, Thomas, and Eyal Weizman. 2012. *Mengele's Skull: The Advent of Forensic Aesthetics*. Frankfurt: Sternberg Press.

Kennedy, Paul. 2009. "Report Following a Public Interest Investigation into a Chair-Initiated Complaint Respecting the Death in RCMP Custody of Mr. Robert Dziekanski." In *Commission for Public Complaints against the Royal Canadian Mounted Police*, 21. Ottawa: Government of Canada.

Ketcham, Christopher. 2011. "A Season in Hell." *Salon.com*, 4 January 2012. http: //www.salon .com/2001/09/19/dust/.

Kikuchi, Daisuke. 2017. "Ex-Tepco Execs Plead Innocent as 3/11 Nuclear Negligence Trial Kicks Off." *Japan Times* (National News).

Kim, Hun Joon, and Renée Jeffery. 2014. *Transitional Justice in the Asia-Pacific*. New York: Cambridge University Press.

Kim-Cohen, Seth. 2016. *Against Ambience and Other Essays*. London: Bloomsbury Academic.

Kinoshita, Shuichi. 2008. *Structural Colors in the Realm of Nature*. London: World Scientific Publishing.

Kirby, Vicki. 2017. "Matter out of Place: 'New Materialism' in Review." In *What if Culture Was Nature All Along?*, ed. Vicki Kirby, 1–25. Edinburgh: Edinburgh University Press.

Kirschenbaum, Matthew G. 2008. *Mechanisms: New Media and the Forensic Imagination*. Cambridge, MA: MIT Press.

Kirsten, Campbell. 2013. "The Laws of Memory: The ICTY, the Archive, and Transitional Justice." *Social and Legal Studies* 22 (2): 24.

Kittler, Friedrich A. 1999. *Gramophone, Film, Typewriter*. Trans. Geoffrey Winthrop-Young and Michael Wutz. Stanford: Stanford University Press.

Kostin, Igor. 2006. *Chernobyl: Confessions of a Reporter*. New York: Umbrage Editions.

Krauss, Rosalind. 1981. "The Photographic Conditions of Surrealism." *October* 19 (Winter): 3–34.

Kuhn, Randall. 2009. "Tsunami and Conflict in Sri Lanka." Josef Korbel School of International Studies, University of Denver.

Kunuk, Zacharias, and Ian Mauro. 2010. "Inuit Knowledge and Climate Change." Isuma TV.

Kurgan, Laura. 2002. "New York, September 11, 2001, Four Days Later …" In *Ctrl [Space]: Rhetorics of Surveillance from Bentham to Big Brother*, ed. Thomas Y. Levin, Ursula Frohne, and Peter Weibel. Karlsruhe: ZKM.

Kurgan, Laura. 2013. *Close Up at a Distance: Mapping, Technology, and Politics*. New York: Zone Books.

Lardner Jr., George 1973. "Haig Tells of Theories on Erasure." *Washington Post*, 7 December, A01.

Latour, Bruno. 2004. "Why Has Critique Run Out of Steam: From Matters of Fact to Matters of Concern." *Critical Inquiry* 30 (Winter): 23.

Latour, Bruno, and Peter Weibel. 2005. *Making Things Public: Atmospheres of Democracy*. Cambridge, MA: MIT Press.

Laursen, Wendy. 2016. "Winners and Losers in Deepwater Horizon Payout." *The Maritime Executive*.

Lavallee, Guillaume. 2013. "Drones Take Toll On Mental Health." *China Daily*, 8 April, http: // www.chinadaily.com.cn/cndy/2013-04/08/content_16381701.htm.

League of Nations. 1925. "Protocol for the Prohibition of the Use in War of Asphyxiating, Poisonous or Other Gases, and of Bacteriological Methods of Warfare." United Nations Office for Disarmament Affairs, Geneva.

Lenoir, Timothy. 2002. "Makeover: Writing the Body into the Posthuman Technoscape Part Two: Corporeal Axiomatics." *Configurations* 10: 373–374.

Leopold, Aldo. 2001. "The Land Ethic." In *A Sand County Almanac: With Essays on Conservation*. New York: Oxford University Press. Originally published 1949.

Leslie, Esther. 2005. *Synthetic Worlds: Nature, Art and the Chemical Industry*. London: Reaktion Books.

Leslie, Esther. 2016. *Liquid Crystals: The Science and Art of a Fluid Form*. London: Reaktion Books.

Levi, Primo. 1997. *Conversation and Interview*. Turin: Einaudi.

Levin, Sam, Julia Carrie Wong, and Luke Harding. 2016. "Facebook Backs Down from 'Napalm Girl' Censorship and Reinstates Photo." *The Guardian*, 9 September, Tech. https: //www.theguardian.com/technology/2016/sep/09/facebook-reinstates-napalm-girl-photo.

Levin, Thomas Y. 2002. "Rhetoric of the Temporal Index: Surveillant Narration and the Cinema of 'Real Time.'" In *Ctrl [Space]: Rhetorics of Surveillance from Bentham to Big Brother*, ed. Thomas Y. Levin, Ursula Frohne, and Peter Weibel. Karlsruhe: ZKM.

Lewis, Libby. 2005. "Rose Mary Woods, Devoted Nixon Secretary, Dies." National Public Radio, Washington, DC.

Liebovich, Louis. 2003. *Richard Nixon, Watergate, and the Press: A Historical Retrospective*. Westport, CT: Praeger.

Lies Agreed Upon. 2011. [Film]. Ratnayake, Minoli. dir. Sri Lanka: Ministry of Defense.

Lippit, Akira Mizuta. 2005. *Atomic Light: Shadow Optics*. Minneapolis: University of Minnesota Press.

Locard, Edmond. 1930. "The Analysis of Dust Traces. Part I." *American Journal of Police Science* 1 (3): 276–298.

Lumb, Rebecca. 2010. "Reunited with the Vietnamese 'Girl in the Picture.'" *BBC News*, 17 May, World / Asia Pacific. http: //news.bbc.co.uk/1/hi/world/asia-pacific/8678478.stm.

Lutts, Ralph H. 1985. "Chemical Fallout: Rachel Carson's Silent Spring, Radioactive Fallout, and the Environmental Movement." *Environmental History Review* 9 (3): 210–225. doi: 10.2307/3984231.

McChrystal, General Stanley. 2013. *My Share of the Task: A Memoir*. London: Portfolio Penguin.

McCormack, Derek P. 2017. "Elemental Infrastructures for Atmospheric Media: On Stratospheric Variations, Value, and the Commons." *Environment and Planning D: Society and Space* 35 (3): 418–437.

McGreal, Chris. 2011. "Richard Nixon Transcripts Reveals Fury over Partially Erased Watergate Tape." *The Guardian*, 10 November. https: //www.theguardian.com/world/2011/nov/10/richard-nixon-transcripts-fury-tape.

McLagan, Meg, and Yates McKee, eds. 2012. *Sensible Politics: The Visual Culture of Nongovernmental Activism*. New York: Zone Books.

McNeill, David. 2011. "Why the Fukushima Disaster Is Worse than Chernobyl." *The Independent*, 29 August, Asia.

McNichol, Tom 2002. "Richard Nixon's Last Secret." Accessed 25 November. http: //www.wired.com/wired/archive/10.07/nixon_pr.html.

McVeigh, Karen. 2013. "Drone Strikes: Tears in Congress as Pakistani Family Tells of Mother's Death." *The Guardian*, 29 October, World. https: //www.theguardian.com/world/2013/oct/29/pakistan-family-drone-victim-testimony-congress.

Majumder, Sanjoy. 2005. "Sri Lanka's Tsunami Aid Politics." *BBC News*, 21 March, http: //news.bbc.co.uk/go/pr/fr/-/1/hi/world/south_asia/4367935.stm.

Marks, Laura U. 2000. "The Memory of Things." In *The Skin of Film: Intercultural Cinema, Embodiment and the Senses*. Durham: Duke University Press.

Marmaroli, P., X. Falourd, and H. Lissek. n.d. "A UAV Motor Denoising Technique to Improve Localization of Surrounding Noisy Aircrafts: Proof of Concept for Anti-collision Systems." Ecole Polytechnique Fédérale, Lausanne.

Martini, Edwin A. 2012. *Agent Orange: History, Science and the Politics of Uncertainty*. Amherst: University of Massachusetts Press.

Masco, Joseph. 2006. *The Nuclear Borderlands: The Manhattan Project in post-Cold War New Mexico*. Princeton: Princeton University Press.

Massumi, Brian. 2002a. "On the Superiority of the Analog." In *Parables for the Virtual: Movement, Affect, Sensation*, 336. Durham: Duke University Press.

Massumi, Brian. 2002b. *Parables for the Virtual: Movement, Affect, Sensation*. Durham: Duke University Press.

Matheson, Kelly. 2015. "Video as Evidence Case Study: Filing Long after a Crime in Croatia." witness.org. Accessed 7 September. https: //blog.witness.org/2015/02/video-evidence-case-study -crime-croatia/.

Miller, Jonathan. 2009. "Sri Lanka Execution Video: Evidence of War Crimes?" London: Channel 4 News.

Miller, Stephen Paul. 1999. "Politics in the Watergate Era." In *The Seventies Now: Culture as Surveillance*, 414. Durham: Duke University Press.

Mnookin, Jennifer L. 1998. "The Image of Truth: Photographic Evidence and the Power of Analogy." *Yale Journal of Law and the Humanities* 10: 1–74.

Morelle, Rebecca. 2012. "The Hum that Helps to Fight Crime." *BBC News*, 12 December, Science and Environment.

Morris, Errol, dir. 2008. *Standard Operating Procedure*. USA: Sony Classics.

Mufson, Steven. 2010. "Altered BP Photo Comes into Question." *Washington Post*, 20 July.

Murphy, T. S. 1998. "Quantum Ontology: A Virtual Mechanics of Becoming." In *Deleuze and Guattari: New Mappings in Politics, Philosophy and Culture*, ed. Eleanor Kaufmann and Kevin Jon Heller, 211–229. Minneapolis: University of Minnesota Press.

Nancy, Jean-Luc. 2005. *The Ground of the Image*. Trans. Jeffrey Fort. New York: Fordham University Press.

NAIIC. 2012. *The Official Report of The Fukushima Nuclear Accident Independent Investigation Commission*. Tokyo: The National Diet of Japan.

NARA. 2002a. "National Archives Releases 500 Hours of Additional Nixon White House Tape Recorded Conversations." Press release, US National Archives and Records Administration, February 14. www.archives.gov.

NARA. 2002b. "White House Tapes 3rd Chronological Release January 1972–June 1972." Nixon Library, 7.

NARA. 2003. "Archivist Accepts Watergate Tape Panel Recommendations." Press release, U.S. National Archives and Records Administration, 8 May. http: //www.archives.gov.

National Research Council. 2005. *Oil Spill Dispersants: Efficacy and Effects*. National Research Council, Division on Earth and Life Studies, Ocean Studies Board. Washington: National Academies Press.

Nixon, Rob. 2011. *Slow Violence and the Environmentalism of the Poor*. Cambridge, MA: Harvard University Press.

No Fire Zone. 2013. [Documentary]. Callum Macrae. dir. UK: Channel 4.

O'Brian, John. 1996. "Bruising the Public Eye." In *Voices of Fire: Art, Rage, Power, and the State*, ed. Bruce Barber, Serge Guilbaut, and John O'Brian, 3–22. University of Toronto Press.

Okumura, Takeshi. 2003. "The Material Flow of Radioactive Cesium-137 in the U.S. 2000." US Environmental Protection Agency, Washington.

Olsen, Bjørnar. 2010. *In Defense of Things: Archaeology and the Ontology of Objects*. Lanham, MD: Rowman and Littlefield.

Oppenheimer, Joshua, and Joram Ten Brink, eds. 2012. *Killer Images: Documentary Film, Memory and the Performance of Violence, Nonfictions*. London: Wallflower Press.

Paglen, Trevor. 2016. "Invisible Images (Your Pictures Are Looking at You)." *New Inquiry* 11 (8 December).

Parikka, Jussi. 2015. *A Geology of Media, Film and Media*. Minneapolis: University of Minnesota Press.

Parisi, Luciana. 2013. *Contagious Architecture: Computation, Aesthetics, and Space*. Cambridge, MA: MIT Press.

Patton, Paul. 1997. "The World Seen from Within: Deleuze and the Philosophy of Events." *Theory and Event* 1 (1): 1–13.

Peters, John Durham. 2015. *The Marvelous Clouds: Toward a Philosophy of Elemental Media*. Chicago: University of Chicago Press.

Petraco, Nicholas, Thomas A. Kubic, and Lisa Faber. 2007. "The Microscopic Analysis of World Trade Center Dust." Trace Evidence Symposium poster session, National Forensic Science Technology Center, New York, 15 August.

Petryna, Adriana. 2002. *Life Exposed: Biological Citizens after Chernobyl*. Princeton: Princeton University Press.

Petryna, Adriana. 2004. "Biological Citizenship: The Science and Politics of Chernobyl-Exposed Populations." *Landscapes of Exposure: Knowledge and Illness in Modern Environments* 19: 25–265.

Pottage, Alain. 2011. "Law Machines: Scale Models, Forensic Materiality and the Making of Modern Patent Law." *Social Studies of Science* 41 (5): 621–643. doi: 10.1177/0306312711408484.

Povinelli, Elizabeth A. 2016. *Geontologies: A Requiem to Late Liberalism*. Durham: Duke University Press.

Pringle, Thomas. 2014. "Photographed by the Earth: War and Media in Light of Nuclear Events." *European Journal of Media Studies* 3 (2): 131-54.

Purdy, Ray, and Richard Macrory. 2003. "Satellite Photographs: 21st Century Evidence?" *New Law Journal*: 337–338.

Pyle, Richard. 2000. "Trang Bang Revisited (excerpts)." *AP*, 9 June 2008, 2. http: //digitaljournalist.org/issue0008/ng7.htm.

Rabin, Robert L. 1989. "Tort System on Trial: The Burden of Mass Toxic Litigation." *Yale Law Journal* 98 (813): 813–829.

Rajasingham, K. T. 2006. "Bring LTTE Leaders to International Criminal Court for War Crimes against Children." World Institute for Asian Studies, Last modified 29 July, accessed 31 August 2015. http: //www.asiantribune.com/index.php?q=node/1303.

Rancière, Jacques. 2004. *The Politics of Aesthetics: The Distribution of the Sensible*. London: Continuum.

Reprieve. 2012. "17.03.2011 Jirga Drone Strike." In *Witness Declarations*, ed. Usama Khilji. Islamabad, Pakistan: Reprieve and Foundation for Fundamental Rights.

Roberts, Sarah T. 2012. "Social Media's Dirty Work: Contextualizing the Facebook Screening Controversy." *The Illusion of Volition: Critical inquiry and reflection at the intersection of our analog and digital worlds*, 21 August. https://illusionofvolition.com/2012/02/26/social-medias-dirty-work-contextualizing-the-facebook-screening-controversy/.

Russell, Bertrand. 1967. *War Crimes Tribunal in Vietnam*. New York: Monthly Review Press.

Russia Today. 2013. "Lethal Buzz: US Air Force Developing Insect-size Drones." Last modified 20 February 2013, accessed 22 June 2013. http: //rt.com/news/air-force-tiny-drones-190/.

Sadasivan, S., M. Gurubasavaraj, and S. Ravi Sekar. 2001. "Acoustic Signature of an Unmanned Air Vehicle—Exploitation for Aircraft Localisation and Parameter Estimation." *Aeronautical Development Establishment Bangalore*—560 093 51 (3): 279–283.

Scheeres, Julia. 2002. "Video Forensics: Grainy to Guilty." *Wired*. Accessed 30 January. https://www.wired.com/2002/01/video-forensics-grainy-to-guilty/.

Schuck, Peter H. 1987. *Agent Orange on Trial: Mass Toxic Disasters in the Courts*. Enl. ed. Cambridge, MA: Belknap Press of Harvard University Press.

Schuppli, Susan. 2013. "The Most Dangerous Film in the World." In *Materialities*, ed. Krzysztof Gutfranski. Gdańsk: Wyspa Progress Foundation / Wyspa Institute of Art.

Schuppli, Susan. 2014. "Deadly Algorithms: Can Legal Codes Hold Software Accountable for Code that Kills?" *Radical Philosophy* 187 (September/October): 2–8.

Schuppli, Susan. 2016. "Dirty Pictures." In *Living Earth Field Notes from the Dark Ecology Project 2014–2016*, ed. Mirna Belina and Arie Altena. Amsterdam: Sonic Acts.

Schuppli, Susan. 2017. "The Subterfuge of Screens." In *Et maintenant regardez cette machine*, 148. Montreal: Musée d'art contemporain de Montréal.

Schwartz, Louis Georges. 2009. *Mechanical Witness: A History of Motion Picture Evidence in U.S. Courts*. Oxford: Oxford University Press.

Sengupta, Somini. 2015. "UN Grants Deferral in Inquiry." *International New York Times*, 17 February, Asia Pacific.

Serle, Jack, and Chris Woods. 2013. "Secret US Documents Show Brennan's 'No Civilian Drone Deaths' Claim Was False." *Covert Drone War*.

Serres, Michel. 1982. *Hermes: Literature, Science, Philosophy*. Ed. Josué V. Harari and David F. Bell. Baltimore: Johns Hopkins University Press.

Shaw, Ian G. R. 2016. "Scorched Atmospheres: The Violent Geographies of the Vietnam War and the Rise of Drone Warfare." *Annals of the American Association of Geographers* 106 (3): 688–704. doi: 10.1080/00045608.2015.1115333.

Sherwin, Richard K. 2007. "A Manifesto for Visual Legal Realism." *New York Law School Public Law and Legal Theory* 40: 1–18.

Shevchenko, Vladimir. 1986. Chernobyl: Chronicle of Difficult Weeks. In *The Glasnost Film Festival*. USSR: The Video Project.

Shiva, Vandana, Ana Luz Valadez, Diana Murcia, Blanca Chancoso, Cecilia Cherréz, Nnimmo Bassey, Delfín Tenesaca, Alberto Acosta, and Líder Góngora. 2010. "Lawsuit on Behalf of the Rights of Nature under the Principle of Universal Jurisdiction." Constitutional Court of Ecuador, Quito.

Sloterdijk, Peter. 2009. *Terror from the Air*. Los Angeles: Semiotext(e).

Smith, John N., Robin M. Brown, William J. Williams, Marie Robert, Richard Nelson, and S. Bradley Moran. 2015. "Arrival of the Fukushima Radioactivity Plume in North American Continental Waters." *Proceedings of the National Academy of Sciences* 112 (5): 1310–1315. doi: 10.1073/pnas.1412814112.

Solomon-Godeau, Abigail. 1991. *Photography at the Dock: Essays on Photographic History, Institutions, and Practices*. Minneapolis: University of Minnesota Press.

Spiegel, Jennifer Beth. 2013. "Subterranean Flows: Water Contamination and the Politics of Visibility after the Bhopal Disaster." In *Thinking with Water*, ed. Cecilia Chen, Janine MacLeod, and Astrida Neimanis, 84–103. Montreal: McGill-Queen's University Press.

Spivak, Gayatri Chakravorty. 2003. *Death of a Discipline*. New York: Columbia University Press.

Sri Lanka's Killing Fields. 2011. [Documentary]. Callum Macrae. dir. UK: Channel 4.

Sri Lanka's Killing Fields: War Crimes Unpunished. 2012 [Documentary]. Callum Macrae. dir. UK: Channel 4.

Sri Lanka: New Video Evidence of Grotesque Violations. 2014. [Documentary]. Callum Macrae. dir. UK: Channel 4.

Stellman, J., et al. 2003. "The Extent and Pattern of Usage of Agent Orange and other Herbicides in Vietnam." *Nature* 422 (17 April): 681–687.

Stengers, Isabelle. 1997. *Power and Invention: Situating Science*. Trans. Paul Bains. Minneapolis: University of Minnesota Press.

Stengers, Isabelle. 2007a. "Diderot's Egg: Divorcing Materialism from Eliminativism." *Radical Philosophy* (144).

Stengers, Isabelle. 2007b. "Divorcing Materiality from Physicality." In *Conference Materials + Materialisms*. Birkbeck, University of London: Radical Philosophy.

Steyerl, Hito. 2009. "In Defense of the Poor Image." *E-Flux* 10: 9.

Stone, Christopher D. 1972. "Should Trees Have Standing—Toward Legal Rights for Natural Objects." *Southern California Law Review* 45 (2): 450–501.

Stone, Deborah A. 1987. "Agent Orange on Trial: Mass Toxic Disasters in the Courts." *Journal of Health Politics, Policy and Law* 12 (2): 371–375. doi: 10.1215/03616878-12-2-371.

Stover, Eric, and Harvey M. Weinstein. 2004. *My Neighbor, My Enemy: Justice and Community in the Aftermath of Mass Atrocity*. Cambridge: Cambridge University Press.

Strawser, Bradley Jay. 2010. "Moral Predators: The Duty to Employ Uninhabited Aerial Vehicles." *Journal of Military Ethics* 9 (4): 342–368.

Suisman, David. 2015. "The Oklahoma City Sonic Boom Experiment and the Politics of Supersonic Aviation." *Radical History Review,* January (121): 169–195.

Takahashi, Tess. 2006. "Impure Film: Medium Specificity and the North American Avant-Garde (1965–2005)." PhD diss., Brown University.

Tamen, Miguel. 2001. *Friends of Interpretable Objects*. Cambridge, MA: Harvard University Press.

Tamil Guardian. 2015. "War-Affected Tamils Call on US to Support International Accountability Mechanism." *Tamil Guardian*, last modified 28 August 2015, accessed 31 August 2015. http: //www.tamilguardian.com/article.asp?articleid=15723.

Tavares, Paulo. 2014. "Nonhuman Rights." In *Forensis: The Architecture of Public Truth*, ed. Forensic Architecture, 553–572. Berlin: Sternberg.

Thurston, Thomas. 1996–2009. "Hearsay of the Sun: Photography, Identity, and the Law of Evidence." *American Quarterly in collaboration with the American Studies Crossroads Project at Georgetown University and the Center for History and New Media at George Mason University*.

Time. 1973. "The Secretary and the Tapes Tangle." *Time*, 10 December, 11.

Torchin, Leshu. 2012. *Creating the Witness: Documenting Genocide on Film, Video, and the Internet*. Minneapolis: University of Minnesota Press.

TPIY. 1999. "Mission française d'expertise médico-légale: Kosovo été 1999." *OTP Reference* (#K0176281), 57.

Tyrkin, Stas. 2001. "In Stalker Tarkovsky foretold Chernobyl." *Komsomolskaya Pravda*, 23 March, accessed 4 January 2008. http: //www.acs.ucalgary.ca/~tstronds/nostalghia.com/TheTopics/Stalker/sharun.html.

UN News Center. 2010. "Deeming Sri Lanka Execution Video Authentic, UN Expert Calls for War Crimes Probe." United Nations, New York.

United Press International. 2008. "Dog Takes the Stand in French Court." United Press International, 10 September.

United States Court of Appeals. 2001. Danny Lee Kyllo v. United States. United States Court of Appeals for the Ninth Circuit 99-8508. Washington, DC: Supreme Court of the United States.

United States District Court. 1984. In re Agent Orange Product Liability Litigation. 597 F. Supp. 740 (E.D.N.Y. 1984). United States District Court for the Eastern District of New York.

United States Supreme Court. 2010. Citizens United v. Federal Election Commission. No. 08-205. Washington, DC.

Van Lier, Henri. 2007. *Philosophy of Photography*. Leuven: Leuven University Press.

Van Wyck, Peter C. 2004. *Signs of Danger: Waste, Trauma, and Nuclear Threat*. Minneapolis: University of Minnesota Press.

Van Wyck, Peter C. 2011. *The Highway of the Atom*. Montreal: McGill-Queen's University Press.

Vanhanen, Janne. 2001. "Loving the Ghost in the Machine/Aesthetics of Interruption." ctheory. Accessed October. http: //www.ctheory.net/articles.aspx?id=312.

Vaughan, Adam. 2016. "Renewables Made Up Half of Net Electricity Capacity Added Last Year." *The Guardian*, 25 October. https: //www.theguardian.com/environment/2016/oct/25/renewables-made-up-half-of-net-electricity-capacity-added-last-year.

Vicente, José Luis de, Honor Harger, and Josep Perelió, eds. 2011. *Invisible Fields: Geographies of Radio Waves*. Barcelona: Actar.

Vidal, Fernando. 2007. "Miracles, Science, and Testimony in Post-Tridentine Saint-making." *Believing Nature, Knowing God / Science in Context* 20 (3): 481–508.

Virilio, Paul. 1989. *War and Cinema: the Logics of Perception*. Trans. Patrick Camiller. London: Verso.

Virilio, Paul. 2000. "The Primal Accident." In *The Politics of Everyday Fear*, ed. Brian Massumi, 211–218. Minneapolis: University of Minnesota Press.

Virilio, Paul. 2007. *The Original Accident*. Cambridge: Polity Press.

Vismann, Cornelia, and Geoffrey Winthrop-Young. 2008. *Files: Law and Media Technology*. Stanford: Stanford University Press.

Vulliamy, Ed. 2004. "New Battle Breaks Out over Serb Death Camp." *The Guardian*, 2 December, 3, News. https: //www.theguardian.com/uk/2004/dec/02/balkans.

Walton, Marsha. 2005. "Scientists: Sumatra Quake Longest Ever Recorded." *CNN*, Science. Accessed 18 August 2015. http: //edition.cnn.com/2005/TECH/science/05/19/sumatra.quake/index.html.

Warren, Stephen G. 1982. "Optical Properties of Snow." *Reviews of Geophysics and Space Physics* 20 (1): 67–89.

Webb, J. H. 1949. "The Fogging of Photographic Film by Radioactive Contaminants in Cardboard Packaging Materials." *Physical Review* 76 (3): 375–380.

Weeratunga, Lalith. 2011. Report of the Commission of Inquiry on Lessons Learnt and Reconciliation. Democratic Socialist Republic of Sri Lanka, Colombo.

Weinstein, Jack B. 2005. Memorandum, Order and Judgment re: Agent Orange Product Liability Litigation. MDL No. 381, United States District Court Eastern District of New York, Brooklyn.

Weizman, Eyal. 2011. *The Least of All Possible Evils: Humanitarian Violence from Arendt to Gaza*. London: Verso.

Weizman, Eyal. 2018. *Forensic Architecture: Violence at the Threshold of Detectability*. New York: Zone Books.

Wiener, Norbert. 2007. "Cybernetics in History." In *Theorizing Communication: Readings across Traditions*, ed. Robert T. Craig and Heidi L. Muller. London: SAGE.

Wieviorka, Annette. 2006. *The Era of the Witness*. Ithaca: Cornell University Press.

Wigley, Mark. 2016. *Buckminster Fuller Inc.: Architecture in the Age of Radio*. Zurich: Lars Müller.

Wilder, Kelley E. 2009. "Photography and the Art of Science." *Visual Studies* 24 (2): 163–168. doi: 10.1080/14725860903106161.

Wilshire, William L., and David Chesnut. 1993. "Joint Acoustic Propagation Experiment (JAPE-91) Workshop." NASA Hampton, Virginia.

Woods Hole Oceanographic Institute. 2014. "Deepwater Horizon." In *Oil in the Ocean*. Woods Hole, MA: Woods Hole Oceanographic Institute.

Yusoff, Kathryn. 2019. *A Billion Black Anthropocenes or None*. Minneapolis: University of Minnesota Press.

Yuzon, Ensign Florencio J. 1996. "Deliberate Environmental Modification Through the Use of Chemical and Biological Weapons: 'Greening' the International Laws of Armed Conflict to Establish an Environmentally Protective Regime." *American University International Law Review* 11 (5): 793–846.

Zalasiewicz, Jan, Mark Williams, Colin N. Waters, Anthony D. Barnosky, and Peter Haff. 2014. "The Technofossil Record of Humans." *Anthropocene Review* 1 (1): 34–43.

Zetterberg, Hans L. 1996. "Public Opinion and Nuclear Energy: Sweden after Chernobyl." Eleventh Annual Symposium of the Uranium Institute, London, 2–4 September.

Zierler, David. 2011. *The Invention of Ecocide: Agent Orange, Vietnam, and the Scientists who Changed the Way We Think about the Environment*. Athens: University of Georgia Press.

Index

The letter *f* following a page locator denotes a figure; the letter *p* denotes a photograph.